JUDAISM

IN PERSIA'S

SHADOW

A Social and Historical Approach

Jon L. Berquist

Wipf and Stock Publishers
EUGENE, OREGON

To Laura Rey

Wipf and Stock Publishers
199 West 8th Avenue, Suite 3
Eugene, Oregon 97401

Judaism in Persia's Shadow
A Social and Historical Approach
By Berquist, Jon L.

ISBN: 1-59244-308-7
Publication date 8/12/2003
Previously published by Fortress Press, 1995

CONTENTS

PREFACE

THIS BOOK BEGAN WITH my attempts to understand the development of Israel's history and theology. So many of the proffered solutions produced a linearity that disturbed me; the progression never seemed that simple to me. My search for an answer brought me to a methodological quandary. How can one cope with the categorical divide between literature and history?

Over time, I developed a conviction: literature and history are both human productions, and the people who lived historical life in ancient Israel were the same ones who wrote the first versions of today's biblical texts. Of course, it is not that easy—often an elite minority produced the texts, and so a text reflects the social relationships of its origins. In other words, I had to understand the society of the ancient world to make sense of the history and of the literature, and the study of society required the tools of sociology.

After this choice of method, a nagging problem still lingered. I sensed that there was something radically different between the typical texts of the Hebrew Bible and those from the late Hellenistic period. The descriptive studies of different genres and the intertestamental history of religions left too much unexplained for me, and so I sought to understand the changes in society that occurred after Israel's exile. The project first concentrated on early postexilic prophecy, but what I really wanted to know was bigger than that. How did society change after the exile?

With reluctance, I delved back into history, where the Groningen Achaemenid Workshop was producing numerous articles about the historical features of the Persian Empire. Combined with sociological and anthropological tools for understanding the developments of states, empires, and colonies, I gained the language to frame the question: How did Judah's transformation into Yehud, the Persian colony, affect its ideology, its self-understanding, its religion, and its rhetoric, and how did this new form of religion work both to maintain and to oppose the society in which it took this shape?

This book expresses my attempt to answer this question. As with any answer, it participates in the assumptions of its related question. First, I assume that public life in Jerusalem changed because of the Persian Empire's dominance of Yehud and that this difference in public life affected the religion's inheritance and application of its past traditions. Thus the book first moves toward an understanding of the social mechanisms of Persia's imperial domination and Yehud's colonial existence. Second, I assume that all society (including ancient Israel) is dynamic and that the tendencies toward social cohesion are approximately as many as toward social dissolution. Sociology's functionalist and conflict paradigms are both simplifications that heuristically describe *parts* of society, but not all. To understand Yehud, one must examine both the institutions that functioned to keep society in order *and* those that struggled across the grain, producing conflict at every level. Third, I assume that religion is an integral part of a society's ideology, and thus religion is also integral to its social organization and its appropriation of the economic infrastructure. Just as all social analysis must be economic, all social analysis must be religious.

Starting from these assumptions, I found a richness in Persian Yehud that bedazzled me, and still does. My colleagues keep hearing explanations for Israel's society that lead to some basis in Persian history; my friends laugh at me for tossing Achaemenid anecdotes into otherwise light conversation. The Persian Empire produced a pluralistic context in which Judaism survived, grew, and flourished, and the faith of Yahweh was never the same, in any of its expressions. Without the monarchy's direct support, the religion sought other means of social expression. These two centuries produced historiography, prophecy, wisdom, apocalyptic, songs, and short stories as the religion and the society reconnoitered new domains of possibility.

More than two and a half millennia later, we still struggle in our various religious communities with the proper relationships of church and state—and I would argue that we keep coming up with the same answers and the same confusion that Yehud experienced. Since there was no government to identify itself completely with the religion and to enforce it, diversity became one of the hallmarks of the Jewish tradition, and belief in this God continues still today, in many forms and with many expressions, keeping alive that vital diversity. On the western fringes of the Persian Empire, our ancestors of faith first learned to live within this diversity and to organize their communal lives in varying relationships to politics and other aspects of society. Their lessons continue, and so do our attempts to understand the nature of the problem.

Another way of saying this is that it is difficult to return from Babylon. The Persian road out of exile held plenty of rough spots for these ancient travelers. In addition, once they reached their Promised Land, they did not fully know what to expect. How could they construct life together? In theological terms, could God really make life new? These questions have haunted me, as well. After years as an outside observer in Persian Yehud, my heart sings for Laura Rey, who brought me back to experience life from the inside, in the present. Although our road has had its rough spots, and I admit that some of the terrain looks uncertain, I rejoice in the realities and promise of life together. In dedicating this book to her, I wish to affirm that there is life after exile, and that it is more wonderful than one could imagine.

I would like to acknowledge my gratitude to those under whom I did my graduate work in Hebrew Bible at Vanderbilt University's Graduate Department of Religion: James Barr, James Crenshaw, Peter Haas, Walter Harrelson, Douglas Knight, Shemaryahu Talmon, and Renita Weems. Walter Harrelson's direction of the dissertation as well as his patient persistence with me in the years afterward has shaped this project in more ways than I can count—and, on more than a few pages, less than he would wish. Also, colleagues through the graduate program have been helpful not only in encouraging me while in Nashville, but in the time since, especially Loren Crow, David Odell-Scott, and Marti Steussy. Several persons at Fortress Press were indispensable: Charles Puskas, Marshall D. Johnson, Cynthia L. Thompson, and Lois Torvik. The library staff of Phillips Graduate Seminary, the University of Tulsa, and Vanderbilt University all proved immensely supportive throughout this process. I owe a special word of thanks to the Southwest Commission on Religious Studies for granting me their Junior Scholar Research Award in 1991–92, which enabled me to tie many of the loose ends a bit tighter. The ends still loose, the strands yet unconnected, and the knots tied clumsily still remain my responsibility.

ABBREVIATIONS

AB	Anchor Bible
ANET	James B. Pritchard, ed., *Ancient Near Eastern Texts Pertaining to the Old Testament, with Supplement,* 3d ed. (Princeton, N.J.: Princeton University Press, 1969).
ATD	Das Alte Testament Deutsch
BTB	*Biblical Theology Bulletin*
BZAW	Beihefte zur *Zeitschrift für die alttestamentliche Wissenschaft*
CAT	Commentaire de l'Ancien Testament
CBQ	*Catholic Biblical Quarterly*
FOTL	Forms of Old Testament Literature
HSM	Harvard Semitic Monographs
HUCA	*Hebrew Union College Annual*
JAAR	*Journal of the American Academy of Religion*
JBL	*Journal of Biblical Literature*
JNES	*Journal of Near Eastern Studies*
JQR	*Jewish Quarterly Review*
JSOT	*Journal for the Study of the Old Testament*
JSOTSup	Journal for the Study of the Old Testament—Supplement Series
NCBC	New Century Bible Commentary
OTG	Old Testament Guides
OTL	Old Testament Library
SBL	Society of Biblical Literature
SBLDS	SBL Dissertation Series
SBLMS	SBL Monograph Series
SWBA	Social World of Biblical Antiquity
VT	*Vetus Testamentum*
WBC	Word Biblical Commentary
ZAW	*Zeitschrift für die alttestamentliche Wissenschaft*

PART I

INTRODUCTION

CHAPTER 1

PERSPECTIVES ON THE POSTEXILIC PERIOD

RECENT YEARS HAVE SEEN an increase of interest in Israel's postexilic period. Certainly scholars have been quick to realize both the new information available for study and the severe limits to our knowledge of the postexilic era. The approximate boundaries of the period are commonly established. The destruction of Jerusalem (587 B.C.E.) resulted in the removal of certain Jerusalemites to Babylonian territory, but within two generations (539 B.C.E.) the Persian Empire defeated Babylonia and offered opportunities for some of the exiles' children and grandchildren to migrate to the Jerusalem area. This intermingling of the separated strands that derived from monarchic Judah continued in a postexilic community under Persian rule for about two centuries, until Persia's defeat in 333 B.C.E. Although these outlines are clear, the exact nature of the community's life and faith during these two centuries requires careful analysis.

In addition to being aware of the data and its limits, scholars begin their analysis with general orientations that organize the material and predispose the analysis in certain directions. The essential question concerns the important influence upon the literature and community of Yehud.[1] Should we search for such explanatory influences within Israel's history of development or among other issues, such as the effects of Persian rule? Are internal or external factors the chief cause of Yehud's experience?[2]

Wellhausen's Synthesis

Julius Wellhausen set the agenda for the study of postexilic religion, just as he did for many other realms of Hebrew Bible scholarship.[3] Wellhausen depicted ancient Israelite religion, especially during the earlier periods, as being very closely connected to the life of people. The true worship of Yahweh was a natural expression and extension of people's lives, but this faded late in the monarchy. In the postexilic period, institutionalized religion completely eclipsed this natural form of worship, as centralization removed religious practices from local life settings.[4]

In Wellhausen's view, the relationship of the religion to people's lives was the chief variable throughout the history of Israelite religion; the members of the postexilic community kept religion separate from the land and thus from daily life. Two reasons can be noted for this separation, according to Wellhausen. First, the postexilic religious community's memories of exile haunted them, and the weakness of their political reality disallowed any guarantees that they could continue to possess their restored land. They developed a form of religion that would not depend upon such an unknown quantity as possession of a certain plot of land, and thus their religion evolved into greater abstraction with a corollary durability in the face of political uncertainty.

Second, the postexilic community believed that aberrant religious practices of their ancestors in the late monarchy caused their misfortunes. For this reason, the people wanted to be different from the way of life and self-governance that had transpired earlier. They believed the critique of the eighth-century prophets was correct; reliance on political and military independence was the path to disaster, and they must avoid that path.[5]

Thus the separation of religion from its natural basis was also a distancing from the practices of the past rulers as well as a construction of a religion that was less geographically and politically dependent. This resulted in the development of a religion that was not tied to nationalist politics, to international alliance building, or to any other trappings of state. The members of the sixth- and fifth-century religious community would have, in Wellhausen's view, understood this depoliticization of religion to follow from the teachings of the eighth-century prophets. However, Wellhausen sees this separation of religion and government as part of the denaturalization of the religion. The people's religion diverged from the real-life basis of daily existence, including family life, agriculture, and economics, as well as politics.[6] Thus this separation was primarily conditioned by factors internal to the religious community.

The distancing of the postexilic religion from its preexilic antecedents was, however, also externally conditioned, being a result of certain social and political pressures introduced by the Persian government. In Wellhausen's view, the internal, intentional aspect of the separation did not conflict with external, circumstantial influences. The two were complementary. The internal factors caused the Jerusalemites to abhor the establishment of a new state, and this matched Persian policy, which would not allow such independent political activity anyway.[7]

Thus the separation between religion and daily life that was envisioned and created by these early returnees was intentional, not forced, and yet fully in accord with the exigencies imposed by the circumstance of foreign rule. Within this context, the separation expressed itself in institutional modes rather than in an ideological fashion. In other words, the separation of past and present was a break with the governmental forms of the past, making the separation visible to the foreign rulers, since the people's continued survival required such appearances.

For these reasons the people instituted new religious forms of organization.[8] The law's development as an institutional means to protect and preserve the religion forbade new interpretations and thus disallowed prophecy's new innovations.[9] According to Wellhausen, the law killed prophecy. The resultant organizational form for the people was a theocracy, dictated by the acceptance of certain past religious traditions, with the rejection of the political forms of monarchic Israel, as was to some extent required by Persian politics.[10] Institutional discontinuity combined with a reappropriation of ancient ideology and religious tradition, producing a new governmental and societal form with an ideology that stressed that this society was not new.

Wellhausen's understanding of the nature of the postexilic Yehudite community summarizes itself in one quotation: "The Mosaic theocracy, the residuum of a ruined state, is itself not a state at all, but an unpolitical artificial product created in spite of unfavourable circumstances by the impulse of an ever-memorable energy: and foreign rule is its necessary counterpart."[11] Yehud is a shattered community that takes an artificial form, shaped by its past but rejecting ideologically any continuity of form with that past, deeply influenced by the needs of surviving in the political context of foreign rule. This institutionalization is one of Wellhausen's chief insights.[12]

Postexilic religion distanced itself from its natural roots in the land, as an intentional response to internal factors, because the people wanted to be different from the old ways that had led to destruction and to allow themselves to survive other potential disasters by making the religion abstract and institutionalized. Furthermore, Persian political control allowed and shaped this separation of religion from other aspects of life. Wellhausen's historical reconstruction draws from and thus explains the influences of the people's past, the presence of new international political realities, and the conflict between the inhabitants and the repatriates of the land.

Much of Wellhausen's theology of the early postexilic period centers on the concept of the law. Wellhausen reconstructed a historical situation that required ideological continuity with past tradition in combination with an institutional separation from the past, thus creating a theocracy that was a "residuum of a ruined state."[13] In the same way, the theological content of the preexilic times continued into the postexilic period, but this content was strictly contained within a new institution: the law. This law expressed and encapsulated the old religious traditions and thus preserved, objectified, and limited the religious life of the earlier times.

From this analysis of the institutionalization of the religion of the people comes Wellhausen's central evaluation: "The Mosaic theocracy appears to show an immense retrogression."[14] Although at times Wellhausen praises the law's ability to protect the ancient religion, the weight of his assessment consistently falls on the negative, restrictive aspects of the law.

> *At the restoration of Judaism the old usages were patched together in a new system, which, however, only served as the form to preserve something that was nobler in its nature, but could not have been sacred otherwise than in a narrow shell that stoutly resisted all foreign influences. That heathenism in Israel against which the prophets vainly protested was inwardly overcome by the law on its own ground; and the cultus, after nature had been killed in it, became the shield of supernaturalistic monotheism.*[15]

Wellhausen never brought the positive and negative effects of the law into balance. Always, he perceived the negative effects to be greater than the positive results. The law's perturbation of the ancient religion through institutionalization was abhorrent to Wellhausen, whose own personal background had left him with a strong anti-institutional bias.[16] In his opinion, the dependence of the postexilic period upon institutions was in great contrast with the ancient, personal faith of the Israelites. "The ancient Israelites acted according to 'the uncommon freshness of their impulses' with the divine power imbuing them as individuals, whereas after the exile the outward norms and the established institutions overwhelmed the vitality of the individuals."[17] Wellhausen's attitude toward Judaism as a whole was extremely negative, and this attitude pervades his writings and limits its objective results.[18] Certainly Wellhausen's theological statements should be taken with great hesitancy. This does not require, however, that his historical reconstructions should be rejected.[19]

Subsequent Historical Reconstructions

Much later scholarship on the early postexilic period reflects both Wellhausen's understanding of institutionalization, its internal causes, and Persia's external cooperation. These influences can be traced throughout the subsequent century of scholarship.

Whereas Wellhausen emphasized the increasing institutionalization due to internal causes, Martin Noth stressed the external factors that influenced Judea in this period, especially Persian policy. Even religion should be understood from this perspective, since Yehud's external political tutelage drove its inhabitants to the interior dimensions of personal spirituality. The Persian Empire, according to Noth, took advantage of this tendency and gained its subjects' loyalty by the wise policy of encouraging their religion.[20] This Persian policy allowed the religious life of the people to take on ever greater autonomy, while keeping any and all forms of political independence in abeyance. Thus Persian policy, not the internal continuation of a centuries-old shift of religion away from its natural base, caused the increasing centrality of the Temple vis-à-vis politics.[21]

The priestly influence grew, and Noth understood such influence in the light of the high priest's status as a Persian official. The community also depended on Persia for its own internal regulation. Although the Deuteronomistic code was in effect, it could not be enforced, since it assumed a politically independent community. When the need for reorganization was recognized, the impulse for this societal restructuring came from the exiles still living in Babylonia, such as Ezra and Nehemiah.[22] These eras of restructuring under the direction of high priests and scribes were not instances of internal institutionalization, as Wellhausen would argue, but examples of external manipulation of Yehud within the narrow confines of Persian design, according to Noth.[23]

The community was structured around the goal of Deutero-Isaiah. That ideal formed the motivation for the community's reformation and served as the gauge for success. This was an internal factor, and even though this goal was not reached, it was the controlling factor in the community's nature and self-definition throughout the early postexilic period, according to John Bright.[24] External factors, such as the Persian imperial policies, set a general framework in which Yehud was extremely free to operate; thus most influences for social developments were internal.[25]

Yehezkel Kaufmann's analysis of the postexilic period focused on temple and cult. Before the exile, the cult was naturalistic, and thus all the people participated in it eagerly. In the early postexilic period, temple and cult symbolized the people's reverence for God.[26] Despite occasional neglect of the temple, the cult succeeded in purifying the religion from idolatry.[27] The internal religious nature of the community was thus homogeneous. In this restoration of the community's cultic life, political factors played only a slight role. Postexilic Jews understood Persia's policies of repopulation as effects of God's pleasure with the people. Thus internal factors, such as piety, caused Persian policy. The internal factor of religion controlled the development of the community.[28]

Like Noth, Peter Ackroyd emphasized the importance of Persian political influence upon the postexilic community. Persian policy was not tolerant, since harsh ruthlessness could also be used.[29] However, the Persian government frequently and successfully used conciliation to discourage rebellion.[30] Ackroyd argued, against Noth, that the influence of Persian policy upon Yehud did not mean that Babylonian Jews were responsible for the temple. Instead, he suggested that such a view was the opinion of the Chronicler rather than a reflection of actual events.[31] The anticipation of the new age, encouraged by Haggai and Zechariah, led to the reconstruction of the temple, which provided a new focal point for the community. Although Jerusalem and its temple formed a center for Jewish life, the increased geographic dispersion of the Jewish people meant that the Jerusalem temple was a center only in a loose sense. Consequently, Judean hopes of a new age were frustrated and religious devotion declined.[32] This presented a continuous development of the temple as a religious symbol. "In fact the postexilic period represents a natural development from the thought of the exilic age in the direction of a right understanding of the nature of the presence of God of which the Temple is the most potent symbol."[33]

In these matters of thought, symbolism, and religious expectation, Ackroyd stresses the internal causal factors of continuity with the past and connectedness between politics and religion. He emphasizes that Persia kept close scrutiny over its provinces. Although Persia could redirect Judean life at any point, the impetus for change often came from within the Judean society. In fact, almost all of the recorded early postexilic events developed from internal factors within the limits set by Persia.

In recent years, Paul D. Hanson has offered a new reconstruction of early postexilic history. The destruction of 587 B.C.E. and its resultant national trauma ended the previous social differences and shattered the precarious balance of power between various groups. Several competitive power groups arose. After the exile, a hierocratic party returned to Palestine with the express purpose of building the temple, supported by a Persian mandate.[34]

This hierocratic group exerted significant influence and gained a quick advantage in the struggle for power, since it offered a more pragmatic plan for the reconstruction of the community than did other, more theoretical groups. The hierocrats struggled against certain disciples of the prophets, especially followers of Deutero-Isaiah, who still held the egalitarianism and universalism of the prophetic ideal. These visionaries challenged the hierocrats, and this opposition is the chief dynamic of the early postexilic period in Hanson's reconstruction, as the hierocrats became increasingly subject to secular interests and to concerns about their own power.[35]

As the two groups polarized and as the balance of secular power shifted to the hierocrats, their attacks on the visionaries became increasingly severe and effective, until the two groups completely separated.[36] Hanson's historical reconstruction of the early postexilic period thus diverges greatly from Wellhausen's depiction. Scholarly consensus emphasized the nearly unanimous self-rearrangement of the community into a new pattern of life that centered on the rebuilt temple. In Hanson's view, a hierocratic group grasped power very early in the postexilic period and used that power to gain more influence, until they rigidly controlled the entire community. The events of the period were not unquestioned; they were the results of a bitter struggle for community control. This one social sector imposed a new community structure, over increasing opposition by the rest of the society.

Hanson's reconstruction almost completely dismantles Wellhausen's hypothesis, with one highly notable exception: Hanson fully maintains Wellhausen's idea of institutionalization. Wellhausen reconstructed a process of institutionalization that turned the idealism of the early prophets into pragmatic plans.[37] Wellhausen, despite his marked theological predisposition against institutionalism, saw the postexilic institutions as somewhat passive. Hanson argues that the postexilic hierocratic institutions actively suppressed opposition in their pursuit of power and social control.

Hanson's argument completely reorients the question of causation. The chief dynamic of the early postexilic period was a competition between two groups, creating an internal causation for the majority of social events and structures. However, external factors enter this portrayal in that the hierocratic group was able to gain official Persian support for its plans. In Hanson's treatment, the Persian government never interferes independently in the life of the Judean community; instead, the hierocratic group mediates all such Persian influences. The hierocrats actively seek and receive Persian intervention in their favor for specific projects, such as the rebuilding of the temple. Thus Hanson reverses the direction of causation. The hierocrats can and do cause Persian policy, and they use that power of policy for advantage in their internal struggles.

Despite the persuasiveness of Hanson's reconstructions and the extent of its acceptance, more recent historians of the early postexilic period have consistently emphasized the Persian Empire's external influences upon the Jerusalem community. Geo Widengren argued that times of internal dissension within the empire led to messianic expectations within the community around 520 B.C.E., but not that the dissension caused political unrest.[38] Persian interests and policies were the chief influences upon Jerusalem; the presence or absence of certain policies affected the social situation of the Judean community. Widengren also noted distinctions among various spheres of social life; Persian policy created controlling external influences in political, linguistic, and ideological matters, whereas internal factors were more important in cultic and social items.[39]

J. Maxwell Miller and John H. Hayes emphasized that the "vigorous life" of the community had continued in Judea throughout the exile, and therefore discontinuity is not a likely explanation.[40] Because the Persian Empire as a whole was stable in the early postexilic period, this was also the case in Yehud.[41] Thus the external factors are dominant in Miller and Hayes' depiction of the early postexilic period. Persian policy controlled many aspects of the Judean community, both directly and indirectly, through the appointment of officials to supervise and govern. Even many of the internal factors were mediated through Persian-appointed officials, and thus these too were subject to external considerations.

Eric M. Meyers discussed two major elements in early postexilic Yehud: the return of significant numbers of exiles and the response of the Yehudite leadership to this and other elements of Persian policy. The first generation's response to the Persian policies (522–486 B.C.E.) was "a pragmatic and tolerant attitude toward Persian rule."[42] This was a very stable period, controlled by Persian policy and by the leaders' response. The second generation of Yehudite leadership (486–445 B.C.E.) faced a much different situation of instability and uncertainty, because Persia had turned its attentions elsewhere. The difficulties of ethnic self-definition combined with religious corruption and economic decline to create a chaotic social condition. Nehemiah's arrival formed a new, third generation of leadership "as part of a larger Persian effort to fortify the routes to the coastal lands and Egypt."[43] Thus, Persian intervention, both in its presence and in its absence, presented the chief dynamic for the postexilic period.

Summary

The general outline of Wellhausen's historical reconstruction of the early postexilic period and its religion has been repeated throughout the majority of subsequent scholarship. Judea in the early postexilic period abandoned its desire for political independence and instead formed itself as a religious community, centered in the rebuilt temple in Jerusalem. Wellhausen perceived the chief influences for this new understanding and new structuring of the community to be internal, including the institutionalization of the religion that had begun with the centralization of the cult, which removed the religion from its roots with the people and the land. The external factors of Persian policy coincidentally allowed the community to reshape itself in the directions intended by the internal factors. Later, the distribution of causation became a major issue in the scholarship. Noth stressed the external influences of Persian policy as the controlling factor; Ackroyd argued for a greater balance between the two types of causes.[44]

Another issue in scholarship, the degree and nature of institutionalization, sustained a debate that reflected this phenomenon's centrality in Wellhausen's depiction. Bright understood the majority of Israelite history to contain significantly developed institutions, and thus the postexilic period could not be considered to be more institutionalized than any other period. Of course, there were differences in the nature of the institutions, and in the balance between the various institutional sectors, as the priesthood grew to increased significance vis-à-vis other institutions, but Judean religion did not become more institutionalized, according to Bright. Kaufmann agreed both with Wellhausen's concept of institutionalization and with his view of the decline in religion, but not with any causal connection between the two. The institutionalized form of cultic worship was not theologically bankrupt and could have been observed with great fervor and piety.

Hanson differed greatly from Wellhausen on both issues. Hanson argued for internal causation, with the desire of the hierocrats to build a temple impacting Persian policy. Also, Hanson described institutions that pursued power in order to subjugate the opposing, noninstitutionalizing groups.

Yehud, the Persian Colony

The variety of perspectives points clearly to a central problem in any study of Yehud. Were the chief factors that caused or contributed to Yehud's specific character internal or external? Our initial answer to that thorny question will shape the rest of this study, and yet such answers do not come easily. Certainly Yehud experienced both internal and external influences at different times within its development, and these influences varied in strength and direction.

Yehud was a Persian colony.[15] In political arenas, its greatest influences were external. Persia's size and power could overwhelm the tiny province of Yehud, and so it was possible for the external causes to be completely determinative of Yehud's life. Yet Yehud also was heir to traditions that shaped its character. Although Persia controlled Yehud, Yehud was still only a colony, with some degree of political self-determination, even if Persia limited its options severely. Yehud formed its own society, complete with internally determined goals, activities, norms, and values, as well as its struggles and conflicts. The community formed this society out of the building blocks of its own traditions and customs, struggling to create itself out of the various opinions and actions of many constituents.

Yehud experienced its political establishment through the activity of Persia's imperial expansion and administration, but the community maintained and transformed itself through the dynamics of internal social formation. From this perspective, there is no "exile" (absence of people from the land) followed by "restoration" (a failed goal of return to self-rule in the old fashion, by elites who come from Babylonia). Instead, there are only shifts in the level and nature of political organization. Imperial political goals shaped Yehud in an attempt to create a new sense of identity suitable for a colony, but these external pressures combined with internal factors of continuity and opposition.

Notes

1. The term "Yehud" reflects the Persian name for the province or area that included Jerusalem and its environs. The use of this term differentiates Jerusalem and "Judah" during the postexilic period from the independent Judah of the monarchy as well as from Judah in other periods. Also, "Yehud" restricts the analysis to the period of Persian rule (539–333 B.C.E.).

2. In modern science, experimental method allows for repetition of connected events, in order to develop arguments of causation. However, social-scientific investigation of past phenomena does not allow such repetition. This means that the direction of causation must remain indeterminate, even though we can notice instances of probable correlation. For this reason, the direction of causation is not a result of study but is a perspective that organizes evidence prior to study.

3. Julius Wellhausen, *Prolegomena to the History of Ancient Israel* (New York: Meridian Books, 1957). For a recent evaluation of the impact of Wellhausen's work upon the scholarship of the Hebrew Bible and other fields of study, see Douglas A. Knight, ed., *Julius Wellhausen and His "Prolegomena to the History of Israel," Semeia* 25 (Chico, Calif.: Scholars Press, 1982).

4. See Douglas A. Knight, "Wellhausen and the Interpretation of Israel's Literature," *Semeia* 25 (1982): 26. Note the influence of Wellhausen upon the views of Israelite religious institutionalization in Max Weber, *Ancient Judaism* (Glencoe, Ill.: Free Press, 1952). Also, Gerhard von Rad shared the view that the postexilic prophets were so far removed from the traditional religion and that the populace was so detached from true faith that the tradition could be made relevant only with great difficulty (*Old Testament Theology*, 2 vols. [New York: Harper & Row, 1962–65], 2:264).

5. Wellhausen, *Prolegomena*, 420.

6. Ibid., 494. Wellhausen states that this is the reason for the restored communities' insistence on "ethnic" separation between the former exiles and those who had remained in the land. Only

those who had returned from the exile in Babylon have sufficient separation from the preexilic type of religion and community that was still being practiced by those who had remained in the land. Although there were still ethnic connections between the two groups, this natural connection was denied in favor of new, abstract religious ties.

7. Ibid., 420.

8. Ibid. This is the insight developed by Paul D. Hanson (*The Dawn of Apocalyptic: The Historical and Sociological Roots of Jewish Apocalyptic Eschatology*, rev. ed. [Philadelphia: Fortress Press, 1979]; *The People Called: The Growth of Community in the Bible* [San Francisco: Harper & Row, 1986]; "Israelite Religion in the Early Postexilic Period," in *Ancient Israelite Religion: Essays in Honor of Frank Moore Cross*, ed. Patrick D. Miller, Jr., Paul D. Hanson, and S. Dean McBride [Philadelphia: Fortress Press, 1987], 485–508). Hanson understands an institutionalization of postexilic religion among the hierocrats, set in opposition to the eschatological visionaries.

9. Wellhausen, *Prolegomena*, 403. Note the assumption that prophets were charismatic, uncontrollable innovators, a view that echoes throughout Weber, *Ancient Judaism*. Cf. the recent reflections in Frederick E. Greenspahn, "Why Prophecy Ceased," *JBL* 108 (1989): 37–49.

10. Wellhausen's position here agrees with that of Abraham Kuenen, *The Prophets and Prophecy in Israel*, trans. Adam Milroy (Amsterdam: Philo Press, 1969), 185.

11. Wellhausen, *Prolegomena*, 422.

12. Knight, "Wellhausen and the Interpretation of Israel's Literature," 32.

13. This has drawn sharp criticism from Jewish scholars, such as Yehezkel Kaufmann, *History of the Religion of Israel*, vol. 4, *From the Babylonian Captivity to the End of Prophecy*, trans. C. W. Efroymson (New York: Ktav, 1977), 455–56.

14. Wellhausen, *Prolegomena*, 422.

15. Ibid., 425. For the continuing effects of this interpretation, see Lester L. Grabbe, "The Jewish Theocracy from Cyrus to Titus: A Programmatic Essay," *JSOT* 37 (1987): 117–24. For a critical appraisal of Wellhausen's opinions, see Knight, "Wellhausen and the Interpretation of Israel's Literature," 33.

16. See also John H. Hayes, "Wellhausen as a Historian of Israel," *Semeia* 25 (1982): 55.

17. Knight, "Wellhausen and the Interpretation of Israel's Literature," 32.

18. Lou H. Silberman, "Wellhausen and Judaism," *Semeia* 25 (1982): 75–78.

19. In the light of the problematic nature of Wellhausen's theology of Judaism, it is surprising and disturbing that a great deal of subsequent theological reflection on the postexilic period echoes his negative evaluation of postexilic religion. Nevertheless Wellhausen's general negative evaluation of the religious value of the period has remained more widely accepted than his precise historical formulations.

20. Martin Noth, *The History of Israel*, 2d ed., trans. P. R. Ackroyd (New York: Harper & Row, 1960), 304.

21. Ibid., 314–15.

22. Ibid., 315–18.

23. John Bright, *A History of Israel*, 3d ed. (Philadelphia: Westminster Press, 1981), 343–49, argued that postexilic Yehud manifested no greater a degree of institutionalization than monarchic Israel did, even though the institutions changed.

24. Ibid., 341–62.

25. John Bright, *The Kingdom of God: The Biblical Concept and Its Meaning for the Church* (Nashville, Tenn.: Abingdon Press, 1953), 156–62. This echoes the opinions of von Rad, *Old Testament Theology*, 2:281. The opinion mostly repeats Wellhausen.

26. Kaufmann's view of the change in the postexilic cult parallels Wellhausen's institutionalization, although he rejects Wellhausen's theology.

27. Kaufmann, *History of the Religion of Israel*, 4:213, 438.

28. This is also expressed in Zechariah's visions, which developed from a "hidden messianic mood" and portrayed two realms, an earthly realm controlled by Persia and a heavenly realm ruled by God. It was only the heavenly realm that was significant for the community's self-understanding and formation (Kaufmann, *History of the Religion of Israel,* 4:302–3).

29. For a more recent statement of this position, see Amélie Kuhrt, "The Cyrus Cylinder and Achaemenid Imperial Policy," *JSOT* 25 (1983): 83–97.

30. Peter R. Ackroyd, *Israel under Babylon and Persia,* New Clarendon Bible, Old Testament 4 (Oxford: Oxford University Press, 1970), 165.

31. Ibid., 169–71.

32. Ibid., 172–73, 180–81.

33. Peter R. Ackroyd, *Exile and Restoration: A Study of Hebrew Thought of the Sixth Century B.C.*, OTL (Philadelphia: Westminster Press, 1968), 248.

34. Hanson, *Dawn of Apocalyptic,* 212, 226.

35. Ibid., 255–66, 278.

36. Cf. the earlier and closely related view of Otto Plöger, *Theocracy and Eschatology,* trans. S. Rudman (Richmond, Va.: John Knox Press, 1968). Also, see the related notion of the elimination of eschatology as developed by von Rad, *Old Testament Theology,* 2:297.

37. Wellhausen, *Prolegomena,* 420.

38. Geo Widengren, "The Persian Period," in *Israelite and Judean History,* ed. John H. Hayes and J. Maxwell Miller (Philadelphia: Westminster Press, 1977), 489–538.

39. Ibid., 538.

40. J. Maxwell Miller and John H. Hayes, *A History of Ancient Israel and Judah* (Philadelphia: Westminster Press, 1986), 445.

41. Ibid., 448–60.

42. Eric M. Meyers, "The Persian Period and the Judean Restoration: From Zerubbabel to Nehemiah," in *Ancient Israelite Religion: Essays in Honor of Frank Moore Cross,* ed. Patrick D. Miller, Jr., Paul D. Hanson, and S. Dean McBride (Philadelphia: Fortress Press, 1987), 509.

43. Ibid., 516.

44. Within the wider arena of Persian or Achaemenid studies, this question received the focus of Heleen Sancisi-Weerdenburg and Amélie Kuhrt, eds., *Achaemenid History IV: Centre and Periphery. Proceedings of the Groningen 1986 Achaemenid History Workshop* (Leiden: Nederlands Instituut voor het Nabije Oosten, 1990). Most works on Achaemenid history emphasize the importance of the center (and thus the influence of external factors on the peripheries); for a chief example, see M. A. Dandamaev and Vladimir G. Lukonin, *The Culture and Social Institutions of Ancient Iran* (Cambridge: Cambridge University Press, 1989).

45. The colonial concept is not new, although its sociological implications have not been sufficiently explored. The historical insights of Geo Widengren, J. Maxwell Miller and John H. Hayes, and Eric M. Meyers all have moved in this direction, as has the discussion by Norman K. Gottwald, *The Hebrew Bible: A Socio-Literary Introduction* (Philadelphia: Fortress Press, 1985), 409–594.

CHAPTER 2

SETTING THE STAGE: EXILE AND DIASPORA

BABYLONIA CONQUERED JUDAH AND carried the population into exile in 587 B.C.E., where the Jews lived until Persian liberation in 539 B.C.E. Despite the simplicity of that statement, the actuality of the process and the nature of exile prove to be much more elusive. The southern kingdom of Judah had experienced a slow decline, and its relationship with Babylonia was complex long before the conquest and exile. Furthermore, the specifics of the exile itself are unclear. How many Judeans were removed to Babylonia? Who was taken and who was left behind? How was life in Babylonia different from life in Judah? How did life in Judah change as a result of the exile? How did the transition from Babylonian imperial rule to Persian imperial rule impact both the Judean and the Babylonian communities? These questions provide the basis for a new understanding of the exile.

The Collapse of Monarchic Judah

In 722 B.C.E., Assyria conquered Samaria, the capital of Israel, immediately to Judah's north. Judah and Israel had existed as separate nations for just over two centuries, but Israel's destruction had grave implications for Judah, which escaped a similar fate only by capitulating to Assyria, including an occupation in 711 B.C.E. At times Judah had served as Israel's vassal and at other times as Israel's ally. After the destruction of Samaria, neither of those relationships was possible. Instead, Judah was left to navigate the problems of international politics alone.

Was Judah independent after Israel's destruction? Despite the Judean kings on the Davidic throne, larger world powers frequently intervened. In addition to their occupation in 711 B.C.E., Assyria besieged Jerusalem in 701 and had a strong military presence in Judah in 679, 677, 674, 670, and 664.[1] In subsequent years, Assyria posed less of a threat to Judah because of its own troubles, resulting in Babylonian conquest in 625 B.C.E. When Assyria withdrew, Egypt filled the power vacuum, exercising some control over Judah for at least 635 to 610 B.C.E. (2 Kings 23:28-30). After 604, Babylonia had gained ascendancy, and Judah's kings were Babylonian vassals. In 587 B.C.E., Babylonia besieged Jerusalem (2 Kings 25). Jerusalem never regained its independence or its status as a separate vassal in the face of Babylonian might. Throughout this entire period, Judah was rarely an independent state; for most of the time, it existed as a vassal or a dominated ally of a larger power, whether Assyria, Egypt, or Babylonia.

The Destruction of Jerusalem

Early in 597 B.C.E., Babylonia deported a large contingent from Jerusalem, including King Jehoiachin and many of the elites and officials of Judah (2 Kings 24). In 587, Babylonia once more advanced on Jerusalem, breaking a siege of at least eighteen months by breaching the walls of Jerusalem (2 Kings 25). The invading army dismantled the walls, burned the city, executed many of the rulers, and deported a number to more central Babylonian territory.

How severe was the destruction of Jerusalem in the early sixth century? Typical opinions have emphasized its severity. Consider, for example, this quotation from John Bright: "The land had been completely wrecked. Its cities destroyed, its economy ruined, its leading citizens killed or deported, the population consisted chiefly of poor peasants considered incapable of making trouble."[2] Such a quotation represents utter devastation, with a near impossibility of any continuing society. Bright later cautions that this disaster and its disruption of Judean life should not be minimized, and he further asserts that the people who remained in Judah were too depopulated and too helpless without their leaders to organize themselves or to follow true religion.[3] From this interpretative perspective, Judean life was over. Although there were inhabitants, there was no society in the Jerusalem area after 587 B.C.E.

The evidence, however, does not support such a conclusion. Certainly the devastation was great, and the effects on Judean society were immense. It does not follow, however, that there was no social organization. A more pertinent question deals with the type of society present in the Jerusalem area from 587 to 539 B.C.E.

Certainly there was great damage to the physical accomplishments of monarchic Judah. The walls of Jerusalem fell and many buildings were demolished or burned. In all likelihood, the Babylonian army targeted the buildings of military, political, economic, and symbolic importance, such as the palace, the temple, and other governmental sites. Without walls, the city remained unable to protect itself against foreign invasion, and thus its ability to dictate its own foreign policy declined as well as its ability to store safely precious items within the city.

In all, Jerusalem experienced a sharp depopulation. Estimates have varied widely, but there may well have been 250,000 in Jerusalem before 587 B.C.E. and only half that or even as low as 20,000 or fewer inhabitants during the middle of the exile.[4] Many scholars prefer the lower figure as being more reflective of the archaeological data.[5] However, this does not represent the death or deportation of the Jerusalem population; instead, it may well indicate the deurbanization of the city dwellers. The biblical evidence indicates that Babylonia "carried away all Jerusalem" (2 Kings 24:14a), but the text then corrects this impression of totality almost immediately: "no one remained, except the poorest people of the land" (2 Kings 24:14b; cp. 2 Kings 25:12).[6] Furthermore, the text asserts the continuing presence of local leadership, in the form of Zedekiah (2 Kings 24:17-18). Although the Deuteronomistic narrative emphasizes the totality of the military action, it must also admit that the action was not at all total. The destruction of the great houses by fire (2 Kings 25:9) may well involve only the wealthiest portions, and the wall may only have been breached at a limited number of places (2 Kings 25:10). Repeatedly throughout the rest of 2 Kings, the reader discovers more persons left around Jerusalem.

What becomes clear is not the total devastation of Jerusalem and the removal of all of its inhabitants but rather the removal (through death and deportation) of the upper strata of Jerusalemite and Judahite society. Babylonia killed or captured the wealthy, the landowners, the temple officials, the military leaders, and the political governmental elite, but not the majority of the people. The poor people remained. Babylonia seems to have devastated the city of Jerusalem and its wealthy, powerful occupants while leaving a substantial portion of the populace behind, who continued their work as laborers in the fields outside Jerusalem. The destruction did not noticeably affect the rural or poor constituencies of Judah. The reader of the biblical text gains the opposite opinion only because of the text's unbalanced emphasis on the "important" people of Jerusalem, among the ruling classes. Many of them went to Babylonia.

Babylonian Life

Life was quite different for the Jews whom Babylonia deported. It represented a highly significant change in the pattern of their daily existence from the lives they had known in Jerusalem and environs. These exiles had been elites; they had been the urban people with significant employment in the palace or the temple, or they had been the larger landowners with considerable wealth and social power. For them, exile meant not only a geographic displacement but a removal from their sources of power that had formed the basis of their self-concept. No longer were they the rulers; they were now the subjects of a world empire.

Babylonia itself left almost no record of its treatment of exiles, but there are clues about exilic life. Ezekiel depicts exile as a mostly rural event; his locale is near an irrigation canal in an agricultural area, and he refers to elders, apparently representing villages and other small communities of Jewish exiles.[7] Deutero-Isaiah focuses on the religious practices of the exiles and their Babylonian captors and depicts the sort of temple life that indicates the city of Babylon itself as a locale. This supports the assertions of 2 Kings 25 that the Babylonian Empire deported the king and the officials to the imperial palace in Babylon (2 Kings 25:11, 27-30). Thus it seems that some of the exiles lived in the capital and were involved in governmental activity, whereas others were primarily agricultural and rural.[8]

Such a division of the exilic population makes sense in the light of typical imperial tendencies and goals in deportations. Imperial policies tend to involve the acquisition of labor forces subjugated into areas of imperial need.[9] In 587 B.C.E. the Babylonian Empire's greatest needs reflected their expansionist policies: government and food. Those exiles from Judah with governmental experience (including temple service) would have worked within the Babylonian palace and temple system. The empire would have sent other exiles to new fields, where they could organize themselves in any way possible so long as they produced enough food to pay their in-kind taxes. This parallels the two groups attested in the Hebrew Bible.

As was the case with all of the ancient empires, Babylonia required a substantial bureaucracy in order to operate its expanding holdings. Both palace and temple needed experts in bureaucratic, imperial functioning as well as persons with foreign experience. The Jewish exiles who had worked within the government before, as well as those with priestly experience, would have met this imperial need. Certainly Judah's last king sat at the emperor's table for the rest of his life; it is unlikely that this was merely a position of honor. It seems more reasonable to think of the Jewish king as contributing to matters of state in an advisory capacity. Other Jewish governmental officials would have served similar functions in other levels of the bureaucracy. For instance, the ancient world had such low literacy rates that there was a special value upon any person who could write. Perhaps Judah's scribes found employment within the palace and temple as Babylonian scribes, continuing their same line of work but for a new employer. Likewise, the Babylonian temple system would have found attractive the inclusion of trained personnel. Although the religious systems were different, and although the Babylonian priests might well have seen the worship of Yahweh as a conflicting religion, syncretism was well entrenched and should not be discounted. Certainly Deutero-Isaiah gives the impression of a close knowledge of the Babylonian temple system, perhaps also indicating the high level of involvement of some Jews with that system.[10]

In the rural areas, Babylonia's interest was the increase of food production. Imperial strategy involved the intensification of core agriculture rather than dependence on colonial food sources. As a part of this strategy, Babylonia had been opening more of its land for production. The empire may not have farmed the area between the Tigris and Euphrates rivers before the early sixth century. This dry area required extensive irrigation for proper growing, and so it proved to be a more expensive project than agriculture nearer to the main rivers. At some point in time, the Babylonian Empire contributed the labor to provide the irrigation and then transplanted client populations in the newly irrigated region in order to farm the land and bring it into production. This intensification of the land both supported and required expansionist imperial policies.

Perhaps the Ezekiel communities of rural people were persons required to farm as part of the intensification process. If so, it becomes evident why they complained about exile more than did the city group, as reflected in Deutero-Isaiah. Whereas the urban exiles condemned the acculturation to Babylonian practices, the rural exiles had a simpler task of cultural resistance, since they lived in their own, semiautonomous communities, but their lifestyles had undergone the greater change. The urban exiles might have continued in roughly the same line of work, but the rural exiles had not been farmers before the exile. All of the exiles came from Judah's upper social strata, especially the governmental officials, operatives in the Jerusalem temple, the military's lower and middle echelons, wealthy landowners, and influential merchants. If the employees of palace and temple were relocated to Babylon, then the rural areas would have been populated with landowners, merchants, and military officials. None of them would have been primarily involved with food production in their Judean lives; instead, the exile to the farm would have reoriented their whole lives. This rural group experienced much greater change.

Neither the urban nor the rural exilic groups were slaves. Babylonia did not depend on slaves for the economic operation to any large extent. However, Babylonia did require intensification, and the rural exiles may have experienced extreme taxation in order to maximize Babylonia's profit. Even though these exiles were farming in the middle of Mesopotamian fertility or practicing their trades within the world capital, all of the exiles experienced a severe discontinuity with their pasts. The reconstruction of community in the midst of such social disruption would have been of the most fundamental importance.

Life in Judah

The change in life for those who remained in Judah was also disruptive but of a very different nature from that experienced by the deportees. Although the capital city had faced destruction and although the rural areas had also undergone pillaging during the siege of Jerusalem, much of the land was either untouched or reusable within a growing season. Jerusalem's population decreased remarkably, but the rural areas show rather little change in population throughout this period. In fact, the effects of the exile on the Judean peasantry seem minor.[11]

Although the effects on the rural people would have been only minor, there seems to be the presence of low-level Babylonian imperial administration. The Hebrew Bible records the name of the first local administrator, Gedaliah (2 Kings 25:23-26). As a recently conquered area, Judah would still need to pay taxes, and thus there would be a government in place. There is no evidence to suggest that the withdrawal of the Babylonian army necessitated the removal of the imperial administrative structure, and if that structure stayed in place (perhaps in an altered form), there was at least some sort of social structure operative in exilic Judah.

The social structure continued to include some hierarchicalization. Village elders remained and were probably as influential as ever in organizing local life. The native central elites who had labored to create a unified kingdom were gone, but the more local forms of society were still present. With this lower level of social organization and a thin overlay of imperial bureaucracy at the top, the rest of society's local institutions and some of its regional ones probably remained intact. Family life, cultural traditions, modes of economic productivity, behavioral norms and values, ideological assumptions, and local religious rituals probably were among these cultural constants. The removal of the elite meant the end of national ideology, military conscription, obligatory temple worship, and other elements of social centralization, but it is difficult to assess the degree to which these social institutions had ever penetrated rural Judah. Their cessation during the exile may have affected the rural population very little indeed.

The destruction of the temple did not end worship. Although Babylonia had deported the priests from the central national shrine in Jerusalem, there is no evidence that the worship of Yahweh (and other deities) in high places and villages had ever ceased or that it was threatened by the Babylonian incursions. One should not assume that all priests went into exile; probably only those priests who had connections to the Jerusalem temple were taken. These priests continued to represent the Jewish religious heritage in the Jerusalem area, despite the removal of the temple. There may well have been continued ritual sacrifices on the temple mound as well as in the rural areas.[12] The removal of the temple cultic apparatus may have had very little effect on religion as the rural Jews practiced it.

In the economic arena, the rural inhabitants of Judah would still need trade in similar amounts as during the monarchy. Without a centralized Jerusalem government and merchant elite to manage such trade, it may well have been more haphazard, unless other groups (such as the Babylonian administration or the elites from an adjacent area) intervened to do so. Trade probably continued, although at a reduced level, serving as an organizing factor for the rest of the economy by continuing economic ties to the larger world.

Thus, in political, economic, social, and religious areas, the exile was a severe change to Judean society, but it was not a categorical end of that society or a complete transformation. The depopulation and deurbanization of Judah must have altered the society, but many of the decentralized functions of the society would have continued with very little change.

Persia and Babylonia

Although Babylonian conquest in far regions of Palestine had created the exile, such imperial strength did not last long. In the decades after Jerusalem's destruction, Babylonia waned quickly. The rise of another empire, Media, threatened to take away Babylonia's influence in the Mesopotamian region. Nabonidus, the king of Babylon, made an alliance against the Median Empire with one of Media's vassals, Persia. Quite possibly, Babylonia did not take Persia seriously, since it had not been the world power that Babylonia had once been, and since it was a barbarian tribe from the north, an area that Babylonia had never considered a significant threat to its own imperial security. Assisted by the alliance, Babylonia directed its attention toward the west and south, entering into successful battles against Syria and other regions under nominal Babylonian control. Persia's king, Cyrus, then attacked Media, led by his father-in-law, Astyages.

From 555 to 550 B.C.E., this alliance was effective in expanding Babylonian and Persian territory at Media's expense. In 550 B.C.E., Cyrus' Persian forces took Ecbatana and effectively controlled the earlier Median Empire. From this position of power, Cyrus attacked the Median Empire's western holdings, surrounding Babylonia by 547 B.C.E. Despite Nabonidus' strategic retreat southward into Arabia, Cyrus succeeded in defeating the whole of Babylonia by late 539 B.C.E. The near decade of Persian threat to Babylonia created a slow, gradual war, often noted for its use of propaganda and internal dissent.

With the defeat of Babylonia, the Persian Empire took control of the former empires of Babylonia and Media. Under the Persian Empire, a number of changes took place in imperial administration. The time of exile soon ended, and the character of Judah's existence changed once more.

Notes

1. John H. Hayes and Paul K. Hooker, *A New Chronology for the Kings of Israel and Judah and Its Implications for Biblical History and Literature* (Atlanta: John Knox Press, 1988), 71–83.

2. Bright, *History of Israel*, 331.

3. Ibid., 343–45.

4. The larger figure reflects the largest number offered by Daniel Smith, *The Religion of the Landless: The Social Context of the Babylonian Exile* (Bloomington, Ind.: Meyer-Stone Books, 1989), 32. The smaller figure can be found in Bright, *History of Israel*, 344.

5. Most recently, see Joseph Blenkinsopp, "Temple and Society in Achaemenid Judah," in *Second Temple Studies: 1. Persian Period*, ed. Philip R. Davies, JSOTSup 117 (Sheffield: JSOT Press, 1991), 43–44.

6. All scripture references are from the NRSV unless otherwise noted. In some cases, I have substituted "Yahweh" for "the LORD."

7. Ezekiel's inaugural vision was located near the irrigation canal, Chebar (Ezekiel 1:1). He frequently interacted with local elders (see Ezekiel 8:1; 14:1).

8. For the districting of the Jews in Babylonia, see M. A. Dandamaev, *A Political History of the Achaemenid Empire* (Leiden: E. J. Brill, 1989), 61.

9. For perspectives on the control of distant labor resources in secondary state formation, see Barbara J. Price, "Secondary State Formation: An Explanatory Model," in *Origins of the State: The Anthropology of Political Evolution*, ed. Ronald E. Cohen and Elman R. Service, 161–86 (Philadelphia: Institute for the Study of Human Issues, 1978). The use of labor follows the principles of competitive exclusion, as discussed by Robert L. Carneiro, "Political Expansion as an Expression of the Principle of Competitive Exclusion," in Cohen and Service, *Origins of the State*, 205–23. For an examination of irrigation's labor requirements, see Jonathan Haas, *The Evolution of the Prehistoric State* (New York: Columbia University Press, 1982), 146–50.

10. Isaiah 44:9-20; 46:1-7.

11. Peasants rarely suffer when the governments change in ancient worlds, because their existence is day-to-day no matter what policies are adopted. See Eric R. Wolf, *Peasants*, Foundations of Modern Anthropology (Englewood Cliffs, N.J.: Prentice-Hall, 1966).

12. Daniel Smith, *Religion of the Landless*, 34–35.

PART II

THE INFLUENCE OF IMPERIAL POLITICS

CHAPTER 3

CONQUERING BABYLONIA AND THE WEST: CYRUS (539–530 B.C.E.)

THE PERSIAN EMPIRE EXISTED as a separate entity for just over two centuries, during which it expanded to contain an area larger than the world's previous empires. Such an immense political unit inevitably included conflicts and change. Empires were never static; they were constantly in flux through their development and decline. By the competition of various interests and the intrusion of political power throughout the pre-existing and evolving social systems, the empire developed its social forms in changing ways.

The construction of politics is an artificial process, in which a new self-identity (in this case, the notion of an empire) overlays the reality of disparate communities. Cyrus' successes in imperial development created a sense of a Persian Empire that conflicted with the various power groups throughout the space occupied by this fluctuating entity. The movements of an army and the realignment of trade and tribute patterns mark the construction of an empire, as do the imposition of law codes and their enforcement structures. The effects of such a developing empire appear not only in the political structures of the core but also in the ramifications of imperial expansion upon the periphery. Thus the study of Cyrus' imperial expansion will focus on the construction of politics in the centers of the imperial administrative and military apparatuses and also in the colonies, such as Yehud.

The History of Cyrus' Reign

Cyrus

Having begun as a chieftain of one of Media's vassals in 559 B.C.E., Cyrus spent two decades establishing the core of his new empire and defeating the only nearby competitor, Babylonia.[1] Through his conquests of the Median and Babylonian empires, Cyrus gained a formidable area to rule, from Asia Minor and Palestine to the borders of India.[2] This formed the largest empire that the ancient world had known to that point in time; Cyrus later gained control over large portions of the Arabian Peninsula.[3]

Cyrus' administrative style demanded little change from Babylonia and its territories, including Palestine and the Jerusalem area. Although there may well have been a more forceful subjugation of other regions, the Persian Empire did not dismantle or reorganize the parts of the former Babylonian Empire. The priesthoods of various peoples throughout Cyrus' empire regained their former strength and reinstated their former cultic practices. Cyrus allowed most regional administrators (under the Babylonian system) to stay in their places.[4]

Cyrus' chief imperial expansion therefore was not administrative. The growth of law and of bureaucratic systems for imperial enforcement was not highly significant. In most ways, Cyrus' reign as the first Persian emperor represented little or no change from the previous Babylonian imperial involvement with the periphery. Instead, his chief expansion was military. Under his leadership, the Persian Empire gained control through attack upon the previous Babylonian imperial structure; Persia then replaced Babylonia as a nearly identical administration of the distant colonies. Cyrus seems to have planned attacks against Egypt as well, but he never conducted the attack, which would perhaps have necessitated a change in administrative structures in order to integrate a colony previously unsubjugated by Babylonia. Instead of focusing on Egypt, Cyrus looked to the eastern borders, attacking the nomadic Central Asian tribes of the Massagetai.[5] Since these tribes lacked central organization, the imperial reorganization was minimal.

Throughout his reign as Persian emperor, Cyrus focused his attention on the addition of new territory to the empire. Usually the conquered lands paid tribute to Persia in identical structures and amounts as they had previously paid to Babylonia. In the eastern areas, Cyrus required more organizational skills in order to coerce the payment of tribute from other peoples that had never existed as imperial colonies. Still, the systems of imperial organization found in the late Babylonian Empire and the early Persian Empire encouraged Cyrus to expand territorially through military conquest while almost ignoring the potential for social transformation, administrative change, and economic intensification in the imperial colonies. Military expansion served as the most efficient means for increasing imperial income; Cyrus' Persian administration chose to retain past sources of tribute without administrative change and to annex new areas that presented little military resistance.

The Edict of Cyrus

The so-called Edict of Cyrus (Ezra 1:2-4 [in Hebrew] and 6:3-5 [in Aramaic]) reflects one of the few extant legal documents from Cyrus' administration.[6] Although the historicity of both of these documents has rightly been questioned, Cyrus also erected a cylinder with similar information. According to this inscription, Cyrus asserts,

> *I returned to (these) sacred cities on the other side of the Tigris, the sanctuaries of which have been ruins for a long time, the images which (used) to live therein and established for them permanent sanctuaries. I (also) gathered all their (former) inhabitants and returned (to them) their habitations.*[7]

This inscription of Cyrus accords with the general thrust of the decrees that the Book of Ezra attributes to this same emperor. First, the Persian Empire allowed and perhaps encouraged the immigration of colonies' earlier inhabitants, and second, the empire also facilitated the return of religious objects. One question arises: Why did Cyrus' empire undertake such policies? Some scholars have suggested that the Persian Empire was more open to religious freedoms than were previous empires, and others have argued that the Persians shared a monotheism with the Jews and thus possessed a certain sympathy for the Yehudites' religion.

Both of these assertions prove to be problematic. There is no indication that Cyrus or any of the other Persian emperors were monotheistic. To the contrary, they worshiped the deities of each land in which they traversed. Both Cyrus and Cambyses "worshipped all the Persian and foreign deities of their empire, they believed in their power and tried to gain their favours."[8] These emperors did publicly profess devotion to the Persian deity Ahuramazda, but they also praised the powerful beneficence of Yahweh, Marduk, and other gods. Thus the Persian support for Jewish religion in Jerusalem did not spring from a special loyalty to monotheistic religions. Indeed, Cyrus sponsored the restoration of temple objects and he rebuilt temples throughout Babylonia, Elam, and Assyria.[9] Similarly, Cyrus also encouraged the return of foreigners, such as the Phoenicians, the Elamites, and the Jews.[10]

Furthermore, the policies of the Persian Empire seem to be no more sensitive to human rights and religious freedoms than were the administrations of its predecessors.[11] Cyrus showed no interest in the autonomy of his subjects. Instead, his intent in the edict, preserved in different forms on a cylinder and in the Book of Ezra, involved the disposition of goods throughout the controlled empire. The decrees emphasize imperial domination, as expressed in the centralized ability to move populations and property, including symbolically valuable religious property. Cyrus' interest was the enhanced control of the empire, not the religious freedom of his subjects. The mode of Cyrus' control of resources reflects the imperial organization in the time of his reign.

Cyrus' Interests

In general, Cyrus maintained the Babylonian administration apparatus inherited from the previous world empire. However, there were many significant differences. Cyrus avoided the maximization of tribute and the excessive violence of the Assyrian and Babylonian empires.[12] He also moved the dependent imperial populations closer to the peripheries. These changes in policy reflected fundamental shifts in the perception of imperial organization, even though these shifts never progressed beyond their nascent stages in Cyrus' administration.

Babylonian imperial administrative strategy involved centralization; the empire practiced intensification of resources by moving populations toward its own center, where they would farm land that was otherwise underutilized. This kept the Babylonian peripheries weak and placed their populations in areas that the Babylonian armies could more easily defend. In contrast, the early Persian Empire encouraged the subject peoples' movement *away* from the center toward the peripheries. The populations that would have proved to be most mobile were those whose life under Babylonia had been the most tenuous: the recent exiles. Persian policy did not call for forced or speedy relocation; instead, it created a system of values in which relocation became an attractive option for small minorities of the population over the period of several decades. Persia realized that the weakened, underutilized peripheral colonies could not assume the burden of quickly, radically increased populations; instead, Persia encouraged a slow movement.

What could Persia gain from this slow shift to the periphery? The movement of population allowed for the boundaries to build strength. This posture of population deployment accompanied an organization of territorial expansion. The ability of the colonies and peripheries to support traveling armies would greatly increase, assisting Persia's increased dependence on military expansion for the imperial budget. The empire would intensify its border operations and explore possibilities for annexing local territory. Quite possibly, the first acts of the Persian Empire would have been to export sufficient leadership into the outlying areas to ensure their payment of tribute and their loyalty in the face of border wars.

Cyrus' interests in the movement of population and the return of religious artifacts reflected the larger tendencies of the empire to expand its borders. A preparatory step toward such conquest would be the strengthening of the borders and neighboring areas, such as Jerusalem. A more robust and secure population in these areas increased the possibilities for tribute and peace along the military supply routes. Since temples were involved in the collection of tributes and taxes as well as in the ideological grounding of the society, the periphery received a certain level of support for rebuilding its religious institutions. Cyrus intended that the support of Jerusalem and other similar areas would assist his policies of imperial expansion.

These policies remained unemphasized, as befitting the generally low level of imperial intensification expressed by Cyrus' Persian Empire. Cyrus decreed that native populations could return, but there was no widespread return or any administrative support to force or encourage strongly a large population movement. Cyrus intended a low-level increase of peripheral populations and administrative capabilities, and so he allowed returns. This created a slow influx of population into the Jerusalem area over a lengthy period of time.

At the end of his reign, Cyrus turned his attentions increasingly toward the eastern reaches of the empire. In these areas, he followed his pattern of imperial gain through conquest of already organized people groups. By annexing these semideveloped peripheries and requiring them to pay tribute, Cyrus enhanced his population, mercantile, and fiscal bases. In the earliest times of the empire, these were the most cost-effective ways of expanding. Whereas the Babylonians had redirected populations in order to enhance their empire through the intensification of previously occupied land, Cyrus' Persian Empire moved the populations toward the peripheries to annex new territory. In battle in the east, Cyrus died in 530 B.C.E.

Yehud as a Province

Cyrus' administrative structuring of the provinces allowed for a slow increase in Yehud's population through the emigration of Jews from Babylonia. From extant records, it seems that few Jews emigrated in Cyrus' time, but perhaps as many as 45,000 went by the early years of Darius, and 50,000 more by 458 B.C.E.[13] According to Ezra 2:64-65, a total of

49,797 persons arrived with the Persian governor Sheshbazzar in Jerusalem as a result of Cyrus' ordered emigration.[14] However, Ezra's historiography should be considered suspect at best. The books of Ezra and Nehemiah contain records about the middle of the fifth century as well as recollections from the late sixth century; the memories of the earlier time of Cyrus seem to be much less accurate. Ezra's assertion of nearly fifty thousand emigrants may be a correct figure for the number who had moved by the completion of the temple construction, but the thought of one large caravan at a single point in history cannot be accurate. Even if these figures are correct, then the Sheshbazzar emigration may well represent those Babylonian Jews who were present in Jerusalem in 521 B.C.E., and in that case these fifty thousand emigrated at an average rate of fewer than three thousand a year into Jerusalem and its environs.

The gradually increasing population of Yehud did not exist as a unified society. Presumably, the most obvious division would have been the tensions between the emigrants and the natives. Jerusalem was not an abandoned city during the reign of the Babylonian Empire. To the contrary, there was a continuation of worship and a small population. It may have taken the entire reign of Cyrus and his successor, Cambyses, to reach a numerical balance between the native and the immigrant population within Yehud. If so, then the slow shift in power would have been apparent over a period of decades. In the midst of a gradual power shift between the native and immigrant groups, Jerusalem would have experienced at first a deadlock of action and then a slow overcoming of a lingering resistance.

Certainly the differentials in power between the groups complicated this shift in societal influence. Because the immigrants into Jerusalem from Babylonia included Persian governmental officials, this group gained in power more quickly than it grew in numbers. Still, the Persian Empire under Cyrus had not established a sufficiently strong centralized government to allow for the high-level imposition of imperial will. By necessity, the local rulers of Yehud governed with the support of the populace.

A further question arises about the nature of group interactions within Yehud during Cyrus' reign. One would expect frictions between the natives and the immigrants, but perhaps other divisions existed within this community. The lack of evidence makes the consideration of further distinctions extremely problematic, especially with regard to the native population, which is much less represented in the extant literature. However, the immigrants arrived from a community that did leave other records. The Jews in the Babylonian exile did not represent a unified group themselves. Biblical records include a portrayal of a somewhat rural, agricultural group in Ezekiel and a more urban group in 2 Kings 25. Some of the exiles, especially those connected to the royal family, lived in the Babylonian king's palace. Others, including local priestly families and communal elders such those depicted in Ezekiel's prophecy, plus merchants, former military officers, landowners, and others, resided in the farming areas of central Babylonia, where crop production remained the chief concern of communal life.[15] This difference between the former ruling class's life in Babylon itself and the other groups' experience in the fields of Babylonia may well mark a significant variation in attitudes and loyalties. If so, then the immigrants of Cyrus' Jerusalem may reflect this division, separating along the lines of urban, political orientations versus rural, agricultural segments of the exilic population. In matters of imperial administration, the political leaders of the immigrants may or may not disagree significantly with the others. The social solidarity of the immigrant group cannot be safely assumed. As a result, the Persian-appointed political leaders of Yehud would need to create and manage coalitions, combining the interests of the Persian Empire, the agriculturally based groups in Yehud, and the native populations of Yehud.

Despite the differences between the urban and the rural immigrants, the religion of Yahweh continued in each group. At least, both of these immigrant types associated themselves with priests and counted priests as parts of their numbers. Probably the priests who aligned with the urban, political concerns descended from priests and priestly families who lived in Jerusalem and worked from a power base within the capital and the official state temple in late monarchic Jerusalem. Other priests who had not worked within the national temple may well have been deported along with the rural agriculturalists. These local priests would have been much less familiar with the workings of the Jerusalem temple, and then in Babylonian the rural priests had fewer opportunities to participate in the worship of Bel or other Babylonian deities. Although both the urban and the rural priests would have upheld a related form of Yahwism, and although each would have faced similar possibilities for syncretism, it appears that both the rural and the urban priests maintained a closely related theology and practice.

The social interests of these three groups with regard to the Persian Empire follow directly from their past involvement with the empire. The natives represent a conservative force; their life had continued in exile and now they experienced the same sort of administrative governmental overstructure. For these natives, there were no changes except in personnel, and so their investment with the *status quo ante* affected their laissez-faire reaction to the minor shifts of the early Persian Empire. They desired as few changes as possible in the new imperial administration. The rural Babylonian Jewish immigrants, along with the priests, would have sought much the same thing. Their experience of farming in the exile would have been one of state control; perhaps these individuals chose themselves for the emigration to Yehud with the intention of escaping oppressive state control in their agriculture. Thus the priests and the rural immigrants would have worked to minimize Persian interference and involvement in Yehudite life. The political appointees of the Persian Empire, however, would have had a very different investment in their social situation, since their employment and their lives depended upon loyalty to the Persian emperor. Thus they would have worked to enhance Persian influence, as the emperor demanded. Cyrus demanded little change, and so for the time of his reign, there were few tensions between these three groups of early postexilic society. None of these groups wished or attempted to reconstitute the social life from Jerusalem's monarchical, preexilic period. All groups invested themselves away from governmental affairs at the imperial level.

The specific changes under Cyrus' administration prove extremely difficult to determine. Whereas bureaucratic reorganizations under later emperors left annals and created shifts in epigraphic titles, Cyrus' military model for management produced few records. The best assumption, therefore, is that there was little change. Certainly the situation in the time of Darius (after 521 B.C.E.) bespeaks little difference from the late exilic condition of Jerusalem and environs. In the late sixth century, Yehud was still a split and fragmented society, wrestling with questions of rebuilding after the exilic depopulation (see Haggai). Had Cyrus' time produced great change from the exilic patterns of social life, then presumably the situation at the beginning of Darius' time would not have appeared so much like the exile.

The issue of Jerusalem's temple construction illustrates well the extent of the few changes that resulted from Cyrus' administration of the newfound Persian Empire. Cyrus allows the temple to be rebuilt and permits the movement of personnel and some goods in order to encourage the temple construction (Ezra 1–2).[16] However, the construction does not occur; not until Darius' reign some eighteen years later does construction begin, according to Haggai and Zechariah. The purpose of Cyrus' permission for temple construction included intensification and garrisoning. The lack of emphasis for this project is not surprising; Cyrus' interests were on the unconquered territories toward the east. Darius' reasons for building a temple were different, and at that time the construction project began in earnest and reached its conclusion. Under Cyrus, there was permission for emigrants from Babylonia to Yehud to reestablish and fortify Jerusalem society, but there was no great investment in either infrastructure or administrative apparatus.

In short, there is little indication that there were significant changes in the condition of Yehud as a result of Cyrus' rise to power. Instead, the temple was not built and there was no sudden influx of population. The changes begun during Cyrus' reign were gradual, and Jerusalem did not experience their full effects until much later. The life concerns of Yehud's population would not include much consideration of the international movements of armies, nor the intricacies of imperial politics, since neither held much import for daily operations in this distant colony. The internal strife between the natives and the immigrants would have continued to build its frustrations, but even this was a slow process of change rather than a climactic confrontation.

The true effects of Cyrus can be seen in the years of preparation in Babylonia rather than in the change of life in Palestine. Cyrus spent considerable effort in propaganda to gain the support of various Babylonian constituencies in the years before his conquest of Babylonia. The exilic Jewish community was far from an exception. Cyrus was well known by at least some of the Jews in exile, and some of the writings of the Jews longing for Cyrus' rule have even become canonical within the Hebrew Bible. Thus the search for Cyrus' influence needs to begin in Babylonia. There was no restoration of a Jerusalem community, either in terms of a civic-political community or in terms of a temple-faith community. Cyrus' propaganda in Babylonia, however, strongly impacted (at least parts of) the exilic Jewish communities, providing a redefinition of reality and modifying the Jewish communities' self-definition in lasting ways.

Literature from Cyrus' Reign: Second Isaiah

Isaiah 40–55 derives from the exiles' experience in Babylonia, and at least some parts of it date from Cyrus' reign as Persian emperor.[17] As such, it represents a separate document from Isaiah 1–39, most of which reflects an eighth-century Judean prophet, and Isaiah 56–66, which deals with the workings of Jerusalem in the time of Darius (see below). Within Isaiah 40–55, whose author can conveniently be called Deutero-Isaiah, Cyrus' name appears twice,[18] and Babylonia or its inhabitants receives direct mention nine times. The close connections between this writing and its historical context seem clear.

A more difficult question is the social location of Isaiah 40–55. Within the different groups of the Babylonian Jewish exiles, different social locations offered varying perspectives on the matrix of social interactions; Deutero-Isaiah's location within that matrix determined much of the prophet's range of responses to society. Certain clues as to social location exist within the text itself. First, the multiple references to Cyrus indicate an international political bent to Isaiah 40–55. The prophet refers to the emperor as God's anointed, chosen one (Isaiah 45:1) and promises divine support for Cyrus' actions (Isaiah 45:3). Yahweh's intercession in favor of Cyrus proceeds in clearly militaristic, imperialistic fashion, referring to God's victory over other strong nations and powers (Isaiah 45:2).

The prophet desires Cyrus' political success, and this clearly aligns Deutero-Isaiah with the political concerns of the Babylonian-based Jews who descended from Jerusalem's royal family and entourage. God proclaims that Cyrus' success is not for the emperor's own good but for that of God's servant Jacob. The prophet anticipates a political gain for the Jewish audience if Cyrus succeeds in his battle against the Babylonian Empire. The expectation of some degree of political ascendancy marks Deutero-Isaiah's audience as members of Babylon's Jewish political elite. Likewise, the availability of information about Cyrus' progress as Babylon's attacking enemy indicates access to information about international events, and this argues for a base in Babylon near the political courts.

The political emphasis in Isaiah 40–55 is not the text's only indication of social location, however. There are repeated references to Babylonian worship of idols. The worship of the Babylonian gods Bel and Nebo receives special attention (Isaiah 46:1), and the text repeatedly mocks idolatry (see especially Isaiah 40:19-20; 44:9-20). The inclusion of cultic concerns would certainly reflect a priestly contingent within the prophet's audience. But are these urban or rural priests? Such a question may well be unanswerable, but the lengthy discussion of the practice of idol fashioning (Isaiah 44:9-20) probably indicates that these Yahwist priests knew substantial portions of the Babylonian practice of worship. It seems likely that Deutero-Isaiah reflects priests in Babylon, who were near enough to the national shrines that they could watch the making of idols as well as their worship. Isaiah 40–55 focuses not only on the worship of idols but on their crafting, which in all likelihood would have been more centralized.

If this analysis of social groups is correct, then Isaiah 40–55 derives from the urban Babylonian Jews, including both politicians and priests. Agriculture and other such concerns receive little attention throughout the document, and this reinforces the analysis of social location. Deutero-Isaiah's audience included Jews who worked within the palace and within the temple system of Babylon, and the document's emphases reflect the interests of these Jews in the coming of a new world power to overthrow the Babylonian Empire for which they worked.

Cyrus fought against the Babylonian Empire on many fronts at once. The direct military campaign was only one of these. Cyrus also worked to stir dissent within Babylonia through the use of propaganda among a variety of minority groups within the empire. The condemnation of the Babylonian Empire and the praise of Cyrus were familiar themes throughout a range of Persian-produced literature.[19] Josephus even claims that Cyrus read Isaiah 40–55 and approved of its content for use with the Jewish Babylonian communities.[20]

Cyrus used such propaganda to weaken the Babylonian Empire from within. Babylon's empire had brought large populations of deported persons into the midst of Babylonia, and many of these deportees may well have proved difficult to control. Thus Cyrus could use the dissent of these ethnic groups to undermine popular support for the Babylonian Empire. It is impossible to suggest how much impact this had upon the dissolution of Babylonian morale and structure, but the attempt to influence the outcome of the battle and to develop an ideological and religious legitimation for the nascent Persian Empire seems clear. M. A. Dandamaev argues that these propagandistic religious texts were written by Babylonian priests employed by Cyrus after Persia's initial successes.[21]

Was Deutero-Isaiah, then, written by a Babylonian priest? It seems unlikely that an ethnic Babylonian priest who worshiped Bel or one of the other Babylonian deities would have produced Isaiah 40–55, since this document condemns Babylonian priestly efforts and values in ways that other Cyrus propaganda avoids. In these matters of content, as well as in issues of style and form, Deutero-Isaiah appears more traditionally Jewish and Yahwist than Babylonian or Persian. However, the question is appropriate. What were the loyalties of Deutero-Isaiah, and in what types of religious systems did he function?

Politically, Deutero-Isaiah favored the Persian Empire that Cyrus was creating. This prophet granted religious approval to Cyrus in the form of Yahweh's own authority for this human's rule. Although Cyrus' reign would create political benefits for the Jews of the Babylonian court, there was no mention in Deutero-Isaiah's writing of a possible restoration of the Davidic monarchy in a renewed Judean nation. Deutero-Isaiah was not pro-nationalist or pro-Davidic; he was pro-Persian, with the argument that the fortunes of the Babylonian Jews, if not all Jews, would be best under Persian rule.

Religiously, Deutero-Isaiah supported a monotheistic, priestly form of Yahwism. Although there is a concern with a rebuilding of a temple in Jerusalem (Isaiah 44:28), the main religious concern is the separation of Yahwism from the other religions pervasive in Babylon. Just as there was little political attention to the creation of a new Jewish nation, there was little concern with the construction of a new temple in Jerusalem. Deutero-Isaiah's loyalties lie with the Persian Empire's concern for efficient administration of the provinces, not with any supposed attempt to separate from the world empire. Still, Isaiah 40–55 evidences attitudes of religious intolerance. Whereas Cyrus seems to have accepted almost any religion at all within his empire, Isaiah 40–55 remains exclusivistically Yahwist (Isaiah 44:6-8; 45:14-15).[22] One cannot argue that Deutero-Isaiah is a Persian lackey, producing the propaganda that mirrors future Persian policy. Instead, it seems that this prophet argued for Jewish support of Persian ascendancy for selfish reasons, foreseeing a future where the Jews in Babylon could regain control of Jerusalem within the context of a wealthy, lush Persian Empire and where the worship of Yahweh, the one God, could proceed apace.

Within this prophetic desire, Isaiah 40–55 depicts Cyrus as the mighty and virtuous messiah who will vanquish Israel's foes and restore them to fortune (Isaiah 44:24—45:7). Cyrus' portrait shows him to be without flaw, receiving God's complete and unquestioning support. Yahweh guarantees Cyrus' success and promises about miracles as of old in order to ensure this Persian's military and political victories. This support of Cyrus forms the most important political theme within the document, but several other themes are also of great importance to the understanding of the thought of Deutero-Isaiah. Perhaps the most striking of these themes is the argument against idolatry, as already mentioned. Within this setting of the rejection of idols, the prophet praises Yahweh. Zion's independence and flourishing are essential for Deutero-Isaiah, within the context of Persian rule and Cyrus' leadership. Throughout Isaiah 40–55, the prophet combines motifs from Israel's earlier sacred traditions, such as creation and the exodus, in new and invigorating expressions of theology. Last, Deutero-Isaiah considers a servant, and this enigmatic figure is certainly one of the important contributions of this document.

Idolatry

Repeatedly, Deutero-Isaiah turns the prophetic rhetoric against the making of idols. The satirical treatment of idol construction points toward the absurdity of such craft and worship.[23] With these polemics, Isaiah 40–55 argues against the Babylonian religious practices surrounding the Jewish community faithful to Yahweh. Idolatry appears prominently in Isaiah 40:18-20; 42:8; 44:9-20; 45:16; 45:20-21; 46:1-2; and 48:5.

The main thrust of these passages is the superiority of Yahweh over any worship of idols or images. Thus, when Deutero-Isaiah begins the first discussion of idolatry, the initial question is: "To whom then will you liken God?" (Isaiah 40:18). Idols are considered as a possible comparison for Yahweh but are rejected because they are humanly constructed objects. Such an evaluation of Yahweh's superiority becomes clearer in other texts, such as the declaration that "I am the LORD, that is my name; my glory I give to no other, nor my praise to idols" (Isaiah 42:8). Specifically, Yahweh is the God who can save the people, but idols are incapable of saving anyone (Isaiah 45:20-22).

Deutero-Isaiah rarely selects any appropriate worship practices for encouragement; instead, the prophecy focuses entirely on the practices to avoid. Idol manufacture and divination are effectively forbidden through the sarcastic presentation of those who perform such tasks. The prophet emphasizes the inability of idols to foretell the future, through statements such as Yahweh's claim:

> *I declared [such things] to you from long ago,*
> *before they came to pass I announced them to you,*
> *so that you would not say, "My idol did them,*
> *my carved image and my cast image commanded them."*
> *(Isaiah 48:5)*

Not only are the idols incapable of performing salvation but they are also equally insufficient to foretell or announce salvation. Idols are useless throughout the process of discovering and experiencing salvation (Isaiah 46:7; 47:13). This emphasis combines with the frequent statements of God's ability and decision not only to create salvation but also to predict its arrival accurately (Isaiah 40:21; 41:22-23; 42:9; 43:9; 44:7-8; 45:21).

Much of the specifically satirical development of the anti-idolatry passages concentrates on the physical details of the crafting of images. Nowhere is this stronger than in Isaiah 44:9-20. Perhaps the most striking of the satirical criticisms within this passage deals with the use of wood:

> *[The carpenter] plants a cedar and the rain nourishes it. Then it can be used as fuel. Part of it he takes and warms himself; he kindles a fire and bakes bread. Then he makes a god and worships it, makes it a carved image and bows down before it. Half of it he burns in the fire; over this half he roasts meat, eats it and is satisfied. He also warms himself and says, "Ah, I am warm, I can feel the fire!" The rest of it he makes into a god, his idol, bows down to it and worships it; he prays to it and says, "Save me, for you are my god!" (Isaiah 44:14b-17)*

Human agency marks the use of wood as fire for warmth and cooking; the prophet insinuates that the same human agency is at work in the production of an idol and the worship of it. Because the idol is a human construction, its ability to save is false. The prophet seems to argue that, just as the wood has no value for warmth except that a human act upon it, so an idol has no function or capability for salvation except what humans do to it. Even Bel and Nebo, great gods of the Babylonian pantheon, cannot prevent the actions that humans do: thus humans will carry away these idols into captivity (Isaiah 46:1-2).

As the Jews were struggling to understand the exile, in which they witnessed their own temple furnishings being carried away into captivity, along with themselves in bondage, they moved frequently to notions of radical freedom for God. God can act in many ways; no one can act upon God. Deutero-Isaiah makes the opposite argument regarding Babylonian idols; they are not free, they do not act, they cannot control themselves or their populaces, and they will be taken into exile against their putative will. This contrasts with Yahweh, who may be resident in exile (as in the images offered by Ezekiel 1–2), but who is present in any location only by divine choice. This theological and ontological difference between Yahweh and the idols reinforced the conviction that Yahweh could (and would) save the Jews, whereas the imperial might of Babylon had no ultimate power behind it. On the social level, this produced the expression of Cyrus as messiah, God's chosen and anointed one who would achieve God's plan of salvation from Babylonia for the Jews. Even though the Jews did not have the political ability to save themselves, God would save them, and the *modus operandi* of that salvation would be a surprising one—the intervention of a foreign enemy against the Babylonian Empire.

Praising God

Many of the anti-idolatry passages lead directly into discussion of Yahweh's grandeur. The condemnation of idolatry that begins with "To whom then will you liken God?" (Isaiah 40:18; cp. 46:5-7) develops into a hymn of praise:

> *Have you not known? Have you not heard?*
> *Has it not been told you from the beginning?*
> *Have you not understood from the foundations of the earth?*
> *It is he who sits above the circle of the earth,*
> *and its inhabitants are like grasshoppers;*
> *who stretches out the heavens like a curtain,*
> *and spreads them like a tent to live in;*

who brings princes to naught,
and makes the rulers of the earth as nothing.
Scarcely are they planted, scarcely sown,
scarcely has their stem taken root in the earth,
when he blows upon them, and they wither,
and the tempest carries them off like stubble.
To whom then will you compare me,
or who is my equal? says the Holy One.
Lift up your eyes on high and see:
Who created these?
He who brings out their host and numbers them,
calling them all by name;
because he is great in strength,
mighty in power,
not one is missing.
(Isaiah 40:21-26)

The power of God to act as God chooses—unlike the idols—is clear within this passage. Yahweh is the God who answers to no one, who did not learn anything from any person or deity (Isaiah 40:14).

Thus humans have no position from which they can criticize God. Just as there is an ontological distinction between God and idols, there is an identical gulf between Yahweh and humanity. The emphasis on God's holiness serves to underscore the vast difference.[24] God is the Holy One, beyond compare with any mortal or with any other god. Thus humans who interfere with the divine intention for life will suffer the consequences of such disagreement. There is no ability to stand in the way of God.

Woe to you who strive with your Maker,
earthen vessels with the potter!
Does the clay say to the one who fashions it, "What are you making"?
or "Your work has no handles"?
Woe to anyone who says to a father, "What are you begetting?"
or to a woman, "With what are you in labor?"
Thus says the LORD, the Holy One of Israel, and its Maker:
Will you question me about my children,
or command me concerning the work of my hands?
I made the earth,
and created humankind upon it;
it was my hands that stretched out the heavens,
and I commanded all their host.
I have aroused Cyrus in righteousness,
and I will make all his paths straight;
he shall build my city
and set my exiles free,

not for price or reward,
says the LORD of hosts.
(Isaiah 45:9-13)

This passage combines the radical inability of humans to resist divine activity with the holiness and creation themes. Because God made the earth, God controls human life there, and humans are like the potter's clay that cannot argue with its master.[25] Creation and holiness language combine to emphasize God's ability to control human destiny. The chief example of such control is the immediate political situation, in which God appoints Cyrus and offers him protection and success in his defeat of the Babylonian Empire. The practical consequences of divine transcendence develop in the human, political, international realm.

The praise of God derives naturally from God's decision to save. That decision repeats itself throughout the text in a variety of ways. God reminds the people of prior announcements to save (Isaiah 40:21; 42:9; 44:8; 45:21). The promise is irrevocable, and so the praise should follow naturally, by God's intention and command.

Turn to me and be saved,
all the ends of the earth!
For I am God, and there is no other.
By myself I have sworn,
from my mouth has gone forth in righteousness
a word that shall not return:
"To me every knee shall bow,
every tongue shall swear."
(Isaiah 45:22-23)

God's salvation occasions human praise of God. One should note that even the creation language does not lead into praise for the nature of God, nor do the Deity's past acts stir praise. Instead, the promise of salvation in the immediate future provides adequate reason for praise. When God's people experience God's salvation, which will involve restoration to the city of Jerusalem and the establishment of the exiles in a new, fruitful life there, then there will be praise. This becomes the climax of an extended hymn of participial praise:

Thus says the LORD, your Redeemer,
who formed you in the womb:
I am the LORD, who made all things,
who alone stretched out the heavens,
who by myself spread out the earth;
who frustrates the omens of liars,
and makes fools of diviners;
who turns back the wise,
and makes their knowledge foolish;
who confirms the word of his servant,
and fulfills the prediction of his messengers;

who says of Jerusalem, "It shall be inhabited,"
and of the cities of Judah, "They shall be rebuilt,
and I will raise up their ruins";
who says to the deep, "Be dry—
I will dry up your rivers";
who says of Cyrus, "He is my shepherd,
and he shall carry out all my purpose";
and who says of Jerusalem, "It shall be rebuilt,"
and of the temple, "Your foundation shall be laid."
(Isaiah 44:24-28)

Thus the reestablishment of a Zion community is the climax of the divine activity, which began with creation and continued its expression within the context of worship and prophecy. For such acts of God on behalf of the exiles, the prophet offers deepest praise.

Zion's Independence

God's activity on behalf of the Jewish exiles is not limited to Cyrus' conquest of the Babylonian Empire. Yahweh intends that Cyrus resettle the exiles in Jerusalem. This focus on Jerusalem (or Zion, as Deutero-Isaiah more commonly refers to the city) brings the activity of God into concrete political action.

The emphasis on Jerusalem occurs from the very start of Isaiah 40–55. God sends out a command to an individual:

Comfort, O comfort my people,
says your God.
Speak tenderly to Jerusalem,
and cry to her
that she has served her term,
that her penalty is paid,
that she has received from the LORD's hand
double for all her sins.
(Isaiah 40:1-2)

The comfort of salvation for this prophet points toward Jerusalem. The emphasis is strange, since the audience consists of Babylonian Jews. However, the promise to these exiles is that they will receive the land of Yehud; the audience will be the comfort for Jerusalem. The prophet depicts an emigration from Babylonia to Yehud, so that the exiles can take over a Persian colony. Deutero-Isaiah defines this occupation as good news for Jerusalem (Isaiah 41:27), even though one might reason that the native inhabitants of Yehud would have disagreed.

The occupation of Zion takes on a grand scale, affecting even nature.

Thus says the LORD:
In a time of favor I have answered you,
on a day of salvation I have helped you;
I have kept you and given you
as a covenant to the people,

to establish the land,
to apportion the desolate heritages;
saying to the prisoners, "Come out,"
to those who are in darkness, "Show yourselves."
They shall feed along the ways,
on all the bare heights shall be their pasture;
they shall not hunger or thirst;
neither scorching wind nor sun shall strike them down,
for he who has pity on them will lead them,
and by springs of water will guide them.
And I will turn all my mountains into a road,
and my highways shall be raised up.
Lo, these shall come from far away,
and lo, these from the north and from the west,
and these from the land of Syene.
Sing for joy, O heavens, and exult, O earth;
break forth, O mountains, into singing!
For the LORD has comforted his people,
and will have compassion on his suffering ones.
(Isaiah 49:8-13)

To this statement Zion responds (Isaiah 49:14), indicating that the foregoing was an address to Zion itself. The prophet interprets the gift of Jerusalem to the exiles as salvation, clearly reflecting the exilic perspective. God will reapportion the land, which the native inhabitants occupied, by giving it to the exiles upon their return. The exiles have been like prisoners, like those in darkness, but they will receive bountiful blessings and will transport themselves along God's highway. At the sight of the occupation of Jerusalem even nature will burst forth into joyful singing and praise.

Likewise the filling of the "desolate" places within Yehud will be comfort (Isaiah 51:3). Deutero-Isaiah does not consider the plight of the inhabitants of the land, even though they would far outnumber the emigrants. The Babylonian Jews' claim to the land of Yehud would be the only claim worthy of consideration. The restoration of Jerusalem is not necessarily a concrete change in the economic or other status of the city but is an occupation of the city by a new group of people, the exiles.

The exiles' presence brings a freshness to Jerusalem. Zion will be a new city once God's salvation is at work within it.

Awake, awake,
put on your strength, O Zion!
Put on your beautiful garments,
O Jerusalem, the holy city;
for the uncircumcised and the unclean
shall enter you no more.
Shake yourself from the dust, rise up,
O captive Jerusalem;

loose the bonds from your neck,
O captive daughter Zion!
. . . .

How beautiful upon the mountains
are the feet of the messenger who announces peace,
who brings good news,
who announces salvation,
who says to Zion, "Your God reigns."
Listen! Your sentinels lift up their voices,
together they sing for joy;
for in plain sight they see
the return of the LORD to Zion.
Break forth together into singing,
you ruins of Jerusalem;
for the LORD has comforted his people,
he has redeemed Jerusalem.
The LORD has bared his holy arm
before the eyes of all the nations;
and all the ends of the earth shall see
the salvation of our God.
(Isaiah 52:1-2, 7-10)

The purification of Jerusalem embodies God's redemption. No undesirable elements enter this pure city to defile it. Who are the uncircumcised and the unclean whom God bans from the revitalized city? They may well be foreigners, but it is also possible that the ostracized group is the native inhabitants of Yehud, whom the exiles regarded as foreigners. In either case, the promised restoration of Jerusalem renders the city fit for the occupation only of the exiles. God's choice to restore negates other threats, whether from Yehud's inhabitants who claim ancestral lands or by the Babylonian powerful. The exiles form an elite to whom God gives the sole right to live in the new Jerusalem.

Combining Traditions

Deutero-Isaiah displays an affinity for combining ancient traditions in creative ways. Whereas earlier prophets did borrow motifs from Israel's religious heritage, Deutero-Isaiah not only borrows them but also combines them in ways that were unique. Chiefly, Isaiah 40–55 depends upon the creation and exodus narratives for traditional material.

Creation images abound in Isaiah 40–55. Much of the creation language appears in the context of praise. The identity of God as creator forms the basis for the declaration of God's current nature, as grounded in the past activities of creation as well as the enduring intention of those creative acts.

For thus says the LORD
who created the heavens
(he is God!),
who formed the earth and made it
(he established it;

he did not create it a chaos,
he formed it to be inhabited!):
I am the LORD, and there is no other.
(Isaiah 45:18)

At times the creation theme functions as an opposing counterbalance to the anti-idolatry themes. Creation demonstrates divine agency, whereas idolatry only points toward human agency, which is fleeting. Humans make idols; Yahweh makes humans. This essential difference of function not only expresses Deutero-Isaiah's ontology but points to the uselessness of idols and the ability of Yahweh alone to save the exiles effectively, through the chosen implement of Cyrus.

Exodus themes are also prevalent. Deutero-Isaiah refers to the miracles of devastation against Egypt before the exodus itself (Isaiah 50:2b–3); these provide examples of the power that Yahweh will use to overcome Babylonia. Then the exiles will flee Babylonia as Moses' band fled Egypt.

Go out from Babylon, flee from Chaldea,
declare this with a shout of joy, proclaim it,
send it forth to the end of the earth;
say, "The LORD has redeemed his servant Jacob!"
They did not thirst when he led them through the deserts;
he made water flow for them from the rock;
he split open the rock and the water gushed out.
(Isaiah 48:20-21)

Thus the exodus tradition also brings to bear the wilderness experiences, understood here as a time of Yahweh's profoundly caring provision. Just as Yahweh cared about the people after Egypt, so will God provide what these exiles need for their trip to Jerusalem. Not only will God provide, but God will greatly simplify the journey, by straightening the curves in the highway and leveling the mountains along the path (Isaiah 40:3; 43:14-21; 49:11; 51:10).

The combination of these creation and exodus themes shows the theological innovation of Deutero-Isaiah. Creation demonstrates God's power, agency, and ability; exodus retells of God's provision and care for the journey. Together, these themes speak of God's ability to do what God decides to do.

But now thus says the LORD,
he who created you, O Jacob,
he who formed you, O Israel:
Do not fear, for I have redeemed you;
I have called you by name, you are mine.
When you pass through the waters, I will be with you;
and through the rivers, they shall not overwhelm you;
when you walk through fire you shall not be burned,
and the flame shall not consume you.
For I am the LORD your God,
the Holy One of Israel, your Savior.

I give Egypt as your ransom,
Ethiopia and Seba in exchange for you.
Because you are precious in my sight,
and honored, and I love you,
I give people in return for you,
nations in exchange for your life.
Do not fear, for I am with you;
I will bring your offspring from the east,
and from the west I will gather you;
I will say to the north, "Give them up,"
and to the south, "Do not withhold;
bring my sons from far away
and my daughters from the end of the earth—
everyone who is called by my name,
whom I created for my glory,
whom I formed and made."
(Isaiah 43:1-7)

This passage, framing the exodus traditions with statements of creation at each end, emphasizes that God's caring nature and salvific decision are grounded within God's ability to perform such acts of salvation. The mixing of these traditions may well represent an attempt at a coalition of forces within the exilic Jewish community. Creation elements resided more typically within the priestly strands of ancient Israelite religion.[26] The exodus stories, however, originated within more political arenas of Israel's life.[27] Certainly within Isaiah 40–55, the exodus traditions function in more political ways, drawing a parallel between Moses' rescue from Pharaoh and Cyrus' rescue from Babylonia. The creation language, however, adheres to the Deity, arguing for the salvation on the basis of divine character rather than divine action within the human realm. Could there be here an attempt to communicate the news of the exiles' impending return using traditions and arguments that the priests and the politicians would have heard from within their own specialists' communities?

Deutero-Isaiah seems to be aware of the mingling of these streams of tradition. At times, the "former things" refer to past events in Israel's history, the foretelling of which prove the religious tradition and the reliable nature of God (Isaiah 41:22; 43:9; 46:9; 48:3). In other places, the "former things" contrast with the new things that God is now doing (Isaiah 42:9; 43:18).[28] These last two instances are interesting in that they express the newness that Deutero-Isaiah performs rhetorically.

Do not remember the former things,
or consider the things of old.
I am about to do a new thing;
now it springs forth, do you not perceive it?
I will make a way in the wilderness
and rivers in the desert.
The wild animals will honor me,
the jackals and the ostriches;

for I give water in the wilderness,
rivers in the desert,
to give drink to my chosen people,
the people whom I formed for myself
so that they might declare my praise.
(Isaiah 43:18-21)

The salvation is new, but it is also grounded in creation and exodus. Although God has saved the people in times past, the new actions of salvation are completely new and worthy of praise. The newness consists of a new time as well as a new leader—Cyrus.

The Servant

The most fervently contested sections of Deutero-Isaiah are those that depict a mysterious figure, often entitled the Servant. Scholarship usually isolates four passages as referring to this Servant: Isaiah 42:1-4; 49:1-6; 50:4-9; and 52:13—53:12. The most persistent question is the identity of this servant. Was it the prophet, or Cyrus, or Israel?[29]

The first Servant passage (Isaiah 42:1-4) announces that God has chosen and does support a servant whose task is to bring justice to the nations. Even though the servant does not speak loudly or do direct damage, the servant will persist until justice reaches the corners of the earth.

The Servant speaks in the first person in the second Servant passage (Isaiah 49:1-6). God selected the Servant before birth (cf. Isaiah 49:1b with the slightly earlier Jeremiah 1:5) but has hid the Servant away, waiting for the right time. The Servant's goal is the restoration of the exiles to Jerusalem.

The opposition against the Servant receives attention in the third passage (Isaiah 50:4-9). Even though God gives wisdom to the Servant, others of the world abuse the Servant. In the end, however, God will intervene and will bring the Servant into confrontation with the abusers; the Servant's victory is assured.

The final Servant passage is the longest (Isaiah 52:13—53:12). The Servant suffers a painful, humiliating death, but through death the Servant saves the exiles. For this reason, God counts the Servant as a success.

Throughout these Servant passages, the most obvious contemporary referent is Cyrus. Although there are elements that would apply equally well to the prophet, the cosmic scope of the Servant's salvation matches well with the descriptions of Cyrus' political salvation. Persia's defeat of Babylonia would cause a return for the exiles and a restoration for Jerusalem; the Servant's function is identical to that of Cyrus, at least in the first two passages. The third and fourth passages are classically more difficult to explain, because they focus on the isolation and destruction of the Servant. The third passage (Isaiah 50:4-9) could very sensibly derive from a time when Cyrus' attack on Babylonia was advancing, but when Cyrus himself had not appeared. The forms of siege warfare that Persia implemented might have kept Cyrus waiting on the periphery of battle with a sizable portion of the military force. Then, when the siege began to break through the specific weaknesses of the Babylonian defense, Cyrus would lead an advance. In those times of waiting, there is great sense for the third passage's discussion of patient, wise waiting in the face of apparent defeat but with assurance of eventual victory. Perhaps the fourth passage (Isaiah 52:13—53:12) derives from the time after the death of Cyrus. The poem would overplay the pain and tragedy of his death, but it would still point out that Cyrus' activities, including his sacrifice at death, worked to the advantage of the exiles who experienced salvation through the work of Cyrus, the messiah, God's Servant.

Conclusion

Cyrus' reign as the first Persian emperor involved the conquest of adjoining empires, the chief of which was the Babylonian Empire. Although Cyrus made few changes in the way that colonies such as Yehud experienced their imperial administration, Cyrus did have a significant impact through the advancement of propaganda and publicity within the empires that he attempted to conquer. Cyrus appealed to minorities and dissent groups, such as the Jewish exiles in Babylonia.

Deutero-Isaiah wrote in Babylon during Cyrus' rise to power and perhaps even slightly after this emperor's death. The prophet's concerns dealt with the problems of idolatry and the goal of return to Jerusalem, a goal that Cyrus supported. In this way, the goals of the exiles and the goals of Cyrus overlapped. The prophet depicted Cyrus as God's servant and messiah, the chosen one who would bring salvation to the exiles. For this reason, Deutero-Isaiah offered almost complete, unquestioning support of Cyrus' plans, while emphasizing constantly that Cyrus was nothing more than a special tool in God's hands, intended for the salvation of the Jews.

Deutero-Isaiah's prophecies may well have brought together an alliance of the priestly and political factors among the Jewish exiles. Together, these groups worked toward the day when they could resume control of their own colony, the colony of Yehud where the current exiles' grandparents had been born. Through the Edict of Cyrus, the exiles received imperial permission to emigrate.

The immigrants entered Jerusalem with imperial encouragement but with little imperial support. They found themselves slowly joining a native population that did not welcome the arrival of their new overlords. Cyrus' intentions of repopulating the imperial periphery proceeded very slowly. Soon Cyrus' attentions turned to the east, and there seems to have been little attempt to change the realities of life in Yehud.

Two factors were creating long-term change, however. The first factor was the slow influx of a Babylonian-born populace. As the native and immigrant populations began to equalize themselves, the tensions grew, and those tensions can be seen with more clarity in the time of Darius, the third Persian emperor. The second factor of long-term change was the introduction of Deutero-Isaiah's ideology, with its strong injunctions against idolatry and with its equating of God's will with Persian policy. This equivalence continued in prophetic perception for several decades, shaping the entire religion's response to political authority. The Judeans did not rebel, and there is no evidence to suggest that they revolted at any point in this era. Instead, the ruling class felt its loyalties toward Persia, even though those loyalties were strained when the resources proved not to be forthcoming; likewise, the native rural class felt its loyalty to itself, not to any bureaucratic structure, and so they did not revolt either. Yehud arranged for itself a certain degree of autonomy, although it was very limited and was strictly within the control of the newcomers who had emigrated from Babylonia. The power of this immigrant group would only increase in years to come.

Notes

1. See Richard N. Frye, *The History of Ancient Iran,* Handbuch der Altertumswissenschaft III/7 (Munich: C. H. Beck, 1984), 94–96; and Ephraim Stern, "The Persian Empire and the Political and Social History of Palestine in the Persian Period," in *The Cambridge History of Judaism,* vol. 1, *Introduction, The Persian Period,* ed. W. D. Davies and Louis Finkelstein (Cambridge: Cambridge University Press, 1984), 70.

2. Dandamaev, *Political History,* 33.

3. Ibid., 59.

4. Ibid., 55. See also I. Eph'al, "Syria-Palestine under Achaemenid Rule," in *The Cambridge Ancient History,* vol. 4, *Persia, Greece and the Western Mediterranean, c. 525 to 479 B.C.,* ed. John Boardman, N. G. L. Hammond, D. M. Lewis, and M. Ostwald, 2d ed. (Cambridge: Cambridge University Press, 1988), 147.

5. Dandamaev, *Political History,* 66.

6. See E. J. Bickerman, "The Edict of Cyrus in Ezra I," in *Studies in Jewish and Christian History, Volume I,* ed. E. J. Bickerman (Leiden: E. J. Brill, 1976), 72–108. Bickerman argues for the historicity of both documents, each reflecting a different style of administration in the times of Cyrus and Darius. See also Eph'al, "Syria-Palestine under Achaemenid Rule," in *The Cambridge Ancient History,* 4:151.

7. See *ANET,* 316.

8. Dandamaev, *Political History,* 57.

9. Ibid., 54.

10. Diodorus XIII.22.3.

11. Kuhrt, "Cyrus Cylinder."

12. Dandamaev, *Political History,* 54.

13. Ibid., 64.

14. A mostly parallel list in Nehemiah 7:66–67 indicates a slightly larger number, 49,942.

15. See the agricultural images in Ezekiel 17 and 34, for example. These metaphorical images would have seemed out of place in the writings of an urban prophet, such as the exilic Isaiah.

16. Of course, Ezra also narrates Samaritan opposition to the construction plans (Ezra 4), and many scholars have interpreted a strong Jewish desire to build a temple followed by a strong opposition that shuts down the construction project for over a decade and a half. However, Ezra's account contradicts itself, first proposing that the emperor Artaxerxes stopped the construction that Darius later restarted, even though Artaxerxes reigned *after* Darius (Ezra 4–5), and then asserting that the construction never actually stopped (Ezra 5:16). Overall, the historiography of Ezra appears to argue tendentiously to defend the nonconstruction of the temple before Darius.

17. See John L. McKenzie, *Second Isaiah,* AB 20 (Garden City, N.Y.: Doubleday & Co., 1968); Claus Westermann, *Isaiah 40–66, A Commentary,* OTL (Philadelphia: Westminster Press, 1965); and R. N. Whybray, *Isaiah 40–66,* NCBC (Grand Rapids: Wm. B. Eerdmans Publishing Co., 1975).

18. Isaiah 44:28; 45:1. Some English translations also render "him" in the first line of 45:13 as "Cyrus," which certainly seems to be the correct referent.

19. Dandamaev, *Political History,* 53.

20. Ibid., 53.

21. Ibid.

22. But see Joseph Blenkinsopp, "Second Isaiah—Prophet of Universalism," *JSOT* 41 (1988): 83–103. However, Whybray argues that Israel was not a missionary to the nations (*Isaiah 40–66*, p. 31), against the position of McKenzie (*Second Isaiah*, lvii, lxv).

23. Thomas Jemielity, *Satire and the Hebrew Prophets*, Literary Currents in Biblical Interpretation (Louisville, Ky.: Westminster/John Knox Press, 1992).

24. The phrase "Holy One" (or a variant thereof) appears in Isaiah 40:25; 41:14, 16, 20; 43:3, 14, 15; 45:11; 47:4; 48:2; 49:7 (2); 54:5; and 55:5. This term links Deutero-Isaiah with Isaiah of Jerusalem, who used the term fourteen times. "Holy One" refers to Yahweh only sixteen times in the rest of the Hebrew Bible.

25. Deutero-Isaiah may have been aware of Jeremiah's development of the potter and clay image (Jeremiah 18:1–11), although Jeremiah develops this as a more thoroughly negative image of God's destruction of the people and does not include Deutero-Isaiah's emphasis on God's radical otherness.

26. This assumes that P was written or at least in process before this time. Also, McKenzie argues for Deutero-Isaiah originating the concept of Yahweh as creator (McKenzie, *Second Isaiah*, lix).

27. Consider that J and E are both court-based propaganda.

28. Cf. Isaiah 48:6-7, in which God creates new things for the people's consideration.

29. Much classic Christian interpretation sees the Servant as a prefiguring of Jesus Christ. Certainly Christian tradition has used many of the images of Isaiah 52:13—53:12 (and, to a much lesser extent, the other Servant passages) to describe the Christ-event. Some Jewish interpretation understands the Servant as a messianic figure.

CHAPTER 4

STABILITY AND STAGNATION: CAMBYSES (530–522 B.C.E.)

WITH CYRUS' DEATH IN the eastern reaches of the newly founded Persian Empire in 530 B.C.E., Cambyses became the second Persian emperor. Cambyses had served as the heir apparent to the throne almost from the beginning of Cyrus' reign. Even though the Persian Empire was a new entity, this Achaemenid family had controlled the throne of Persia for generations, and so the rules of dynastic succession were firmly in place. Cambyses became the local ruler for Babylonia by at least March 538 B.C.E., and Cyrus returned to the traditional Persian capital of Ecbatana. Cambyses not only held responsibilities for the administration of Babylonia (including the Beyond the River province that included Yehud) but also managed larger affairs of the Persian Empire while Cyrus was away at battle.

During 530 B.C.E., while Cyrus was fighting the Massagetai in the battle that would result in his death, Cambyses was located in Babylonia ruling the empire and continuing to consolidate his rule. He followed the Elamite custom of marrying his sisters, Atossa and Roxana.[1] This centralized power for Cambyses by denying himself any brothers-in-law or nephews who could serve as loci for power plays against the imperial throne. By several accounts, Cambyses took the further step of murdering his brother, Bardiya.[2] By August of 530 B.C.E., when Cyrus' death became known within the Persian Empire, Cambyses' succession was assured.

Cambyses inherited an empire little changed from Cyrus' experience, and Cambyses himself instigated almost no changes in imperial structure or activity. Like Cyrus, Cambyses presided over the military expansion of the empire's boundaries. Instead of continuing Cyrus' mostly successful but ultimately fatal campaigns against the eastern borders of the empire, Cambyses turned west.

Cambyses' chief contribution to the Persian Empire was the conquest of Egypt in 525 B.C.E. Egypt became a continuing problem for the empire, however, because it revolted often and successfully. Persia never controlled Egypt for very long or with a great deal of certainty, but Persia did usually reconquer Egypt and gain from its vast and varied resources. This initial campaign used naval power for the first time and also brought the first involvement of the Greeks into regional warfare; both of these developments would prove problematic and costly to the Persian Empire over time.

Cambyses spent several years preparing for the attack against Egypt. The Persian Empire did not use the land route to Egypt, which would have led very near Yehud.

Although land warfare was the traditional mode of the Persian military, it presented problems when applied to Egypt, because of the desert in the Sinai Peninsula and because of the need to cross the Red Sea. Instead, Cambyses brought the Persian army by land to the Syrian coast, where they constructed boats with the help of Greeks, whom Persia also hired as mercenaries. When weather allowed, Persia sailed to Egypt, engaging in a major battle at Pelusium. Cambyses proceeded and captured Memphis in 525 B.C.E.[3]

Realizing that holding Egypt might be even more difficult than capturing it, Cambyses stayed in Egypt for multiple seasons in order to consolidate his rule over this new territory.[4] He gained royal titles in Egyptian inscriptions, such as "King of Egypt, King of Lands."[5] Quite possibly, Cambyses planned to stage a conquest of the rest of Africa from an Egyptian base. There were small-scale attacks against Carthage and Ethiopia, but supply proved to be an insurmountable problem for Cambyses, despite some initial successes.[6]

Cambyses' extended stay in Egypt placed him at the extreme southwestern corner of the Persian Empire. With the emperor absent, the Persian Empire began to experience internal dissent. Upon the announcement of Cambyses' return, a revolt took place in Persia in March 522 B.C.E., gaining quick control of Babylonia and the central part of the Persian Empire. Supposedly, Bardiya led this revolt. The matter is the subject of great historical uncertainty. In one possible scenario, Bardiya had never been murdered, and he chose the time of his brother's return to stage a revolt; Cambyses then started the legend of Bardiya's murder to discredit his brother by asserting that Bardiya was really Gaumata, an impostor and usurper. On the other hand, it is possible that Bardiya's murder had been factual but had been kept secret to prevent embarrassing stories about Cambyses as a fratricide. Then, Gaumata seized upon the availability of the Bardiya role and conducted a revolution as a non-Achaemenid, forcing Cambyses to reveal the story of his sordid past. Neither story can be considered certain; convincing historical evidence is lacking.[7]

Cambyses hurried back from Egypt to Persia, returning along the same sea and land path that he had traveled with the army a few years before. The Bardiya/Gaumata controversy changed its character radically when Cambyses died in Syria on the journey back to Persia, where he would have fought to regain his kingdom.[8] In the spring of 522 B.C.E., Bardiya was able to take control of most of the central portions of the Persian Empire, if not all of it.[9] Bardiya cemented his popularity by removing all taxes for three years and forbidding costly foreign wars.[10]

Cambyses' rule over the Persian Empire's central portions ended even before he died with Bardiya's successful revolt (even though the revolt turned out to be only temporarily successful). Thus the eight-year reign of this second Persian emperor can be seen in two phases. First, from 530 to about 526 B.C.E., Cambyses served as a caretaker emperor, changing none of his father's policies or practices. Second, from 526 to 522 B.C.E., he concentrated on the establishment of Persian imperial authority over Egypt, at the far southwestern extreme of the Persian Empire.

Cambyses' Interests

The two phases of Cambyses' career as Persian emperor relate to two assumptions that appear to undergird his actions in office. First, Cambyses assumed that the proper role of the emperor was to maintain the gains of the past. Second, he assumed that the most important task for an emperor was to conquer other nations. These two assumptions controlled the results of his time as emperor and mark his own interests in fulfilling this political role.

Cambyses' assumption of imperial maintenance brought about an empire that worked to conserve the gains of the past. Cyrus' accomplishment was the production of a thin veneer of political unity, bringing new geographical areas under the Persian banner. Cambyses strove to maintain the imperial control over these areas. Control, however, required funds. Cyrus' source of funds was income taken from other nations through battle as well as the continued tribute afterward. Cambyses operated as a caretaker, however, and did not work to conquer new areas in the first phase of his imperium. Thus the only sources for funds to maintain the size and character of the Persian Empire were taxation and tribute. As imperial size increased under Cyrus, more funds were needed, but Cambyses was not enlarging the empire, and so management now required more funds derived from a stable base. The only solution was the raising of taxes among the existing subjects of the Persian Empire. At the same time, Cambyses did not increase the imperial administration, either in services to encourage participation in imperial structures or in regulation to enforce compliance. This combination of responses proved unpopular; revolt was unsurprising.

Cambyses' second assumption was conquest. When he was heir apparent, his role was to stay in Babylonia, at the old royal palace at Sippar, while Cyrus went on military campaigns. This model persisted into Cambyses' rule; the emperor's job was to engage in battle. This role served Cyrus well as a means for increasing the imperial borders, but this strategy reached natural limits as the Persian Empire surpassed the size of any previous empire. The requirements for an empire of this size soon outstripped the technology for imperial management—whether military, mercantile, administrative, or communicative. Cambyses had difficulty in managing this vast empire, but he also felt a need to engage in conquest. His chosen direction for conquest was Egypt.

Egypt formed, in the perception of the Persians, the last remaining threat to their empire. Cyrus had conquered north to sparsely populated barbarian hill country and south to the waters of the Persian Gulf and the Indian Ocean as well as the impassable deserts of Arabia. He had extended the imperial boundaries toward the east through India and close to the impenetrable mountains of Mongolia, but in the west Cyrus had gone no farther than the reaches of the old Babylonian Empire, including Syria and Palestine. The west would be the frontier of significance for Cambyses' reign.

Egypt represented an important target for conquest in another sense as well. For the Babylonian Empire and for the Assyrian Empire before them, Egypt had been the one large kingdom that had been unconquerable. The distances were always too great and Egypt was always too strong to submit to the Mesopotamian-based world empires. Instead, Egypt maintained its own power base, squabbling with the Mesopotamian empires over the territories on their joint borders, such as Judah. As long as Egypt remained independent, Persia could not depend on its continued control of the eastern Mediterranean and the seaports for merchants there. For this reason if for no other, the conquest of Egypt was essential to the long-term stability of the Persian Empire.

The Egyptian Campaign and Yehud

In 526 B.C.E., Cambyses launched an initiative against Egypt. It took until 525 B.C.E. for the forces to reach Egypt, and Cambyses succeeded in conquering this important region in a very short time. The three years of consolidation of rule in Egypt may well speak to some continuing troubles in pacifying and controlling the populace of this nation with an ancient history of independence, but Cambyses proved successful, at least until his death.

The Army's Approach

The Persian army traveled a path that would take them to the Syrian coast, where they waited and built boats with the help of Greek mercenaries. From the northeastern coast of the Mediterranean Sea, the Persian navy sailed to Egypt. Apparently the Egyptian army had gained intelligence of the Persian army's approach but had assumed that Persia would follow its usual tactics of land campaigns. Egypt mistook not only the location of Persia's arrival but also the timing, since the water-borne soldiers arrived months earlier than expected.

As a nonintended result of the naval strategy, the Persian army and its supply lines completely avoided the area around Yehud. Since the Palestinian colonies had no contact with the passing army, they felt none of the myriad effects that the near passage of such a huge military formation would have caused. This added to Yehud's stability throughout the reign of Cambyses. None of this emperor's military or administrative concerns affected Yehud, except for the generalized increases in taxation throughout the Persian Empire.

Success and Defeat

The Persian army won a difficult but decisive battle early in 525 B.C.E. Soon Persia captured Memphis, and Egypt submitted with a lesser loss of life than expected. Cambyses enjoyed success; the last significant portion of the world became part of the Persian Empire, and his boundaries, income, and influence greatly exceeded that of his father Cyrus and the earliest Persian Empire. Cambyses succeeded in grand fashion.

Despite the wonders of the success, defeat was close behind. Because of the assumption of endless military conquest without consolidation, Cambyses attempted to expand his gains in new directions. At first he attempted to conquer toward the west, attacking Libya; later, his efforts pointed south, as he worked down the Nile River into the Ethiopian areas. In both cases, Cambyses failed, in large part because the supply lines became impossible to maintain over such great and increasing distances. Despite success, his assumption that expansion should continue without limits brought about the failure. For nearly three years, throughout most of 525–522 B.C.E., Cambyses failed repeatedly to move the Persian Empire into new territories. By the end of his life, he had succeeded in one military campaign and then failed in everything subsequent to the Egyptian victory; by the end, even the core of the empire was in revolt, and Cambyses seemed powerless to stop it.

Long-Term Effects

In the short term, Cambyses' campaign against Egypt produced strong results. Persia gained control of this vital region, including tribute payments and military control. These benefits to Persia were short-lived, however. Once Cambyses left Egypt and then died, Egypt revolted and regained its independence. The long-term effects of this war took on another dimension.

First, this was Persia's first military experience with two important elements: naval warfare and Greek mercenaries. Both of these elements became crucial in the next century of Persia's history. Especially after 480 B.C.E., Persia turned its attention to battling the Greeks for control of the northeastern Mediterranean Sea; this conflict became formative in classical Greek and Hellenistic society and eventually brought about the downfall of the Persian Empire. Naval warfare became the key to the continuing Greek-Persian conflicts; although Persia learned these technologies and tactics from the Greeks and used them successfully, Greece maintained an advantage in sea battles that was often decisive.

The second set of long-term effects finds its best expression in the revolution that followed. The pattern of administrative neglect accompanying military conquest became too costly for Persia to maintain over the decades. Although Persia would still attempt this pattern, its self-limitations already became manifest. Especially important in this connection was the difficulty of maintaining lengthy supply lines. Cambyses experienced repeated failure in large part because of the army's inability to control such extensive supply lines. At the same time, Cambyses' military campaign embodied a policy of refusing to change the priorities of the previous administration. This left Yehud unaffected for nearly a decade. Although taxes were high, the Jerusalem society was able to control its own destiny and fell into established patterns that proved long-lasting, even though they could be (and were) changed through imperial administration at later times. The battles in other parts of the empire meant peace and stability for Jerusalem and Yehud during the time of Cambyses' reign. Although there was revolt throughout the empire, Yehud remained stable, and in its stability Yehudite society tended toward stagnation.

Stability and Stagnation

As the Persian Empire under Cambyses resisted change throughout its core and shifted its military resources without approaching Palestine, Yehud experienced a time of calm. Immigration may have continued throughout Cambyses' time, although there is little record of any of Yehud's activities during this decade. The stability offered an opportunity for slow, steady change throughout Yehud, probably including the assimilation of the immigrants and a continuing stratification between the immigrant and native sectors of the community.

The absence of imperial attention to Yehud in this period allowed Yehud to pursue its own identity and its own goals. Cambyses continued Cyrus' policies that gave Yehud freedom to develop in most ways possible. Immigration, reorganization, and construction were all possible. This encouraged Yehud to choose its own path, and its choice perhaps shows the most internally motivated choices that it ever made.

During this time, Yehud chose not to construct a temple. Although Cyrus had given permission for such construction, sensing the political and administrative advantages of a Jewish temple in Jerusalem, the residents of Yehud chose not to build a temple. Presumably religion continued, including the worship of Yahweh through sacrificial means at the ruins of the temple. Certainly society continued, but without a newly constructed temple to centralize and formalize that social existence. Yehud's organization continued, much as the rest of the empire's patterns, as a loosely connected social group. With this unstructured environment and lack of significant change in the patterns of life in Yehud, it is unsurprising that we possess no extant literature from Yehud in Cambyses' time.

Notes

1. A. T. Olmstead, *History of the Persian Empire* (Chicago: University of Chicago Press, 1948), 87.
2. Geo Widengren, "The Persians," in *Peoples of Old Testament Times,* ed. D. J. Wiseman (Oxford: Clarendon Press, 1973), 321.
3. A. R. Burn, *Persia and the Greeks: The Defence of the West, 546–478 B.C.*, 2d ed. (Stanford: Stanford University Press, 1984), 86; Olmstead, *History of the Persian Empire,* 88; and Widengren, "The Persians," 320.
4. Edda Bresciani, "Egypt and the Persian Empire," in *The Greeks and the Persians from the Sixth to the Fourth Centuries,* ed. Herrmann Bengtson, trans. Phyllis Johnson (New York: Delacorte Press, 1968), 332–35; Olmstead, *History of the Persian Empire,* 88–90; and Widengren, "The Persians," 321.
5. William Culican, *The Medes and the Persians* (London: Thames & Hudson, 1965), 60.
6. Burn, *Persia and the Greeks,* 86–87; and Olmstead, *History of the Persian Empire,* 89.
7. Maurice Meuleau, "Mesopotamia under Persian Rule," in *The Greeks and the Persians from the Sixth to the Fourth Centuries,* ed. Herrmann Bengtson, trans. Robert F. Tannenbaum (New York: Delacorte Press, 1968), 357; and Olmstead, *History of the Persian Empire,* 92–93, 108–10.
8. Burn, *Persia and the Greeks,* 93; and Widengren, "The Persians," 321.
9. Olmstead, *History of the Persian Empire,* 107.
10. John Manuel Cook, *The Persian Empire* (London: J. M. Dent & Sons, 1983), 216; and Olmstead, *History of the Persian Empire,* 93.

CHAPTER 5

ENFORCING IMPERIAL RULE: DARIUS (522–486 B.C.E.)

PERSIA'S SECOND EMPEROR, CAMBYSES, died in Syria while returning from a lengthy administration of the newly conquered province of Egypt. Babylonia had rebelled against the Persian Empire even before Cambyses started his return journey. Cambyses' ruling assumptions of maintenance and conquest had caused the Persian Empire to begin its collapse; after Cambyses, even the original dynasty was on the brink of extinction.

The accession of Darius to succeed Cambyses as Persian emperor was difficult, but it eventually passed the mantle of imperial power to a new type of ruler. Darius was a member of the extended Achaemenid family, but he was not of the line of Cyrus and Cambyses. Darius brought more innovation to the imperium than simply a new set of genes, however. His management style and administrative goals appear to be sufficiently different from those of his predecessors that the differential effects on the entire empire should not be underestimated. There are also other significant differences to Darius' reign, including the introduction of Greece as enemy, a factor that became of increasing importance throughout the rest of Persian imperial history. Darius reigned for nearly four decades, about twice as long as Cyrus and Cambyses combined. Although Cyrus was certainly formative for the Persian Empire as its first emperor, in many ways Darius molded the Persian Empire into the structures and patterns that shaped the rest of its existence.

Darius' contributions to Yehud and the development of Jewish religious tradition are vast. He sponsored publications of laws throughout the empire and may well have supported the codification of Israelite law as well. Darius' military campaign against Egypt exerted the imperial presence very near to Yehud, certainly causing some economic and political effects. In addition to these influences, the time of Darius saw the writing of at least three prophetic texts from the Hebrew Bible: Haggai, Zechariah 1–8, and Isaiah 56–66.

The History of Darius' Reign

Accession

Gaumata had usurped the imperial throne from Cambyses very early in 522 B.C.E., first organizing a revolt in Babylonia and then consolidating his rule in Persia. Sparse records shed no light on the extent of the rebellion into the further reaches of the empire, but certainly the central parts were well controlled by Gaumata. Many portions of the core population were pleased with Gaumata's rule. He had removed levies and taxes for a period of three years, and he promised to avoid wars to reduce costs.[1] If these reports are accurate, then Gaumata's strategy reversed Cambyses' assumptions about imperial rule and instead emphasized a decrease in imperial bureaucracy and a lack of conquest. Even though Gaumata thus avoided Cambyses' mistakes by reverting to their antitheses, Gaumata still chose a path that would have led to the dissolution of the empire.

Darius represented another option. Darius was a member of the extended Achaemenid family but was not the heir to the throne, even in Cambyses' absence. By tradition, young Darius had been Cambyses' spear-bearer during the Egyptian campaign.[2] Darius, however, did not wait for Cambyses and the remainder of the entourage to travel back to Persia together. As soon as Darius heard about Gaumata's revolt in Babylonia, Darius began the trip back, and so he arrived long before the full Persian army.

Darius formed a conspiracy in Persia with other nobles who favored a strong imperium. Whereas Gaumata's support came from the lower and middle classes (whose vulnerability to taxation and military conscription was higher) as well as the lower levels of the nobility and the priestly castes (such as the Magi), Darius' cabal involved a small number of the highest-ranking nonroyal nobles.[3]

With the help of his coconspirators, Darius succeeded in killing Gaumata on September 29, 522 B.C.E. Cooperation among the Seven Great Houses of nobles, of which Darius and the Achaemenids were the chief, characterized Darius' rule as emperor.[4] Darius contracted the groups allowed into the ruling elite, moving toward an aristocratic oligarchy. Persian ethnicity became an important prerequisite for all top administrative posts throughout the empire's history.

By the time that Darius killed Gaumata, much of the work of reuniting the Persian Empire had already occurred. Darius' accession was, in some senses, a counterrevolution, with the royal family taking power once more, along with the help of the traditional sources of Persian power. Together, the Seven Great Houses would have controlled so much of Persia itself that the death of Gaumata would have created an instant retrenchment of power. Although there were still military battles to be fought in order to allow the Persian imperium to regain its control over the provinces, Darius did not undertake the recentralization of power by himself but rather in the context of a strong aristocracy and a reliable system of governmental aides. This structure of government would create the most profound changes within the Persian Empire's history. But first, the rebellions of the provinces required Darius to address the military concerns of reuniting the empire.

The Suppression of Revolts

The military threats to the unity of the Persian Empire were extremely severe. Gaumata's usurpation threatened the ability of the empire to retain its provinces. Although Gaumata attempted to build a union by negating Cambyses' ruling assumptions of maintenance and conquest, Gaumata's strategy backfired. Without the services supplied by taxation and without the threat of Persian military force (since Gaumata had promised not to use the army at all), the provinces saw no reason to remain connected to the Persian Empire. Under Gaumata's leadership, provinces fled the imperium from one end of Cyrus' empire to another. Darius' counterrevolution centralized authority by empowering a very small elite group, and revolt continued. Only the use of harshest force brought several of the provinces back into the empire. In the meantime, Darius was involved in the suppression of revolts throughout the empire. Within the first few years of his reign, Darius undertook military action in almost every region: Elam, Babylon, Parsa, Media, Assyria, Egypt, Parthia, Margiana, Sattagydia, Saka.[5]

Darius took the Persian throne on September 29, 522 B.C.E., and immediately addressed the rebellion of Babylonia, the first region to support Gaumata. Darius achieved an immediate victory over Babylonia on October 3, 522 B.C.E., and then proceeded to take back Media by the end of the year.[6] However, retaking Babylonia permanently proved more difficult; Babylonia revolted again on December 13, 522 B.C.E., under the leadership of Nebuchadnezzar IV, Nabonidus' son, and Darius reasserted imperial authority over it on December 18, 522 B.C.E.[7] For over two months near the end of 521 B.C.E., Nebuchadnezzar V revolted against Darius, but again Darius proved victorious. By November 27, 521 B.C.E., Darius had taken firm control of Babylonia, which never again revolted in Darius' time.

Media revolted again and remained independent from January through May of 521 B.C.E. Armenia also freed itself and stayed separate from the Persian Empire for months. Egypt had rebelled against Persia as soon as Cambyses died, and Darius did not reconquer it until the middle of 519 B.C.E., significantly after his reconquest of the rest of Cambyses' empire.

One of the strategies that Darius used with great effectiveness was the rebuilding of temples throughout the empire. On the infrastructural level, this created imperial building projects within the areas affected by revolts; as with any public works project, temple construction increased employment and brought funds from the general bureaucracy into local control. On the ideological level, Darius appeared to support a variety of local religions, and he gained the good will of various temple administrations throughout the imperial provinces. As did the previous and subsequent Persian emperors, Darius sought recognition by local temples as the manifestation of the local deity or as the one whom that deity chose for religious and political leadership. This created a popular following, at least among many of the religiously oriented members of any subject population. Darius gained much popular support by following this program in multiple regions of the empire.

Despite the success of temple support as a strategy for pacifying populations, military suppression also proved repeatedly necessary. Almost every region within the Persian Empire required some military action within the first two years of Darius' reign. Even Babylonia revolted three times (led by Gaumata, Nebuchadnezzar IV, and Nebuchadnezzar V). In the case of this largest of the Persian regions, Darius held control for over 80 percent of his first eighteen months in power, and still Babylonia required the use of the Persian army three times in order to restore loyalty. Military response to local pressures is notoriously inefficient and costly. Thus it is not surprising that Darius soon turned to other means for promoting imperial unity and stability.

Assertion of Imperial Power

By the end of 521 B.C.E., Darius had reconquered all of Cambyses' Persian Empire, except for Egypt, which had been under Persian control for only a few years while Cambyses was actually present there. Darius had succeeded in reintegrating the main territories of the empire, even if Egypt remained outside the sphere of Persian influence. Although Darius had quickly and efficiently squelched the accession revolts, the reality of these rebellions still existed within the empire. The revolts proved that Cambyses' assumptions of maintenance and conquest were inadequate for the task of keeping together such a far-flung and diverse empire. Instead, as Darius apparently realized, a different form of connection was essential. Had Darius continued Cambyses' ruling assumptions, Darius probably would have faced a constant set of rebellions, as the force needed to unify such a large area through military means alone proved too much for a maintenance-oriented empire to survive. It would have been inefficient and, eventually, insufficient for Darius to keep provinces within the empire by force.

Instead, Darius found another set of assumptions by which to rule. Whereas Cambyses emphasized maintenance and conquest, Darius operated through organization and taxation. Cyrus and Cambyses strove to add new territories; Darius worked to maximize the effectiveness and benefit to the empire that each region provided. Darius thus reorganized the empire into twenty provinces, each with its own governmental structures, although each reportable to the emperor. The emperor could assign variable rates of taxation to the individual provinces (called satrapies), thus maximizing the benefits provided by each. This administrative system located Persian-born and Persian-raised officials in each satrapal office, so that Darius kept close contact with each local administrator. Enforcement of law could occur at any location or level. The person of the emperor provided the empires' ideological unity, but local administrators with loyalty enforced by the emperor supplied the structural unity.

This bifurcation of symbolic and structural unity allowed for increased centralization of imperial power at the same time that more administrative functions moved to the satrapies. Within his first two years of reign, Darius built and occupied a new palace in Susa.[8] This centralized the symbols of imperial power, but the functions of the imperial bureaucracy were another matter. Darius' organizational system of satrapies decentralized many of the functions of regular administration. For these satrapies, Darius appointed many new governors. Darius usually appointed ethnic Persians for governorships as well as for most other important administrative positions. Certainly all of Darius' appointments were made from those loyal to the throne. Personal loyalty to the emperor became a vital criterion for governmental roles, but the functions of leadership devolved to lower levels of bureaucracy and to the local officials. At the local level, Darius allowed some cooperation with native officials.[9] However, Persian control was always present. Native officials held positions of even the smallest authority only by the choice of the imperial Persian bureaucracy; only with evidence of direct personal loyalty to Darius could any leader take any position. Even though the work was done within the context of this new administrative structure, the centralization of ultimate power under Darius was far more advanced than under the Persian Empire's first two leaders.

The issue of personal loyalty has no clearer expression than in Darius' publication of an official autobiography. This biography praises Darius, lists his accomplishments, demonstrates his power over all of the satrapies, and exonerates him from any wrongdoing in the accession. Extant copies exist in the Akkadian language on a Babylonian monument as well as in Aramaic on papyrus from the island of Elephantine in the Nile River, where a group of Jews much later served as a mercenary military garrison for the

Persian Empire.[10] From one end of the empire to another, the subjects of Persia had access to copies of Darius' autobiography, translated into their own native language.

The autobiography probably dates from 520 B.C.E., once Darius had subdued all of the accession revolts. By that time, Darius had reunited the empire militarily and had reorganized the imperial structure into satrapies; the autobiography celebrates these accomplishments. The most striking version of the autobiography appears at Behistun, where it communicates the story of Darius' rise in three languages and a series of inscribed depictions. The massive inscriptions in rock were high above a major highway in the Persian Empire, so that those passing nearby on the highway would see the depictions, even though they could not read the written forms unless they climbed the rock. The impressive nature of the physical representation of the autobiography as well as the content of the text itself serves to underscore its message of Darius' vast power and personal authority to rule.

Personal authority was not the only mode of asserting imperial power. The empire charged the satrapal governors and local officials to codify and follow a law. Whereas Cyrus and Cambyses ruled by *fiat* alone, Darius moved the empire toward a legal base. This allowed for greater imperial influence on daily life as well as a partial standardization throughout the empire. The shift to law also furthered Darius' tendencies toward decentralization, since local officials could administer most facets of the law.

Darius did not attempt to create one law for the entire empire, although his administration did focus on some standardization. "The King's Law," as it came to be known, varied slightly from region to region. In each location, Darius' officials used various sources of local tradition and law to form large sections of the law code. Thus each province and each region with an extant legal tradition provided at least some of its own imperial law. Certainly there were other influences, such as the Code of Hammurabi and other traditional Babylonian laws, but localities had input into the law-making process.[11] Within Yehud, the later reference to the King's Law in Ezra 7:26 probably indicates the version of the King's Law that was in place within Yehud as a result of Darius' codification; presumably, this law reflected earlier Israelite traditions but also received its final form by scribes in the service of the Persian imperium.

This attempt to standardize laws within regions and within the empire as a whole earned Darius the epithet of "Lawgiver." Many of the laws were in place very early in Darius' reign; others seem to have taken longer. For instance, the codification of Egypt's laws did not occur until 495 B.C.E.[12] In reality, he did not create very many laws but instead provided an administrative structure through which each region could codify its own traditions. Once codified, however, these laws took on imperial force, and Darius reserved the right to enforce them as he needed and desired.

The establishment of law codes greatly enhanced the standardization of imperial administration, as did the creation of regional governmental structures. An efficient bureaucracy minimized the need for the emperor's personal attention to local situations, while still maintaining control over every corner of the empire. At the same time, a cult of personality grew around Darius, through the autobiographies, the myth of Darius the Lawgiver, and the need for absolute personal loyalty for anyone in the vast imperial bureaucracy's employ. Through all of these mechanisms, Darius strengthened and asserted his imperial power and then turned to issues of expansion.

Expansion

After the consolidation of the empire through the establishment of his own imperial authority, Darius reintroduced the Persian imperial tradition of conquests. In 519 B.C.E., two and a half years after he became emperor, he took Saka, and then Hinduš.[13] This concentration on the eastern ranges of the Persian Empire completed the assertion of power over the areas where Cyrus had briefly held sway and also greatly increased the income of the Persian Empire's colonies, since these regions were perhaps among the wealthiest. Further impulses east proved impractical; Persia never crossed the Mongolian mountains or entered ancient China itself.

Many interpreters have assumed that Darius then began to think about conquering Greece. Although the imperial motives cannot be reconstructed, Darius' next military movement was against Egypt. Certainly, any large-scale move against Greece would have required a loyal Egypt on the southern coast of the Mediterranean, and so this may or may not have been an intentional first step toward Greece. Darius did consistently avoid two-front wars. As the threats from the east were firmly under imperial control, Darius saw that Egypt was still in revolt and must be conquered for political and military reasons, and so he prepared for an invasion of Egypt.

Although the Egyptian campaign did not begin as such until 519 B.C.E., the preparations had started years earlier. Darius gained a reputation as an informed planner, and in accord with this image, he delayed the conquest of Egypt until circumstances allowed for more than conquest. His plans resulted in the long-term, nearly permanent control of this vital region in the southeastern Mediterranean Sea. Darius avoided the mistakes of his predecessor, Cambyses, whose conquest of Egypt was notoriously short-lived.[14] Darius began to concentrate on a multifaceted empirewide strategy to control Egypt as early as 521 B.C.E. and placed his son, Xerxes, as crown prince and ruler of Babylonia.[15] With the increased income from the eastern reaches of the Persian Empire and the administration of imperial core firmly under Xerxes' leadership, Darius turned full attentions to the west, with the goal of Egypt's conquest and control.

Darius understood conquest to require more than military preparation. Cambyses had been a brilliant military commander, and his surprisingly quick naval attack against Egypt had proved wildly successful. Darius knew that such a fast takeover did not guarantee at all the larger goals of the empire. Cambyses could rule Egypt as long as he stayed physically present, accompanied by a large army, but such strategies for control would be far too expensive in comparison to the tribute monies gained. Instead, Darius chose paths that would result in the expansion of the empire by full integration of an Egyptian province. Toward this end, Darius utilized a wide range of his imperial resources to bring Egypt under Persian sway.

When Cambyses had been in Egypt in or after 525 B.C.E., he had met and recruited Udjahorresnet, who had commanded the Egyptian navy in its defeat by Persia. Cambyses placed Udjahorresnet in charge of the medical and theological school at the Sais temple.[16] Apparently Udjahorresnet accompanied Cambyses during his fatal return. Darius may well have met Udjahorresnet while both served in Cambyses' Egyptian court, or they may have met during Darius' earliest years as emperor. Nevertheless Darius sent Udjahorresnet back to Egypt in 520 B.C.E., with instructions and funds to rebuild the Sais school.[17] This was a bold move; at this point, Egypt was not part of the Persian empire, but Darius was willing to allocate funds and personnel for construction projects in this rebel territory.

Like Cyrus before him, Darius used religion and native traditions to construct an image of the Persian emperor as beneficent ruler, causing significant portions of local populations to ally themselves with Persia without military expenditures. Just before Darius' arrival in Egypt, the Apis bull died, initiating one of the great transitional moments for Egyptian religion as the people searched for the new specially marked bull to be installed in the bull's religious shrine. Darius offered a hundred gold talents to the person finding the next bull to become the Apis bull.[18] When Darius entered Egypt with the Persian army behind him, there was no significant military conflict. Instead, the Egyptian people welcomed Darius and crowned him Pharaoh.[19] Darius also dedicated the epitaph of the former Apis bull on August 31, 518 B.C.E., increasing his popularity.[20]

These tactics allowed for minimal military losses while forming a foundation for an extended period of Persian rule of Egypt. Darius did not conquer the Egyptians; he won their loyalty as their benefactor. Especially, the emperor's strategy focused on influential subgroups within Egyptian society, such as the priests of the Sais school and of the Apis bull. These groups experienced the strong financial benefits of allegiance to Darius; as long as the imperial money kept flowing into the temple coffers, the priests were willing to guide public opinion to support the Persian Empire. With and through the priests and other leaders of similar influence, Darius controlled Egypt and brought it into line as a loyal Persian province.

Even though Darius arranged a nonmilitary coup regarding Egypt, the Persian Empire still prepared a military campaign. This campaign presented numerous logistical problems, especially in the area of supply and defense of that lengthy supply line. Cambyses solved that problem through a heavy dependence on Greek and Phoenician mercenaries, but Darius seems to have maintained a more ethnically pure army. Cambyses' naval attack also saved time and bypassed Palestine and the Sinai Peninsula. Darius, on the other hand, marched the army through all of these territories at great length. Whereas Cambyses chose surprise, Darius opted to let Egypt know the size and timing of the army; Darius' plan had marked psychological effects.

This slow style of military campaign necessitated extensive preparations. The supply line would be vulnerable to attack by local provincial peoples, such as those in Palestine.[21] To prevent such possibilities, Darius used tactics identical to those in Egypt to prevent rebellions or resistance along the way from Persia. Darius was better informed about the various regions of the empire than his predecessors. He relied on several people who formed a "staff of specialists on provincial affairs whom he could retain as advisers or send out to act as his agents."[22] These included Udjahorresnet in Egypt and Datis the Mede.[23] Later, Darius used the same policy in employing Histiaeus of Miletus (Aegean affairs, dispatched to the Ionian revolt) and Demartus (the exiled king of Sparta).

In Palestine, Darius' policies meant allowing the rebuilding of the Jerusalem temple.[24] Darius sent Zerubbabel, a young courtier with ethnic ties to the Jews, as governor of Jerusalem, accompanied by Joshua the high priest, in early April of 520 B.C.E., reaching Yehud in August of 520 B.C.E.[25] Along with the prophets Haggai and Zechariah, Zerubbabel served the interests of the Persian Empire by encouraging temple construction and loyalty to the empire and by urging the surplus production of foodstuffs to feed the approaching army. The administrative changes to Yehud and other areas along the army's route produced stable governments with little chance of untimely revolt and also allowed for preparation for the upcoming military campaign.

Whereas the results of Cambyses' campaign were primarily military, Darius' effects were chiefly administrative. The Egyptians accepted him as Pharaoh, solidifying Persian rule of Egypt and the loyalty of the citizens, at least in part. Within government, the Egyptian campaign brought or returned to power several local governors, such as Udjahorresnet and Zerubbabel, who were now part of the Persian Empire's far-flung administrative structure. Each of them ruled from rebuilt temples or schools in former national capitals now reconfigured as provincial headquarters. Although they shared no ethnic connection with the Achaemenid family, they acted loyally to the empire and enforced the imperial will within their own territories. This system of government formed one of Darius' chief contributions.

Within this administrative system, Darius sought a codification of law. He left Egypt by the summer of 518 B.C.E., placing Aryandes in power with instructions to place Egyptian law into the popular vernacular.[26] Darius also ordered such reorganization of legal codes within Babylonia. This imperial decree seems to emphasize the distribution of local laws on scales wider than done previously. Darius' ancient reputation as lawgiver is partially correct, then; although he did not write his own laws or widely enforce a standardized Persian law throughout the vast empire, he did order localities and provinces to standardize their own laws and to publish them in forms more accessible to others besides the priests.[27]

Darius also commissioned construction projects other than local temples, schools, and governmental centers. He ordered the digging of the first canal at Suez, thus linking the Mediterranean and the Indian Ocean, both of which were borders for Darius' empire.[28] This greatly increased the possibilities for maritime trade, and the seafaring peoples benefited greatly from this expansion of the empire. The Phoenicians and others not only profited from trade; they engaged in exploration to the east and gained valuable experience in the use of boats.[29] Naval trade and battle capability continued their increase in importance. The enhanced naval power propitiated by the Suez canal supported Darius' eventual conquest of Ionia in Greece and Indus in India.[30] Darius did, however, continue his land campaigns, threatening Scythia (in south Russia) and Libya and exercising some control over these regions.[31]

Darius' campaign against Egypt was the most directly significant factor of the imperial expansion for the small province of Yehud. However, Egypt proved such a little problem for the Persian army, because of Darius' campaign of propaganda and preparation, that military attentions soon turned elsewhere. With Darius' increasing emphasis on the Mediterranean and on naval power, the growing city-states of Greece formed the next logical opponent. Persia's other expansions under Darius included other directions, such as the Libyan excursions to the southwest, the threats against Scythia to the north, and the capture of parts of India to the east, but Greece provided a special temptation. Following the pattern of Cyrus, Darius chose to attack already settled areas in order to subsume their civilization and administration wholesale. Cyrus used that strategy exclusively, whereas Darius also developed the strategies of intensification of previously loosely organized regions. Greece's special position as the last remaining highly organized border region earned it Darius' close attention.

The long-range significance of Darius' campaigns against Greece cannot be underestimated. The true impact, however, appears during the reigns of other emperors. Darius' own contributions to Persia's war against Greece were modest beginnings, but they started the Persian Empire down a path of escalating conflict with the Greeks. This conflict did not end until a Greek, Alexander from Macedonia, conquered the whole of the Persian Empire in 333 B.C.E. What Darius had begun as a small-scale imperial expansion ended as Persia's destruction almost two centuries later, and the wars between Persia and Greece soon consumed all of Persia's military, administrative, and creative energies.

Darius spent 512 B.C.E. in Sardis, attempting to influence relations with the Greeks. Ionia was stabilized, and Darius' own brother Artaphrenes was placed as satrap of Sardis and Ionia, but the rest of Greece was left alone. Over the next several years, Darius continued to dabble in Greek politics.[32] Various Ionian revolts were crushed, but Persia lost a major battle at Marathon in 490 B.C.E., proving that Greek hoplites could defeat Persian light cavalry.[33] The Greek citizen-farmers serving in required military service in the defense of their hilly homelands proved superior to the Persian military machine, heavily dependent upon mercenaries and extensive supply lines for the warriors and their horses. The battle of Marathon has been rightly understood as a turning point in Greek-Persian relations. Persia never adjusted its military technology to defeat Greece, which continued a pattern of military innovation, especially in naval technology. The Persian Empire, throughout much of the rest of its history, struggled to maintain its tenuous hold over Greece, and this ever-failing attempt resulted in a world empire's stalemate with the Greeks on the very western fringe of their empire.

Consolidation and Administration

The military campaigns of Darius formed only part of his contributions as Persian emperor. Not only did he conquer new territories and bring them under the Persian aegis but he also reorganized the existing territories. The system of twenty satrapies as local units of government proved quite effective, but Darius also undertook other actions.

Darius began the building of Persepolis as a new capital. Previously, the Achaemenid emperors had ruled from Pasargadae, which was built on the site of Cyrus' defeat of Astyages. Persepolis, four miles to the south of Pasargadae, was the site chosen for all later palaces of the Persian Empire. Persepolis functioned as a dynastic, ritual center (especially for the New Year festivals and other religious ceremonies of communal and imperial solidarity), whereas Susa, which was more accessible to trade routes and transport, continued as the administrative capital.[34] Ecbatana, Babylon, and other cities were influential provincial capitals and functioned as major trade centers. Despite the presence of many other important sites throughout the empire, Darius devoted large amounts of time and finances to the construction of Persepolis. The work on the new capital city continued from 512 to 494, with the bulk of it done in 503–497 B.C.E.[35]

Many scholars have suggested that Darius was a monotheist, possibly along the lines of Zoroaster, but that for political reasons he maintained a pluralistic, polytheistic empire.[36] It proves impossible to guess Darius' own religious inclinations, but the effects of religion throughout the empire can be readily seen. Many provinces of the Persian Empire referred to Darius as a local deity, as Egypt recognized Darius as Pharaoh and thus as at least a relative of the gods. Darius apparently did nothing to stop this worship of himself in any of the provinces. At the same time, there is no evidence that Darius forced any of the provinces to worship him. This laissez-faire attitude toward religion coupled with a sharp understanding of the governmental effects of religion. The political gains from the various recognitions of Darius as a local deity were heartily accepted. There was no religious standard set by the emperor, nor were any religions or types of religion preferred or encouraged, but Darius took political advantage of religious propaganda in as many circumstances as feasible.

Darius' rule also had economic effects. Darius set new standards for weights and measures as well as making some other relatively limited fiscal reforms.[37] These standardizations, along with new routes of travel and a general atmosphere of peace throughout the empire, allowed for increased trade, with subsequent effects on prosperity and economic unity of the empire. Furthermore, trade enhanced the imperial coffers and directed the wealth increasingly into the hands of merchants and those who controlled the merchants and the valuable goods. Despite all of this attention to increasing trade, Darius developed no unified economic policy and no standardization of lifestyles.[38] Still, the empire grew economically and maintained enough of its identity (since Cyrus' time) as a frontier empire, expanding to include new territories, new tax bases, and new markets, that the economy remained robust throughout Darius' time.

In Darius' time began the Persian emphasis on politics within the imperial family. Darius had six wives. One was a daughter of one of the Seven, and her marriage may well have been for political alliance. Certainly the marriages to three of Cyrus' daughters were an attempt to unite the imperial lines and to assure the solidarity of Darius' dynasty. The most powerful of Darius' wives was Atossa, who was the mother of Xerxes, who would be the next emperor.[39]

Darius' key defeat of the Greeks at Marathon had occurred in 490 B.C.E., and within a few years Darius was preparing another assault on Greece. In the second half of his reign, he had proven unable to conquer new lands, and thus the static empire could not easily produce the increased income necessary for another major military campaign. Darius thus turned inward and raised taxes throughout the empire in 486 B.C.E., especially in Babylonia and Egypt.[40] Egypt revolted rather than pay the higher tribute. This introduced a crisis unlike any of those since Darius' accession and consolidation: Egypt had removed itself from the Persian fold and Greece remained an unconquered threat to the west. In November of 486 B.C.E., before he could address these threats to the unity of the Persian Empire, Darius died at the age of sixty-four.

Yehud under Darius

Effects of Reorganization

Darius' reorganization of the Persian Empire into twenty satrapies marked an important departure from previous imperial policies. Both Cyrus and Cambyses had functioned entirely within the dichotomy of conquest versus maintenance. Either the empire was expanding militarily through the violent annexation of neighboring states or the empire was static, with very little attention paid to the administration of the far-flung bureaucracy. Under Darius the terms shifted significantly. Certainly Darius was also involved in conquest, but his government utilized administrative options other than warfare in degrees previously unknown. Through the creation of a formalized bureaucratic structure, Darius was able to control production and trade, and thus imperial income, with sources besides conquest.

The approach to Egypt serves as a clear example of this shift in imperial policy. Whereas Cambyses designed a purely military strategy for conquest and rule, Darius used the army in conjunction with other administrative assets. Propaganda, combined with funding for construction projects and the support of partial local autonomy in religious and regional affairs, won the allegiance of the Sais school in Egypt. This produced two results: Darius took Egypt without military losses, and a native ruling class was already in place and loyal to the Persian emperor. Thus political measures substituted for military control.

The same administrative policy should also be visible in the province of Yehud. Darius would have avoided military threats to Yehud because such actions were economically expensive. Instead, Darius' administrative contacts with Yehud would have taken the form of the installation of local governors (such as Zerubbabel and his helpers) and rhetorical support for the Persian Empire (such as that offered by Haggai and Zechariah). The goals of such administration would have been the same goals that Darius supported throughout the empire: intensification of production and the regular payment of taxes. These would have been especially important during the campaign against Egypt in 521–518 B.C.E.

At root, Darius changed the definition of good government from speedy conquest (Cyrus) and/or mere maintenance (Cambyses and Gaumata) to notions of maximal taxation and loyal dependence. Yehud would not have been under military threat but would have enjoyed relative autonomy under the leadership of rulers loyal to Persia, as long as Yehud participated in the intensification and taxation of its resources and labor.

Military Movements

Even though the Persian Empire would not have posed a direct military threat to Yehud, the presence of the Persian army as it marched toward Egypt would have affected the life of Yehud and its inhabitants to a large degree. Darius' military campaign against Egypt was a massive undertaking. Since Darius postponed the Egyptian campaign until after his forces had suppressed the revolts in the east, the entire imperial army was available, and almost certainly the military contingent accompanying Darius to Egypt was huge. The army's route took it through or very near to Yehud on both its approach to and its removal from Egypt during 519–517 B.C.E.[41] In all probability, the army would not have passed through Yehud but near it; the sea route would have been more easily passable than the mountains at Jerusalem. However, some high-ranking officials, perhaps including Darius, probably did visit Jerusalem and Yehud proper. Certainly the presence of the army in the Yehud area would have caused the empire to take note of this small province, to assure the empire of provincial loyalty.

The presence of this army would have terrified the inhabitants of Yehud. An army of this size, representing a world empire's major force, would not have been this close to

Jerusalem since Babylonia besieged and conquered the city in 587 B.C.E. Even Cambyses' army never went that far south; its naval strategy caused it to avoid Palestine entirely.[42] Under Darius, the largest army in the world's history marched on the path toward Egypt, bringing fear to those along the path, such as Jerusalem.[43]

Many scholars have argued that the restart of temple construction activity was a reaction to the uncertainty of the time surrounding Darius' accession and that perhaps there was a strong revolutionary undercurrent among the people of Yehud. Timing is troublesome for any rebellion theory. By the middle of 521 B.C.E., the revolts throughout the empire were over, and Darius had undertaken major reorganizational and consolidating steps during 520 B.C.E. The construction of the Second Temple, begun at the very end of 520 B.C.E., can hardly be considered a timely reaction to the revolts that had been widespread in the middle of 522 B.C.E., two and one-half years earlier, and that had been pacified eighteen months earlier.[44] Second, there is no evidence of Zerubbabel's supposed revolt.[45] Perhaps most important, the presence of the Persian army would have prevented any revolt. Persian control of the area, through military and other means, was at its height.

The Persian Empire spent large amounts of economic resources to support its military venture into Egypt.[46] Sufficient foodstuffs for the army's needs could not have been transported along with the army from Persia to Egypt. Rather, such food would have to be grown along the way. Thus Yehud and the many other regions through which the army would pass would have been required to provide an enormous amount of food for the soldiers.[47] This feeding of the army would have been a significant economic drain upon Yehud. Even the seizure of the fields for a short period of time would not have been sufficient for the army; the fields must have been placed in higher production at least several months in advance of the army's arrival. This would have produced a severe economic drain upon the populace. It is possible that the construction of silos for grain storage during this period was part of the production of surplus in preparation for the army.[48] If this is the case, the economic and other effects would have been known in advance of the army's arrival, and thus the army's forthcoming presence would have been announced and expected.

The required food could have been produced only at substantial cost to Yehud. However, the Persian imperial treasury seems to have been willing to reimburse the province, at least partially, for the costs of the food. Some of the reimbursement would perhaps have been understood as construction projects, including the temple and the grain silos. If there were other reimbursements, such as coinage or commodities, this income would not have been distributed to the persons whose agricultural production had fed the army; rather, the funds would have been given to the temple leadership that was under Persian control.[49] Thus the military passage would have resulted in economic redistribution, with rural areas being responsible for additional labor and the surplus of that labor being presented to Yehud's elite.

Temple Construction

A strengthened administrative base along the army's path would have facilitated the creation of food supplies. The army's safe passage required stable administrations along the way, and thus Persia funded the construction and maintenance of a new Jerusalem temple.[50] Although Cyrus allowed temple construction, the Jerusalemites did not build until Darius ordered it. The natives in Jerusalem during the exile had continued sacrifices and worship upon the ruins of the temple; this seemed sufficient to them.[51] The immediate motivation for the temple construction, then, is threat of force. This links the temple construction more closely to Persian imperial policies than to Yehudite internal debates. As a center for Persian administration, the temple would assure tranquillity and supplies for the Persian army as it passed nearby on the way to Egypt. The Persians funded the construction of Jerusalem's Second Temple for humanitarian reasons.[52] At the same time, the temple was a symbol of Yehudite and Persian unity and of Persian favor toward Yehud.[53]

For the faithful Yahwists of Yehud, both natives and immigrants, however, the construction of the Second Temple held a very different range of meanings. This event was so important, in political, economic, and religious spheres, that it maintained a rich multivalence of meaning for all involved.

The construction of a temple allowed for a variety of functions to be met in a single building: imperial government, financial administration, and renewed worship of the people's deity. The multivalence of this building and the symbolic uses of it were one of the chief social factors of the period. As the chief location of new social resources, it would attract the types of power and influence, political, economic, and religious, that were able to transform society. Within this temple, both the governor and the priest attended their roles, as did a wide range of faithful adherents to the religion of the people. Thus the temple was a work of the people as well as a work of the Persian imperial government, although in different ways.

The Growth of Official Life

Darius' reign saw the establishment within Israel of an official Persian presence within the political and religious arenas. With the construction of a temple came an official religious body's control of the temple work. The key local players in this issue were Zerubbabel and Joshua.

Zerubbabel was the Persian-appointed governor for Jerusalem and Yehud. Increasingly, scholars are questioning the assumption that Zerubbabel was a Davidide with monarchic aspirations that can only attain fruition by armed conflict with the Persian Empire. First, the Book of Haggai never identifies Zerubbabel as a Davidide. The text mentions his father, Shealtiel, agreeing with Zechariah and Ezra, but provides no other details. First Chronicles 3:16-19 asserts that Jeconiah, Judah's last king, had seven sons, including Shealtiel and Pedaiah. Pedaiah's lineage receives further attention, and the Chronicler lists Zerubbabel as *Pedaiah's* son. The disagreement of these texts about Zerubbabel's lineage is disconcerting. Thus there is no clear evidence that Zerubbabel was the grandson of Judah's last king, or even that he was Davidic.[54] Zerubbabel was a political official appointed by Persia and subject to Persian rule, as administered through a satrapal system that made Zerubbabel directly responsible to a Syrian official who was in turn responsible to the Babylonian satrap. He had served in the court of Cambyses and possibly also in that of Cyrus.[55] The governor served as the administrator in charge of temple construction, military provisioning, and financial management.[56] As such, Zerubbabel would have had key access to the most significant free-floating resources of the time.

Many of the Yehudites recognized the need to maintain a cult that was agreeable to the Persian overlords.[57] Others comprehended the possibility for religious independence despite the political domination, and still other faithful Yahwists understood an irrelevance in politics as long as the temple worship would be restored.[58] Thus there was a variety of religious opinions concerning the connection of temple and politics, and likewise a variety of religious images. Many of these, deeply rooted in the ancient Yahwistic religious traditions, expressed these opinions.

Zerubbabel's position was dependent upon the continuing acceptability of his performance by Darius. This would have been even more important during Darius' two visits through the Yehud area during the Egyptian campaign.[59] Any appearance of rebellion would have been removed easily by the massive armies present in the area. Zerubbabel, then, should be understood as a loyal Persian official, although with ethnic and other ties to the growing community of immigrants in Yehud. He was chosen on the basis of his loyalty to the Persian Empire, and that loyalty was continually monitored and enforced.[60] His responsibilities and powers were limited to the discharge of Persian policy in the Yehud area, which included the construction of a temple for administrative purposes and the preparation of sufficient foodstuffs for the anticipated army. It should thus be unsurprising that Zerubbabel does not appear in any records after these tasks are completed. The rhetoric surrounding Zerubbabel should be interpreted within the context of this loyalty to the Persian Empire's goals of intensification.

The priests were led by a high priest, Joshua. According to Ezra 2:2, Joshua accompanied Zerubbabel from the Babylonian court to Jerusalem, for the purpose of rebuilding the temple. It is unclear whether Joshua had a role in the temple construction in the same official sense that Zerubbabel did. However, it is very likely that Joshua was officially appointed by the emperor to oversee the temple functioning, as was the usual practice. If so, then Joshua was selected by Darius for the same type of loyalty to Persia that Zerubbabel was seen to possess.

Joshua's responsibilities were not identical to Zerubbabel's. As high priest, Joshua would have governed the religious practices of the temple. Through controlling the activities of other priests, Joshua would have had more direct contact with matters of public opinion and consensus, whereas Zerubbabel would have been expected to concentrate more on the bureaucratic matters of imperial provincial governance. These were new issues for Zerubbabel and the priesthood. Likewise, the relation of the other priests to Joshua is also unknown.

Certainly Joshua fulfilled a vital social role for Yehud and the Persian Empire. Through the Persian-funded temple, Joshua had amazing abilities to impact the populace's forms of worship. Because of his loyalty to Persia, it may well be that the empire influenced some of the high priest's treatment of the people. The advent of official religion, which Darius continued to fund, mandated a temple religion that supported Persian politics. The Persian-appointed high priest would structure the religious experience so that the inhabitants found a message consonant with obedience to the Persian Empire. Although the temple remained autonomous, there would have been a constant implicit threat to the temple leadership, requiring obedience to the Persian standards. Such an official religion served both the empire and the people, by bringing them together in a common task.

Together, Zerubbabel and Joshua created a public, official life for Yehud. Although there had been inhabitants of the Jerusalem area throughout the exile, these two leaders marked the return of an officially recognized society. This social structure depended upon Persian political support and also served to popularize the goals of the Persian Empire. Zerubbabel and Joshua were the representatives of Yehud to Persia, but they were also the embodiment of the Persian Empire within the sight and hearing of Yehud's inhabitants.

Literature from Darius' Reign

Scholarship dates three pieces of literature from Darius' reign: Haggai, Zechariah 1–8, and Isaiah 56–66. These prophetic texts deal at considerable length with the temple and with its construction as a new locus of social resources. Prophecy gravitates toward influential social locations as well as toward areas of unresolved tension, and both existed in the temple construction project. The temple functioned as an economic center, as a political symbol, and as a religious focus for worship. The temple's political, economic, and religious resources attracted prophets, who used them as the starting point for religious thinking and speaking. In this way, both Haggai and Zechariah were intimately connected to the temple construction project. Third Isaiah's relationship to the temple, as will be discussed below, was much more complex.

The approaching army also concerned Haggai and Zechariah. Since the army's passage required a large-scale mobilization of Yehud's agricultural resources, then the majority of the people would have known of the army's approach. These two prophets dealt with the panic by people afraid of military destruction. However, they did not directly oppose the Persian Empire or its manifestations.[61] Yehud's leaders supported Persian rule because of religious freedom, the freedom to return to the land, and other benefits that were granted by Persian policy, as well as for the more immediate reasons of survival and political advancement.[62]

Haggai

The Book of Haggai contains numerous dates that firmly place it within the earliest time of Darius' reign. These dates represent August through December of 520 B.C.E., a time after the cessation of Darius' accession-related revolts and before the movement of the Persian army through Palestine on the way to Egypt. Haggai's sermons fit the time of military preparations for the Egyptian campaign and deal very specifically with the issues related to that preparation. Several passages within the book deal with the Yehudites' perception that Persia threatens them with war. Haggai argues strenuously for a peaceful posture and for producing the required surplus of grain for the army's passage. The book also discusses the commanded construction of a Second Temple in Jerusalem.

Warfare

The Book of Haggai frequently uses military images, and scholarship has often debated the referents of these images. A popular consensus interprets the military passages as indicating an eschatological hope that Jerusalem will vanquish the Persians and other nations of the world. This connects to postulations about a Yehudite rebellion under Zerubbabel's leadership. However, the chances of a rebellion are very low, and the military action most directly affecting Yehud is the Persian campaign against Egypt, which brought huge armies through Palestine along the same route that was used by the Babylonians when they attacked Jerusalem. The nearness of the approaching army would have brought fear to the inhabitants of Yehud, but Haggai argues against fear, encouraging the people to see Persia's involvement as a prelude to glory.

> *For thus says Yahweh of Hosts,*
> *"Once again—it will be a little while—*
> *then I will be shaking the heavens and the earth,*
> *the sea and the dry land.*
> *I will shake all the nations,*
> *and the desirable things of all nations shall come in.*
> *I will fill this house with glory," says Yahweh of Hosts.*
> *"To me belongs the silver, and to me belongs the gold,"*
> *an oracle of Yahweh of Hosts.*
> *"The glory of this house in latter times*
> *will be greater than the former times,"*
> *says Yahweh of Hosts.*
> *"In this place I will gave peace,"*
> *an utterance of Yahweh of Hosts.*
> *(Haggai 2:6-9)*[63]

In this unit, Yahweh makes five succinct statements: (1) Yahweh will shake the universe; (2) Yahweh will fill the temple with glory; (3) the temple's glory will be greater than that of earlier times; (4) this glory is related to silver and gold; and (5) in the temple, Yahweh will provide peace. Scholarship usually understands the shaking as a prophecy of Jerusalem's military conquest of the Persian armies and resultant booty.[64] Persian military movements, however, cast a different interpretive light upon this literary evidence. In the context of a massive army passage near the province of Yehud, the "shaking" of the world (Haggai 2:6-7) may not refer to battle per se but to the marching of the armies nearby. If so, the glorification of the temple is not achieved through military conquest but through other means, such as patronage by the Persian Empire. The text itself describes the temple's glory in financial terms (2:8) rather than in terms of political independence gained through battle. The near presence of the army, described as the shaking of the world, is the precursor for the blessings that will pour into the temple, including the financial benefits. Stated in political terms, the Persian military campaign is the reason that the empire paid the community to rebuild the temple.

Yahweh will provide peace for the temple (Haggai 2:9), so that the Persian armies pass by Jerusalem without any damage. In fact, the relationship is almost causal; as long as the newly constructed temple is present and finished when the army arrives in the region, then it will not attack Jerusalem. The new temple keeps the people safe. Yahweh acts through the temple's presence to bring safety and blessing to the Jerusalem community. Yahweh causes peace, through the tool of the Persian Empire.

> *And the word of Yahweh came a second time to Haggai,*
> *on the twenty-fourth of the month, saying:*
> *"Say to Zerubbabel, the governor of Judah:*
> *'I am causing the heavens and the earth to quake.*
> *I will turn aside the throne of the kingdoms,*
> *and I will exterminate the strength of the kingdoms of the nations.*
> *I will turn aside*[65] *the chariotry and its riders,*
> *and the horses and their riders will go down;*
> *each by the sword of the other.*
> *In that day,'*
> *an oracle of Yahweh of Hosts,*
> *'I will take you, Zerubbabel, son of Shealtiel, my servant ,'*
> *an oracle of Yahweh,*
> *'and I will place you as a signet, because you have I chosen,'*
> *utterance of Yahweh of Hosts."*
> *(Haggai 2:20-23)*

This oracle concludes the Book of Haggai with an unequivocally supportive statement for the Persian-appointed governor, Zerubbabel. The standard scholarly position describes Zerubbabel as the potential leader of a nationalist rebellion against Persian rule during the time of revolts surrounding Darius' accession, whether by his own initiative or at the prophet's urging; after this victory, Zerubbabel would rule over a restored Israel as Yahweh's appointed monarch on the ancient throne of David, expressing a contemporary, popular messianic eschatological expectation.[66]

When Haggai presented this oracle near the end of Darius' second year (Haggai 2:10, 20), Darius' early problems with accession had ended and the Persian Empire had embarked upon the Egyptian campaign. Throughout the early planning phases of that campaign, Darius waged a pitched political battle designed to create loyalty along the path. Within that plan, Zerubbabel provided Darius with loyal leadership that encouraged the inhabitants of Jerusalem to stockpile grain to the feed the army, to build a temple that would allow more effective administration of the region, and to accept the approach of a massive army. Perhaps this last point was the most problematic. The army would have created substantial fear, forcing the local governor, Zerubbabel, to work hard to pacify the population. This oracle works toward that goal of pacification.

First, the oracle claims that Yahweh will shake the world (Haggai 2:21). There is no need for rebellion, since Yahweh controls world events. This is hardly a call to arms; it emphasizes faith in Yahweh's abilities to protect the people amid the tumult of a passing army. Under Yahweh's control, there will be extermination for the strength of the kingdoms of nations. The text does not claim complete eradication of the Persian Empire and its administrative apparatus; instead, Yahweh will destroy the strength of the kingdoms of the nations. This strange phrase may well refer to imperial armies, not to the political systems of those empires. Furthermore, the phrase is redundantly plural, with both kingdoms and nations. It is sensible to understand this as a reference to more than one empire. The envisioned destruction includes both the nations involved in the warfare; there is no sense in Haggai 2:21-22 of a Jerusalemite victory over a foreign army.

The empires participating in this prophetically depicted carnage are the same two world powers involved in the historical battle. Five years earlier, Persia had conquered Egypt, but Egypt rejected Persian control very shortly thereafter. Jerusalem had stood in awe of Egyptian military prowess for centuries, and such events only confirmed this conception. A reasonable expectation for the outcome of Persia's renewed Egyptian campaign would be massive destruction on both sides. Haggai's prophecies reflect this expectation through the references to massive destruction of the strength of the kingdoms of nations. Both mighty powers, Persia and Egypt, will meet their match in each other, and each will die by the sword of the other (Haggai 2:22).

In this context of promised safety from military threat, Yahweh declares that Zerubbabel is God's servant and signet (Haggai 2:23).[67] The use of the term "signet ring" reverses Jeremiah 22:24, in which Yahweh removes Judah's last king, there called Coniah. In Haggai 2:23, Zerubbabel receives that role from which Coniah fell, but such a role is very limited. Coniah was a puppet ruler with some administrative responsibilities but very little autonomy (2 Kings 24:10–16). As signet, Coniah was a tool for a world empire, and Haggai 2:23 places Zerubbabel in this role. Only a ruler with unquestionable Persian loyalty could prevent Persia from destroying Jerusalem on its way to Egypt. With Zerubbabel as leader, Persia will turn aside and attack Egypt, leaving Jerusalem unharmed and fulfilling Yahweh's desire.

Fertility

Several passages within Haggai address the Persian army's expenditure of grain grown by the Yehudites. These texts focus on decreased consumption, using the language of agricultural fertility.[68] The prophet is analyzing the ecological and economic condition of Yehud.[69] The overarching intention of the Book of Haggai is to offer theological support for the construction of the Second Temple, and so the payment of the high grain taxes leads, in Haggai's rhetoric, to God's glorious presence in the Persian-built temple.

> *"Now! Set your hearts from this day and forward.*
> *Before the placing of a stone upon a stone*
> *in the temple of Yahweh,*
> *before they were, when one came to a heap of twenty,*
> *there were ten.*
> *When one came to the winevat, to the trough, to scoop out fifty,*
> *there were twenty.*
> *I struck you, all the work of your hands,*
> *with scorching and with mildew and with hail.*
> *But none of you were toward me,"*
> *an oracle of Yahweh.*
> *"Set your hearts from this day and forward,*
> *from the twenty-fourth day of the ninth month,*
> *from the day you established the temple of Yahweh.*

Set your hearts.
Is the seed still in the storage pit?
Even[70] *the vine and the fig and the pomegranate and the olive tree,*
do they not yield?
From this day I will bless you."
(Haggai 2:15-19)

This unit begins with "set your hearts" (Haggai 2:15), repeating an emphasis throughout Haggai on human choices. Throughout Haggai, the call to set the heart, to make a conscious decision, combines with economic issues and fertility language, which form the context in which the decision must be made.

The unit's first section (Haggai 2:15-17) contains a retrospective. The prophet describes the limited market availability of basic staples, then the unit claims that Yahweh struck the people and damaged their work. As in the related texts, production may have remained at relatively high rates, but the imperial policies of stockpiling grain for the approaching army limited consumption to the level of bare subsistence, so that basic supplies were not sufficiently available for daily needs (Haggai 2:15-16). The stated reductions of 50 percent and 60 percent probably do not represent exact amounts, but they indicate the severe scope of the problem. Even a small decrease in supplies would have greatly endangered the livelihood of many, but when policy decreases consumption by 50 percent or more, survival proves difficult.

The remarks in Haggai 2:17 represent meteorological problems that intensified the economic difficulties. These three scourges (scorching, mildew, and hail) receive no other mention in Haggai, and so seem distinct from the main concern. Perhaps weather had endangered the increased production, causing enough loss of crops that survival no longer seemed possible. In that context, the people had to decide which activities would receive their greatest attention: the stockpiling of grain, the construction of the temple, or food for daily life. Faced with such choices, none of the people oriented themselves toward Yahweh and the construction of the temple (Haggai 2:17b); instead, they prioritized other tasks. Haggai refuses to compromise and insists that the people do everything. In the prophet's view, Yahweh is the source of the meteorological disasters. Once again, the people's resistance to Persian policy is equated with a rejection of the Deity.

Haggai 2:18-19 forms the second of this unit's sections. This section begins, as did the previous one, with the call to set the heart, but here the prophet connects that call to the specific date of the temple's establishment. Once again, the completion of the temple construction is implicit, and fertility images express the reasoning for this project. Two rhetorical questions lead to the promise of divine blessing (v. 19).[71]

The first question is syntactically straightforward: "Is the seed still in the storage pit?" The term here for "storage pit" is rare and may be a technical term for the Persian-constructed grain storage pits.[72] The expected answer to this question, however, proves problematic. If one assumes a positive answer, then grain is still in the silos, presumably after the army's departure, and this grain assures the coming fertility.[73] If the answer is negative, then the Persian army has passed through the region, leaving no grain behind. If so, the approaching army no longer poses a threat; the danger is over and the people have survived.[74] In either reading, Haggai 2:15-19 follows the army's passage near Jerusalem, leaving the inhabitants of the city alive, although impoverished.

The second question follows upon the first: "Even the vine and the fig and the pomegranate and the olive tree, do they not yield?" Here the expected answer is positive; the trees *do* bear fruit. This list of fruits in production gives hope for the future, because there is still time to harvest these crops before the season ends. With these staples and luxury items, a revitalized economy is at hand.[75] God's blessings are not only future promises but present realities, as soon as the Persian armies pass without harming Jerusalem.

Temple Construction

The point throughout the Book of Haggai is the necessity of the temple construction project. Direct statements to this end appear in Haggai 1:2, 8, 12; 2:3, 9, 15, 18. Both Yahweh and the Persian Empire desire that Yehud construct a temple that will function in political and religious means to solidify the colony. Those leaders and residents who support the project find blessing; curses and destruction await those who resist the will of God and Persia. The construction of a temple must have been a project that the people hesitated to do; thus there was a need to encourage them strongly in this direction. It is reasonable to assume that the residents of Yehud understood that the temple would benefit others, such as the Persian Empire and the priests appointed by Darius, more than it would advantage the workers. The Second Temple was controversial, but Haggai's prophetic arguments for construction, including the focus on Persia's strong desire and support as well as Yahweh's divine call to build, proved persuasive. History records that the people of Yehud built the temple and that the Persian army passed by without known harm to the colony of Yehud.

Zechariah 1–8

The first eight chapters of the book attributed to Zechariah reflect the writings of Zechariah, the son of Berechiah (Zechariah 1:1,7), who prophesied during 520–518 B.C.E., mostly after overlapping slightly with the prophet Haggai (Ezra 5:1; 6:14). These contemporaneous prophets shared many concerns, such as the construction of the Persian-funded temple, which God supported. Haggai and Zechariah also expressed the common conviction that Darius' approaching army would not destroy Jerusalem but would pass nearby on its way to attack Egypt. Throughout the writings of both prophets, one finds repeated emphasis on the difficulties of establishing the new community of Yehud at the intersection of Persian politics and Yahwistic tradition, within the context of immigrants and native inhabitants who had survived the exile in Palestine.

Zechariah 1–8 expresses these concerns in a manner vastly different from the Book of Haggai. The bulk of Zechariah's writing records visions that the prophet saw, along with some interpretive comments that an accompanying angel provided. Whereas Haggai exists squarely within the prophetic tradition of direct political discourse in representation of God's own voice in earthly community debates, Zechariah was a visionary who dreamed of the divine realms and reported these findings to the people during the time that the Persian Empire's army was marching through the surrounding territory on its way to Egypt. In the midst of this time of crisis, the prophet assured that the Persian army offered no threat to Yehud, because God determined international events.

The Visions of the Horses

In Zechariah 1:7-17, the prophet sees four horses and riders who report to God. An angel attends Zechariah, and when the prophet asks the angel about the meaning of the vision, one of the riders addresses them: "We have patrolled the earth, and lo, the whole earth remains at peace" (Zechariah 1:11b). At this time in February 519 B.C.E., the Persian army was marching or preparing to march toward Jerusalem, but the prophet proclaims that there is no cause for alarm here; all is at peace. Not only does the angel state this but Zechariah hears Yahweh's comforting words to the angel, who then interprets Yahweh to the prophet:

> *I am very jealous for Jerusalem and for Zion. And I am extremely angry with the nations that are at ease; for while I was only a little angry, they made the disaster worse. Therefore, thus says the LORD, I have returned to Jerusalem with compassion; my house shall be built in it, says the LORD of hosts, and the measuring line shall be stretched out over Jerusalem. Proclaim further: Thus says the LORD of hosts: My cities shall again overflow with prosperity; the LORD will again comfort Zion and again choose Jerusalem. (Zechariah 1:14b-17)*

Yahweh's loyalties are clearly directed toward Jerusalem, with full realization of Yehud's present problems as the Persian army marches closer. Yehud is not one of the nations at ease, but Yahweh will return with compassion to Zion. This passage defines God's compassion as activity to rebuild the temple and to increase Jerusalem's prosperity. These would have characterized the Persian efforts within the city. The Persian need for administrative and storage facilities in the light of the army's passage necessitated the building of a temple. Yahweh's choice of Jerusalem is tantamount to a saving act, such as the survival of the city in the face of the approaching army. The promises also extend into the future; Yahweh's choice of Jerusalem will soon manifest itself, in the passing by of the army, and then prosperity follows, as Persia allows Jerusalem to keep more of its own production for itself, once the army receives its food.

Zechariah's next vision expands on these concepts of divine protection for Jerusalem. In Zechariah 1:18-21, the prophet sees horns, which symbolize the nations and armies (principally, Babylonia) that destroyed Jerusalem in 587 B.C.E. The angel explains that craftspersons have arrived to scare off the horns and to prevent destruction. These craftspersons build the temple; their presence shows the loyalty to God's desire and to the Persian Empire that will keep Jerusalem safe. When the Yehudites cooperate with those who were building the temple, then there will be safety for all.

Much later in Zechariah's prophecy the image of the horses returns. This second vision (Zechariah 6:1-8) is not identical to the first one (1:7-17). In the second vision, the horses pull chariots as they examine the four corners of God's earth. Their report comes in the concluding verse:

> *Then [the angel] cried out to me, "Lo, those who go toward the north country have set my spirit at rest in the north country." (Zechariah 6:8)*

This passage dates to February 519 B.C.E., just as do the materials from chapter 1. As the Persian army gathers far to the north, God investigates the situation and evaluates the army as a nonthreat, as a state of rest and peace. Through the interpreting angel, Yahweh's messenger reports this reality to Zechariah. Even though the inhabitants of Yehud would have known that Persia was amassing an army to walk near Jerusalem, Yahweh assures them that there is no threat. The Persian army presents no danger.

Throughout these texts and others, Zechariah addresses what would have been the chief concern of the inhabitants of Jerusalem and Yehud, and the prophet continually argues that Yahweh is in full control of international events and that there is no problem. Even these approaching armies are not true problems in God's sight. Yahweh remains fully aware of the situation and approves of what is happening. This powerful theological affirmation of the Persian Empire's action attempts to persuade the populace into the acceptance of Persian policy for religious reasons. Religion and politics are thoroughly mixed in Zechariah's mystical visions.

Issues of Leadership

In Zechariah 3–4, the prophet devotes attention to the matter of Jerusalem's leadership. He introduces two figures: high priest, Joshua, and the governor, Zerubbabel. Both appear to be Persian-born Jews with direct connections to the temple construction project and thus to the preparations for the army's approach. The Persian Empire would have required both to enforce different parts of Persian policy in Jerusalem. Zechariah's political philosophy supports both of these officials, with some sort of sharing of power between them, but his presentation of each is distinct. Many scholars have envisioned a dyarchy that collapses into a rule by the high priest after the removal of Zerubbabel, but there is insufficient evidence for such a view. Instead, these two figures each play major roles within Yehudite society, and the general submission to the leadership of each is vital for Yehud, but in different ways. Zechariah does not equate the two or even present them in the same passage.

Zechariah observes the high priest, Joshua, who stands in the presence of God and Satan (Zechariah 3:1-10). Satan opposes Joshua, but God shows divine favor for the priest, forgives his sins, and clothes him with new, rich garments. An angel repeats God's promise to give Joshua control of the temple, since God intends to bring a day of purity and prosperity to the land through Joshua (Zechariah 3:9). This vision provides unflagging support to Joshua, equating submission to this Persian-appointed priest's authority with God's plan and identifying any political opposition to Joshua with the work of the Accuser, Satan.

In Zechariah 4:1-14, the prophet examines the temple furnishings that symbolize God's protection of Jerusalem's inhabitants. In large part, this protection comes through the governor, Zerubbabel, whose work is described in an oddly inserted section (Zechariah 4:6-10a). Zerubbabel began the temple construction, and God firmly supports his completion of the project (Zechariah 4:9). In this vision's hyperbole, Zerubbabel levels mountains and brings the people to rejoicing. The temple construction proceeds "not by might, nor by power, but by [God's] spirit" (Zechariah 4:6). The military might of Persia and its economic power are not the real reasons for the temple; they are only God's agents. This section concludes with the statement that there are two anointed ones who serve God in a special way. Presumably, these two are Joshua and Zerubbabel, since the prophet thereby closes a section that has discussed each of them at length.

One more passage depicts the prophet's particular political thoughts. Zechariah 6:9-15 oddly envisions the crowning and enthronement of a priest rather than a king. This oddity, along with the text's mention of *two* crowns, has caused many scholars to wonder whether an earlier version of this story included Zerubbabel, but the branch symbolism has already been connected to Joshua,[76] and both of these leaders have legitimate roles in the temple construction. There is no reason to read a rejection of Zerubbabel into this emphasis on Joshua. Both are God's agents in temple construction; Zechariah refers to the harmony between temple and throne (Zechariah 6:13). The prophet envisions a unified leadership structure that extends into the administration of the Persian Empire, and the prophet values this leadership for its effectiveness in bringing prosperity and respect to the colony of Yehud. Because of the work of Joshua and Zerubbabel, God will save Jerusalem, as long as the people fulfill God's will through obedience to these, their leaders, and through them to the Persian Empire.

Life after the Persian Army's Departure

Zechariah also presents images of Jerusalem's future, apparently referring to the times after the passage of the Persian army when the promised prosperity would be manifest. In Zechariah 2:1-5, the prophet sees the construction of the city and hears an angel's declaration that the new Jerusalem would have no walls. At a social and economic level, this points to a degree of prosperity so great that no walls could contain the population. In political terms, this position echoes the Persian policy that the colonies could not fortify themselves. Theologically, Zechariah emphasizes that God will be a wall of fire around the city, protecting it without physical barriers. Again, Persian policy and divine command coalesce. God's own activity effectively saves and maintains Yehud. At that point, Jews from the north (i.e., from Babylonia and Persia) receive a special invitation to immigrate to Jerusalem (Zechariah 2:6-13). Once these newcomers arrive, God will inhabit Jerusalem and live in the people's midst.

Zechariah throughout his prophecy emphasizes that Yahweh's protection extends to the inhabitants of Yehud and to Jews throughout the Diaspora, as long as they obey the Persian policies of temple construction and military nonresistance. The prophet portrays God as completely controlling international events, and the effect of such theological rhetoric is the strong support of the reigning power, who receives this image of God as religious legitimation for its political goals.

Isaiah 56–66

The reign of Darius introduced certain social conflicts into Yehud. Primarily, the threatened introduction of a large military force produced a tension of fear and apprehension, probably causing many inhabitants to wonder whether feeding that approaching army was a wise action. Similarly, the requirement to build the temple would have caused social division, since the natives of the Jerusalem area had lived and worshiped for almost three-fourths of a century without a temple. Haggai and Zechariah 1–8 respond to the social conflicts with strong theological support for the Persian Empire's plans, including direct mention of the Persian-appointed leaders within Jerusalem, the governor

Zerubbabel and the high priest Joshua. Isaiah 56–66 represents a very different sort of response.

Isaiah 56–66 records the conflict much more fully, by preserving the different voices within this internal Yehudite social division. The various groups present their own views on the social problems of the day in four cycles of increasing stridency, and by the end two groups merge to reject the views of the third. Whereas Haggai and Zechariah 1–8 repress the voices of dissent, Isaiah 56–66 preserves those voices and then drowns them out in utter rejection and condemnation.

The major division within Yehudite society was that between the natives and the immigrants. The natives had organized themselves loosely during the time of Babylonian domination, and their society had become adequate to their own needs before the arrival of the Persian immigrants. As the immigrant group increasingly received the Persian Empire's favor, their political power grew and their ability to overpower the more numerous immigrants expanded. However, the immigrants themselves were not a unified group. It consisted both of persons with priestly orientations and those of urban and political interests. The priestly immigrants probably included those who had worked in the Babylonian temple system through the exile, who probably were descendants of the priests of monarchic Jerusalem. The political immigrants would have included descendants of the royal court officials, who had served in Babylonian and Persian royal service for their earlier careers, as well as merchants and other persons whose fortunes were tied to the political and economic success of the Persian Empire. Although these immigrant groups shared many experiences and opinions, they were not equivalent groups and they possessed several important differences in orientation.

The natives' livelihood was tied to the land, and most of their concerns were very practical. For them, an important element of religion was the regulation of land usage and the promises of continued production. Thus social justice and righteousness concepts permeate their thinking, based on the rich traditions of earlier prophets and the other ancient Israelite traditions. The priestly immigrants would have been the strongest supporters for the temple construction and the beginning of "correct" sacrifices. Their discussion would center around ideas such as Sabbath, kosher rules, and correct sacrifices as well as concepts of Zion, God's holy mountain, and the light (of God's law) that proceeds from Zion. The political immigrants focused their concerns on the future of Jerusalem, including the construction of the city, the prosperity in terms of new wealth, political agreements such as covenants, and the need to punish enemies and bring foreigners into controllable positions. Perhaps the wedding images fit into this group's orientation, as a metaphor for a new relationship between God and people, as also was the case with the image of servanthood. Also, this group was the most likely to have preserved the political concerns of the earlier Isaiah traditions, and so Third Isaiah's quotations from First and Second Isaiah came from the political immigrants.

These groups presented their views and argued their positions in four cycles of increasing rhetorical violence. Each cycle marks its end with an attempt at intermediation, in which short passages integrate the distinctive language of the groups. By the end of the fourth cycle, intermediation between all three groups becomes impossible, because the discourse has diverged so radically, and so the two immigrant groups combine their rhetoric into a final rejection of the natives.

Cycle One (Isaiah 56:1—57:21)

The first cycle contains Isaiah 56:1—57:21. The priestly immigrants begin the dialogue with Isaiah 56:1-8, which reads as a programmatic manifesto: "Thus says the LORD: Maintain justice, and do what is right, for soon my salvation will come, and my deliverance be revealed. Happy is the mortal who does this, the one who holds it fast, who keeps the sabbath, not profaning it, and refrains from doing any evil" (Isaiah 56:1-2). Such a statement could hardly anger anyone within the Jerusalem community, although perhaps the high emphasis on Sabbath observance would have been controversial in very early post-exilic faith. However, the radical nature of the priestly agenda enters immediately thereafter: eunuchs and foreigners are to be included, even as ministers, in violation of traditional purity codes.[77] The reason may have been obvious and urgent to the first hearers of this text: many of the temple functionaries within the Babylonian religious system, as well as many of the Persian court officials, were eunuchs and would have been considered foreigners to the natives.

The natives respond in Isaiah 56:9—57:2. They begin the attack, calling the priests wild animals who come to devour, blind sentinels, and silent dogs (Isaiah 56:10). The use of the word "shepherds" (Isaiah 56:11) to describe these evil ones clearly indicates the leadership role assumed by the natives' priestly opponents, who promise prosperity (Isaiah 56:12). Instead, the righteous natives perish while no one cares, while the rich rest on their couches (Isaiah 57:1-2).

The priestly immigrants join the fray with their response in Isaiah 57:3-13, calling the natives the offspring of an adulterer and a whore. Such origin insults would have been the language of attack for genealogically-minded priests. The fertility religion of the natives receives sharp condemnation (Isaiah 57:5-10), as does idolatry (Isaiah 57:13). The priests emphasize the need for the right religion, which only they can mediate. Thus they promise at the end that "whoever takes refuge in me shall possess the land and inherit my holy mountain" (Isaiah 57:13b), in the Zion and inheritance language long tied to priestly concerns.

The final move of the cycle is toward intermediation. The prophet attempts to combine these various concerns into a fused position. Salvation is promised; God claims to dwell "in the high and holy place, and also with those who are contrite and humble in spirit" (Isaiah 57:15). The language represents the self-understanding of both groups. The intermediation concludes with a promise of "Peace, peace, to the far and the near, says the LORD; and I will heal them. But the wicked are like the tossing sea that cannot keep still; its waters toss up mire and mud. There is no peace, says my God, for the wicked" (Isaiah 57:19-21). Thus the intermediation affirms both positions, despite their vast differences, but declares clearly that those who war against each other are wicked. This passage comes close to a validation of pluralism, or at least a pact to disagree agreeably.

Cycle Two (Isaiah 58:1—59:21)

The second cycle begins again with the priestly immigrants in Isaiah 58:1-14, but they now direct their argumentation to the political immigrants. The nature of fasting takes the primary attention, as the priests instruct others that the proper fasting is not an act to sway the Deity's will but a series of acts of social justice and compassion to the poor (Isaiah 58:3-10). The promise, typical of the priests, is of a coming light (Isaiah 58:10).

When the political immigrants demonstrate the proper compassion, then God will rebuild the city—which is this group's chief goal. In a summary, the observance of the Sabbath will result in adequacy of food (Isaiah 58:13-14).

In Isaiah 59:1-15a, the natives respond with their analysis of the political requirements of the day. Iniquity has separated the politicians from God. Whereas the priests call the politicians to correct ritual, the natives label them as sinners. They are guilty of the excesses and abuses of power, in much the same terms as the eighth-century prophets accused their era's leaders (Isaiah 59:3-8). They reverse the priests' declaration of a coming light: "We wait for light, and lo! there is darkness; and for brightness, but we walk in gloom. . . .We wait for justice, but there is none" (Isaiah 59:9, 11).[78] The natives end with a stinging indictment: "Truth is lacking, and whoever turns from evil is despoiled" (Isaiah 59:15a).

The political immigrants join the discussion for the first time in Isaiah 59:15b-20, with a direct response to the natives. They admit that God is displeased with the lack of justice, but they celebrate God's ability to save in military fashion. The politicians' God is a skillful tactician whose mighty acts in the international scene prove God's redemption.

The final intermediation is short, consisting only of Isaiah 59:21. It combines the politicians' term of covenant and the natives' term of spirit. To be sure, these terms are general, which serves to show the severity of the rift in dialogue: the only agreement to be reached is in extremely general terms. At this point, it is not surprising to find the balance of the dialogue shifting. The immigrants demonstrate an ability to work together, but the natives are increasingly isolated from the immigrant positions.

Cycle Three (Isaiah 60:1—65:8)

The third cycle exacerbates the growing rift. Encompassing Isaiah 60:1—65:8, this is the longest of the cycles and alternates primarily between the priestly immigrants in Isaiah 60:1-3, 13-15 and the political immigrants, whose voice becomes clearly heard in Isaiah 60:4-12 and in Isaiah 60:16—63:19, the largest single block within Isaiah 56–66. Both groups attempt to persuade the natives through glowing promises. For the priests, these promises include the chosenness of God's light (Isaiah 60:1-3) and the glory of a beautiful temple in Zion (Isaiah 60:13-15).

The political immigrants develop their promises in much greater detail. They focus on continued immigration expanding the population (Isaiah 60:4, 8-9, 22), radically increased wealth (Isaiah 60:5-7, 11, 16-17), a rebuilt city with effective walls (Isaiah 60:10, 18; 61:4; 62:6, 10), and the control of other nations (Isaiah 60:12; 61:5-11; 62:2; 63:1-6). God's spirit is upon these politicians to bring salvation through practical means to those who need it so desperately, because they have so little (Isaiah 61:1-3). The message of the politicians is not without hints of condescension. They believe that they are God's appointees to bring salvation to the natives.

The natives disagree, offering their rebuttal in Isaiah 64:1-12. They shriek for the heavens to split and for God to descend; their images are nigh unto apocalyptic. They sense that they are losing the battle and wish for divine intervention as their only chance at salvation. Whereas the politicians depict God's intervention as through a mighty arm to redeem and raise up the people, the natives see clearly God's destructive potential (Isaiah 64:3, 9). They admit their sin and realize that they are economically and spiritually diminished. Even though there are no people who represent God (a direct condemnation of the immigrant groups), they confess their faith (Isaiah 64:8) and then beg God to cease silence and to act, lest the people continue to suffer yet new injustices by the hands of the oppressive immigrants (Isaiah 64:12).

The priests offer a short invective against the native cult in Isaiah 65:1-7. The natives admitted their uncleanness, but the priests' response offers a divergent interpretation of the sins of the natives. They claim that God was ready to save but that the natives continued rebellion (Isaiah 65:1-2). Instead, they continued their pagan practices of fertility religion (Isaiah 65:3-7).

The intermediation is brief. Isaiah 65:8 quotes God promising not to destroy the whole cluster of grapes (or the entirety of Jerusalem), because there is a blessing in it. Although God condemns the infighting that tears apart the community, God insists that there is a blessing inside. Theologically, this relativizes the rest of the material, since it raises the level of debate to that of ultimate concern. At the same time, it offers a hope for all concerned: destruction is not at stake, no matter how great the disagreement becomes. Unfortunately the debate retreats from this position and devolves into rejection.

Cycle Four (Isaiah 65:9—66:24)

The fourth cycle begins at Isaiah 65:9 and concludes at the end of the book, in Isaiah 66:24. The political immigrants offer a vision of a restored Jerusalem community, with an enlarged population and great agricultural fecundity. Others will suffer death, starvation, drought, and shame (Isaiah 65:12-13). The politicians propose a split between God's "servants" and the accursed audience (Isaiah 65:15). But this divisive judgmentalism disappears quickly, as they envision a new creation in which all are accepted and find a peaceful prosperity (Isaiah 65:17-25).[79] This vision of community offers a potential for coexistence, in terms of material prosperity.

The natives know that such will not be for them. In their next attack, Isaiah 66:1-6, they inveigh against the temple construction project. Their objection is theological: God has no need of a temple, and those who participate in temple sacrifice are perverse and wicked. Those who tremble at God's word and claim to desire God's glory, that is, the priests and the politicians, are actually God's enemies, whom God will shortly destroy (Isaiah 66:5-6). With these harsh words, the split is complete, and no fusion of perspectives is possible.

The political immigrants admit the troubles in their final statement, Isaiah 66:7-14. Of course there is pain in the birthing of this new society, but it is temporary. True prosperity is at hand, despite the squabbling of the masses. The natives respond with a final rejection in Isaiah 66:15-16: God will arrive in anger and destroy the people by fire. At this point, they have made the transition into the apocalyptic desire for all flesh to receive destruction. The priestly immigrants in Isaiah 66:17 retaliate in kind: God will destroy those who practice disgusting acts of perverse religion.

The final act of intermediation, Isaiah 66:18-24, binds together the two immigrant views, bringing only condemnation to the natives. Gathering of the population brings glory among the nations, as all peoples of the earth arrive with proper gifts and offerings for God. Some will be priests. The new creation will bring all peoples to worship on Sabbaths and new moons. As the nations arrive for worship, they will pass by the stinking, smoking corpses of God's opponents, the natives. With the closing of the book, the battle is won.

Visions of Community

Each of the three groups possesses a certain vision of the proper and divinely ordained community, and these visions control the perceptions of the group. The priestly immigrants desire a community centered on temple. This requires, in practical terms, the construction of a Second Temple. The practices of Sabbath and kosher foods are also essential for this community. Their invective is strongest on two points: those who have sacrificed in hills and valleys (i.e., not in a temple building) and those who have eaten unclean foods.

The priestly immigrants are also strongly emotional about a radical inclusion, in violation of monarchic standards of purity. These priests desire the inclusion of eunuchs and foreigners as priests and cultic servants. Their interest is clear. Many of the immigrants who had served in temples or in courts in Babylonia would have been castrated as an occupational requirement. Combined with the natives' sense that the immigrants were foreigners, the inclusion of foreign eunuchs was a necessity for the immigrants. Their influence was one of the strongest inputs toward inclusivity in Israelite religion; it is ironic that this emphasis on inclusivity resulted in division and rejection.

The political immigrants concentrate on the material aspects of life. They may well have been aligned with the Persian imperial concerns of government, emphasizing a productive colony that could pay its taxes well and that would stay content as Persian citizens. This required prosperity, and these politicians envisioned a community of wealth, ensconced in a strong and protected city with enough food for even the poorest. If this kind of society required the creation of a new heaven and a new earth, so be it. As social engineers, these politicians saw few bounds, but they realized that they had the support of the resourceful Persian Empire and needed only to fund the success of ten to fifteen thousand persons in Jerusalem.

The native vision of community requires that they be left alone. The natives lived on the plots of land where they, their parents, and their grandparents had farmed. Stability and noninterference are typically the chief goals of peasant and village classes. The natives had been worshiping in places of their choosing; they found no need to listen to the priests who insisted that a temple was a requirement. The natives had been farming on their own, perhaps with little beyond subsistence; they had no patience with the politicians who promised prosperity but really thought in terms of Persian taxes and expensive governmental construction projects.

The natives' faith resided in traditional categories. Compassion, justice, and righteousness receive frequent mention. This is not an ethical religion divorced from sacrifice and ritual; certainly the priests are right that the natives engage in worship. For both natives and immigrants, true faith in God requires both ethics and ritual as inseparable elements of the one faith. The natives reject the temple, but not ritual. Instead, they express their chief differences in an understanding of justice and righteousness. Primarily for the natives, these concepts refer to nonoppression and the lack of hierarchy, or to God's intervention to destroy the wealthy. The immigrants think of justice and righteousness as effective policy and a distribution of goods that provides a bare adequacy for all.

The Struggle for Control

The key dynamic of this period, as represented in Isaiah 56–66, is a struggle for control of the society. This literature depicts that struggle at the ideological level. The struggle is made more difficult because of the inability of each group to understand the language of the others. Each uses a specialized vocabulary that communicates *within* its own group but offends those on the outside. For instance, the priests talk about a light dawning from Zion, but the natives reverse that image. The words do not communicate across the boundaries of worldviews.

Instead of intermediation, two groups form a coalition that forces the third group into an untenable "minority" position. The priestly and political immigrants began with noticeably different concerns, which were not so much in conflict with each other as they were focused on widely different issues. Possibly these two groups originated in different areas of Babylonia and in different exposures to and acceptance of Babylonian culture.

The resultant conflict is not a struggle between hierocrats and visionaries.[80] All three groups are envisioning community in strikingly new terms, whether we consider the natives' vision of nonhierarchy, the priests' vision of inclusion and light from Zion, or the politicians' vision of a new creation. None of these are pragmatic concerns, nor is Ezekiel 40–48, which provides an alternative vision of community with ties to all three of these Isaianic visions. The conflict exists along a divergence between natives and immigrants.

This split may begin as a separation of interest groups, but it moves into class conflict. The elite immigrants have the ability to enforce their desires, and in Isaiah 56–66 they enforce their positions ideologically, through a rhetoric of violence against the native worldview. In this recognition of class-based conflict, Paul Hanson is right. The group with the possibility of direct access to the Persian imperial resources wins. The immigrants suppress the native voices.

The remarkable thing about this text, however, is that it *preserves* the losing voices in the struggle. This record of conflict is rare in Israelite literature; usually the opposition positions are not extant. Why did these three positions continue to exist side by side in the written tradition? Such a question cannot receive a definitive answer, but some possibilities can be advanced. Each of the three groups expressed a concern for community. The priests, as well as the others, envisioned a togetherness for all inhabitants that went beyond agreement. Perhaps this impulse, still present in the text, was able to preserve the losing options in ways that are not entirely sympathetic but that are still extant. A second alternative is that there never was a complete victory of any group. Although the natives lost the rhetoric and lost the battle to prevent temple construction, they still outnumbered the elites and controlled food production. Perhaps this provided some sort of equal footing, on account of which all positions remain preserved. As a third alternative, perhaps the Persian Empire required a report of the progress toward temple construction in Jerusalem and Isaiah 56–66 was composed as a summary of the differing viewpoints, making concessions to the opposition forces but emphatically stating the government's ability to deal effectively with dissent. This option might be the most realistic, since Persia's concerns about rebellion in the provinces would motivate the imperial demand for a report. The religious nature of the temple project then allowed the canonization of the records of debate about that construction, as occurred with Ezekiel 40–48, Haggai, and Zechariah 1–8.

Summary

Darius' reign saw a great expansion in the Persian Empire, as Egypt entered the fold of loyal provinces and as Greece became the target of future attempts at expansion. Darius also reorganized the empire, breaking the previous assumptions of conquest or stagnation and shifting the empire toward the increased exploitation of existing resources, including the use of local religions to reward and motivate provinces. These gains and shifts in the Persian Empire had numerous effects upon Yehud within the time of Darius and in the years that followed.

Three recorded prophets spoke to Yehud during the early years of Darius' reign: Haggai, Zechariah 1–8, and Isaiah 56–66. In effect, Haggai and Zechariah argued for submission to Persian will as a means toward pleasing God and receiving God's desire for the reconstruction of Jerusalem and Yehudite society. Third Isaiah more clearly shows the growing exclusion of native voices within the social struggles of adjustment to Darius' imperial policies and the expansion of the population of Jerusalem. Throughout all of these prophets, a single social issue emerges. During Darius' reign, the control of Yehudite society passed from the large native population to the smaller immigrant group, led by those sent by Darius (such as Zerubbabel and Joshua) in order to organize Yehud more effectively for Persian benefit.

Force and Violence

The most visible manifestation of violence was Darius' march against Egypt. The slow progression of this huge force exerted pressure to submit to Persian will, not only upon Egypt but also upon Yehud and the numerous other colonies along or near the army's path. Persia attacked neither Egypt nor Yehud, but the presence of such a large army exerted strong force nonetheless. The army's presence threatened an immediate violent reaction to any independent action, and thus there was a sharply controlling aspect to the army's nonviolent presence. The reorganization of Yehud as a Persian colony took place under this sort of coercion.

Beyond the physical violence threatened by the nearby army, Yehud experienced rhetorical violence. The suppression of divergent views becomes most obvious in Isaiah 56–66, especially in the concluding cycle's condemnation of the native group. Haggai and Zechariah 1–8 also commit a sort of violence through their claims of divine support for partisan positions. After the widespread official acceptance of their rhetoric, it became impossible to oppose the Persian Empire without also opposing God and God's will for Jerusalem. This form of priestly and political immigrant religion became the only allowed official religion within Yehud, and these groups combined to capture the rights to the older traditions. Soon all religious traditions of ancient monarchic Israel, at least those extant, bore the stamp of a strongly Jerusalemite bias. This bias may have existed before, during the closing years of the monarchy, but in Darius' reign that became official and quite possibly became the published official view, if Darius published a set of Yehudite laws as was done for other provinces.[81] These rhetorical moves combined to remove a set of possibilities for faith and social life and to reinterpret older scripture in the light of the provincial, legal, priestly base for the new society of Yehud.

Ramifications for Biblical Interpretation and Faith

The effects of this capture of older traditions by a priestly-political immigrant group reach far into the future of the biblical traditions of faith. Darius' Yehud became the lens through which later biblical communities viewed their earlier history. The dissent groups before and during Darius' time are most difficult to perceive, even though some reconstruction remains possible.

The development of a nonmonarchic temple religion is by far the most significant result of Darius' time as emperor of Persia. Yahwism had grown as a religion under the strict control of a local monarchy, whether in Samaria or Jerusalem. The exile and beginning of the Diaspora introduced a severe challenge to this religion by separating it from its cultic service to the Israelite or Judean state. Although there were many responses to the exile, the winning solution was the one that Darius implemented: a nonmonarchic temple cult. The temple would serve the empire, including its local manifestation within the provincial administration, but the community would not organize itself politically around a local monarchy that controlled the temple. Instead, the temple leadership would increasingly gain autonomy for several centuries; religion and politics would become increasingly separate phenomena within Yehudite society, despite several contrary moments in the next half millennium. At times, the political government would support the temple and at times the empire would remove that support, but the existence of a temple no longer depended upon a local king's desires. A separate temple became the most common norm for Judaism and for Christianity afterward.

The appearance of a canon began during this time as well. During Darius' codification of laws, a set group of scriptures emerged as the religious tradition of Yehud's temple to Yahweh. In previous times, the court had maintained religious and historical traditions through its scribes and employed priests. At this time, the temple developed its own control over the preservation and recording of religious traditions, at first with the support of the Persian Empire. Over time, this developed into a religion that identified itself as people of the book. Along with the growth of a canon-based religion was the use of prior traditions to establish and prove viewpoints. The political immigrants offered quotations and interpretations of the older Isaiah traditions in order to support their own visions of how the Yehudite community should operate. The formation of canon resulted in the use of canon to interpret modern situations. With the shift toward addressing current problems with previous scripture came the tendency to write less new material, and over the next centuries this resulted in a slow closing of the canon. Certainly there were still many more portions of the canon remaining to be written at the end of Darius' reign, but the beginnings of the conceptual base regarding canon, which would eventually allow the notion of a closed canon, had already occurred.

The shifts to temple and canon as centers of the Yahwistic religion set the bases for later Jewish and Christian faith in many respects. Both of these developments began in Darius' time, but the full shape of both temple and canon did not occur for many centuries. Darius' reign as Persian emperor created a reorganization of community life in Jerusalem that greatly affected the development of the religion of Yahweh, and thus this little-known period of history functions as one of the greatest watersheds in the development of both Judaism and Christianity.

Notes

1. John Manuel Cook, "The Rise of the Achaemenids and Establishment of Their Empire," in *The Cambridge History of Iran,* vol. 2, *The Median and Achaemenian Periods,* ed. Ilya Gershevitch (Cambridge: Cambridge University Press, 1985), 216.

2. Widengren, "The Persians," 322.

3. Herodotus 3.73. See also Cook, "The Rise of the Achaemenids and Establishment of Their Empire," 210.

4. The involvement of the Seven Houses in Darius' conspiracy may well have had an ethnic motivation. Cyrus' line of the Achaemenids was a mixture of Median and Persian ethnic groups, whereas Darius' line of the imperial family had remained purely Persian. The Seven Great Houses represented a strongly Persian ethnic group, but Gaumata (by most accounts) was Median. See Cook, "The Rise of the Achaemenids and Establishment of Their Empire," 217; and Culican, *The Medes and the Persians,* 65.

5. Olmstead, *History of the Persian Empire,* 110. See also T. Cuyler Young, Jr., "The Consolidation of the Empire and Its Limits of Growth under Darius and Xerxes," in Boardman et al., *Cambridge Ancient History, 2nd ed.,* 4:57–66.

6. Burn, *Persia and the Greeks,* 100; and Meuleau, "Mesopotamia under Persian Rule," 357.

7. Meuleau, "Mesopotamia under Persian Rule," 357.

8. Olmstead, *History of the Persian Empire,* 119.

9. Ibid., 133.

10. Ibid., 116–17.

11. Ibid., 120–28.

12. Ibid., 222.

13. Cook, "The Rise of the Achaemenids and Establishment of Their Empire," 220.

14. Widengren, "The Persians," 323.

15. Meuleau, "Mesopotamia under Persian Rule," 359.

16. Bresciani, "Egypt and the Persian Empire," 334; Olmstead, *History of the Persian Empire,* 90–91; and Culican, *The Medes and the Persians,* 59.

17. Culican, *The Medes and the Persians,* 71.

18. Olmstead, *History of the Persian Empire,* 142.

19. Widengren, "The Persians," 323.

20. Culican, *The Medes and the Persians,* 71.

21. Ibid., 69.

22. Cook, "The Rise of the Achaemenids and Establishment of Their Empire," 223.

23. Ibid.

24. Widengren, "The Persians," 323.

25. Olmstead, *History of the Persian Empire,* 136. It is possible that Zerubbabel had been in place earlier, perhaps during Cambyses' time. See Culican, *The Medes and the Persians,* 70.

26. Burn, *Persia and the Greeks,* 105; Cook, "The Rise of the Achaemenids and Establishment of Their Empire," 221; and Olmstead, *History of the Persian Empire,* 142.

27. The effects of this publication of the law upon Yehud and the development of the canon will be examined below in chapter 9.

28. Widengren, "The Persians," 324.

29. Burn, *Persia and the Greeks,* 115.

30. Widengren, "The Persians," 324; and Olmstead, *History of the Persian Empire,* 144–45.

31. Olmstead, *History of the Persian Empire,* 147–49; and Widengren, "The Persians," 325.

32. Olmstead, *History of the Persian Empire,* 151–61.

33. Widengren, "The Persians," 325.

34. Richard N. Frye, *The Heritage of Persia* (Cleveland: World Books, 1962), 97; Cook, "The Rise of the Achaemenids and Establishment of Their Empire," 237–38; Olmstead, *History of the Persian Empire,* 172–84; and Culican, *The Medes and the Persians,* 89.

35. Olmstead, *History of the Persian Empire,* 178.

36. Olmstead, *History of the Persian Empire,* 195; but see Frye, *The Heritage of Persia,* 26.

37. Olmstead, *History of the Persian Empire,* 185–94; and Cook, "The Rise of the Achaemenids and Establishment of Their Empire," 271.

38. Culican, *The Medes and the Persians,* 135–48.

39. Cook, "The Rise of the Achaemenids and Establishment of Their Empire," 226.

40. Olmstead, *History of the Persian Empire,* 227.

41. Widengren, "The Persians," 323.

42. Olmstead, *History of the Persian Empire,* 88–89; H. T. Wallinga, "The Ancient Persian Navy and Its Predecessors," in *Achaemenid History I: Sources, Structures and Synthesis,* ed. Heleen Sancisi-Weerdenburg (Leiden: Nederlands Instituut voor het Nabije Oosten, 1987), 47–77.

43. The Persian army may have reached 120,000 warriors (not counting mercenaries), according to Dandamaev and Lukonin, *Culture and Social Institutions,* 223. In contrast, the population of Jerusalem and its environs may have totaled 10,000 to 15,000 persons. See Magen Broshi, "Estimating the Population of Ancient Jerusalem," *Biblical Archaeology Review* 4 (1978): 10–15.

44. The view of Leroy Waterman, "The Camouflaged Purge of Three Messianic Conspirators," *JNES* 13 (1954): 77, that information traveled so slowly in the ancient world that the news of Darius' completed accession would not have reached Haggai when the prophet spoke 2:20–23, must be rejected as counterfactual. Cf. Herrmann Bengtson, "The Persian Empire and the Greeks ca. 520 B.C.," in *The Greeks and the Persians from the Sixth to the Fourth Centuries,* ed. Herrmann Bengtson, trans. John Conway (New York: Delacorte Press, 1968), 13: only seven days were needed for the transmittal of any message within the empire. E. J. Bickerman, "La seconde année de Darius," *Revue Biblique* 88 (1981): 23–28, recognizes the problem with a supposed rebellion in 520 B.C.E. and thus dates Haggai 2 to October to December of 521 B.C.E., which corresponds to the last known revolt of Babylonia. Zechariah 1:7 is the next text in chronological order, from February 26, 520 B.C.E., and announces the return of the imperial peace.

45. This point is widely but not universally accepted. See Stern, "The Persian Empire and the Political and Social History of Palestine in the Persian Period," 72; Richard T. Hallock, "The 'One Year' of Darius I," *JNES* 19 (1960): 36–39; Eric M. Meyers, "The Persian Period and the Judean Restoration," 513; Carol L. Meyers and Eric M. Meyers, *Haggai, Zechariah 1–8,* AB 25B (Garden City, N.Y.: Doubleday & Co., 1987), xxxix–xl; Carl Schultz, "Political Tensions Reflected in Ezra-Nehemiah," in *Scripture in Context: Essays on the Comparative Method,* ed. Carl D. Evans, William W. Hallo, and John B. White, Pittsburgh Theological Monograph Series 34 (Pittsburgh: Pickwick Press, 1980), 233.

46. Olmstead, *History of the Persian Empire,* 135–41.

47. This thesis was developed for the Egyptian campaign of Cambyses by I. H. Eybers, "The Rebuilding of the Temple according to Haggai and Zechariah," in *Studies in Old Testament Prophecy,* ed. W. C. van Wyk (Potchefstroom: Pro Rege Press, 1975), 18; and to a lesser extent by Joyce G. Baldwin, *Haggai, Zechariah, Malachi: An Introduction and Commentary,* Tyndale Old Testament Commentaries (Downers Grove, Ill.: Inter-Varsity, 1972), 16. For the opinion that Darius' Egyptian campaign left a positive agricultural and economic impact upon Yehud, see Kaufmann, *History of the Religion of Israel,* 245.

48. Lawrence E. Stager, "Climatic Conditions and Grain Storage in the Persian Period," *Harvard Theological Review* 64 (1971): 450.

49. The evidence for Persia's financing of the Yehud province exists in the influx of funding for the temple and associated construction projects and cultic practices, as demonstrated in the sudden possibility of these activities. No evidence exists for the reimbursement of the individuals who fed the armies, except for negative evidence: the general populace seems to be facing economic hardship, according to Haggai, and such would presumably not have been the case had imperial reimbursement been policy.

50. The administrative function of the Jerusalem temple is clear in Nehemiah 13:10-13, where Levites and priests operate as treasurers, as well as in Nehemiah 13:4-9, where Nehemiah conflicts with another regional governor, Tobiah, about the latter's rights to have an office in the temple.

51. Niels Peter Lemche, *Ancient Israel: A New History of Israelite Society*, Biblical Seminar 5 (Sheffield: JSOT Press, 1988), 222.

52. For this position, see Franz Josef Stendebach, *Prophetie und Tempel: Die Bücher Haggai—Sacharja—Maleachi—Joel*, Stuttgarter Kleiner Kommentar, Altes Testament 16 (Stuttgart: Verlag Katholisches Bibelwerk, 1977), 9–10; and Jacob M. Myers, *The World of the Restoration* (Englewood Cliffs, N.J.: Prentice-Hall, 1968), 50–51. The benefit that the ruling Yehudites received (power due to the increase of new resources) and the religious "freedoms" enjoyed by the people (ability to worship in a restored temple) were both incidental to the Persian goals for the temple construction.

53. Kuhrt, "Cyrus Cylinder," 94–95, accepts this argumentation for the motivation of Persian construction projects. She argues against the idea that the Persians were inclined to assist the Yehudites on other grounds: "The assumption that Persian imperial control was somehow more tolerable than the Assyrian yoke is based . . . on the limited experience of one influential group of a very small community which happened to benefit by Persian policy." This position is also supported by Noth, *History of Israel*, 302: "The Persian kings . . . respected the traditions and character of the subject-peoples, but certainly not out of benevolent tolerance. Needless to say, they kept the real power in their own hands." See further Klaus Koch, *The Prophets*, vol. 2, *The Babylonian and Persian Periods*, trans. Margaret Kohl (Philadelphia: Fortress Press, 1982), 159.

54. The possibility of a harmonizing genealogy by the Chronicler cannot be dismissed. Genealogies often reflect contemporary political alignments rather than genetic information; see Robert R. Wilson, *Genealogy and History in the Biblical World* (New Haven, Conn.: Yale University Press, 1977). The political necessities of the Chronicler's time may have caused alterations in the reporting of lineages. Note also the assertion by Miller and Hayes, *A History of Ancient Israel and Judah*, 456: "Zerubbabel was a non-Davidic Jewish leader whom the Chronicler has made into a member of the Judean royal family."

55. Ackroyd, *Exile and Restoration*, 147, argues for the appointment of Zerubbabel near the end of Cyrus' reign.

56. David L. Petersen, *Haggai and Zechariah 1–8, A Commentary*, OTL (Philadelphia: Westminster Press, 1984), 45–46, argues that the meaning of "governor" at this early time may not indicate an official position within the Persian government, as the role label would indicate later, after Darius' administrative reforms. Petersen sees both Zerubbabel's and Joshua's authority as tied to their genealogical qualifications for leadership. For a stronger recent statement of Zerubbabel's authority, see Meyers and Meyers, *Haggai, Zechariah 1–8*, xxxviii.

57. See Willy Schottroff, "Zur Sozialgeschichte Israels in der Perserzeit," *Verkündigung und Forschung* 27/1 (1982): 46–68.

58. This latter option approaches the depiction of Zechariah by Walter Harrelson, "The Trial of the High Priest Joshua: Zechariah 3," *Eretz-Israel* 16 (1982): 116*–24*.

59. Othniel Margalith, "The Political Role of Ezra as Persian Governor," *ZAW* 98 (1986): 111, points out that leaders such as Ezra (and Zerubbabel) may have had families in Persia who were held hostage against these leaders' loyalty.

60. After Zerubbabel, subsequent governors had no ethnic Yehudite connections. See N. Avigad, *Bullae and Seals from a Post-Exilic Judaean Archive,* Monographs of the Institute of Archaeology at the Hebrew University of Jerusalem, 4 (Jerusalem: Hebrew University Press, 1976). Even for Zerubbabel, ethnicity was not as determinative a factor as Persian loyalty.

61. Eric M. Meyers, "Persian Period and the Judean Restoration," 512: "Both the prophets Haggai and First Zechariah presuppose the hegemony of Persian authorities in all local affairs . . . . In other words, there seems to be a complete readiness to accept the apparent largesse of a Persian government that had earlier authorized the return of the exiles to their homeland and the rebuilding of their religious sanctuary."

62. This is not to be confused with the much less convincing argument that the Persian government supported Yehud because of respect for Yahwistic monotheism.

63. All quotations from the Book of Haggai are the author's translation.

64. Petersen, *Haggai and Zechariah 1–8,* 69; cf. Hanson, *Dawn of Apocalyptic,* 175–76.

65. This word, *hpk*, is usually translated "overthrow," but more sensibly means "turn aside," in accord with 2 Kings 5:26; 9:23, where the reference to changing a chariot's direction is clear. Yahweh will *turn aside* the Persian forces that approach Jerusalem. Thus the army will bypass Jerusalem and will attack Egypt; Jerusalem will be safe and will have nothing to fear from the Persian forces.

66. Samuel Amsler, *Aggée, Zacharie 1–8,* CAT 11c (Neuchâtel: Delachaux et Niestlé, 1981), 18; Karl Elliger, *Das Buch der zwölf kleinen Propheten,* vol. 2, *Die Propheten Nahum, Habakuk, Zephania, Haggai, Sacharja, Maleachi,* ATD 25 (Göttingen: Vandenhoeck & Ruprecht, 1950), 93; Joseph Blenkinsopp, *A History of Prophecy in Israel from the Settlement in the Land to the Hellenistic Period* (Philadelphia: Westminster Press, 1983), 233; and Hanson, "Israelite Religion in the Early Postexilic Period," 495.

67. Petersen interprets "servant" as a royal, Davidic motif *(Haggai and Zechariah 1–8,* 103), but Meyers and Meyers understand the servant as God's instrument, not as one who initiates his own power *(Haggai, Zechariah 1–8,* 68).

68. Gary A. Anderson, *Sacrifices and Offerings in Ancient Israel: Studies in Their Social and Political Importance,* HSM 41 (Atlanta: Scholars Press, 1987), 116–26, has concluded that fertility language often serves symbolic functions, referring to failings of cult, not to literal meteorological disasters. However, he is clear that this famine language is not used without historical referents and argues for internal political fragmentation as the cause for reduced production, which would be solved through the more efficient political administration resulting from a renewed, centralized temple cult (pp. 123–24). The temple was also attached to fertility through more mythological means (pp. 124–25). Cf. Delbert R. Hillers, *Treaty-Curses and the Old Testament Prophets,* Biblica Orientalia 16 (Rome: Pontifical Biblical Institute, 1964), 28–29.

69. Hans Walter Wolff, *Haggai: A Commentary,* trans. Margaret Kohl (Minneapolis: Augsburg Press, 1988), 43–44; cf. W. A. M. Beuken, *Haggai-Sacharja 1–8: Studien zur Überlieferungsgeschichte der frühnachexilischen Prophetie,* Studia semitica neerlandica 10 (Assen: Van Gorcum, 1967), 196.

70. Reading *wĕʿōd* for MT *wĕʿad,* following LXX. Cf. Wolff, *Haggai,* 59; Petersen, *Haggai and Zechariah 1–8,* 87; Meyers and Meyers, *Haggai, Zechariah 1–8,* 64.

71. Wolff begins the last clause with the adversative "but," and reasons that an asyndetic transition provides an emphatic contrast (*Haggai,* 59). This argumentation remains unconvincing, especially in the light of the difficulties in the prior questions. An emphatic contrast would require a clear, unambiguous adversative, not the lack of copulative.

72. The etymology is uncertain. Although connections to words for "throat" provide a graphic understanding of a pit (Mitchell Dahood, *Psalms II: 51–100,* AB 17 [Garden City, N.Y.: Doubleday & Co., 1968], 35), a derivation from *gwr,* "to sojourn," is sensible, since a *mĕgûrâ* provides food for travelers. This question is probably unsolvable, since the only other instance, Psalm 55:16, is textually uncertain.

73. Meyers and Meyers argue that this provides the seeds to plant for the next season (*Haggai, Zechariah 1–8,* 80).

74. The negative answer is to be preferred, in order to contrast with the second question's affirmative answer. The presence of the negative particle in the second question indicates the contrast.

75. Meyers and Meyers, *Haggai, Zechariah 1–8,* 64–65.

76. Many scholars understand the Branch in Zechariah 3:8 to refer to Zerubbabel. However, the verse begins with a redirection of the voice, which now addresses not only Joshua but also those colleagues called to witness Joshua's anointing. These colleagues are an "omen of things to come," and Joshua, God's servant, the Branch, is the thing that is to come, the event to which the omen colleagues point and testify.

77. Leviticus 21:17-20 and Deuteronomy 23:1.

78. The talk of sin in Isaiah 59:12-13, then, is ironic or perhaps sarcastic, as indicated by the complaint of justice's *reversal* in Isaiah 59:14.

79. Note the quotation from Isaiah 11:7-9.

80. Against Hanson, *Dawn of Apocalyptic* and *The People Called.*

81. See chapter 9, below.

CHAPTER 6

THE EMERGENCE OF PLURALISM: XERXES (486–465 B.C.E.)

PERSIA'S FOURTH EMPEROR, XERXES, ruled during a period of history more frequently remembered from the Greek perspective, as Persia battled its western neighbors for control of the borders between them. Although Greece was the eventual victor in these battles, Persia was still the stronger force at this time and throughout most of the fifth century; Greece increased its size and power but did not come close to matching the immensity or largesse of Persia. Internally, Xerxes maintained most of the policies that Darius had developed, including the growing emphasis on intensification of the colonies. As conquest became less possible for the Persian Empire, the need for funds grew and pressured the empire to raise those funds from the increased taxation of existing colonies. Xerxes also stopped the support for a variety of Darius' projects, trying to conserve funds through reductions in spending, especially spending in the colonies. Persians, on the other hand, grew in legal privileges throughout this period, to the detriment of other ethnic groups in the empire.

Thus Yehud under Xerxes' reign experienced less of the construction and imperial support than the colony had known during Darius' time. Malachi reflects this situation of a populace struggling to understand its nature as a community and as a religion in the midst of a less supportive empire. Whereas Darius' time witnessed the construction of a temple that existed without the monarchy, the temple in Xerxes' time existed as an institution without support from the imperial powers. Religion became much more of a voluntary part of a pluralistic lifestyle within a huge and diverse empire. This new feature of Yahwistic religion transformed its practice, as can be seen through the community's struggles in this period.

The History of Xerxes' Reign

Darius' lengthy reign had fixed several of the key features of the Persian Empire. After Darius, the boundaries of the empire never grew significantly, and Greece remained the enemy until the empire's end. Policies of tolerance and intensification remained consistent in generality if not in implementation throughout the empire's duration. However, there were also problems that required the immediate attention of Darius' successor, including the independence of Egypt and Greece.

Accession

Darius had been a usurper from a collateral line of the Achaemenid family, the same family as that of Cyrus and Cambyses. Despite his own accession in violation of direct genetic ties, Darius succeeded in establishing a dynasty, aided in large part by the length of his reign and by his specific effort to strengthen one of his sons into an imperial candidate. Of Darius' several sons, the eldest was Artobazanes, a grandson of Gobryas. Darius had indicated Artobazanes as the successor by at least 507 B.C.E., very early within Darius' reign. Darius then fathered a child through his wife Atossa, who was Cyrus' daughter and Cambyses' sister and wife. Darius had taken several of Cambyses' wives as his own, in order to symbolize the passage of power to the new emperor, but none were of previous royalty as was Atossa. As soon as Atossa's son, Xerxes, was old enough to assume elements of command, Darius placed him in a new palace in Babylon. This would have been when Xerxes was about twenty, in 498 B.C.E. For the next twelve years until his accession, Xerxes served as satrap of Babylonia, the second most powerful position in the Persian Empire.

There are relatively few indications of difficulties at Xerxes' accession. There are ample instances of art depicting Darius and Xerxes, indicating that Darius may have held numerous public appearances and invested in significant propaganda to show that Xerxes was the heir apparent to the Persian throne. Perhaps the empire expected Xerxes to be the next emperor and thus the unsurprising accession provided little opportunity for rebellion. Egypt had already revolted late in Darius' reign. All of these appear to be unrelated to Xerxes' new role as emperor. In 485 B.C.E., Xerxes' armies marched toward Egypt and recaptured it in January of 484 B.C.E. with little difficulty.[1] Thus within the first months of his reign, Xerxes ruled over a united and loyal empire.

Persian Centrality

Xerxes' administration emphasized the importance of Persia over against the classical claims to authority and status presented by other ethnicities and nationalities. Cyrus had inherited a Babylonian style of government, and all of Persia's first three emperors honored that previous system. In many cases, the Persian emperors left in place Babylonian officials over the colonies. Likewise, under Cyrus and Cambyses the Medes had a certain prominence, which began to decline in the time of Darius, whose Achaemenid lineage had not mingled with the Medes. Xerxes furthered the process of favoring Persia and increasingly excluding persons of other groups.

As this process of Persian centralization occurred gradually, Babylonia revolted, in 482 B.C.E. Megabyzus, the great Persian general and Xerxes' brother-in-law, quickly took Babylon. In order to establish Persian dominance and to squelch Babylonian nationalism, Megabyzus smelted down the eighteen-foot-tall gold statue of Marduk, which weighed eight hundred pounds. Through Megabyzus' violent responses to the Babylonian revolt, Persia ended Babylonia's independence as a satrapy, being annexed to Assyria, according to some records. After this revolt, Xerxes did not even allow Babylonians to serve in the army, removing their right to choose a mercenary career.[2]

The Persian centralization of the empire went far beyond the diminished treatment of the Babylonians. More Persians took positions of power throughout the empire, especially in politically sensitive situations such as provincial governorships. Tax structures throughout the empire shifted to favor Persians and to increase the taxation upon all other ethnic and national groups. As Xerxes completed the temple built by Darius and continued to pour huge amounts of funds into the construction of Persepolis, others throughout the empire experienced higher taxes, and in some cases these taxes created very deleterious effects upon local societies.[3] Xerxes' administrative organization allowed for much greater intensification than Darius had achieved, in large part because of the removal of non-Persians from favored status and the use of all other peoples toward increased production of food and other items for the purposes of taxation.[4]

Temple Destructions

Xerxes followed a religious policy distinctly different from that of his father, Darius. Darius' reign had been marked not only with tolerance for other faiths but with a high degree of assistance for some of the trappings of religion. For instance, Jerusalem's temple was not only a religious space, it was also a public area. For reasons of administrative efficiency, Darius funded the Jerusalem temple so that Yehud would have better local government and thus aid in the Persian Empire's moves toward intensification. Yehud gained a religious temple from this arrangement, and under Darius the empire funded a variety of such temples throughout the realm. Xerxes changed that policy radically. Not only did Xerxes withhold funds from the construction and operation of temples in the Persian Empire but he was involved in the destruction of these temples in many places in order to decrease local senses of nationalism that could center around temples. In several places where there had been revolts during his time, Xerxes destroyed the local temples in attempts to remove the local administrative centers that had temporarily become autonomous. The destruction of temples was not so much a religious act as a political act to remove the base of power for rebels and the nationalistic feelings and organization that these rebels could foster. Although such distractions also had religious results, these may well have been side effects rather than the targeted consequence of Xerxes' action.

Yehud's case seems to have been without revolt. There is no indication through biblical or Persian records that there was a destruction of the temple that had been built during Darius' time, nor is there any remembrance of a revolt shortly after 485 B.C.E. or at any other time in the Persian Empire. However, it does appear that Yehud's temple suffered a radical decrease in funding, and thus the temple experienced a protracted time of financial problems. These issues form one of the themes of the Book of Malachi.

Administration and Economics

Xerxes' administrative policies furthered the doctrine of intensification and moved into division and usury. Darius' satrapal system had allowed for much more efficient taxation of the entire empire. Xerxes continued the fragmentation of the former Babylonian Empire by separating the Beyond the River region from Babylonia.[5] This separation of administrative units removed much of Babylonia's historic power base and became part of Xerxes' consistent policies of removing authority from the Babylonian regions.

One of the richest sources for the reconstruction of this period's economics is the Murashu documents, which emphasize the economic changes of this period. Toward the end of Xerxes' reign, the Murashu family ran banking and loan services in Mesopotamia, and some of their records have survived. Darius' issuance of imperial coinage had slowly degraded the value of Babylonian money; by the end of Xerxes' reign, there was little wealth or economic power left in Babylonia. Interest, which had been at 10 percent during the Babylonian period and had risen to 20 percent during the reigns of Cyrus and Cambyses, skyrocketed to 50 percent in the Murashu documents. The Murashu records also show that even at this time, generations after the Edict of Cyrus in 538 B.C.E., many wealthy Jews remained in Babylonia and participated actively in the economy.[6] In 467–466 B.C.E., there seems to have been a shortage of wine and sheep, causing trouble in the king's Persepolis treasury.[7]

These indications hint at growing economic trouble throughout Xerxes' reign. The Persian Empire under Darius had moved to intensification as a replacement for the income lost by the cessation of conquest. Xerxes attempted to fund fruitless military campaigns toward the west as well as expanded governmental bureaucracies within the center of the empire, and the only source of funds was taxation. Over time, the tax increases overwhelmed the ability of the Persian imperial economy to grow; the results included high interest and the depletion of assets. By the end of Xerxes' reign, not even the increased taxes could pay for the imperial expenses.

Wars with Greece

The Persian-Greek wars continued during Xerxes' rule as emperor. Darius had lost the battle of Marathon but had not given up hope of taking Greek territory. These Greek lands to the west not only limited Persia's ability to control the Mediterranean Sea but also presented tempting locales for further intensification. Had the wars ever been successful, the Persian Empire could have funded its own internal costs and an expanded economic base throughout the empire for decades to come; the increases in trade alone would have driven the economy and imperial unity to new levels of energy. Persia's huge potential gains from the conquest of Greece kept attracting the interest of Persian emperors, even though the meager military achievements in that region indicated the low chances for Persian success. Also, Persia recognized that an independent Greece threatened the imperial territories in adjacent areas.[8]

Early in his reign, Xerxes signed a treaty with Carthage to prevent Sicily and South Italy from assisting Greece. This policy proved somewhat successful in containing the Greeks so that Persia could press a winning attack against them. However, Xerxes sought revenge for previous defeats and performed acts of suppression similar to what had worked in Babylonia. Throughout the rest of the empire, Xerxes had been ruthless in responding to rebellions, destroying the sacred symbols and the power structures of provinces such as Babylon. With a similar policy, Xerxes ordered the burning of Athens. However, Athens presented a situation that was categorically different from that of Babylonia. Whereas Babylonia had been a longtime province of the Persian Empire, having fallen to Cyrus over half a century before Xerxes' acts of destruction, Greece was a newer enemy with clear memories of having withstood Persian aggression before. The Greeks perceived the burning of Athens as an atrocity that served only to harden Greek resolve. Their literature and propaganda now portrayed Darius as a sensible hero and Xerxes as a monster.

To prepare for the final invasion of Greece, Xerxes took temporary residence in Sardis in 481 B.C.E. Persia won a major battle at Thermopylae, only to suffer a severe setback at Salamis on September 22, 480 B.C.E. Still, the Persians led more and more attacks with its huge army, although always with limited success. The Greeks formed the Delian League in 478 B.C.E. as protection against Persia, and the Greeks soon began to be more aggressive in their campaigns against Persia.[9] In many ways, the battles of the first ten years of Xerxes' reign represent the turning point in Persian-Greek relations; Greece continued to improve its position for the next century and a half, until Alexander defeated Persia entirely in 333 B.C.E.

Palace Intrigue and Xerxes' Inattention

The attention placed on Greece was accompanied by a lack of attention on the more central areas of Persian rule.[10] This was combined with Xerxes' antiprovincial attitude. No longer were the older civilizations and the wealthier areas accorded any advantage within the empire.[11] Thus Babylonia again revolted, although Xerxes' general, Megabyzus, was able to stop the rebellion.[12] Such revolts occurred in 484 and 482 B.C.E.[13]

Toward the end of his reign, Xerxes turned his attention inward, no longer visiting the troops in battle and ignoring the doings of his generals. Instead, he gave more of his time to the numerous harem intrigues. Darius had married several women, but Xerxes began the practice of monogamy, as was practiced by the later Persian kings. Xerxes married only one woman, but he maintained a harem of over 360 concubines from the provinces.[14] Stories abound about Xerxes' loves and losses, including affairs with numerous wives of relatives and court officials. One story relates that Xerxes fell in love with the wife of his brother Maistes but that she did not love him. In order to keep her closer to the palace, Xerxes married her daughter Artayante to his son Darius. Xerxes then fell out of love with his sister-in-law and in love with his niece and new daughter-in-law, Artayante. The queen's anger at the entire situation followed, and Xerxes was caught in a complicated set of alliances and enmities throughout the court.[15]

These palace intrigues cost Xerxes' concentration on the concerns of rule, and soon the edges of the empire began to unravel. After great losses in 466–465 B.C.E., the Asiatic Greeks left the Persian Empire and joined the Delian League. This nullified Xerxes' hard-won gains to the west and cut heavily into the imperial treasury's income. In response to the seeming ineffectiveness of the emperor, Artabanus conspired and assassinated Xerxes in bed late in 465 B.C.E.[16]

Yehud Under Xerxes

After Darius erected and dedicated the Second Temple in Jerusalem during 520 to 515 B.C.E., the social situation in the colony of Yehud changed. Darius' attempt to conquer Egypt was successful, and this radically transformed the status of Yehud within the Persian Empire, changing both the political and the economic situation. Whereas Yehud had been a border colony, the addition of Egypt to the Persian Empire made Yehud no longer a border but a trade corridor. The completion of the temple even more directly affected the religious dimension of life in Yehud. The years of wondering about the temple's impact were over, and now the people experienced the construction's ramifications.

Palestine had experienced Darius' aggressive passage through its land. After Darius' pursuit, the military avoided the area of Palestine; for the next thirty-five years, the main body of the Persian military force was absent from any of the areas around Yehud. Yehud was sufficiently inland to escape the military presence of the coastal trade routes, and yet some of the economic effects of increased sea trade would have reached Jerusalem. Thus the latter part of Darius' reign offered few military or economic changes that would have impacted Yehud's internal development.

In 485–484 B.C.E., Xerxes marched upon Egypt and went through Palestine twice.[17] The effects of this military venture, however, were not as visible in Yehud as were the effects of the travel of Darius' army through the area of Palestine. Prophets such as Haggai and Zechariah presented images of Darius' time with significant military metaphors, but no such literature depicts Xerxes' march toward Egypt. This military incursion probably produced an enforcement of Xerxes' new imperial policies in Yehud. Within five years of the Egyptian campaign, Xerxes' attention had turned against Greece, where Persia fought a war of attrition and continuing loss. By the end of Xerxes' reign, the Delian League controlled European Greece and parts of westernmost Asia.[18] Thus Persia under Xerxes slowly lost influence in the northeastern Mediterranean.

Persian policies toward the provinces varied from one emperor to the next. Darius' attitude approached a laissez-faire posture, allowing local rule as long as ultimate Persian control maintained itself, encouraging local religion, and at times financing local altar services from the imperial treasury. Xerxes brought a sudden change to this imperial policy, with a profoundly antiprovincial attitude that removed much local control and placed most social functions under strict ethnic Persian supervision.[19] This antiprovincial attitude resulted in the destruction of many temples throughout the empire, but this level of imperial encroachment did not occur in Jerusalem. However, financial support for local religious practices ceased.[20] There is no record that during Xerxes' reign any provincial and area rulers had ethnic or religious ties to Yehud, as the traditions attribute to the earlier Zerubbabel and to the later Ezra and Nehemiah.[21]

In all likelihood the two generations of the early postconstruction era saw a continuation in emigration of Jews from Babylonia and Persia to Yehud. Although emigration occurred throughout the period, it would not have been uniform. This continued yet varying population movement should be seen as a minor part of the general fluctuations of population throughout the empire. The evidence for an increase of Yehud's population in Xerxes' time is scant; it appears that whatever immigration occurred had little social consequence.

The temple continued to play a major role in the political functioning of Yehud after the construction project was finished. The temple was the locus for Persian imperial agents, such as provincial governors and financial administrators. Furthermore, internal battles for control of the economy and the political allegiances of the Yehudite populace would have necessarily concerned the temple, although other social locations could have originated such struggles. Of course, the temple continued its role as the chief institution for the perpetuation of the ancient faith. The most influential external influence upon the temple politics would have been the sudden shift in temple policy at the beginning of

Xerxes' reign, ending Darius' funding of local cults at provincial shrines. This would have resulted in a sudden shortfall of funding for the temple and for the priests. Temple functions would have to be sharply curtailed at once, or other sources of funding internal to Yehud would have to be located and exploited immediately. Most likely, some combination of these two financial solutions were applied. In the following years, the situation once again stabilized, at a lower level of public expectation for the temple. This seems to have been the case upon the arrival of Ezra and Nehemiah.

In the economic sphere, the inactivity of the Persian Empire's interference in the western provinces during the latter reign of Darius and most of Xerxes' reign produced not stability but consistent decline.[22] Darius had stressed the importance of intra-imperial trade for the economic well-being of the empire. Through Darius' reign, the taxation upon this trade was one of the key sources of income, and provincial financial administrators situated in local temples became responsible for the collection of this tax. By the end of Darius' reign, there were increasing amounts of Greek pottery to be found in Yehud, indicating increased trade through the Mediterranean.[23] By the early years of Xerxes' reign, it is possible that direct trade with Greece did not meet with imperial approval and thus may have declined, reducing some of the income for the temple as it taxed such trade. It is clear, however, that such trade continued.

These factors, which certainly had adverse effects throughout the Persian Empire, brought gradually increasing economic pressure to bear especially upon the inhabitants of the more distant, poorer provinces such as Yehud. Xerxes reacted to this diminished economic health and productivity of the empire. By redirecting to the central imperial coffers the taxes that were collected by the provincial shrines and the imperial funds that were used to support these temples, Xerxes hedged the decline of the ethnic Persian economy by depleting the resources of the provinces. Whereas Darius' policy emphasized intensification, Xerxes worked toward depletion of local economies. Egypt responded to this policy of depleting taxation with revolt, in an unsuccessful attempt to protect its economy of more substantial resources than the other distant provinces. In other areas of the empire, Xerxes' policies catalyzed the factors of economic decline.[24]

In religious matters, the indirect effects of imperial policies in military and economic matters can be seen. Both Darius and Xerxes allowed high degrees of autonomy among the religious communities of the Persian Empire. They differed in one key regard: Darius allowed imperial funds to support the cults, whereas Xerxes ended this practice to counter the drain upon the imperial treasury.[25]

Xerxes inherited Yehud at a time when the military absence created a lack of direct manipulation but also when economic policies had resulted in a slow decline. Yehud's only steady income from the empire was a result of Darius' policy to spend Persian funds to support the temple in Jerusalem. Yehud's economic conditions of the early fifth century perhaps expressed an increasing separation between the priests, as well as others who derived their income from the temple, and the laity of Yehud, whose economic well-being was tied to the other imperial policies. Such an economic division, accompanied by a difference in political power and support, would also have produced an increasing social differentiation.

When Xerxes removed imperial funding for the temple, the priests suddenly lost the economic vector of their social support, calling forth a realignment of society in postconstruction Yehud. Yehud experienced an isolation from the Persian Empire. While the colony was still subject to imperial will and paid taxes under imperial threat, the empire substantially reduced its direct intervention. Figures such as Zerubbabel were not present, and so there were no such direct inputs into Yehud's life. Instead, the power groups that had arisen on the basis of connection with Persia, such as the priests, no longer could depend upon that connection to the extent that they could before. Similarly, the lesser degree of Persian attention and intervention resulted in an increased pluralism within Yehud, as positions of power decreased in their ability to enforce social norms.

Literature from Xerxes' Reign: Malachi

Only one document from the Hebrew Bible represents the time of Xerxes' reign. Many scholars debate the dating of even this one document, the Book of Malachi. Although most commentators recognize the early postexilic nature of this short book, others have placed it as early as the late monarchy.[26] The book clearly deals with the current status of the priesthood and also introduces apocalyptic themes, which some scholars have dated significantly later than the rest of the book.[27]

This book has been traditionally attributed to a prophet named Malachi. However, the book's title, "The word of Yahweh to Israel by Malachi," may be misleading. Quite possibly, the name in the title is a transcription of a comment in Malachi 3:1: "See, I am sending my messenger to prepare the way before me." The term translated "my messenger" is "Malachi." Probably this book is anonymous, and a later compiler took the title from Malachi 3:1 as a name for this nameless prophet. The book lacks a prophetic call narrative, genealogical information, and biographical data, affirming a sense of anonymity. Indications of the prophet's historical and social location must come from elsewhere.

The concern with the priests provides the necessary historical reference, in connection with Xerxes' reforms of temple funding. Suddenly the reduction in temple income forced a decision: would the costs of temple worship decrease to match the available funds, or would the available monies increase to make up for the lost revenue? If income increased, what would be its source? Apparently the society considered all of its options. Some people did not want to pay for full worship that was in accordance with priestly codes; they thought that God would still accept less costly worship. Malachi argues that God would accept only the best worship, faithful to the oldest traditions. The prophet then encouraged priests and laity to rise to the challenge together.

The Book of Malachi uses a distinctive form to express its concerns, organizing its six main units into sets of questions and answers. Each unit begins with a categorical statement by God, followed by the people's reactive rhetorical question. The prophet then answers with God's voice addressing the issue at hand. Units sometimes repeat the cycle of questions and answers (Malachi 1:6-7; 2:7-8). This disputational form allows for the depiction of a social debate not only through the content of the prophecies but through the medium as well. In the confusing context of change resulting from Xerxes' policy innovations, questions and answers arise, troubling the people who debate back and forth about the merits of divergent definitions of and approaches to their common problems.

Critique of the Priests

Since Xerxes' chief impact upon Yehud was the removal of temple funds, it is not surprising that Malachi's largest unit addresses priestly functioning. Malachi 1:6—2:9 expressed grave concerns about the current status of the priests' sacrifices and offerings and condemned them harshly before calling them to a renewed commitment for their vital task. Malachi understood a temple that connected intimately to the rest of the community; in this conception the prophet followed earlier Israelite traditions about holiness. The unit divides into two distinct sections. Malachi 1:6-14 condemns the priests for their failings; Malachi 2:1-9 continues to chide them but offers a path for the correction of the problem.

The key issue throughout this unit is the opportunity to restore proper worship and the character of the community that engages in such worship. The indictment in the unit's first half is undeniably harsh as Malachi argues against those who would block true worship. The indictment focuses on the ways in which the priests have defiled themselves, and Malachi phrases the condemnation in terms of respect.

> *A son honors his father, and servants their master. If then I am a father, where is the honor due me? And if I am a master, where is the respect due me? says the LORD of hosts to you, O priests, who despise my name.*
> *(Malachi 1:6a)*

The prophet initially depicts the problem not as an economic decision or as the violation of purity codes or worship regulations. Instead, the issue is at root one of respect. The priests have acted disrespectfully toward God. As the question-and-answer format requires, the priests respond with a question of denial, suggesting that they have not disrespected God. The format repeats, and then the charges become specific. The priests have not given God the due respect, because they have sacrificed unacceptable animals. These priests offer blind, lame, and sick animals, thinking they will be good enough for God even though they know that such sacrifices would never be accepted as taxes to be paid to the governor (Malachi 1:8). Yahweh's own animals are chosen from the wasted animals of the flocks, not from the best specimens, as is God's due.

Malachi affirms the ancient priestly codes that the priests should know: the priests must not offer crippled and diseased animals to God (Leviticus 22:17-25). In Malachi's perspective, the problem is more than a refusal to give God at least the same level of respect that the priests give the governor. At root, the problem is deeper: the priests are not living in accordance with their own regulations as priests.[28] Even though they know the proper worship, they do not perform it.

Malachi opens into expansive rhetoric against the priests, first imploring them to seek God's graciousness while unquestionably placing the blame upon the priests. The prophet subsequently rejects the priests for their behavior:

> *Oh, that someone among you would shut the temple doors, so that you would not kindle fire on my altar in vain! I have no pleasure in you, says the LORD of hosts, and I will not accept an offering from your hands.*
> *(Malachi 1:10)*

Malachi radicalizes the situation. Because the priests offer inadequate sacrifices, God will accept nothing from them. The argument depicts the problem as an all-or-nothing dilemma; because the priests do not adhere to the strictest form of the regulations, God rejects them completely, even to the point of wishing that someone would shut down the temple practice altogether. If any among the priests were arguing for a reduced level of ritual, allowing lesser expenses to react to the cessation of external funds, they would have felt the sting of Malachi's critique. The prophetic rhetoric rules out such middle positions.

Not only does the prophet condemn the priestly religion in and of itself but Malachi continues to compare it against the worship of God throughout the world, asserting that God's name receives proper offerings among the nations (Malachi 1:11). Certainly, throughout the period of the Persian Empire, Yahwistic worship spread throughout the imperial borders, but referring to God's worship as "from the rising of the sun to its setting" is nothing short of hyperbole. Malachi uses this rhetorical flourish to critique the Jerusalem temple priests, who fail their own standards and show themselves to be less than those who pontificate at shrines of incense to Yahweh throughout the world.

After this stunning, two-pronged critique of the priesthood, Malachi repeats the brunt of the accusation before turning the condemnation to the laity. Those who consider it a weariness to bring their sacrifices to God will find their own offerings rejected (Malachi 1:13). With these words, Malachi echoes his prior disappointments with the priests, but now the rhetoric progresses to include a new group.

> *Cursed be the cheat who has a male in the flock and vows to give it, and yet sacrifices to the Lord what is blemished; for I am a great King, says the Lord of hosts, and my name is reverenced among the nations. (Malachi 1:14)*

God curses those who have the resources to bring unblemished animals but who hoard their wealth.[29] There is never condemnation for the poor who lack the ability to give pure animals, here or elsewhere in the Hebrew Bible (Leviticus 5:7-13; 14:21-22; 27:8). The prophet's scathing critique affects only those who make active choices to offer less than they have to their God. The laity who withhold funds and goods from the temple worship receive the same harshness of condemnation as the priests. The laity become the objects of Malachi's wrath because of their bringing inadequate animals to the temple; the temple priests receive the same derision because of their willingness to offer such animals in the worship service. Both should be contributing nothing but their best. Malachi sees both priests and the laity as responsible and thus culpable for the quality of worship in the temple.

The outline for Malachi's solution becomes visible already, halfway through this unit of condemnation and before the direct mentions of solutions arise. If the priests and the laity are both at fault for offering less than their best and thus producing sacrifices that do not bring forth divine acceptance, then the only possible solution will be for both priests and laity to improve the condition of their offerings. In the face of reduced funding from the Persian Empire, they must band together to insist on nothing but the best worship materials for their service of God in the temple of Jerusalem. Nothing but the best will be accepted by God, and so both priests and laity must offer nothing but their best.

Malachi's solution appears simple, and yet one-sided; certainly other voices within the faithful community would have suggested some sort of compromise, a possibility for worship to continue in less expensive modes, but this appears to be exactly the object of Malachi's condemnation.

The unit's second half returns to the subject of the priests who have offered inadequate sacrifices (Malachi 1:7-8, 12-13). Malachi does not lessen the level of attack but now offers them a solution. The prophet calls them to live by their own highest standards. This critiques the priests in the light of their own priestly traditions, just as has already started in the oblique references to the priestly regulations in Leviticus. Through this repeated emphasis on upholding the past laws, Malachi sets unwaveringly high standards for the priests, arguing against compromises.

The language immediately turns harsher as the prophet unleashes curses against the priests. Through the prophet, Yahweh threatens them with personal curses as well as the removal of their ability to distinguish blessing from cursing and to cause blessing in the world. Yahweh asserts that the rejection not only will affect them as priests but will extend to their offspring. Furthermore, the priests will become ritually unclean as a direct result of Yahweh's action and will no longer enjoy access to Yahweh's presence.

> *And now, O priests, this command is for you. If you will not listen, if you will not lay it to heart to give glory to my name, says the LORD of hosts, then I will send the curse on you and I will curse your blessings; indeed I have already cursed them, because you do not lay it to heart. I will rebuke your offspring, and spread dung on your faces, the dung of your offerings, and I will put you out of my presence. (Malachi 2:1-3)*

This thoroughgoing critique of threatened curses is unmistakably severe, and yet it is also clearly conditional. The priests are still capable of action that will prevent the curses from falling upon them. Malachi's warnings provide the proper path away from the threatened cursing and into a correct relationship with God that will enable their continued and restored functioning as priests. Malachi offers the priests the terms of a covenant that seems as if it is familiar to them, even though it is not known in the rest of the Hebrew Bible. This covenant of Levi offers the possibility for the priests to return to an acceptable mode of practice, away from their current failings.

> *Know, then, that I have sent this command to you, that my covenant with Levi may hold, says the LORD of hosts. My covenant with him was a covenant of life and well-being, which I gave him; this called for reverence, and he revered me and stood in awe of my name. True instruction was in his mouth, and no wrong was found on his lips. He walked with me in integrity and uprightness, and he turned many from iniquity. For the lips of a priest should guard knowledge, and people should seek instruction from his mouth, for he is the messenger of the LORD of hosts. But you have turned aside from the way; you have caused many to stumble by your instruction; you have corrupted the covenant of Levi, says the LORD of hosts, and so I make you despised and abased before*

> *all the people, inasmuch as you have not kept my ways but have shown partiality in your instruction. (Malachi 2:4-9)*

The reason for Malachi's denunciations is to call the priests back to this covenant, a possibility that still exists for the priests. To the extent that the priests have not followed this covenant, they are chastised and condemned, but only to the degree of their violation (Malachi 2:8-9). The possibility for restoration continues, and Malachi's entire stated raison d'être in this section is to challenge the priests to accept their own responsibility and to return to this covenant.

Even though the Hebrew Bible records no covenant with Levi known by that name, Moses' blessing of Levi contains several parallels of note.

> *And of Levi he said:*
> *Give to Levi your Thummim,*
> *and your Urim to your loyal one,*
> *whom you tested at Massah,*
> *with whom you contended at the waters of Meribah;*
> *who said of his father and mother,*
> *"I regard them not";*
> *he ignored his kin,*
> *and did not acknowledge his children.*
> *For they observed your word,*
> *and kept your covenant.*
> *They teach Jacob your ordinances,*
> *and Israel your law;*
> *they place incense before you,*
> *and whole burnt offerings on your altar.*
> *Bless, O LORD, his substance,*
> *and accept the work of his hands;*
> *crush the loins of his adversaries,*
> *of those that hate him, so that they do not rise again.*
> *(Deuteronomy 33:8-11)*

Three elements of strong similarity appear. First, both Malachi and Deuteronomy call for a rejection of partiality. In Malachi, the partiality of instruction is the final word of condemnation (Malachi 2:9); in Deuteronomy, the priest receives praise for avoiding partiality even to mother, father, and kin (Deuteronomy 33:9). Second, both codes call for the priest to provide instruction to all people (Deuteronomy 33:10a and Malachi 2:6-7). Not only does this avoid the partiality but it emphasizes the role of priest as teacher. This is especially consonant with Malachi's high view of the laity; the priests do not perform magic or have special power, but they do function as the repository for the tradition and as the most important source for the transmission of that tradition. Third, both of these covenants call for the adherence to correct worship (Deuteronomy 33:10b-11a; cf. Malachi 1:7-8). Although such correct worship receives almost no definition or delimitation, both of these writings consider it of utmost importance. The priests are responsible for assuring that the worship of the temple was correct to the best of their knowledge, and the priests as teachers were also responsible for making sure that the laity properly executed their role in worship by bringing nothing but the best animals. The priests must establish the right relationship with the laity, through impartiality, effective teaching, and proper worship.

Even though the priests have stumbled from the ideal and caused others to stumble, the priests can still be faithful. Malachi holds out the possibility for repentance. If the priests legitimately change their actions, then they will once more be functioning within the covenant with Levi, and God will bless their efforts. Although Malachi's rhetoric is almost entirely negative, the possibilities for restoration are clear, and the prophet calls the priests to this kind of energetic, expensive worship and a partnership with the laity that enables such worship. Malachi brooks no compromise with the contingents within the society that approved of a lessening of worship; Malachi insists on nothing but the best in worship, accompanied by the return to the covenant with Levi that established ground rules for priestly interaction with the laity.

Call to Community Effort

Malachi's fifth unit (Malachi 3:6-12) expresses again this desire for the community, both priests and laity, to unite in service of God. Here the emphasis falls much more upon the laity. God charges that they are robbing God, but the people dispute the point, questioning how they are involved in robbing God. God responds with a call to joint effort throughout the community to offer nothing but the best in worship.

> *Bring the full tithe into the storehouse, so that there may be food in my house, and thus put me to the test, says the LORD of hosts; see if I will not open the windows of heaven for you and pour down for you an overflowing blessing. I will rebuke the locust for you, so that it will not destroy the produce of your soil; and your vine in the field shall not be barren, says the LORD of hosts. Then all nations will count you happy, for you will be a land of delight, says the LORD of hosts. (Malachi 3:10-12)*

Malachi has referred to offerings earlier in his condemnation of the priests (Malachi 1:7-8). In Malachi's parlance, these offerings refer to the sacrifices and the other cultic contributions to the worship of God. The term also seems to refer to the taxes paid to the unnamed Persian governor, which would also be donated through the temple (Malachi 1:8). This concords with the wider Hebrew Bible usage of the term as a general denotation of gifts. But Malachi here urges more than the offerings; the prophet insists on full tithes (Malachi 3:10). Tithes are the temple tax paid to the Levites as their only source of income (Numbers 18:20-30). This command would mandate full payment of wages to the temple staff as well as the presentation of right sacrifices for worship. Again, laity and priests appear in partnership, with the laity responsible for funding right worship and the priests responsible for performing it. Many amazing blessings await the community if it unites for the correct temple worship, and in recognition of such blessings all of the nations of the world will assert God's love and blessing for Yehud (Malachi 3:12).

A Day of Judgment

Although Malachi encourages the possibilities for repentance and righteous cooperation, the prophet still realizes the difficulties and unlikelihood of the changes that must transpire. Malachi's sixth unit (Malachi 3:13—4:3) represents a realistic examination of the difficulties preventing social cohesion and also provides rhetoric to encourage cooperation in both positive and negative fashions.[30]

The Book of Malachi recognizes an "inner-group" defined by strict belief, consisting of Malachi and those who agree with the prophet (Malachi 1:2; 3:16; 4:2-3). This "inner-group" partially accepts the lesser belief of others who form an "in-group," whose guilt brings about critique (Malachi 1:6—2:9) but for whom salvation is still possible (Malachi 2:2-4; 3:7, 10, 17-18); God will refine them in the coming divine action (Malachi 3:2-4). There is also an "out-group" that Malachi rejects, calling them "arrogant" or "evildoers"; although they may prosper now (Malachi 3:15), they will be the object of the coming judgment (Malachi 3:5; 4:1).

Malachi 3:13—4:3 centers on the inner-group of those who fear Yahweh, whose names have been written in the book of remembrance (Malachi 3:16). There are also skeptics (Malachi 3:13-15), mentioned in the second person, who will fully resolve their doubts on the day when Yahweh acts (Malachi 3:17-18); because they repent as a result of the prophetic critique, they form the in-group. The out-group of evildoers and arrogant Jerusalemites, consistently referred to in the third person, will be destroyed completely, having been rejected for their lack of any faith (Malachi 2:17; 3:14-15; 4:1).

Malachi 3:17—4:3 presents a contrast between the in-group, with a chance for repentance, and the out-group, who receives nothing but apocalyptic condemnation. The sparing of the in-group depends upon the repentance discussed in Malachi 3:18: "If you return, you shall see the difference between the righteous and the wicked."[31] Return to Yahweh is not only possible, but it becomes the target of the prophet's rhetoric. Repentance solves the problems of discernment presented earlier in the text (Malachi 3:14), and repentance removes the risks of destruction, as the prophet details later (Malachi 4:1-3).

Malachi argues for repentance, and this accords with the prophet's continuing arguments for correct worship. If the people accept the prophetic recommendations for solving their society's problems, including the lack of Persian funding for the Jerusalem temple, then God will recognize their efforts and will reward their faithfulness. Malachi attempts to create a change within the people's lives and thus to alter the action of the community as a whole in the direction of correct worship. Malachi's attitudes and assumptions, however, betray the social conditions of his prophecy. The prophet argues and persuades. Even though in the end of time evildoers will receive the divine wrath and God will destroy them for their lack of faith, Malachi holds out hope for changes in action in the present. In the face of activity deserving of condemnation, Malachi holds out the possibilities for repentance and refuses to reject those who disagree. The prophet recognizes the social debate and honors its terms, consistently stepping back from the strongest types of personal attack or statements of permanent condemnation. Instead, the rhetoric aims to persuade.

Malachi reflects the dawning of a pluralistic world in which the centers of power do not intervene with sufficient force to shape opinion decisively. In fact, under Xerxes, Persian power retreated from Yehud and the imperial intervention decreased, especially in relationship to the temple. Under Darius' reign, a governmental bureaucracy with an army's support would enforce taxes and the temple would receive funds for operation. Now the temple had to collect its own funds, and voluntarism was the only plausible means. The temple could only persuade; it could not coerce. Thus pluralism grew, allowing several responses to the situation. Malachi proposed strict adherence to ancient codes, although the prophet carefully constructed the appeals to focus on the priests' own traditions rather than on some external source of authority. Malachi urged cooperation in a setting where no one could any longer take cooperation for granted.

Religion in a Pluralistic World

Within the increasingly isolated and ignored Yehud of Xerxes' reign, several questions arose. How much acceptance can the religious community grant to those who do not adhere strictly to the regulations of the law? How much commitment does the faith require? Malachi struggled with the answers to these questions in the midst of a pluralistic world where it was impossible to coerce faith and religion.

Malachi allowed a high degree of acceptance, although it was not complete. The prophetic condemnations of evil and incorrect worship were harsh. Still, Malachi preached a reasonable repentance with specific goals. One did not have to agree with every point of Malachi's position or adopt a complicated and nuanced theology; all that Malachi requested was adherence to one's own statements and traditions about worship. For example, Malachi accepted the priests' definition of what good worship should be. There was no attempt to enforce an external code of behavior; instead, the prophet argued for the priests' traditions. This acceptance matched the shift into a more pluralistic form of Yahwistic religion than previously expressed in Israel's religious traditions.

At the same time, Malachi asserted the need for commitment to the religion and to the community of faith. Both priests and laity had roles that impinged upon the other; Malachi charged both groups with upholding their own roles so that blessing could come to all in cooperation. On the other hand, Malachi condemned the faith of those without commitment. A financial commitment commensurate with ability to pay was requisite; Malachi wished those with good animals to bring them instead of lesser beasts for the sacrifice. The prophet required no one to take on an unreasonable level of commitment, but commitment became a requirement for all. In a pluralistic setting where religion depends on voluntarism, each adherent to the faith must possess sufficient commitment to discharge the duties of that one's roles in the religious system. Malachi recognized the increasing pluralism of the religious setting in Yehud and made clear statements about the need to dedicate one's self to the faith and to its practice.

Malachi argued for a vital faith and an active, high-quality temple worship. The seeds of pluralism formed the context in which Malachi's message grew, and thus this prophet pushed the worship of Yahweh into new adaptations, such as a wider acceptance and a focused set of commitments. These new responses fit within the unstable world of Xerxes' reign and kept the religion adaptive through changing times. The questions of proper acceptance and commitment lingered, however, and new solutions entered the social debate during the reign of the next Persian emperor, Artaxerxes.

Notes

1. Olmstead, *History of the Persian Empire,* 214–35.

2. Ibid., 237–45.

3. Ibid., 230.

4. Young, "Consolidation of the Empire," Boardman et al., in *Cambridge Ancient History,* 4:78–79, cannot understand Xerxes' continuation of former policies, and instead interprets Xerxes' "failures" as examples of personal inability to rule. Although Young recognizes the dangers of his dependence upon sources such as Plato, which characterize Xerxes as "foppish" and "court-bred," he seems to err in the same direction rather than examining the sociological factors behind the developing administration of the Achaemenid Empire.

5. Meuleau, "Mesopotamia under Persian Rule," 361.

6. Ibid., 361–75.

7. Richard T. Hallock, "The Evidence of the Persepolis Tablets," in Gershevitch, *Cambridge History of Iran,* 2:603.

8. Dandamaev, *Political History,* 188.

9. Culican, *The Medes and the Persians,* 81; Olmstead, *History of the Persian Empire,* 255–65; Dandamaev, *Political History,* 190–94; and Widengren, "The Persians," 325.

10. Widengren, "The Persians," 326.

11. Meuleau, "Mesopotamia under Persian Rule," 359.

12. Widengren, "The Persians," 326.

13. Meuleau, "Mesopotamia under Persian Rule," 360.

14. Cook, "The Rise of the Achaemenids and Establishment of Their Empire," 226.

15. Olmstead, *History of the Persian Empire,* 266–67.

16. Ibid., 288–89; Dandamaev, *Political History,* 232–37; and Widengren, "The Persians," 326.

17. Olmstead, *History of the Persian Empire,* 234–35. Cf. Ezra 4:4-6. However, some scholars have incorrectly reconstructed a revolt during this time. See Julian Morgenstern, "A Chapter in the History of the High Priesthood," *American Journal of Semitic Languages and Literature* 55 (1938): 1–24, 183–97, 360–77; and idem, "Jerusalem—485 B.C.," *HUCA* 27 (1956): 101–79; 28 (1957): 15–47; 31 (1960): 1–29.

18. See P. J. Rhodes, "The Delian League to 449 B.C.," in *The Cambridge Ancient History,* vol. 5, *The Fifth Century B.C.*, ed. D. M. Lewis et al., 2d ed. (Cambridge: Cambridge University Press, 1986), 34–61.

19. Meuleau, "Mesopotamia under Persian Rule," 359–61; Matthew W. Stolper, "The Governor of Babylon and Across-the-River in 486 B.C.," *JNES* 48 (1989): 297; and Widengren, "The Persians," 326.

20. Olmstead, *History of the Persian Empire,* 235–37. Stolper, "Governor of Babylon and Across-the-River," 296, understands the temple sites to exhibit dilapidation during Xerxes' time rather than outright destruction. This position is consonant with a decrease in imperial funding for provincial temple sites throughout the empire, although it does not prove it.

21. Of course, the argument from silence should be limited. For a recent discussion of the imperial governmental bureaucracy and its implementation in Palestine at the beginning of Xerxes' reign, see Stolper, "Governor of Babylon and Across-the-River."

22. For evidence of western economic activity, see Hallock, "Evidence of the Persepolis Tab-

lets," 588–609; and Bezalel Porten, *Archives from Elephantine: The Life of an Ancient Jewish Military Colony* (Berkeley and Los Angeles: University of California Press, 1968).

23. Culican, *The Medes and the Persians*, 149. See also J. K. Davies, "Society and Economy," in Lewis, *The Cambridge Ancient History*, 5:287–305.

24. In Yehud, the temple's lack of income encouraged the people to fund the temple. The temple encouraged this through rhetoric, not force, and thus this was not taxation. However, it contributed to the depletion of Yehud's economic resources in the same fashion as increased taxation.

25. Roland de Vaux, *Ancient Israel* (New York: McGraw-Hill Book Co., 1965), 2: 403.

26. Julia M. O'Brien, *Priest and Levite in Malachi*, SBLDS 121 (Atlanta: Scholars Press, 1990), favors an earlier date, perhaps as early as 605 B.C.E. For more common opinions, see W. Emery Barnes, *Haggai, Zechariah and Malachi*, Cambridge Bible (Cambridge: Cambridge University Press, 1934); Jon L. Berquist, "The Social Setting of Malachi," *BTB* 19 (1989): 121–26; Théophane Chary, *Aggée—Zacharie—Malachie*, Sources Bibliques (Paris: J. Gabalda, 1969); R. J. Coggins, *Haggai, Zechariah, Malachi*, OTG (Sheffield: JSOT Press, 1987); Robert C. Dentan, "Malachi," in *The Interpreter's Bible* (New York: Abingdon Press, 1956), 6:1117–44; Beth Glazier-McDonald, *Malachi: The Divine Messenger*, SBLDS 98 (Atlanta: Scholars Press, 1987); Paul D. Hanson, "Malachi," in *Harper's Bible Commentary*, ed. James L. Mays (San Francisco: Harper & Row, 1988), 753–56; Andrew E. Hill, "Dating the Book of Malachi: A Linguistic Reexamination," in *The Word of the Lord Shall Go Forth: Essays in Honor of David Noel Freedman in Celebration of His Sixtieth Birthday*, ed. Carol L. Meyers and M. O'Connor (Winona Lake, Ind.: Eisenbrauns, 1983), 77–89; Rex Mason, *The Books of Haggai, Zechariah, and Malachi*, Cambridge Bible Commentary (Cambridge: Cambridge University Press, 1977); and Alexander von Bulmerincq, *Der Prophet Maleachi*, 2 vols. (Dorpat and Tartu: J. G. Krüger, 1926–32).

27. David L. Petersen, *Late Israelite Prophecy: Studies in Deutero-Prophetic Literature and in Chronicles*, SBLMS 23 (Missoula, Mont.: Scholars Press, 1977).

28. Of course, the difference between obeying Persian law and following priestly regulations blurs substantially if the relevant regulations were part of the law codes promulgated by Darius' codification, as was quite likely the case.

29. Many scholars do not recognize the rhetorical shift to the laity as audience, interpreting Malachi as continuing a reference to the priests. However, the redirection of the rhetoric in Malachi 2:1 to focus once more upon the priests upholds the recognition of a shift in the prophet's attention away from the priests to the laity in Malachi 1:14.

30. For a more complete discussion of this unit, see Berquist, "The Social Setting of Malachi," 121–26.

31. NRSV and many other versions translate incorrectly as, "Then once more you shall see the difference between the righteous and the wicked." But see Gesenius, § 159g; cf. Nehemiah 1:9.

CHAPTER 7

INCREASING WESTERN AUTONOMY: ARTAXERXES I (465–423 B.C.E.)

The long reign of Artaxerxes I lasted more than four decades, the second longest reign of the nine emperors of Persia. Artaxerxes I oversaw the Persian Empire through its halfway mark to destruction, even though no one at the time would have recognized the landmark. After Artaxerxes I, the Persian Empire settled into highly predictable patterns and risked little innovation. The stagnation of the empire begins already in Artaxerxes I's time. Cyrus and Cambyses ruled from a groundwork of conquest, and Darius turned to intensification for a similar basis of funding and imperial ideology. Xerxes' policies depleted the empire's colonies of their resources in an effort to redistribute the wealth to the ethnic Persians themselves. Artaxerxes I continued many of his father's policies, focusing the empire clearly on the road to decay and collapse. The Greek wars begun by Darius and continued against increasing odds by Xerxes continued to occupy the imperial attention. Throughout the imperial colonies, local matters drew ever less attention from the empire's core, and local governors took on ever greater powers in their limited rule.

Without conquest, the Persian Empire seemed purposeless, and the Greeks offered a challenge continually besting the efforts of the Persian military. Both Greece and Persia defined themselves increasingly through their mutual conflict. Halfway through the reign of Artaxerxes I, in 445 B.C.E., a Greek historian named Herodotus recited a lengthy history of the Persian Empire and its Achaemenid rulers to date. This history became Greece's chief means of knowing its adversary as well as a key historical source for later writers into the modern era. However, the historiography of Herodotus expresses one other pertinent fact: Greece was defining itself against Persia and against Persian rule and values. The same process appeared within the Persian court itself, as the rulers of the Persian Empire lost an ability to see themselves as anything but the opponents of the Greeks. With Artaxerxes I's century-old empire defining itself only in relationship to its western enemies, the shortening of vision was certain.

The History of the Reign of Artaxerxes I

Accession and Administration

The accession of Artaxerxes I was rooted in the palace intrigues prevalent at the time of Xerxes' latter years. Xerxes had seduced his niece Artayante, who was also the wife of Xerxes' son Darius. Darius appeared the heir apparent after the courtier Artabanus assassinated Xerxes. However, Artabanus did not wish Darius to be emperor, and so he convinced Artaxerxes, a younger son who was only eighteen years old at the time, to assassinate Darius. Shortly thereafter, Artabanus wished to kill Artaxerxes, but this conspiracy was betrayed. Artaxerxes was wounded but Artabanus was killed. Artaxerxes was then able to take the throne and rule as emperor, even though other sons of Xerxes revolted against his rule, such as Hystaspes in Bactria. Artaxerxes retained control of the imperial Persian military and soon squelched these revolts.[1]

The extent of Artaxerxes' empire was almost as large as that of Xerxes. Some of the Greek areas submitted to Persian rule. By 462 B.C.E., Artaxerxes had reinstated the Marduk priests, solidifying his control over Babylonia and at least partially reversing Xerxes' policies toward the priesthood. Some of the Egyptian inscriptions refer to Artaxerxes as Pharaoh. However, Artaxerxes' kingdom was shrinking, as the Persian Empire had begun to do during the time of his father, Xerxes; undoubtedly some of the more distant colonies developed in separate directions and were lost to Persian rule.[2]

Artaxerxes I continued Xerxes' policy of nontaxation for Persians; accordingly, Artaxerxes increased taxes throughout the rest of the empire. By continuing Xerxes' policies of redistribution, Artaxerxes significantly depleted the money supply. Coined money was rare, and loan sharks became common. Local landowners became bankrupt and lost their land, and in most cases Persians became the new landlords. Throughout the empire, the number of small-scale revolts increased markedly.[3] Economy and unity were twin concerns from the time of Artaxerxes I forward.

Most of the empire's attention focused on the Greek wars throughout Artaxerxes' reign, to the exclusion of other items of imperial business. Artaxerxes I did get involved in palace intrigues, as did his father, Xerxes. About the end of 424 B.C.E., Artaxerxes died, within the same week as Queen Damaspia and the Queen Mother, arousing suspicions of foul play.

Egypt and Greece

On the military front, the western borders of the Persian Empire proved increasingly difficult to control. Certainly Artaxerxes' attempts to encourage native religions, against Xerxes' policies, were aimed at increasing the loyalty of the colonies, but the larger issues of the economy remained ignored. The benefits given to the Persian nationals and ethnics removed too much of the wealth from the outlying regions to suit the colonies. Law and order broke down throughout most of the more distant colonies, and Artaxerxes could not dispatch the army to quell all of the disputes. Travel became much more difficult throughout the empire, and it proved especially dangerous in the Mediterranean colonies.

Early in Artaxerxes' reign, Egypt and Greece united forces and revolted against the Persian Empire. Egypt's Pharaoh at the time was Inarus, the son of Psammetichus III, and Athens was under the leadership of Pericles.[4] They allied in 460 B.C.E., and in 459 B.C.E. they attacked and regained Memphis. This provided Athens with a grain supply uncontrolled by Persia. The new alliance attempted fiscal reform in Egypt and restored the use of Egyptian monetary systems instead of Persian imperial coins. However, despite the military strength and the valuable trade alliance between these two regions, the economy did not substantially improve. High interest and voracious depreciation continued; the pattern of depletion that Xerxes had institutionalized proved impossible to stop within a short time span.[5] The new western alliance was incapable of solving any of its own issues beyond military sovereignty and political freedom.

Alliance of Persia and Sparta

Eventually the Persian Empire responded to the new military and political threat on its western flank. In 458–457 B.C.E., Artaxerxes sent a general, Megabyzus, to the Greek city-state of Sparta, which had traditionally been Athens' enemy. Persia offered a great deal of money to Sparta in exchange for an alliance to defeat Athens. The alliance between Persia and Sparta was successful, even though it would more rightly be termed Sparta's mercenary service for Persia. Megabyzus returned to Persia with Inarus and the Greek generals in captivity, but Artaxerxes granted their release in 454 B.C.E. As a reward for his faithful and successful service, Megabyzus was later appointed as satrap of Syria.[6] This marked a turning point in the Persian-Greek struggles for control over their border. The Persian Empire was able to gain a victory over the Greeks, even after its alliance with Egypt, a power that Persia had subdued repeatedly over the past seven decades but that often eluded Persian control. However, Persia could not achieve victory on its own. Only with the help of a local ally could the Persian Empire triumph over the Greeks. This limitation would provide the key to Greek strategy and would prove to be the core of Persia's undoing: Greece's unity was the secret to its survival against the larger Persian military force.

Greece was not long in understanding this situation. In 451 B.C.E., Athens allied with Sparta, and in 450 B.C.E. the allies declared war upon the Persian Empire. Athens and Sparta placed Cyprus under siege, but the siege eventually failed.[7] Eventually, Athens sued for peace at the Persian imperial court of Susa, resulting in the peace of Callias in 449 B.C.E. Megabyzus, who had served as the Persian satrap for many of the western regions after his successes in diplomacy with Sparta, also rebelled, in 448 B.C.E. The Persian armies were unable to retake Megabyzus' territories, but he was weakened and soon rejoined the empire, restating his loyalties to Artaxerxes I.

Despite the setbacks to Greece, Athens then adopted a strategy of slow annexation. Persia was ignoring its western reaches. Although the empire would respond to direct threats, many colonies left the empire through attrition, and Persia never struggled against this slow leakage of provinces. In this way, Athens expanded its territory in western Asia between 445 and 435 B.C.E. After the strenuous Peloponnesian War in 431 B.C.E., Persia again faced less opposition.[8]

Concerns with Borders

In the reign of Artaxerxes I, the Persian Empire increasingly experienced difficulties in maintaining its borders peacefully, especially its western borders. For part of the time, the eastern Mediterranean seacoast would have been Persia's westernmost border and only foothold on that important sea, which Egypt and Greece virtually controlled. The Inarus-Pericles alliance had severely limited Persia's ability to exercise naval power in the Mediterranean. This left areas such as Yehud susceptible to influence and coercion from non-Persian sources and also vulnerable to the Persian desire to hold its remaining western frontier. Both factors increased in their influence upon Yehud and the rest of the Persian Empire's western colonies throughout the reign of Artaxerxes I.

Yehud under Artaxerxes I

Strong Governors and the Fortification of Borders

Yehud suffered from the economic weakness of Artaxerxes' time and also experienced the increasing influence of the Greek city-states and other Mediterranean powers. Yehud's orientation began to shift from east to west. Within the shift of economic influences during these four decades, the evidence requires a distinction. During the early years of Artaxerxes I, the Persian Empire attempted to place additional resources on its western border to support its campaigns against Egypt and Greece. Later, the general weakening of the Persian imperial economy removed Persia from concerns in the southeastern Mediterranean and drove Yehud closer to Greece's economic sphere of influence. This produced the more lasting economic and cultural ramifications for Yehud, but the political and religious impact of Persia's mid-century concerns for Palestine is also great.

In 458–457 B.C.E., Megabyzus brought the Persian army through Palestine and near Yehud on the way to Egypt, where it would attack Pharaoh Inarus and his Egyptian-Greek alliance. During this period, Yehud found itself in the center of three great eastern Mediterranean powers vying for control. This prolonged conflict pinned Yehud in the midst of forces to which it could not compare. The Persian Empire desired to strengthen its loyal colonies along the Mediterranean to compensate for its losses of Egypt and Greece and to stabilize the area until it could force these regions to return to imperial control. Thus Artaxerxes I appointed strong governors to rule Yehud, to rebuild its walls, and to minimize the economic distortions throughout this small colony. The canon preserves some of the effects of these governors and the longer-reaching effects of their policies and religious understandings in the books of Ezra and Nehemiah.

Persia's interest in Yehud and neighboring colonies was a strengthening of the border against further military incursions by Egypt and Greece.[9] At the time of Pericles' and Inarus' alliance, Artaxerxes I increased the level of staffing for the Persian outposts in places like Jerusalem. Likewise, Artaxerxes used the same strategy that had been at least partially effective in Babylonia: he reversed Xerxes' policies and reinstated some funding for religious services in the colonies. Although Artaxerxes did not support religious practices with the same intensity that Darius did, clearly Artaxerxes used leaders with religious position and influence in order to sway populaces and to regain control of local administration, including what transpired through temples. Artaxerxes also ordered and funded fortifications in the outlying western colonies, to assure that the Egyptian-Greek alliance could not gain further territory.

Yehud under the first half of the reign of Artaxerxes I appeared to be a front line of defense against the encroachment of the western allies. Fortifications, higher allowances for local spending, and greater authority exercised by local administrators all depict a coordinated attempt to maintain the loyalty and safety of this border community. Perhaps Persia needed a strong Yehud to counter the increased threat of Greek Phoenicia in 458 B.C.E.[10] However, as soon as the Persian Empire's armies defeated the Egyptians and

Greeks, this attention declined, and Persian attentions to the border areas such as Yehud slowly declined. By the second half of Artaxerxes' reign, Yehud was again alone, and the influences of trade and economics became more important than the distant political and military movements of the Persian Empire.

Lasting Economic Shifts

Within the second half of Artaxerxes' reign, Greece began to be the controlling factor in Yehudite trade and other economic vectors. Olives and grain played important roles in Yehud's participation in the Mediterranean economy, since it is thought that Yehud traded grain to Athens and other Greek city-states for olive products and wine, at least in the latter periods of the Persian Empire, and presumably also in the earlier times. Trade with Greece became of increasing importance throughout the Persian period, and Yehud was forced to barter because of its lack of silver for money.[11] In Yehud, as in most places during the Persian Empire, old modes of production and slavery existed alongside each other.[12]

As Greece recovered from the effects of the Persian wars, its economic influence became greater. The Greek city-states retained a strong naval advantage over the Persian forces throughout Artaxerxes' reign, and this allowed for maritime trade with areas such as Palestine and Phoenicia. Yehud may or may not have been a direct trading partner with the Greek city-states at this time; certainly there was trade at least indirectly, through other seagoing peoples. Yehud produced olives and olive oil for trade with Greece and other areas, and at times sold off Jewish children into the slave trade.[13] Greek pottery began to find its way into the Yehud area at this time in increasing amounts.

Despite the enhanced Greek trade, Yehud's economy seems to have continued to decline. By 456–455 B.C.E., interest had reached at least 12.5 percent, and there is some indication of more common rates in the range between 40 percent and 60 percent through Yehud and the rest of the Persian Empire.[14] Economic collapse was on the horizon for all of the empire's colonies, and Yehud was no exception. Although the trade with the Greek city-states provided another avenue for economic development, Yehud's available options were poor and market pressures encouraged the Greeks to keep Yehud just as poor as Persia would have done. Yehud did not grow wealthy at all through this trade; instead, the impoverishment seems to have increased or at least continued.

Literature from the Reign of Artaxerxes I

Two texts from the reign of Artaxerxes I may well be extant in the Hebrew Bible. The books of Ezra and Nehemiah record the activities of two Persian-appointed governors of Yehud during the reign of Artaxerxes. However, the text does not specify for either of these governors under which Artaxerxes they served. Thus the problems of dating still exist. However, it seems very likely that at least one of these governors served within Artaxerxes' time, and the juxtaposition of the Persian Empire's interests in conflict with those of the Egyptian-Greek coalition provide a helpful backdrop for understanding the work that one of these governors began and the other continued.[15]

Dates of Ezra and Nehemiah

Dating Ezra and Nehemiah proves difficult. The raw data is easily accessible. According to the biblical texts, Ezra served as Yehud's governor beginning in the seventh year of Artaxerxes (Ezra 7:7-8), and Nehemiah served in that same capacity from the twentieth year to the thirty-second year of Artaxerxes (Nehemiah 1:1; 2:1; 5:14). However, that is also where the problem begins. Both texts specify the emperor Artaxerxes; neither specifies *which* of Persia's three emperors named Artaxerxes is the one these texts intend.[16]

Most scholars have placed Nehemiah during the reign of Artaxerxes I, and thus Nehemiah's governorship extended from 445 B.C.E. to 432 B.C.E. Typically, debate concerning Ezra's date has ranged between two chief alternatives. First, Ezra served under Artaxerxes I, and thus Ezra's governorship began in 458 B.C.E. and ended sometime before Nehemiah's rule began in 445 B.C.E. Second, Artaxerxes II appointed Ezra beginning in 397 B.C.E., and thus Ezra arrived after Nehemiah. This second interpretation goes against the implication of the extant texts that Ezra predated Nehemiah, but the texts themselves make no clear statements to that effect.[17] Neither dating alternative is without support. The straightforward reading of the text suggests Ezra's primacy, but many scholars have argued that Ezra's reforms make better sense as furtherance of Nehemiah's (prior) efforts. However, the reforms of both governors function well within the context of Artaxerxes I's early problems. Of course, there may have been situations in the fourth century B.C.E. that fit the descriptions of these governors with even greater accuracy than the mid-fifth century dates during the reign of Artaxerxes I, but such would be an argument from silence. It seems best, therefore, to interpret Ezra and Nehemiah as two governors, in that order, during the reign of Artaxerxes I. Ezra's service began in 458 B.C.E.; Nehemiah follows from 445 B.C.E. to 432 B.C.E.

Both Ezra and Nehemiah functioned as governors of Yehud. Nehemiah 8:9 draws a distinction between Nehemiah as governor and Ezra as priest and scribe. However, scholarly concentration on this terminology obscures the fact that they both exercised civil authority under Persian command. The Persian imperial bureaucracy appointed them both for similar reasons, focusing on the political control of the Yehud area. Whatever their differences, they were both politicians with responsibility for governing the province to keep it in line with Persian interests. Their Persian connections resulted in primary contributions within the political realm, but there were religious dimensions to their concerns as well. Ezra's contributions included a refurbishing of the Jerusalem temple, which at that point was nearly seventy years old. Ezra's group brought gold and silver for the temple, presumably returning things from Artaxerxes' Babylonian treasury that had once ornamented the temple of the Davidic monarchy. Ezra's expedition may well have enjoyed significant backing from the Babylonian Jews, who were well integrated into Babylonian and thus Persian imperial society. Ezra also enforced a fixed interpretation of the King's Law as well as the law of the God of Heaven (Ezra 7:26); the text itself realizes Ezra's loyalties both to political and to religious matters. Artaxerxes I sent Ezra to enforce the law of the Persian Empire and also to provide helpful service to the temple. Thus through enforcement and through religious support, Artaxerxes sought to firm his control of the western borders of his weakened empire. Ezra arrived shortly after the Inarus-Pericles alliance had captured Memphis and had secured for themselves a large and independent grain supply. Ezra's mission was to avoid the spread of the Egyptian-Greek alliance and to retain Yehud as a colony loyal to Persia.

Religious Reforms

Ezra's concerns range directly toward religious reforms. The narrator refers to Ezra as scribe (Ezra 7:6), a title with explicit religious connections. The Book of Ezra begins with the Edict of Cyrus allowing immigration of Babylonian Jews to Yehud; that edict ends with mention of the need to serve the Jerusalem temple (Ezra 1:4). The first six chapters detail the earlier rebuilding of that temple; only then does Ezra himself appear in the narrative. Ezra intended to teach the law of Yahweh to those in Yehud (Ezra 7:10); the text seems to assume that there will be a need for religious reforms once the people understand anew God's law.

Artaxerxes sent a letter with Ezra, with reference to the imperial donations for the temple, intended to provide for a full service of worship (Ezra 7:16-20). Perhaps this shows a direct reversal of Xerxes' policies, which provided no imperial funding for local temples. Certainly Ezra's work involves a new and newly funded attention to correct and legalistic practices within the Jerusalem temple. These gifts included large amounts of gold and silver, primarily in the form of vessels to be used within the worship services. The value of this large gift would have been quite substantial (Ezra 8:24-30). In Ezra's time, these gifts represented the contributions from the imperial court, showing an official financial concern with the enhancement of worship. Nehemiah also made a large personal contribution to temple service in his time, but it seems to have been a gift from the governor's own wealth, not necessarily from the Persian imperial funds (Nehemiah 7:70-72).

The gifts to the temple are not the only changes within the religion during the times of Ezra and Nehemiah. Ezra led the inhabitants of Yehud in an involved service of worship, culminating in an intense confession of faith (Nehemiah 9:1—10:39). Ezra's chief goal seems to have been to increase the popular commitment to the religion and its practice within the temple. This accords well with a reaction early in the reign of Artaxerxes I to the lack of imperial support for local religion that Yehud experienced under the reign of Xerxes and expressed within the Book of Malachi. In finances and in emotional commitment, religion in Yehud declined under Xerxes, and Artaxerxes I attempted through Ezra to strengthen the people's religion, along with other reforms. In all of these ways, Artaxerxes I desired a much stronger presence for the Persian Empire in this frontier colony, and religion proved to be one means toward this end for the emperor, as it did for Darius before him.

The King's Law

The investment of the Persian Empire in Yehud's religious reforms has political reasons. First, the religious system with its bureaucracy of priests and other officials provided a means toward social cohesion and thus loyalty. Perhaps more important, the religion provided a more direct way for Persian involvement in local affairs.

Ezra was an appointee of the Persian imperial government, and he served at the pleasure of the emperor, Artaxerxes I. Ezra thus participated in a dual allegiance, with responsibilities to both God and emperor. Repeatedly, the narrator explains that Ezra was a scribe with loyalty to the law of Yahweh, the God of Heaven (Ezra 7:6, 10, 12, 14, 21).[18] Even with this loyalty, Ezra's occupation was that of a lower-level Persian bureaucrat. Over half a century earlier, the Persian emperor Darius had codified laws throughout the empire, presumably including Yehud, by gathering together prior bodies of local legal codes and reissuing them in edited form as the King's Law. If this was the case in Yehud, then many of the Pentateuchal legislations, both governing social matters and regulating temple functions and religious holiness, were promulgated by Darius with the full authority of the Persian Empire behind them. This inextricably linked the law of God and the law of the Persian Empire. Perhaps nowhere does this become more clear than at the end of Artaxerxes I's letter of approval for Ezra's activities:

> *All who will not obey the law of your God and the law of the king, let judgment be strictly executed on them, whether for death or for banishment or for confiscation of their goods or for imprisonment. (Ezra 7:26)*

Artaxerxes I expresses Ezra's role as enforcing God's law and the king's law; imperial policy assumes no discrepancies between the two. Ezra must maintain social and economic order as well as religious sensibilities. The chief example of legal enforcement within the Book of Ezra deals with mixed marriages, and these receive explicit attention below.

The nature of Ezra's work as scribe and governor was to bring about social cohesion and to ensure that Persian goals succeeded within Yehud. Perhaps Artaxerxes I's greatest fear for Yehud was that the colony might revolt in social chaos; the intensified enforcement of imperial law, including the religious codes appropriate for Yehudite religion to continue in an orderly fashion, would accomplish the regulation of society in ways beneficial to an empire that craved peaceful borders wherever those could be found.

Ezra's enhanced temple worship would have had at least two effects. First, it strengthened the temple system for funneling taxation revenues through the colony and into the larger imperial system. This would have had a differential effect, possibly increasing the income of the wealthier people within Yehud and thus increasing their loyalty to the political status quo within the empire. Second, it increased the amount of correct worship occurring within the Yehudite community, providing a newly revitalized set of social norms and commitments. By depicting the Persian Empire as a government that allowed such historically ethnic forms of religious expression, Artaxerxes attempted to gain the loyalty of the people at a time when other nearby colonies revolted to escape Persian domination. Artaxerxes' plan took the popular allegiance to the religion and used Ezra's joint responsibilities to merge that allegiance into imperial loyalty. To the extent that Yehud avoided the revolts of its neighbors, the policy succeeded.

Fortifications

Although the Book of Ezra mentions the construction of a wall a few times (especially Ezra 9:9), Ezra seems little concerned with fortifications for the city of Jerusalem or the larger colony of Yehud. However, a few years later in his reign (445 B.C.E.), Artaxerxes I sent Nehemiah to make sure that Yehud remained loyal. At this time, the new governor's first task would be not to join the revolt that Megabyzus was leading in the eastern Mediterranean area but to oppose it and to maintain the colony's reliance upon the Persian Empire. Because of this task, personal loyalty to the emperor was probably the chief criterion for choosing the new governor. Nehemiah was a eunuch who had worked in the king's personal service (Nehemiah 1:11). The military nature of Nehemiah's expedition required that an escort of royal cavalry accompany him to Yehud (Nehemiah 2:9). Once there, Nehemiah began a series of fortifications that were hastily completed (Nehemiah 6:15). These new walls require only fifty-two days for their construction, but they achieve their desired goal: the surrounding nations raised their estimate of Yehud's strength, and they were wary of attacking Yehud in any attempt at rebellion.

The Book of Nehemiah's strong emphasis on the building of a wall in Jerusalem demonstrates that the fortification must have been one of the governor's chief tasks. The beginning report of Yehud's condition contains only two details after a mention of general difficulties: the wall is down and the gates have been burned (Nehemiah 1:3). This serves as an initial definition of the problem. Nehemiah then asks Artaxerxes for travel permission plus materials to build gates, a wall, and a governor's residence (Nehemiah 2:7-8). Upon arrival, Nehemiah inspects the walls (Nehemiah 2:11-16). Although the walls were not Nehemiah's only concern, his chief intention and greatest emphasis of attention were upon the construction of fortifying walls for Jerusalem. In fact, Nehemiah later asserts that the wall was his chief priority (Nehemiah 5:16). Although Ezra clearly had a more varied range of interests, Nehemiah focused almost completely upon the fortifications. This reflects a time in Persia's experience when the empire wished to strengthen its position through this part of its vast territory.

Economic and Political Rebuilding

Artaxerxes I worked for greater social cohesion in Yehud and for increased loyalty to and usefulness for the Persian Empire. Toward these ends, Ezra reformed and refinanced the religion, and Nehemiah fortified the city. In both cases, the governors were involved in the social machinery of economic and political strengthening. As it was throughout the empire, Yehud's economy was poor and declining. Other factors complicated the general economic malaise.

Darius' energetic funding of the temple, including the construction project and the services held therein, produced a class within Yehud that depended upon the imperial bureaucracy for its own power and wealth. These priests and governmental officials, many of whom had just emigrated from Babylonia and Persia, became the upper class for Yehud, although these early years did not allow for a great difference between rich and poor. Darius' continued efforts at intensification, however, soon proved successful, and the income differential increased. Xerxes' refusal to support local temples combined with his policy of depletion in order to intensify the class separation in Yehud. Because the Persian Empire no longer provided financial underwriting for the temple, the Yehudite elite encouraged the laity to contribute more money and resources to the functioning of the temple. This maintained the income of the priests while depleting the resources remaining to the rest of the populace, thus expanding the distance between the classes. As Persia continued to deplete the resources of the colonies, the effects struck Yehud differentially, and the rich maintained their power while the poor grew markedly poorer.

The rebuilding of the city walls was Nehemiah's prime task, and it enhanced the separation between the rich and the poor by creating a physical barrier between the urban elites and Yehud's countryside dwellers. In this context, it is striking that the Book of Nehemiah details the people involved in the wall construction; they represent leaders from the tribes (Nehemiah 3). In fact, the priests conduct the organization of the project (Nehemiah 3:1). Those who will live within the walls of the restored city include the priests, the temple servants, merchants, goldsmiths, perfumers, and others—clearly the upper classes of Yehudite society. The rebuilt city exists for the urban elite and their cohorts from Persia; the outlying, unprotected countryside remains for the poorer inhabitants of the land.

Nehemiah recognizes the problems caused by the severe economic dislocation of the populace. Because of the high degrees of poverty experienced by many of the poorer people, they are unable to pay for their debts, and this extreme poverty cuts into the system of taxation that kept the upper classes viable.

> *Now there was a great outcry of the people and of their wives against their Jewish kin. For there were those who said, "With our sons and our daughters, we are many; we must get grain, so that we may eat and stay alive." There were also those who said, "We are having to pledge our fields, our vineyards, and our houses in order to get grain during the famine." And there were those who said, "We are having to borrow money on our fields and vineyards to pay the king's tax. Now our flesh is the same as that of our kindred; our children are the same as their children; and yet we are forcing our sons and daughters to be slaves, and some of our daughters have been ravished; we are powerless, and our fields and vineyards now belong to others." (Nehemiah 5:1-5)*

The governor Nehemiah narrates an instance of economic injustice. The problem represents conflicting interests on the parts of two groups: the "people and their wives" versus the "Jewish kin." The precise identifications of these two groups is unclear. Joseph Blenkinsopp argues that the "Jewish kin" are the elites of the city;[19] this accords well with the fact that the term describes these people not by their Jewish faith but by their Yehudite identity. These elite are the official residents of Yehud; the Persian Empire considers the ruling class to be the ones of import. Regardless of the use of titles for groups herein, the opposition is clear: urban elites are oppressing the rural farmowners in severe ways. The poorer people cannot pay their taxes, and so they mortgage their property to pay the tax. Once the property no longer belongs to them, they have no further assets except their children, whom they then sell into slavery (probably to Greece). The depletion of the rural economy and the heavy taxation to support the local and imperial governments caused the poorer inhabitants of Yehud to sell off their land and their children, and this combined to create virtually all of their income-producing potential for the future.

One does not need to mention the cruelty and inhumanity of these acts. The desperation of persons during this era is obvious. They even sell their own children into slavery in order to keep the rest of the family alive. Persia's economic exploitation of the colonies has here produced a system whereby the colonial occupants cannot produce enough to maintain their own production. The imperial system then feeds upon itself in self-destructive fashion, hastening the end of Persian hegemony and power. However, the situation may well be even more complicated. If the rural inhabitants of Yehud were selling their children to one of the Greek city-states, then Persia's exploitation of Yehudite labor was not only reducing Persia's labor force but forcibly emigrating part of it to Greece, Persia's enemy. It would be possible for slave trade to have accompanied the olive oil trade and other sources of exchange throughout this period. As Greek control of the seas increased, Yehud increasingly involved itself in trade with Greece.

Nehemiah not only recognizes the problem but undertakes significant financial reform in order to curb it. He deals with the nobles, those who have been charging exorbitant interest and driving the populace into bankruptcy.

> *I was very angry when I heard their outcry and these complaints. After thinking it over, I brought charges against the nobles and the officials; I said to them, "You are all taking interest from your own people." And I called a great assembly to deal with them, and said to them, "As far as we were able, we have bought back our Jewish kindred who had been sold to other nations; but now you are selling your own kin, who must then be bought back by us!" They were silent, and could not find a word to say. So I said, "The thing that you are doing is not good. Should you not walk in the fear of our God, to prevent the taunts of the nations our enemies? Moreover I and my brothers and my servants are lending them money and grain. Let us stop this taking of interest. Restore to them, this very day, their fields, their vineyards, their olive orchards, and their houses, and the interest on money, grain, wine, and oil that you have been exacting from them." Then they said, "We will restore everything and demand nothing more from them. We will do as you say." And I called the priests, and made them take an oath to do as they had promised. (Nehemiah 5:6-12).*

Nehemiah's plan involves two stages: the removal of interest from loans and the restoration to the people of the items seized in back payment. The motivation for this radical economic move is that the costs would be greater to the wealthy if they lose their next generation of the labor pool, in which case the elites would have to buy back their workers from around the known world. Nehemiah works from an assumption that the people are unified, at least to the degree that the elites hold at least some responsibility for the wider success or failure of the whole colony of Yehud. If for no other reason, then this may have been conditioned by the Persian Empire's pressure to collect taxes; Yehud must meet its quotas no matter what its population. In Nehemiah 5, the wealthy ones acknowledge their responsibility and pay for a variety of forgiven loans through their own losses. This, however, allows the labor pool to remain constant, and it prevents the Persian Empire from forcing a reduced Yehud local administration to pay taxes even without the primary workers of the society.

Nehemiah calls for a radical rapprochement between the urban elites and the countryside farmers and tenants. Even though the exploitation had been effectively institutionalized, Nehemiah urges the wealthiest people to forgo their interest payments and to refuse to repossess any land.

Regionalism

The separation of Yehud from the influences of its neighbors concerned both Ezra and Nehemiah. Perhaps the clearest ideological expression of this concern comes from Nehemiah: "Should you not walk in the fear of our God, to prevent the taunts of the nations our enemies?" (Nehemiah 5:9). The activities of the people reflect upon the colony of Yehud in the eyes of their neighbors throughout the region. Nehemiah's statement is couched in religious terminology, but the context of that passage deals with economic issues of survival and class struggle. The governor worries about the other colonies of the region and their perception of Yehud's economic management. The surrounding colonies were also subject to Persia, and the records of Yehud's governors indicate clearly that other colonies were prone to reporting on Yehud's behavior to the Persian Empire's central administration. One colony might play itself off another colony, seeking benefits from the empire. Nehemiah strove to be respectable in the eyes of other regions so that his own reputation would not be tarnished; presumably, this would also prevent Persian intervention in local affairs. Persian governmental style allowed this competition to occur, with the effect that each region monitored its neighbors and reported on them in service to Persia; this decreased the need for direct supervision of colonial matters. Furthermore, the Persian policy of colonial depletion since the time of Xerxes kept each colony at the throats of its neighbors, competing for scarce and shrinking resources.

The effects of regionalism appear first in Ezra 4, where neighboring governors in an earlier time desire to join in the construction of the temple, which surely would have been a profitable governmental construction project. The Book of Ezra continued the discussion of regional opposition into the reigns of Xerxes and Artaxerxes (Ezra 4:6-24). The experiences of Nehemiah with this regional opposition were greater. He competed directly with Sanballat and Tobiah, governors of neighboring areas who sought to prevent the fortification construction work in Yehud (Nehemiah 2:10, 19-20).[20] Later, the difficulties with regional officials grew to include the regions of Samaria, Ammon, Arabia, and Ashdod (Nehemiah 4). Almost all of Yehud's neighbors opposed the construction of walls that would fortify Jerusalem. Even though this construction reflected Persia's need to arm certain of its areas against the Greek threats of the time, the local regional officials felt themselves threatened by this fortification of Jerusalem. Nevertheless Nehemiah persevered and quickly finished the repairs to the wall (Nehemiah 6:1-9).

Tobiah returns in a brief notice at the end of the Book of Nehemiah. Yehud's governor returns from a trip to the Persian imperial courts only to find that Tobiah the Ammonite official had begun to reside within the temple, with the support of Eliashib, one of the chief priests (Nehemiah 13:4-9). Nehemiah vigorously removes this foreign threat from the center of Yehud's power.

This story provides an interesting sidelight: Tobiah and Eliashib are related. Two possibilities for this relationship help to explain the nature of the political regional struggles throughout this period. If Tobiah and Eliashib are genetically related, then there are kinship ties connecting Persian governmental officials throughout different regions. In a context of shared ethnicity, this may well indicate that there were Persian ethnic influences within several of these rulers of different colonies. This would reflect the earlier policies of Darius and Xerxes favoring ethnic Persians for leadership positions throughout the empire; all indications suggest that Artaxerxes I continued and furthered these policies by placing more Persians at even relatively lower levels of imperial bureaucracy. Perhaps both Tobiah and Eliashib ruled in part by virtue of their Persian descent, and thus their ethnic ties to the regions that they administered must be questioned. A second alternative is that they were related by marriage. The intermarriage of ruling classes of adjacent areas would not at all be surprising, especially in the context of Ezra and Nehemiah's argument against ethnic intermarriage. This would then provide a clear case for the dangers of such intermarriage practices: alliances made through marriage would allow foreigners to have special access to Yehud's own center of power, possibly undermining the work of Yehud to be a partially autonomous colony under Persia's rule.

The connection between Tobiah and Eliashib cannot be ascertained with reliability, but the threat seems clear. Because of this connection, a foreign official with interests antithetical to Nehemiah's designs for Yehud has gained special access into Yehud. Nehemiah acts decisively to remove this influence from another region. The regional competition that Yehud experienced in Artaxerxes' time resulted in a strongly separationist policy vis-à-vis other regions, which competed for the scarce resources available to the distant colonies during the reign of Artaxerxes I.

Marriage and Ethnicity

Often, commentators have asserted that the problem of intermarriage was the chief social issue to which Ezra and Nehemiah addressed themselves. Although there is a preponderance of other issues, as treated above, intermarriage and the ethnic concerns related thereto provided a concrete example of great importance to both of these governors. However, the texts suggest that the problem and the suggested solution took slightly different form for Ezra than for Nehemiah.

For Ezra, the concern focuses on Yehud's leadership. Yehudite men, including priests, Levites, and officials, have married women from the neighboring areas. The key problem is that the leaders have participated in this intermarriage (Ezra 9:1-2). After Ezra's lengthy prayer and mourning over the problem, one of the people offered a suggestion: the Yehudite men could divorce their foreign wives and reject the children of these mixed marriages (Ezra 10:2-4). The problem focuses on the elites, and there is indication that the inheritance of the children is at least part of the problem (Ezra 9:12). Ezra depicts a harmonious solution by the whole community acting in a plenary gathering, with the intention being "to isolate the assimilationists in the community by a kind of plebiscite."[21] Any conflict is minimal, although a few disagree with this action (Ezra 10:15).

The Book of Nehemiah presents the problem differently. Yehudite men have married women from Ashdod, Ammon, and Moab (Nehemiah 13:23). Whereas Ezra deals with all foreign women, Nehemiah focuses on the marriages that involve the more traditional enemies of Israel. The more specific problem is that the children of such marriages speak only the languages of their mothers (Nehemiah 13:24); without a knowledge of Hebrew or Aramaic, they would not be capable of assuming leadership positions within the community. Nehemiah then offers a comparison to Solomon's problems of dissipating alliances developed on the basis of intermarriage; thus Nehemiah indicates that the problems may involve foreign complicity within issues of colonial policy (Nehemiah 13:25-27). The text then provides an example: the high priest's grandson was the son-in-law of Sanballat the Horonite, a neighboring governor (Nehemiah 13:28). Nehemiah chased these relatives of foreign officials away. The concern to prevent interference from foreign officials of neighboring and competing colonies resonates with the opposition from regionally competitive colonies, as discussed above. Nehemiah does not suggest divorce and thus differs from Ezra in the solution as well as in the precise definition of the problem.

For Nehemiah, the problem is one of native speech and foreign collusion, and the problem is to be solved by the cessation of intermarriage; for Ezra, the problem is of tainted leadership and the resultant dangers of inheritance, and the solution is divorce. Within both of these sources is a concern for the economic and political results of intermarriage among the upper classes. Ezra's list of affected persons, for instance, leans heavily toward the priests and leaders (Ezra 10:16-44). Many scholars have advanced ethnic purity as the reason for this shared emphasis on intermarriage, but this seems strange in the light of the other orientations of these governors. For instance, they are rarely concerned with ethnic issues when dealing with the Persian court with which both of them must have interrelated.

The issues that have appeared throughout the books of Ezra and Nehemiah are matters of regional competition and economic differentiation within Yehud. In both of these issues, Yehud was increasingly isolating itself from other geographic and political entities, and the ruling classes of Yehud found themselves increasingly distant from the economic concerns of the masses. Both of these factors can lead to a concern against intermarriage. Nehemiah's perception of the dangers of intermarriage seems clear: it could produce opportunities for foreign officials to exercise undue influence on Yehud's internal matters (Nehemiah 13:28). In an atmosphere of economic depletion by the Persian Empire's central authority and harsh competition from other regions, regulations against intermarriage would enhance a sense of Yehudite solidarity over against the other regions. The concern would be to solidify political control and economic security within the ruling stratum of Jerusalem society.

Within this context, there would also be concerns about marrying outside one's class. For the landed aristocracy of Jerusalem, most of whom had descended from exiles of a former day, a chief concern would have been to centralize their own control over the land and the wealth. This would require an emphasis on marrying within one's own class. In such a way, each child would have familial connections only to other landed persons; there would be no means for land or resources to be given away to relatives outside the aristocracy. Perhaps Ezra's injunction refers not to foreign women per se but to women who inhabited the countryside of Yehud and were thus socially distant from the aristocratic classes of Jerusalem and the Yehudite elites.[22] This governor's concentration on the families affected by the intermarriage makes sense in this connection.

The economic effects of intermarriage would have been a further depletion of already scarce resources through dissipation into a widening social circle, and the political effects would have included alliances and collusion with other regional governments.

These concerns that related to intermarriage are already documented for Ezra and Nehemiah, and so it seems likely that they were significant factors in these governors' opposition to intermarriage. Of course, there may also be religious reasons for these prohibitions, or concepts of purity and separation. Such ideological and religious factors probably determined the ways in which the governors (especially Ezra) dealt with the situation, since the law of God would thus be the proper religious tool for strengthening the economic and political bases for the community of Yehud.

Conclusions

Throughout their work as governors, Ezra and Nehemiah shared concerns about the economic and political effects of religious and social factors in Yehud's life. Both Ezra and Nehemiah argued against various forms of discouragement and dissipation of societal resources. Their context was the continued depletion of resources by the policies of Artaxerxes I.

Through these two governors the Persian Empire gained a strengthened hold on Yehud and a deeper commitment to law and to autonomous existence. Collusions with other regional governments were exposed and reduced, leaving the loyalties to Persia intact. As the Greek and Egyptian armies and navies influenced the areas of the eastern Mediterranean with increasing effectiveness, and as Greek trade began to influence social attitude and political loyalties, Artaxerxes transferred more resources, including the resources of personnel such as Ezra and Nehemiah, to the small and struggling colony of Yehud. With Yehud's loyalty assured through the influx of funds and political support, the western reaches of the Persian Empire were more secure. Although it was Xerxes' and Artaxerxes' policies that had depleted the economy of the colonies and thus left them more susceptible to outside influences, the new imperial policy increased the social control exercised by governors. These governors utilized political, economic, and religious modes in their administration of Persian imperial policy in Yehud.

Notes

1. Olmstead, *History of the Persian Empire*, 289–90.

2. Ibid., 290–91.

3. Ibid., 291–99; and Widengren, "The Persians," 327.

4. Dandamaev, *Political History*, 238–43.

5. Olmstead, *History of the Persian Empire*, 303–4; and Widengren, "The Persians," 327. See also Cowley's papyrus # 11.

6. Olmstead, *History of the Persian Empire*, 308.

7. Ibid., 309–10.

8. Ibid., 312, 344; Widengren, "The Persians," 327; and idem, "The Persian Period," in *Israelite and Judean History*, ed. John H. Hayes and J. Maxwell Miller (Philadelphia: Westminster Press, 1977), 529.

9. Of course, it is ironic that Egypt and Greece never attempted military incursions at this time, but Artaxerxes I's later inattention to the western reaches allowed for Greece's cultural and economic invasion of the eastern Mediterranean, with far greater and more enduring impact upon Judaism than military invasion might have had.

10. Margalith, "Political Role of Ezra," 111. See also Fritz M. Heichelheim, "Ezra's Palestine and Periclean Athens," *Zeitschrift für Religions- und Geistesgeschichte* 3 (1951): 251–52.

11. Hans G. Kippenberg, *Religion und Klassenbildung im antiken Judäa: Eine religionssoziologische Studie zum Verhältnis von Tradition und gesellschaftlicher Entwicklung*, Studien zur Umwelt des Neuen Testaments 14 (Göttingen: Vandenhoeck & Ruprecht, 1982), 45–47.

12. Heinz Kreissig, *Die sozialökonomische Situation in Juda zur Achämenidenzeit*, Schriften zur Geschichte und Kultur des Alten Orients 7 (Berlin: Akademie, 1973), 115.

13. See Nehemiah 5:5.

14. E. Neufeld, "The Rate of Interest and the Text of Nehemiah 5:11," *JQR* 44 (1953–54): 196–202.

15. See Lester L. Grabbe, *Judaism from Cyrus to Hadrian*, vol. 1, *The Persian and Greek Periods* (Minneapolis: Fortress Press, 1992), 130–38.

16. It is not possible for Nehemiah to have served under Artaxerxes III, since this emperor's reign did not last past twenty-one years.

17. Others have suggested an emendation to the date of Ezra's mission, usually resulting in the thirty-seventh year of Artaxerxes I, or 428 B.C.E. However, this conjectural emendation has no manuscript support and may well create as many problems as it solves. Some scholars have dated both Ezra and Nehemiah to the reign of Artaxerxes II, in which case Ezra would begin 397 B.C.E. and Nehemiah would serve in 384–372 B.C.E. This position receives little support in the most recent literature. For useful and persuasive surveys of the issues, see Joseph Blenkinsopp, *Ezra-Nehemiah, A Commentary*, OTL (Philadelphia: Westminster Press, 1988), 139–44; and H. G. M. Williamson, *Ezra and Nehemiah*, OTG (Sheffield: JSOT Press, 1987), 55–69.

18. The appearance of the phrase "God of Heaven" for Yahweh is quite striking. The narrator places this appellation in the mouth of Artaxerxes (Ezra 7:12). "God of Heaven" may have had a connection to the Persian deity Ahura Mazda. If this connection was strong, perhaps these two gods were equated, at least in the policies of the Persian Empire. Artaxerxes never refers to Yahweh, but only to the "God of Heaven" or by reference to Ezra or Jerusalem. Certainly Persian imperial policy dealt similarly with many local religions, caring less for the theological distinctions between deities than for the political and economic effects of temple systems throughout the imperial colonies.

19. Blenkinsopp, *Ezra-Nehemiah*, 256. The opposite identification is possible, and can be defended with the notion that the "people" often refers to the upper classes. In either case, the tension is apparent.

20. Note that here Nehemiah asserts his authority to build as granted by the "God of Heaven," which may well be a reference to the imperial approval expressed by the Persian emperor in the name of Ahura Mazda.

21. Blenkinsopp, *Ezra-Nehemiah*, 193.

22. This corresponds to the list of ethnicities in Ezra 9:1, which focuses on the old "people of the land" that had inhabited Palestine and especially the Jerusalem area since before the settlement and who continued as problematic even through the monarchy.

CHAPTER 8

STABILITY AND PLURALISM: THE LATE PERSIAN PERIOD (423–333 B.C.E.)

THE HEBREW BIBLE CONTAINS no literature that clearly demonstrates a date in the second half of the Persian Empire, after Artaxerxes I. Certainly much of the extant literature from the Hebrew Bible derives from this late Persian period, but none of the dates is secure. Thus the historical information about this period is of high significance because of its impact on the biblical literature written during this time as well as the material written before and transmitted through this period. However, it proves impossible to trace the precise influences. In general, the Persian Empire declined during its second half. The dissipative wars against Greece continued and intensified. Economic problems became increasingly manifest. The pluralism of the empire increased, especially as areas such as Yehud experienced a greater mix of Greek and Persian cultural influences. These general factors affected the second half of the Persian Empire in varying manners and degrees.

It should also be noted that the quality and the character of the primary sources for the second century of the Persian Empire differ substantially from those available for the first century. In the earlier years, the Persian emperors left a variety of records that are still extant, including inscriptions on monuments as well as larger texts from some recovered archives. There is no such material that chronicles the latter years of the Persian Empire. Furthermore, the wider range of colonial and provincial records is also lacking for the period now in view. Thus the only extensive available sources for the late Persian period are the Greek historiographies, which tell of palace intrigues more than of other events and which tend to focus on the seamier sides of Persian imperial life. The tendencies of these sources tinge the contemporary understanding of late Persian history.

Darius II (423–404 B.C.E.)

Upon the death of Artaxerxes I, the Persian Empire recognized Xerxes II, Artaxerxes' only son by Queen Damaspia, as successor in Susa. Within forty-five days, Secydianus, a son of Artaxerxes I by the Babylonian concubine Alogune, assassinated Xerxes II. Secydianus then demanded that his half brother, Ochus, who had been satrap of Hyrcania and later of Babylon, return to Susa. Most likely, Secydianus meant to kill Ochus.

However, Ochus delayed his return to the capital until he had won over the cavalry's commander, Arbarius. With the support of the imperial military, Babylonia declared Ochus to be the next emperor on February 13, 423 B.C.E. Ochus took the royal name Darius II.[1]

Darius II was a weak king. His wife, Parysatis, who was his half sister, exercised extreme influence upon Darius II, often in directions of cruelty. Throughout the empire, disagreements about the use of power abounded. Egypt provides one of the clearest examples. Under Darius II, a satrap controlled Egypt with strict use of the Jewish mercenary force based at Elephantine. The presence of this military encampment in the middle of the Nile caused a significant irritation to Egypt, which persecuted and repeatedly attacked this mercenary base. As early as 419 B.C.E., Darius II had to command that the garrison be left alone to practice its own religion, as shown by the Passover Papyrus. For political reasons the Egyptians destroyed the Jewish temple of Yahu at Elephantine in 410 B.C.E.[2]

Relations between Persia and the colonies remained tense. A series of rebellions began in 413 B.C.E. with the revolt of Pissuthnes, satrap of Sardis, but most of Greece stayed loyal. A short Median revolt, an attempt by the eunuch Atroaxares to make himself emperor, and a conspiracy in Hyrcania of the king's relatives were all defeated. More wars with Greece and others in the northeastern Mediterranean consumed Persian attention in 410–405 B.C.E. By 404 B.C.E., even Athens had been starved into submission by the Persian general Cyrus (Darius' son) and their Spartan allies, and Persia won the war.[3] In 404 B.C.E., while attempting to defeat a rebellion in Media, Darius fell ill and returned to Babylon, where he died in March of 404 B.C.E.[4]

Artaxerxes II (404–359 B.C.E.)

Arsaces took his grandfather's name, Artaxerxes, upon accession. Artaxerxes II soon faced a revolt in 402 B.C.E., led by his younger brother Cyrus, who had won the loyalty of all Ionia except Miletus and who was supported by ten thousand Greek mercenaries.[5] Many parts of the empire still remained loyal to Artaxerxes II, and the rebellion failed. Near 368 B.C.E., Artaxerxes II faced a much more severe threat, a simultaneous rebellion by several of the satraps. This rebellion was not quenched in Artaxerxes II's lifetime. These extensive revolts nearly brought an end to the Persian Empire.

The Egyptians also revolted. In 405 B.C.E., Amyrtaeus rebelled, and on September 3, 401 B.C.E., the decisive battle between Cyrus and Artaxerxes II was fought. Artaxerxes II was wounded, but Cyrus was killed.[6]

Tissaphernes, the successor of Cyrus in Anatolia, demanded that Ionia recognize the Persian Empire in 400 B.C.E. But the Ionian cities in fear asked Sparta for help, and Sparta issued Tissaphernes an ultimatum. Thus Ionia and Sparta allied themselves together against the Persian Empire. A year of intense fighting produced a standoff, and in 398 B.C.E., a one-year truce was announced for diplomacy. However, these attempts soon proved unsuccessful. Persia reentered the fighting with renewed force. In 396 B.C.E., Tissaphernes returned with more troops as well as with a naval fleet under the direction of Conon. Persia soon succeeded in separating Rhodes from Sparta. The Persian Empire's armies made good progress against the Greeks, but palace intrigue changed the course of the war. Parysatis, the wife and half sister of Darius II, and now the Queen Mother of Artaxerxes II, conspired against Tissaphernes, and the court machinations soon led to his death, leaving the Persian military campaign without a leader.

Unable to pursue the battles further without the military capabilities of Tissaphernes, the Persian Empire offered terms to Greece, and the Greeks turned back and accepted peace and freedom on the condition of the payment of the taxes as dictated in times past. This lasted until 394 B.C.E., when Agesilaus desired a campaign into Cappadocia. Persia, however, had not wasted the intervening year of shaky peace. The Persian Empire had conspired with other nations and had created a European coalition against Sparta. This alliance ambushed the Spartan ships at sea and destroyed them, ending Sparta's attempted revolt.

In 387 B.C.E., the cessation of war in Greece developed into a widespread Pax Persica, in which Persia exerted control throughout the Greek isles. The Persian Empire oversaw the dismantling of the Athenian and Spartan hegemonies, and the Persians forcibly emigrated many peoples into the various Greek cities. Even though the Persians could subdue Greece through the massive use of force, the economy throughout the rest of the empire was sufficiently poor to create widespread unrest. The army could not control the vast stretches of the imperial territory, and so control loosened. Many areas did not revolt, although they were able to exercise enhanced freedoms during this time. The Pax Persica referred not only to a cessation of violence and revolt but to a decrease in direct imperial involvement throughout the colonies and borders of the Persian Empire. Taxes were high, but they may not have been collected with great regularity. To avoid the inciting of riots and rebellions, taxes would remain unmentioned until a more sizable contingent of the army was nearby.

In such fashion, Nepherites I, the founder of the XXIX Dynasty, acceeded to the rule of Egypt at Memphis in 398 B.C.E. He was a worshiper of the ram god, Khnoum. From 400 to 380 B.C.E., Egypt was active in Palestine in attempts to gain independence from Persia. The inscriptions by the Egyptian Neferites I (399–393 B.C.E.) at Gezer and by the Persian general Achoris (393–380 B.C.E.) at Acco and Sidon reflect this Egyptian presence. Again, the Pax Persica of Artaxerxes II demonstrates a lesser degree of interference from Persia in the affairs of the locals. However, Achoris attacked rebellious Egypt, which had learned Greek naval tactics and built new fortifications under Chabrias. The war of 385–383 B.C.E. ended in Egypt's continued independence, and Achoris left inscriptions in Palestine and Phoenicia to indicate his continued rule there. Persian control of Palestine did not extend into Egypt, but the border of the Persian Empire remained beyond Yehud.

A small reversal occurred about 360 B.C.E. Sparta was defeated in the year 362 by pro-Persian Thebes. The Egyptian ruler Nekhtenebef died in 360 B.C.E., and successors were disorganized. This disorganization allowed the Persian Empire its brief respite. For a few years at the end of Artaxerxes II's reign, Persia could maintain its *pax* with reduced effort.

Artaxerxes II had 115 sons from 360 concubines, but only three were sons of Queen Stateira: Darius, Ariaspes, and Ochus.[7] When Artaxerxes II was away at war, Darius as the elder son was appointed heir apparent. However, Tiribazus encouraged Darius in his impatience for his father's death, and they entered into a conspiracy with fifty of the king's other sons. Darius was caught when the conspiracy was betrayed; Artaxerxes II killed him. Ochus deceived Ariaspes into thinking that he had earned Artaxerxes' disfavor, and so Ariaspes poisoned himself. Ochus also arranged the murder of a favorite son, Arsames. In grief, Artaxerxes II died in 359 B.C.E.

Artaxerxes III (359–338 B.C.E.)

Ochus succeeded to the throne as Artaxerxes III because of his machinations in removing competing alternatives. His savagery had already been shown. It was confirmed through his first official act: the murder of all relatives, of all ages and of both genders.[8]

In 356 B.C.E. the Greek allies revolted, and Mausolus of Lycia took Rhodes, Byzantium, and others into a new confederacy, ruling it as a thoroughly hellenized Oriental ruler. This despot had no loyalties or connections to the Persian imperial court. Mausollus, however, convinced the Athenians that he was operating as the representative of Artaxerxes III Ochus, and thus the Greeks were hesitant to attack him. Persia allied itself with Thebes as a Mediterranean naval power. By 355 B.C.E. the Greeks had been subdued through battles, intrigues, and diplomacy.

In Egypt, Nekht-har-hebi undertook a large building campaign, winning the support of the priests. But Artaxerxes III was preparing an Egyptian campaign, first by occupying Phoenicia, where Strato of Sidon was conquered and replaced by Tennes. But after fighting in 351–350 B.C.E., Artaxerxes III retired from the battle, and Nekht-har-hebi was victorious. In Greece, Aristotle argued against allowing the Egyptians to be defeated by Persia, suggesting that such would merely be the prelude to a Persian invasion of Greece. However, Artemisia, satrap of Caria, tricked Rhodes in a major defeat. Sidon revolted after Artaxerxes' inability to conquer Egypt but was suppressed. However, the Phoenicians soon voted to secede from the empire. In Macedonia, a new Greek revolt arose under the leadership of Philip. In 346 B.C.E. continental Greece reached a truce, recognizing Philip as the outstanding leader of the Greek city-states, and the coalition encouraged him to take up arms against Persia.

In 345 B.C.E. Artaxerxes III marched against Sidon as a prelude to another full-fledged Egyptian campaign. In response to the Persian siege, Sidon closed itself off and burned all of itself to ruin, killing its people and leaving Artaxerxes III without plunder to finance further raids. Artaxerxes III then went on to Egypt. He asked Greece for mercenaries. Athens refused, but made a nonaggression pact with Persia. Thebes sent a thousand soldiers, and nine thousand other mercenaries came as well. The whole army was led by Bagohi, Artaxerxes III's chief eunuch. However, Egypt also had hired fifteen thousand mercenaries but refused to attack at the most opportune time, since Nekht-har-hebi had been promised in a dream, on July 5, 343 B.C.E., that it would be best to wait until the coming flood season. Thus the Persians were able to take advantage of timing, and they conquered Egypt. Nekht-har-hebi fled to Ethiopia; Artaxerxes III himself killed the Apis bull and put an ass in its place.

When the Persian Empire under Artaxerxes III reasserted its historic control over

Phoenicia and Egypt, Macedonia and other pro-Macedonian Greeks panicked and feared for their own loss of independence. Philip saw that Persia had just been strengthened immensely, especially in naval military might, and Philip asked for peace with Artaxerxes III. In 341 B.C.E., Athens established an embassy with Persia. This encouraged Persia to send some of its affiliates with Athens to keep Philip limited to Perinthus in 340 B.C.E. At the time that Philip defeated the Greeks at Charoneia (338 B.C.E.), the eunuch Bagohi had the royal physician poison Artaxerxes III.

Darius III (336–331 B.C.E.)

From 338 to 335 B.C.E., Arses ruled the Persian Empire.[9] Arses was a legitimate son of Artaxerxes III Ochus by Atossa. Immediately upon Arses' accession, Philip of Macedon formed a Greek League at Corinth and demanded reparations from Persia for its aid in Philip's defeat at Perinthus. When Arses refused in early 337 B.C.E., Philip became commander-in-chief. By early 336 B.C.E., ten thousand Macedonians began the liberation of Asian Greek cities.

Arses objected to Bagohi's influence and attempted to poison him. This failed, but Arses became a victim of the drought of 336 B.C.E. Bagohi killed all of Arses' relatives and gave the throne to Darius, the satrap of Armenia, who was forty-five years old. Darius III was the son of Arsames, the son of Ostanes, the brother of Artaxerxes II. Thus the Achaemenid imperial dynasty passed into the hands of a distant relative for its last rule. Bagohi found Darius III intractable and attempted poisoning; Darius discovered the ploy and forced Bagohi to drink the cup.

In July of 336 B.C.E., Philip was killed, perhaps by Persian agents, perhaps by Alexander or his mother, Olympias. The throne of Macedon passed to Philip's son, Alexander. The new king Alexander turned first to the problems within Macedonian-occupied territory. However, the intrigues and assassinations in Persia had allowed Egypt's revolt in late 337 B.C.E. Darius attempted the reconquest of Egypt, and he was accepted as king of Egypt on January 14, 334 B.C.E. This placed the power of the Persian troops in Egypt, well to the south of Greece. With this opening, Alexander launched the crusade that his father had wished to start, leading over thirty-five thousand troops in battle against a relatively undefended Persia.[10]

The battle of Granicus, the first battle, was decisive. Most of the Persian generals were killed, and Alexander killed most of the Greek mercenaries who had fought for Persia. Alexander freed the cities they passed, ended taxation, and restored the cities, placing Greek culture in Asia in a new way. After this, Alexander proceeded steadily to the center of the Persian Empire. Persepolis itself was destroyed in February of 330 B.C.E.

Darius III had to overcome revolts by the various subjects and also deal with the threats posed by the rebellious satraps, who by this time wielded power much like that of feudal lords. However, the final blow came not from inside but from the west that had been unconquerable since the time of Darius I, nearly two centuries earlier. Alexander of Macedonia took Asia Minor and then the rest of Persia. By 331 B.C.E., Alexander the Great was the emperor of the known world, and the Persian Empire had reached its end.

Yehud under the Late Persian Emperors

The sure knowledge about Yehud under the last century of Persian rule is embarrassingly small. The sources are meager, whether one examines the Persian material, the biased Greek sources, or the Hebrew Bible records. Still, some patterns appear to be likely.

Yehud's politics probably continued in a form similar to that of the prior century. There are no records of major restructuring in Persian colonial administration. Even though this argues from silence, the form of local governors assisted by appointed priests and other officials seems adequately stable throughout Persian history and the extent of the empire.

Militarily, Yehud probably experienced some occasional pressures from Persia as well as from Egypt which also invaded Palestine in attempts to drive back the Persian control. The conflicting military presence would have been particularly strong at times, such as 401–380 B.C.E., when Egyptian influences over the region were strongest. Also, in 351–343 B.C.E. and 337–334 B.C.E., Persia succeeded in defeating Egypt, and the requisite armies for such a conquest might well have impacted Yehud. However, almost nothing is known about the precise paths of these armies, and so their exact effect on the small colony of Yehud would be most uncertain.

The economics of the Persian Empire throughout this time period probably, although not certainly, represented a slow decline, in accord with the general trends established earlier in the empire's history. As taxation increased to pay for wars of decreasing returns, the colonies and the shrinking tax base of the empire had to support an increasingly higher percentage of the imperial funding needs. This would have encouraged a continuation of the imperial economic practices of depletion. However, at the same time Persia's ability to enforce taxes would have diminished as its hegemony over the most distant provinces faded. Thus taxation may not have become more severe; it may have become more uneven in its distribution.

Culturally, the impact of other regions upon Yehud's culture would have grown. The Egyptian influences during 401–380 B.C.E. would have provided new cultural inputs into Yehudite society. Likewise, the increase in Greek trade would have brought new technology, new styles, and new ideas into the cultural milieu of Yehud. Certainly the literature, ideology, and lifestyles of this period will likely reflect increasing Greek influences.

The religious life of Yehud during the final century of Persian rule would have been affected by the relative autonomy of the colony. Persian control mechanisms were breaking down, and after the interventions of Darius, Xerxes, and Artaxerxes I there are no obvious references to Persian imperial interference with Yehud's free practice of its religion. In all likelihood, this would have increased the variety of expression of that worship, since there would have been no external pressures to choose one type of religious practice over another. Pluralism in religion, especially in the light of an influx of Greek thought, would have flourished as the Persian Empire's influence ended.

Notes

1. Olmstead, *History of the Persian Empire*, 355; and Dandamaev, *Political History*, 258–69.
2. Widengren, "The Persians," 327–29; and Olmstead, *History of the Persian Empire*, 364–66.

3. Dandamaev, *Political History*, 274–85; and Olmstead, *History of the Persian Empire*, 358–70.

4. Olmstead, *History of the Persian Empire*, 371.

5. For a fuller description of the events during the reign of Artaxerxes II, see Widengren, "The Persians," 329–30; and Olmstead, *History of the Persian Empire*, 373–424.

6. Dandamaev, *Political History*, 295–305.

7. Dandamaev, *Political History*, 306, offers higher numbers: 366 wives and concubines and 150 sons.

8. For details of Artaxerxes III's reign, see Olmstead, *History of the Persian Empire*, 424–89; Widengren, "The Persians," 330; and idem, "The Persian Period," 500–501.

9. For further information on the reign of Darius III, see Olmstead, *History of the Persian Empire*, 489–524.

10. Dandamaev, *Political History*, 313–32.

PART III

THE DIALECTICS OF COLONIAL SOCIETY

CHAPTER 9

GOVERNORS AND THE LAW: POLITICAL AND SOCIAL MAINTENANCE

THE PERSIAN EMPIRE USED a legal, bureaucratic style of imperial management in order to create Yehud as a Persian colony. Although the Jerusalem area's transition from Babylonian property to Persian province probably produced a few immediate changes in daily life for most of the occupants, the new empire used law to produce a new organizational entity.[1] Throughout Yehud's time as a Persian province, the Persian imperial administration selected its government and enforced its own laws on the people of Yehud. Of course, this process varied in intensity throughout Yehud's history; at times, Persia's influence was more dictatorial and oppressive, and at other times it was more beneficent. Nevertheless, at all times Persia kept Yehud within this role as province or colony, as constructed by the empire itself.

Organizational structures within Yehudite society contributed to the creation of the province. Power flowed in fixed patterns, and all these patterns shaped social life in the province. There were also significant ideological components, such as law and the concepts of royalty and empire. Other effects of the creation of a province include material and economic impact of population, trade, taxation, and military presence. In all of these ways, the Persian Empire created the entity of colonial Yehud as part of its own program of expansion and imperium. Whereas the inhabitants of the Jerusalem area had been a relatively nonorganized group before the beginning of the Persian Empire, the advent of imperial organization allowed Persia as a state to encroach upon that populace and to transform this group of people into a state of its own, albeit highly dependent upon the more extensive structures of the Persian Empire.[2]

Imperial and Royal Ideology in Colonial Yehud

The intrusion of the bureaucratic, imperial state of Persia's Achaemenid dynasty brought new ideologies to the Jerusalem area. Chief among these were new and revived notions of the state and royalty.[3] Although Jerusalem itself had been the center for the Davidic dynasty and its monarchy for over four centuries, there had been no monarchy, not even as a puppet government, for a half century at the advent of the Persian empire. Thus no one within Yehud had extensive experience and memories of Jerusalem as a state center.

Instead, the inhabitants had spent their lives within a region with a much more informal, almost tribal structure. There were no kings during the exile, even though there were inhabitants and thus a society. The appearance of the Persian Empire meant that this region became once more a part of a state. Even though the state of monarchic Judah was gone, never to reappear in its former reality, these people now experienced both the state of imperial Persia and the state of colonial Yehud as Persia's extension and local manifestation.

The Definition of a State

The reoccurrence of the state in the Jerusalem area ushered in a variety of changes. Existence as a state differs markedly from pre-state experience. At its base, the state is a centralized governmental agency, a collectivity of forces, persons, and goals with related motivations and powers and a shared identity.[4] This centralized government controls the power to enforce laws, to collect taxes, and to conscript labor. States administer these powers over a confined geographic area, and they exercise these powers in the midst of multiple communities within that area.[5] In other words, states are larger than more naturally forming communities, such as small families or tribes. Instead, states contain groups that identify themselves as groups separate from others inside the same state. For individuals, membership in a state is in addition to membership in a smaller social circle; a state is therefore a community of communities that could exist outside a state structure, however related with the larger structure they happen to be.

By this definition of a state, the Persian Empire meets the criteria, and Yehud does by extension. Persia centralized governmental powers into the Achaemenid family, especially the emperor, and the governments designees throughout the empire. Personal loyalty to the emperor became a chief requirement for public service within the imperial bureaucracies, furthering the degree of centralization. Some of the Persian emperors kept the most powerful positions within their own extended family or within families of nobles who had proven their loyalty to the Achaemenid house throughout generations. Certainly the powers of government were highly centralized, especially when one considers the vast geographic expanse of the empire and the slowness of communication across those distances. Throughout the empire, the Achaemenids extended their powers to make and enforce laws, to collect taxes, and to conscript labor. Typically, the empire hired labor for governmental tasks, whether craftspersons for construction work or mercenaries for military service, but conscription was available to the empire. Furthermore, the Persian Empire succeeded in bringing together many smaller communities, as vastly varied as the states of Media, Persia, Babylonia, and Egypt, along with other territories such as India, Palestine, and the northern and eastern boundary areas. Despite the vast cultural, economic, and language barriers between such peoples, the Persian Empire unified them, at least at the governmental level.

Likewise, Yehud exhibited some of the signs of a state, albeit a state dependent upon the Persian Empire as a whole to maintain its own power. Yehud possessed its own centralized governmental agencies, embodied in the person of the governor and located in Jerusalem, working out of the rebuilt temple and supported by that temple's personnel, including the high priest. The extant biblical sources list three governors of Yehud: Zerubbabel, Ezra, and Nehemiah.[6] Presumably there were Persian governors of Yehud at all times throughout the Persian Empire's control of the region. Through these Persian governors and the local resources at their disposal, Persia collected taxes and enforced laws. From the perspective of its inhabitants, Yehud functioned as its own state. The influences of the Persian Empire were not felt directly. Instead, the Persians worked through their agents in Yehudite leadership, and they exercised the local control of government. At times, there may have been extensive freedom about exactly how the local leaders carried out Persian policies.

Yehud also functioned as a community of communities. Even though Yehud itself was small and possessed a low population, there was still substantial variety within the populace. Nehemiah indicates the presence of different langauges among the people (Nehemiah 13:23-24), and the variety of ethnicities and political persuasions is obvious at several points throughout the Persian period.[7] Clearly, Yehud represented several different groups and factions that at times conflicted with one another. There was no general, natural harmony among the inhabitants of Yehud but instead a politically managed unity enforced through the powers of the state, whether the state of Yehud or that of the Persian Empire.[8]

The Introduction and Maintenance of a State

When the Persian Empire introduced the state organization into the Jerusalem area, it created a wide range of changes within Jerusalemite society. The introduction of a state always produces friction and tension. The society inevitably changes as different forms of political organization reorient the society's power relationships, shifting in order to favor groups different from those which had previously received privilege. Although conflict occurs in all introductions of state organizations, not all such societal shifts proceed in the same pattern.

When states extend themselves into nonstate areas by military means, the opposition is clear and often violent. However, this was not the case with Persia's statist intrusion into Jerusalem to form Yehud. Instead, the process relied heavily upon the immigration of a new class of citizens for Jerusalem. These immigrants were distinct ethnically and culturally; certainly there were differences of birth location and language. In general, these immigrants probably considered themselves to be the true inheritors of the Davidic monarchy and Jerusalem's past; they often termed themselves "Jews" in distinction to the inhabitants of the land whose families had not experienced the dislocation of exile at the beginning of the sixth century.[9] Immigration became Persia's chief means for exerting state influence upon Yehud.

The Persian Empire also exercised other means for state extension. As with many state expansions, there is a strong pattern of ideological justification. Persia could have used solely military means for introducing and maintaining its imperial power in Yehud, but military force is always expensive.[10] Instead, the more efficient states such as the Persian Empire rely on symbolic means for the extension of the state organization. Since states are themselves symbolic realities that impinge upon human social structuring, individual commitment to the symbolic universe of state ideology is vital. Once individuals accept state ideology and adhere to the symbolic universe of an empire, their actions tend to reflect their symbol systems. In other words, the inhabitants who believe they are in a state will act in accord with the belief and will then behave according to the desires of the state, as embodied in their leaders.[11]

The symbolic means for extending state authority can vary. Ceremonies and shared rituals are common means for expressing shared symbolic universes, and this ritual construction of reality will be examined in detail below. Similarly, written symbols and the ideological patterns represented therein provide important motivations for the acceptance of the state system. Therefore the attention given below also focuses on the use of writing and rigidly constructed verbal symbol systems, especially the law to be enforced by those governors as extensions of an expanding state. Before we continue to discuss these considerations, however, it is necessary for us to investigate Yehud's particular mode of state development as an extension of a larger state with bureaucratic, imperial organization.[12]

Yehud as a Secondary State

Persia's expansion as an imperialistic state impacted the Jerusalem area through the creation of a secondary state within it, to be known as Yehud. A secondary state results from the intrusion of a developed state into a nonstate area.[13] Yehud's role as a secondary state limited its own development during the Persian period because it could not control its own destiny. Instead, the Persian Empire directed its development in ways that maximized the benefit to the empire. Thus, with each successive emperor, Persia advanced its own exploitation of Yehudite society and economy.[14]

The chief means for imperial domination of Yehud's development as a state came through the appointment of governmental leaders and through the regulation of taxation. The economic effects of taxation were clear; Persia controlled the flow of funds into and out of Yehud by changing taxation rates and alternately funding practices such as temple construction and worship. Governors provided more direct political control over the society, in addition to their primary role of regulating taxes and enforcing the basic laws of the empire. Military presence backed the governors' pronouncements, although there is no clear indication that Persia ever used its army against Yehud itself. Still, the nearness of the army and the knowledge of its ability to devastate the province would have proved to be a continual factor toward stability and loyalty within Yehud.

In most cases, Yehud received as much freedom in its internal affairs as would still allow the Persian Empire to gain the maximum amount of taxation and resources from it. This required that Yehud maintain an internal order. Persia tolerated few threats to its own security; Yehudite loyalty and internal peace were essential. Just as Persia constructed Yehud through its symbolic universe, Persia would have maintained its control over the province through an emphasis on order, including symbols of cosmic harmony. One would expect Yehud to produce literature that emphasized such order, including wisdom literature and other explanations of creation.[15] Creation stories and symbols undergird the perceptions of the status quo by linking contemporary perceptions of reality and social order with a created origin. Creation stories explain current social existence by rooting it in God and God's intentions for the world.[16] Fertility symbols and promises would connect the immediate future's prosperity to loyal actions in the present (see Haggai 2:6-9). All of these literary themes reflect an investment in maintenance of order;

there is an order to all reality, constructed within this reality by the intentions of creation itself, that works in favor of hard work in the service of one's leaders.

A more visible sign of this investment is the temple and other royal construction projects. Darius led the Persian Empire to fund the construction of a temple in Jerusalem, and this provided a physical symbol for the new state community of Yehud. The temple was a physical center for the new state and also functioned as a civic and political locus. Through the temple, the Persian Empire supervised the collection of taxes and issued its laws; around the temple the community of Yehud conducted its debates about its own shifting, adjusting values. Because of taxation and Persian funding, the temple served as a financial interchange between the state of Persia and the secondary state of Yehud.

The temple also served as a symbolic legitimation of the relationship between these states. The temple served as a trapping of royalty, and thus it equated the local Yehudite leadership with the imperium of Persia. Both were involved in the construction in cooperative fashion, and both shared the benefits (both financial and symbolic) of the temple's operation. Thus, when Haggai argued that Yahweh's goals for Yehud were the same as Persia's goals, this prophet prefigured the ideology of the temple, the construction of which he encourages. Furthermore, the temple communicated a rich ideology of the service of God, involving strict rules of morality and means for correcting mistakes. This priestly thought (present in the Second Temple in much the same way as the First Temple of the Davidic Judean monarchy) organized reality in ways that protected the status quo and maintained the already-constructed sense of reality.[17]

Through the temple and the creation, wisdom, and legal literature of the period, Yehud's symbolic construction of reality encouraged the sense of Yehud as a unified state within a much larger world. Morality is a significant theme of this period, as is the maintenance of God's created intentions for the world. All of these symbols describe a reality that is sharply limited; the proper life exists within certain limits of wisdom or morality. Observation of and respect for these limits provides the secret to proper action. This translates well into an ideology for a secondary state, where life itself depends upon the proper levels of productivity for the imperial state. Proper relationships are important, not only between God and humanity and among humans themselves but also especially between Yehud and Persia.

Legitimation of the Persian Empire through Semiroyal Ideology

As Yehud developed as a secondary state as a result of the intrusion of Persian imperial state organization, an ideology grew to match this newfound colonial status. As a state, Yehud developed for itself the trappings of royalty, but these symbols were limited by Yehud's condition as a secondary state in a province of the Persian Empire. Yehud could not express itself as a sovereign nation-state but did develop symbols of social cohesion and of dedication to its leaders.

Perhaps nowhere was this semiroyal ideology clearer than in the case of the governor. The role of governor was exalted as God's special chosen one, at least from the time of Zerubbabel (Haggai 2:20-23). The very preservation of memoirs of Ezra and Nehemiah, two later governors, argues for the positive perception of these figures, even apart from the content of their books. The literature records the great deeds of these two in sharp detail and the highest terms; they are persons of prayer and dedication to God who undertake their activities with no consideration for personal safety or gain but think only of service to God and to the Persian emperor with whose backing they labor.

Despite these positive portrayals, there is no indication of messianism. That is, there is no evidence that Yehud understood any of its governors as political leaders behind whom the populace should rally in rebellion to the Persian Empire.[18] The very language used to discuss the governors emphasized their Persian allegiance. They were called *peḥah*, "governor," instead of some more explicitly royal title such as "king" or "chief."[19] Yehud consistently avoided any reference to kings that could create a perception of competition with the Persian government.[20] Instead, the governors cooperated with Persia in administration of Yehud. In this light, it is not surprising that the three known governors had either Babylonian names (Zerubbabel) or explicit roots in the Persian court (Ezra and Nehemiah). The governors' loyalty attached itself firmly to the Persian Empire who employed them.

Yehud was thus a new political entity, created as a result of Persian expansion and administered in cooperation with Persia for the purpose of supporting Persia's needs for income and border security. Although the state of Yehud was a new creation, the creation was not *ex nihilo*. The immigration of a new elite class provided a group with strong cultural ties to Babylonia and Persia, along with some ethnic, cultural, and religious connections to the long-standing traditions of the Davidic dynasty and its temple. On the other hand, the native Yehudite population continued many of the same traditions from the Judean monarchy. The combination of these traditions produced many of the conflicts in the Persian colony of Yehud. The language and culture descended from the prior centuries, despite the changes through the sixth century. Persian rule also created a number of cultural shifts, but the general mandate from Persia to find an effective, low-expense, indigenous mode of government encouraged Yehud's administration to change as little as possible from the previous culture in the Jerusalem area.

Thus the political legitimation of the new states of Persia and Yehud, as well as their interrelationship, expressed itself in ways that conserved as many elements of the previous symbolic universe while still shifting the emphasis into a support for the new colonial state system. New symbols emphasized the power of the new governmental systems. These tendencies can be seen in the Behistun inscription and other such symbol representations of the new imperial power. At Behistun, the new Persian Empire carved a huge, widely visible statement and portrait of its power, expressing the ability of Darius to conquer those who opposed him. Other symbolic acts, ranging from Cyrus' edict to the varying responses to Egypt's Apis bull, communicated the same perspectives as part of the symbolic universe of the empire.

In order to maintain political order, the Persian state popularized a sense of cosmic order. Local gods received the proper worship under the guidance of the earlier emperors, so that God could bless the establishment of the Persian Empire with proper cosmic order and local earthly fertility, all in service of Persia. Persia's preferred deity was Ahura Mazda, a sky god. Corresponding aspects of local deities became more popular. For instance, the books of Ezra and Nehemiah refer to Yahweh as the God of Heaven, a title rare in the rest of the Hebrew Bible but a title that presents the deity as a guarantor of cosmic order in the same way that Ahura Mazda functioned. God brings harmony between heaven and earth and also in the human realm, when states cooperate for the common good, as defined by the dominant state.

Of course, such symbolic legitimation is never perfect. That is, there are always conflicts and differences of orientation. Isaiah 56–66 records such a conflict, as does Nehemiah 5. When the construction of a symbolic universe to support the empire failed, the Persian Empire had other means of economic coercion and even military force, and the empire used these more costly means to enforce its own will. In Yehud, however, the evidence indicates that at most points in the colony's history it was willing to accept Persian rule in order to keep receiving the favors granted by the worldview of the empire. In other words, Yehud understood its place within the Persian Empire and perceived its own benefit in maintaining that position.

Law

Through its constituent native and immigrant groups, the community of Yehud inherited substantial literary traditions from the Judean monarchy. These literary traditions included legal writings that governed social behavior and religious regulations that legislated the activity of the cult. Legal codes are sets of symbols creating a universe of proper relations among humans, but they also construct a symbolic relationship between the lawgiver and the legal adherent. Israel's heritage of law marked one of its greatest and longest-lasting legacies, but in the Persian period it was much newer and more dynamic.

Orality and Written Documents

Yehud's law existed in both oral and written form. The law had begun during monarchic Israel or earlier as an oral body of information about how communities should deal with certain problems. In the ancient Near East, villages and cities often constructed obelisks on their borders to serve as a written form of that oral law, but literacy rates were so low that written law made little sense for most people. Laws were customs rather than written statements demanding adherence to the letter.

For most of Yehud's inhabitants, written law was still a strange concept. The villagers and the occupants of the rural areas would have had low rates of literacy. The upper classes and those who dwelt in Jerusalem, on the other hand, would have had higher rates of literacy, or at least access to servants or colleagues who could read. For them, written law became more pragmatic, and it allowed for a standardization of the legal codes.

Of course, the writing of law produced situations of differential power. Those who could read and could receive access to the few written copies could know the rules that the society would enforce upon all of its residents. Poor and rural people, on the other hand, had no access to these documents, even though such writings controlled their behavior. The situation was ripe for abuse; those who could read could interpret the law in ways beneficial to their own social class. At best, however, the writing of the law could standardize the societal norms for persons around a wider region. Such commonality of societal norms and laws would create a sense of union among the communities that shared such law, and so a standardized legal code matched well the tendencies of the Persian Empire in constructing social shared identity.

The Persian Empire also used the construction and promulgation of law codes to unify its entire imperial administrative structure. Although apparently there was no attempt to produce one law for the whole empire, Darius I attempted a partial standardization of law throughout the empire's colonies. Under his reign, the Babylonians and the Egyptians, presumably as well as other Persian-ruled colonies, codified their earlier religious and legal traditions and produced single, unified statements of their own native law. Certainly the Persian Empire did have some influence upon the content of that law, but the exact extent is unknown.

The King's Law and the Canonization of Pentateuchal Law

With the presence of imperially produced legal codes in other parts of the Persian Empire, one wonders whether Darius combined earlier Israelite and Yehudite traditions and promulgated them in Yehud as new law. Certainly the presence of "the King's Law" in Yehud argues in favor of this.[21] Darius and subsequent Persian emperors considered one form of Yehud's legal legacy to be normative and thus enforceable by the imperial bureaucracy. This allowed this small province to set its own norms for behavior, while at the same time the Persian Empire had influence upon the general course of its internal affairs. Yehud possessed its own law within the Persian Empire, as did Babylonia and Egypt as imperial provinces.

If Darius combined earlier Israelite religious and legal traditions to produce this King's Law in Yehud, what extant materials formed this document? Such redactional questions lead the scholar to consider the redaction of the Pentateuch. Most scholars agree that the first five books of the Hebrew Bible, Genesis through Deuteronomy, were in much of their final form early in the Persian period. Since this block of literary material contains almost all of the legal codes of the Hebrew Bible, it seems reasonable to assume that Darius' interest would have focused here.

If current redactional theories of the Pentateuch are correct, then the early Persian period saw the final writing of the Pentateuchal materials and the assemblage into their final form, as the last Pentateuchal source (known as P as a reflection of its priestly interests) was put into writing and as the entire volume was edited together.[22] A conjecture can then be offered: Darius assembled these materials and promulgated them in order to support his own imperial project of legal standardization. Although there had been a variety of Israelite and later Yehudite religious texts and even though the editing sponsored by Darius might have changed only little within the texts, the Persian Empire published these documents in an attempt to maintain social order and to define the Yehudites by their own distinctive legal code, now enforced within the confines of the Persian imperial structure.

If this conjecture is right, then the Pentateuch is a strange document, both internal and external at the same time. It is internal in that it represents the old Israelite traditions that had formed monarchic identity and had become the cultural basis for Yehud's own existence, but the Pentateuch is also external in that its final form represents Persia's imposition of a text upon Yehud. Persia not only promulgated a law for Yehud to obey but presented a story that defined who Yehud was. This external definition rhetorically limited Yehud's own self-understanding and kept it within certain ideological confines. With a Pentateuchal story ending at Deuteronomy, Israel existed on the edge of the land, ever poised at the point of entering an autonomous existence. This land was a gift from God—but it was a gift that could be taken away at any moment. As such, God's gift of the land was very much like Persia's gift of the land. If the people obeyed, then they would retain the land, but their sin and rebellion could easily result in destruction.[23]

The internal/external paradox of the Pentateuch reflects well the nature of canonicity. A canon tells one's own story but in a normative way. The canon, through the external process of a community's insistence upon it, forces itself to be the reader's story, displacing other stories and identities. The Persian Empire provided this identity for Yehud, along with the laws that gave specific guidance in daily life. This story provided the official symbolic universe for Yehud's corporate life.[24]

At the same time, the story had less impact on the Yehudites outside Jerusalem. A written text is less able to displace stories of nonliterate people, except more slowly through transmission by the Jerusalemites. In the rural areas, greater dependency upon oral tradition would have resisted the intrusion of this new canon. Still, the priestly influences upon the villagers would have gradually brought the Pentateuchal canon into near-universal acceptance among all Yehudites.

Cosmic Order, Social Order

If the Pentateuch represents a canon both designed and approved by those in cooperation with the Persian Empire, then what can be said about the Pentateuch's themes? Certainly the influence by Persia and the need for a strong role within the Persian Empire would have shaped the text's transmission and canonization and also its content, or at least the ancient reader's sense of dominant themes.

Since the documents contain law, there is a great emphasis on social order. People receive instruction on how to live correctly, so that society does not need to intervene in order to correct behavior. Yehudite law, as with all legal codes at least in intention, strives to minimize deviance and to affirm each person's place within the social order. The Yehudite texts ground this law in a narrative, and the narrative moves toward the same points of social order.

The narrative's beginning is in a creation text (Genesis 1), which moves the bias toward social order in an attempt to assert cosmic order. Each day presents new facets of creation as God's activity in the cosmos moves smoothly onward, expanding until the entire known world exists. As long as people move within that social order, observing the intention of each created thing, then there is prosperity. Humanity's original home was a paradise without conflict and confusion, and God creates each of the human pair just as they always would be.[25]

Both through the law and through the creation account, God's control of the world and God's desire that each human take a divinely preordained place within that world offer dominant themes that reflect the Persian desire for a harmonious, integrated society that would honor its own limits and live within the empire as productive contributors to the greater welfare of the whole. To a great extent, this strategy was successful.

Legal Formation of Yehud as a Religious State

Through the construction of a helpful symbolic universe, the Persian Empire acted to create a colony of Yehud that would cooperate with Persian goals. The Persian Empire also undertook other measures to ensure its goal of social control. These legal and active means created Yehud as a legal and political entity with a religious basis.

The Edict of Cyrus in 539 B.C.E. presented the first legal grounds for a growing community in the Jerusalem area.[26] Cyrus allowed children and descendants of deportees to immigrate to the land of their ancestors, whether that was Yehud or some other territory throughout the empire's growing boundaries. Darius' reorganization of the imperial administrative structure probably first created the political unit called Yehud, but the movement of Yehud's inhabitants into that region began under Cyrus.

Darius' funding of temple worship and construction provided the next political step toward the establishment of Yehud. With an increased influx of people and a new emphasis on funds for the temple, Yehud gained sufficiently in a differential of wealth that it stratified to a larger extent than previously possible. "People do not build civic centers as a form of recreation: the very presence of this type and scale of site intrusion reflects a differential power situation."[27] With increasing wealth and an ever more complex internal social system to match, Yehud continued its internal structuring that resulted in a state of its own, albeit a secondary state within the Persian imperial-colonial system.

The law provided the next step, codifying the behavioral norms of the people and placing in effect the apparatus for direct social control. With the law came the governors and others who could enforce the law as needed. This political might thus connected with judicial and military powers, even though the local government did not have the control of much of this power. Yehud continued to operate as an adjunct of Persia, leaning upon the larger state's power for a variety of self-promoting activities, not the least of which was temple construction.

The most influential political change throughout this period was the introduction of the urban elite. As the immigration continued and increased throughout the first half century of Persian rule, the population of Jerusalem itself over against the population of the region as a whole grew significantly. The reurbanization of Yehud shifted the bases of political power as well as the culture of the colony, producing a predominance of influence among those with experiences in Babylonia and Persia. These new occupants of Yehud possessed a larger worldview and perhaps shared their cultural assumptions and attitudes more with the non-Yehudites of their regions of origin than with the inhabitants of Yehud where they now lived. The introduction of this urban populace with different ethnic connections, different regional experiences, different political affiliations, and different occupations and financial bases produced, over time, a great shift in Yehud's social character. This immigrant class eventually became the group that defined nascent Judaism and shaped its substance and practice over the next centuries. Because of this group's political loyalty to and dependence upon Persia, it increasingly defined Yehud's distinctiveness as a religious function; politically, Yehud was a colony within someone else's empire; religiously, however, Yehud was separate and autonomous, connected in a special way to its God and through God to each other.

The political construction of Yehud was a creative act committed as a result of Persia's own imperial expansion. Persia developed an administrative apparatus with a certain ideology, and that ideology produced a social construction of a new reality, which was Yehud as a Persian colony. This defined the new social body, giving it limits and connections with other bodies, such as the Persian Empire itself but also neighbors such as Samaria, Egypt, and Greece. This construction of a new political reality brings meaning into people's lives and sets the stage for the other institutions as "Yehudite." In other words, the ideological construction of a new political organization produced an objectified or reified understanding of the world and of Yehud as a Persian colony; this in turn resulted in the self-identification of Yehud as a religious group, organized around a temple, maintaining loyalty to its sponsor state, Persia.[28]

Persia's Goals

The goals of the Persian Empire in this political construction of Yehud seem obvious. Persia sought an enhanced tax base and a military buffer on its western fringes. These two concerns repeat throughout the history shared by Yehud and Persia; when Persia needed more funds from its colonies, it changed its provincial policies, and when Persia was concerned about its southwestern border, it shifted its modes of interaction with Yehud. These are typical concerns of a state or empire as it begins the process of secondary state formation.[29] Cyrus and Darius conducted the more direct form of secondary state formation, expanding Persia into Yehud, which was not previously organized as a state, through explicit political incorporation and overt colonialism expressed in economic takeover and control. Other emperors, such as Xerxes and Artaxerxes, involved themselves in a more subtle development of the secondary states through changing economic policies on a larger scale in order to create conditions whereby the colonies transform themselves, such as Yehud did when Xerxes removed funding for the operation of the local Jerusalem temple.[30] In both of these forms of secondary state development, Persia's goals included increased production, and its means involved repopulation with local loyalists who formed a nonagricultural class. Together, these form a policy of intensification, as Persia sought to increase the production out of Yehud so that the empire could receive larger amounts of goods and taxes.

Over time, the nonagricultural elites chose to serve not only Persian intensification but also their own preservation as a secure, landed class. Certainly this was the case by the time of Ezra and Nehemiah, who communicated a stringent class consciousness. Again, this reflects expected patterns of asymmetric culture contact, in which there tends to be increasingly differential access to strategic resources and increasingly stratified social classes. This in turn increases the intensification of the economy, as the work of the lower classes benefits the upper classes. Throughout its history, regardless of the degree of intensification and its associated internal stratification, Persia's treatment of Yehud matches the definition of colonialism: "the capture by a foreign elite of the capital and labor—the surplus energy—of an impacted population."[31]

Imperial states such as Persia are inherently expansionist and conduct their expansion through a colonialism backed by a centralized control of force. Specific goals include the neutralization of potential force by others, the control of resources and labor beyond the borders, and the increased exploitation of client states. Persia gained its own expansion through the creation of colonies like Yehud.

Political Ritual

The establishment of the colony of Yehud proceeded not only through material and symbolic means but also through rituals for the community. Empires prove unable to control the entirety of their regions with only material and military means; they must find additional ways to govern their expanding areas of influence.

A typical ritual move for emperors is the tour or procession of the empire. Through establishing occasional physical presence in most corners of the governed territory, the emperor takes advantage of opportunities for visible presence and for associated rituals to impress upon the citizens the emperor's grandeur and the essential rightness of imperial rule.[32] This becomes even more essential in the empire's periphery, where emotional and governmental ties to the imperial center are fewer and more tenuous. In the reigns of Darius and other Persian emperors, the procession was combined with military movements, increasing the ritual impact by depicting quite clearly the power of the empire as embodied in the emperor's person. These military campaigns linked the emperor's glory with the clear threat of Persian military force. At each stop of the procession, the local colonial governments proclaimed the emperor as the local king, thus preempting the possibility of rebellion. The display of imperial wealth and grandeur must have been quite a spectacle, especially in the poorer regions of the empire.

Ritual not only builds loyalty, often through its impressive and emotional display of excess, but also builds consensus. "Ritual builds solidarity without requiring the sharing of beliefs. Solidarity is produced by people acting together, not by people thinking together."[33] Through the action of common recognition of the emperor on procession, as well as through the range of other ritual actions for building imperial loyalty, the Persian Empire could impress upon the populace the grandeur of the empire without requiring the citizens to agree on anything but the emotional content of the symbols invoked. By working on the emotional level, the ritual bypasses common consent based on intellectual assent. In Jerusalem, the newly constructed temple provided a variety of other rituals that could support not only the worship of Yahweh but the obedience to the Persian Empire. The common recognition of Persian sponsorship would offer such opportunities, even if there was little liturgical emphasis on imperial concerns.

In the wider range of affairs, the empire charged the governors with the assignment of common projects. On the administrative level, this enabled the accomplishment of certain material state objectives. On the symbolic level, it bonded the society through the attached rituals and through the shared involvement in a common goal. It brought consensus of action and thus bonded the populace together in loyalty to the empire, if in nothing else.

Ritual can also replace old symbols with new ones. Through the funding and introduction of a new temple, the Persian Empire gained an opportunity to shape the ritual practices within Yehudite religion; the canonization of Pentateuchal law allowed Persia to shape the details of Yehud's worship and to encourage a ritual practice that enforced the status quo. Through this change in ritual, the empire could alter the perceptions of reality so that the legitimation of the empire continued:[34] even in the midst of social change, therefore, ritual provides opportunities to shift the social hierarchies. The ritual statements by the prophets Haggai and Zechariah allowed for reinterpretations of old faith and a replacement of older hierarchies with new ones. The priestly caste kept its own importance, but the high priest and the governor increased in importance. Ritual, including rituals such as the founding of the temple, depicted the importance of these local leaders and created new relationships of power through the use of these powerful symbols. When Third Isaiah argued for the inclusion of eunuchs in the temple service, even as ministers within the temple, the presence of such persons within the liturgical service would have greatly increased their power within the changing social reality. The argumentation was rooted in theology, but the impact of the ritual would have been firmly entrenched within the politics of the time. Inclusion into the religion, especially within the ministry of that religion, creates powerful symbols of inclusion that can permeate the culture by affirming groups that had been excluded. Thus participation in ritual alters the social reality by shifting concepts of right and wrong, powerful and powerless.

Perhaps the best example of the ritual construction of reality was Ezra's public reading of the law. This brought the Persian-canonized Pentateuchal law into the public mind, thus shifting the ideological basis for activity. The public reading also formed the conception of power groups within Yehud, because it was the public event that sacralized the presence of the elders who came to run Yehud. By equating the law of God and the law of the emperor, Ezra encouraged allegiance to Persia. Furthermore, the dissolution of ethnic intermarriages as a result of the reading of the law shifted the social alliances within the class structure of Yehud.

Sabbath as Political and Religious Symbol

Another possible symbolic shift within the changing Yehudite legal and religious system was the introduction of the Sabbath. The roots of the ritual of Sabbath observance have challenged scholars, but it seems to have had a sudden resurgence in the early Persian period. The Priestly version of the creation story (Genesis 1:1—2:4a) offers the emphases on orderly creation and a permanent, divinely ordained status quo. This story also climaxes the creation in the Sabbath, as if Sabbath rest was not only preordained by God but was the apex and highest purpose of creation.[35] Elements within Third Isaiah emphasize the Sabbath as a key religious observance, over against earlier biblical traditions that showed a monarchic-period interest in the Sabbath without raising it to some dominant status.

As ritual, Sabbath observance offers opportunities to sense solidarity and to thank the powers that grant the time of rest. It limits work and reinforces thoughts that work levels are reasonable; as long as there is time to refrain from work, then the daily work is certainly survivable. Sabbath also provides an easy way for all citizens to have access to temple worship, especially when the Persian Empire required taxes to be paid within the temple. Sabbath provided a solidifying ritual for use in the early postexilic period and beyond; its ability to survive and find relevance in different cultures has been clearly demonstrated by subsequent history. By linking religious devotion with the cycles of work and production, the religion and ritual creation of reality enforced the Persian imperial goals of intensification of productivity. If work and its absence are regularly cycled intentions of God, then the increased production of further work could also be a desire of the Deity. Ritual and politics combine once more for the service of the empire.

Summary

The Persian Empire formed itself as a state and expanded itself into neighboring states in order to fulfill its own internal needs as an imperial power. Through its intrusion into neighboring nonstate organized regions, such as the Jerusalem area, it produced secondary states for the purposes of exploitation of resources. Yehud was such a colony, operated for the benefit of the Persian Empire. Yehud thus organized itself as a state, but its statehood operated within the limits imposed upon it by the empire.

Yehud's organization involved the presence of political leaders such as Zerubbabel, Ezra, and Nehemiah. These officials received their power on the basis of Persian appointment and fulfilled administrative tasks for the purpose of strengthening Persian influence and gain from Yehud. They also possessed ties to Yehudite culture and shared their allegiance with the goal of preserving Yehud as a state of its own, albeit a secondary state dominated by Persia. These governors managed the Persian program of intensification to increase the imperial use of resources.

The politicians also introduced, on Persia's behalf, a new law under the reign of Darius. This law may well be strongly connected to the laws of the Pentateuch in their current form. These laws served to limit Yehud's activities and to define the society in accord with an ethic of not questioning the Persian Empire. The laws produced a sense of status quo in which adherence to this Persian-sponsored law would be likely. Persia's contributions to Yehud's official texts also emphasized other aspects of the status quo, such as creation stories.

Through the temple and the politics associated with the emperor and the governor, Yehud established a series of rituals that also enforced obedience to Persia, although the connections were often indirect and Yehud maintained strong interests in its own survival. Still, these rituals formed the sense of reality desired by the Persian Empire. There is no revolt or attempted rebellion by the Yehudites throughout the two centuries of Persian hegemony. Although other nations experienced such things, Yehud may have escaped such imperial intervention. Through intensification, governors, law, and ritual, Persia maintained a firm control over the Yehudite colony, and the governmental relations provided strength for the colony as well as a sense of stability for internal affairs.

Notes

1. S. N. Eisenstadt, *The Political Systems of Empires: The Rise and Fall of the Historical Bureaucratic Societies,* rev. ed. (New York: Free Press, 1969), esp. 13–32. For an insightful discussion of the specific mid-fifth century implications of the Persian Empire's administrative style, see Kenneth G. Hoglund, *Achaemenid Imperial Administration in Syria-Palestine and the Missions of Ezra and Nehemiah,* SBLDS 125 (Atlanta: Scholars Press, 1992).

2. See Sancisi-Weerdenburg and Kuhrt, *Achaemenid History IV: Centre and Periphery,* esp. Ephraim Stern, "New Evidence on the Administration Division of Palestine in the Persian Period," 221–26.

3. Cf. Heleen Sancisi-Weerdenburg, "The Quest for an Elusive Empire," in Sancisi-Weerdenburg and Kuhrt, *Achaemenid History IV: Centre and Periphery,* 263–74.

4. Of course, the persons who develop and administer a state do not have a perfectly congruous identity, but they do share important parts of a common identity. There is a perceived commonality even in the face of difference and conflict; the inevitable disagreements tend to focus on appropriate means or goals that the combatants usually think *should* be shared even if they are not.

5. Keith W. Whitelam, "Israelite Kingship: The Royal Ideology and Its Opponents," in *The World of Ancient Israel: Sociological, Anthropological and Political Perspectives,* ed. R. E. Clements (Cambridge: Cambridge University Press, 1989), 120.

6. Some passages within the Book of Ezra (1:8; 5:14-16) seem to indicate an earlier governor named Sheshbazzar, although the exact role and date of this figure are uncertain at best. Other governors, such as Sanballat, are known for Samaria, but this seems to have been a separate administrative area for at least most of the Persian period.

7. See the discussion of Isaiah 56–66 in chapter 5 above as well as evidence of conflict in Nehemiah 13:28-30.

8. Specifically, neither ethnicity nor religion provided such a natural sense of unity.

9. See Nehemiah 5.

10. Whitelam, "Israelite Kingship," in Clements, *The World of Ancient Israel,* 121.

11. For a thorough presentation of such acceptance and enactment of ideology, see Peter L. Berger and Thomas Luckmann, *The Social Construction of Reality: A Treatise in the Sociology of Knowledge* (New York: Doubleday & Co., 1966).

12. For theoretical work on the nature of states and state development, see Henri J. M. Claessen and Peter Skalník, eds., *The Early State,* New Babylon Studies in the Social Sciences (The Hague: Mouton, 1978); and Cohen and Service, *Origins of the State.*

13. Price, "Secondary State Formation," 161–86.

14. For other examples of Persia's relations with colonies, see Heleen Sancisi-Weerdenburg and Amélie Kuhrt, eds., *Achaemenid History VI. Asia Minor and Egypt: Old Cultures in a New Empire. Proceedings of the Groningen 1988 Achaemenid History Workshop* (Leiden: Nederlands Instituut voor het Nabije Oosten, 1991).

15. See chapter 11, below.

16. Creation stories not only construct cosmogonies but also defend the status quo of cultic organization, according to Robert B. Coote and David Robert Ord, *In the Beginning: Creation and the Priestly History* (Minneapolis: Fortress Press, 1991).

17. For ideological, symbolic, and ritual means of expressing societal organization, see Mary Douglas, *Purity and Danger: An Analysis of the Concepts of Pollution and Taboo* (New York: Praeger Publishers, 1966), esp. 114–39.

18. Many scholars have argued that Zerubbabel represents such a messianic figure in the depictions offered by Haggai and Zechariah. For a rebuttal of this view and exegetical comments on the relevant texts, see chapter 5 above.

19. Although this second title receives usage in Ezekiel 40–48, there is no mention of a "king" at any point in this literature. In the extant texts, Yehud never envisioned itself with a king and never desired the reestablishment of sovereignty within the Persian period.

20. More accurately, none of Yehud's extant records reflects a competition with Persia for control of the Jerusalem area. Since Persian state expansion created the secondary state of Yehud, and since Yehud controlled most of the populace's modes of writing and literary preservation, it is not surprising that the extant records from official Yehud offer no evidence of opposition to Persia. Indeed, this does not rule out any attempts at rebellion, but any such opposition would have originated outside the elites who ran Yehud. These elites recorded and preserved no significant divergence of opinion, although the preservation of dissident voices in Isaiah 56–66 indicates some minimal admission of difference.

21. See Ezra 7:26.

22. The editing of the Pentateuch, including the existence of multiple sources and the dates appropriate to each layer and to the more general redaction, has received much attention in biblical scholarship, and a variety of positions currently exists. There seems to be no consensus at this time, although many scholars would agree on a final edition of the Pentateuch involving the addition of P at some time in the Persian period. Hayes and Hooker, *New Chronology*, argue for a late monarchic addition of P to the rest of the developing Pentateuchal canon.

23. For the traces in Deuteronomy of Darius' redactional activity, see Laura Rey Spicer, "Post-exilic Additions to Deuteronomy," SBL Southwest Regional Meeting, Dallas, March 1993.

24. In this context, many of the Pentateuchal themes need reinterpretation. Abraham becomes a story of a Babylonian interloper who gains land as an equal with the natives as a result of God's special blessing. Joseph is a good example of collusion with a foreign power, and Moses provides a similar example. (Note, however, the ambivalence toward Egypt—one never automatically does what Egypt tells one to do.) In many of the stories, following the state power and following God become equivalent. See the stimulating proposals of Philip R. Davies, *In Search of "Ancient Israel"*, JSOT Sup 148 (Sheffield: Sheffield Academic Press, 1992).

25. This contrasts the Genesis 2–3 creation story, which most scholars date much earlier. In Genesis 2–3, God creates first man (or human), and then woman as a separate phase of creation. The later telling of the story, more in line with the strong emphasis on social order, shows that God creates both at once, with each in an immutable form.

26. Ezra 1:1-4; 6:2-5.

27. Price, "Secondary State Formation," 171.

28. For the concepts of objectification and reification, see Peter L. Berger, *The Sacred Canopy: Elements of a Sociological Theory of Religion* (New York: Doubleday & Co., 1967), esp. 3–28.

29. Price, "Secondary State Formation," 177.

30. See chapter 6, above.

31. Price, "Secondary State Formation," 171.

32. David I. Kertzer, *Ritual, Politics, and Power* (New Haven, Conn.: Yale University Press, 1988), 23.

33. Ibid., 76.

34. Ibid., 104.

35. See Coote and Ord, *In the Beginning*.

CHAPTER 10

THE PRIESTHOOD'S CAPTURE OF RELIGION: RELIGIOUS MAINTENANCE

DURING THE PERSIAN PERIOD, Yehud defined itself increasingly in terms of its temple and the worship that took place there. Without a monarchy functioning as a central unifying symbol, the temple and the religion gained even more importance as a cultural center than it had experienced during Judah's earlier years. Correspondingly, the priests gained in influence and in control over the society as a whole as the importance of the temple grew.

The temple and its priests functioned as the chief manifestation of the Yehudite religion, but the temple also performed other roles within the culture. It was a symbol for the unity of the populace, serving as a location for rituals of state and imperial solidarity. The temple was also a ground for contesting power, as Nehemiah and Tobiah did.[1] The Persian Empire and its governors used the temple as a place for administrative services and as a locus for the collection of taxes. The temple also contained perhaps the highest concentration of educated persons within the colony, and this group of knowledgeable experts contributed significantly to the direction of Yehud's formation.

In addition to the many roles of the temple, there were other changes within Yehudite religion during the Persian period. The removal of the monarchy and the relative weakening of the local government vis-à-vis the Persian imperial administration allowed the priesthood a freer hand in its own development. Through the two centuries of the Persian Empire's domination of Yehud, the priesthood evolved new forms and expressions of its temple belief system and patterns of practice. The cult itself developed in distinctive ways, and the priesthood gained much more control over the experience of religion among the populace. This priestly capture of religion combined with the other changes of the temple's role in society. These innovations had lasting effects on the Judaisms and Christianities descended from the religion of Yehud during this time.

Theoretical Perspectives on the Cult

Throughout its history, biblical scholarship has suggested a variety of models for the development of Israel's and Yehud's cultic behavior.[2] Sociologists and anthropologists have never reached a clear consensus about how best to understand what transpires within worship and within the temple and priesthood systems that work alongside such worship. Nevertheless these are important issues for consideration. An understanding of worship and temple functioning will prove invaluable for an investigation of the specific forms and changes of worship throughout Yehud's time of Persian imperial domination.

Many of the scholarly suggestions have explained cultic development with evolutionistic models.[3] According to several of these models, religion began among humans in very "primitive" forms that later evolved to more "sophisticated" expressions of religion. For instance, Yehud's practices of sacrifice are overtly ritualistic; religion eventually evolved beyond that into rabbinic Judaism's legal textuality and later mysticism and into Christianity's more spiritual religion.[4] Many religions progress to more advanced states while still holding onto survivals, or artifacts, of previous stages of religion. Thus, although Yehud had developed significant insights into ethical monotheism through its own theological work as well as through its inheritance from the religion of the Judean monarchy, Yehud still practiced temple butchery of live animals as a survival of a more primitive time.

The ideological biases of such evolutionary schemes become obvious. More recent religions are somehow better than ancient ones. Current experience stands at the apex of evolution and thus displaces prior religious practices as insufficient and lesser. These schemas serve to justify the status quo of religious communities today, since they remove any basis for respect from prior religious experiences and elevate current practice into an exalted state. Such evolutionary schemes should be avoided for these ideological reasons, as well as certain practical matters. Evolutionary models may do well in examining changes in religious practice over time, but they do not provide proper detail of analysis within specific moments of history. In the examination of religious forms within the Persian colony of Yehud, one requires a theoretical framework that focuses on how religion functions within Yehud itself. Such a method must connect religion with the rest of its social setting. These sorts of theoretical and methodological perspectives will better inform the search to understand Yehud and its religion.

The sociologist Emile Durkheim offered a considered approach to the analysis of religious practice. Durkheim emphasized the interrelationship of a society's people and its gods, arguing for an interdependence between them. The idea of the sacred represents a society's own self-conception of its strengths and values. Ritual then expresses how gods and humans interrelate within society, since society becomes the proper arena of being for both of them. In Durkheimian terms, Yehud equated Yahweh God with the chief powers of its own society, the Persian Empire and the Jerusalem temple. The religion called for popular acceptance of the governors as divinely chosen figures who spoke the will of God and the policies of the emperor. Likewise, the religion encouraged adherence to the priestly, temple forms of Yehudite religion. Social power becomes religious value in Durkheim's analysis.

Other sociologists emphasize the importance of ritual as the lived expression of cultural and religious myths. Myths provide cosmic legitimation for institutions and belief systems, rooting the social reality in cosmic origins. Ritual shows the relationships embodied by institutions, and rituals encourage the popular acceptance of such myths. In this interpretation of myth and ritual, it is not surprising to find a coercive aspect to ritual. If rituals create assent to myths through an action that embodies a mythic support for an institution, then rituals coerce the acceptance of ideologies of the status quo or of some power group's desires for reality. In all cases, ritual and myth are tied to the same community basis. Both myth and ritual maintain power relationships within the community through uses of symbol and ideology.

Structural anthropology provides a variety of perspectives on myth and ritual and their modes of producing social cohesion. The work of Mary Douglas has been especially persuasive among biblical scholars.[5] Her anthropology emphasizes society's need to protect itself from ambiguity, which inevitably threatens social definitions of reality. For this reason, societies define holiness as wholeness. Wholeness expresses itself in codes of bodily integrity, a perceived need for completeness, and strict definitions of what is clean and thus what belongs in what places. This symbolizes and references social integrity, a desire to maintain the societal status quo in concrete ways. From this perspective, concepts of purity and honor become vital in the analysis of cult. Purity refers to complete, clean objects and the persons associated with them, who then reflect the proper social relations. Honor adheres to persons who maintain this purity within their own conduct and communicate it to others through their honorable, pure actions.

The insights of structural anthropology, including the work of Douglas, perhaps are more helpful when applied to individual lives than when used to understand the social complexities of worship at the Jerusalem temple. Certainly the temple was charged to keep holiness and purity and to communicate these values and commodities to the persons of Yehud, who sought participation in holiness for personal reasons. Religion would provide these people with a sense of assurance, of place in the world, and of personal adequacy. However, how does the temple function for the society as a whole?

Certainly the Jerusalem temple and the cult operative therein functioned to objectify God's presence within the society and to identify God's desires with the political and social needs of Yehud as defined by the elite as well as to provide the personal psychological benefits as structural anthropology recognizes. The temple's operation within society, therefore, takes on the nature of a transaction, in which the elites receive an opportunity to enforce a worldview and the populace receives psychological justification in exchange for its willingness to follow the requirements of the religion. Of course, such are the analytic views held by outsiders;[6] from within the religious system the benefits are defined quite differently, in terms of God's pleasure and covenants with God and with humanity for the betterment of life as well as in terms of human destiny and created design.

This internal definition of the benefits of religion, including Jerusalem's temple cult, points to a different social function. Temple ideology establishes sacred space and sacred activity, which then separates the populace by differentiating between those who participate in such sacred occasions and those who do not. The temple creates social boundaries and in effect splits the world into those who worship and those who do not. Because of the religious content of the worship, the worshipers understand this distinction as a separation between those favored by God and those who are not so favored. The social boundary represents and reflects a theological statement about God's preference for persons and for social groupings. Those who worship correctly are those whom God chooses and those with whom God works in partnership.

From this perspective, the precise content of the worship itself is not particularly significant; what matters is the belief system through which the temple worship offers a particularistic means for reaching God and for aligning oneself with God's endeavors and favor. The act is not as important as the effect of association with God. As with most sociological theories, this explanation does not account for the specific nature of Yehudite worship, but it does focus on the large-scale social effects. Worship operated in such a way that it defined groups of insiders and outsiders. The elite of Jerusalem experienced constant geographic access to the temple, social affiliation with the temple leadership, and sufficient finances to participate in the most lavish of the temple celebrations. Thus they enjoyed a high degree of association with the temple worship practices and became self-defined through the temple activity as within God's favor, as opposed to others who did not worship in this way. Others throughout Yehud who worshiped more sporadically, becaues of limits of geography or funds, were also part of the worshiping community but did not enjoy such a lofty self-definition. Their allegiances were split. At times, the circle of insiders would be drawn to include such persons, but at times the more religiously active urban Yehudites would define the inside group more narrowly to exclude those who did not worship regularly.[7]

Those who never worshiped in the temple and claimed no adherence at all to the worship of Yahweh would have been defined as completely outside the temple system and thus outside the most important social grouping of Yehud. This would include non-Yehudites as well as persons whose practices left them unclean and who thus could not worship within the temple. Not only did the temple provide a locus for the creation of insider/outsider distinctions but it also offered an ideology that allowed for potential exclusion. Those who violated the law could be declared unclean and thus kept outside, as could other social deviants. Through the application of a religious-juridical system, the priests controlled the society's definitions of insiders and outsiders, based at least in part upon individuals' willingness to accept priestly authority and to conform to the norms established by the priests.

In this way, the temple produces a social and religious hierarchy. Close affiliation between the leading political classes and the priests who possessed this religious authority created a unity of the political and religious realms, boosting the strength of the hierarchies and the hierarchical system resulting from each. Thus the temple's functions included the production of a legitimated hierarchy as well as the creation of insider/outsider differentiations. These results of the temple service combined with other functions of Jerusalem's religious system: representing the people's values to themselves through relating them to God, producing myths and supportive rituals that justify the society's institutions, and defining wholeness and purity in attempts to combat social ambiguity and thus to create cultural cohesion.

Priesthood in Colonial Yehud

The Yehudite priesthood of Jerusalem's Second Temple was not the first manifestation of a religious hierarchy. Monarchic Judah had produced an elaborate temple cult that had endured in Jerusalem for over three centuries. This earlier priesthood maintained a contentious existence in the midst of conflict between two powerful priestly families; this difficulty continued throughout the monarchy.[8] The power of the priesthood attracted this sort of conflict by its nature as a social institution of great influence, the control of which could carry immense benefit.

Priests controlled the access to the temple by defining and determining holiness and cleanness. Through the extensive Priestly legislation, that which was included both in the Pentateuch's Priestly source (P) and in the continuing oral traditions of the priesthood, the priests learned the difference between clean and unclean, and they communicated these facts of holiness to the masses, explaining their own failings and recommending remedies for the problems of uncleanness. In many cases, the practical matters of determining cleanness were the responsibility of the priests.[9] Thus priests defined who was clean and unclean and determined who could participate in the temple worship that unified persons with God. Through their control of access to God, the priests possessed a large degree of power.

In the early times of the Second Temple, the canonization of the Pentateuch legislated financial support for the priesthood, in accordance with policies that probably had been in force earlier during the Judean monarchy. Priests received sizable financial consideration for their temple performance.

> *Yahweh spoke to Moses, saying: Speak to the people of Israel, saying: Any one of you who would offer to Yahweh your sacrifice of well-being must yourself bring to Yahweh your offering from your sacrifice of well-being. Your own hands shall bring Yahweh's offering by fire; you shall bring the fat with the breast, so that the breast may be raised as an elevation offering before Yahweh. The priest shall turn the fat into smoke on the altar, but the breast shall belong to Aaron and his sons. And the right thigh from your sacrifices of well-being you shall give to the priest as an offering; the one among the sons of Aaron who offers the blood and fat of the offering of well-being shall have the right thigh for a portion. For I have taken the breast of the elevation offering, and the thigh that is offered, from the people of Israel, from their sacrifices of well-being, and have given them to Aaron the priest and to his sons, as a perpetual due from the people of Israel. This is the portion allotted to Aaron and to his sons from the offerings made by fire to Yahweh, once they have been brought forward to serve Yahweh as priests; these Yahweh commanded to be given them, when God anointed them, as a perpetual due from the people of Israel throughout their generations. (Leviticus 7:28-36)*

The above text offers an example of priestly compensation for services, here limited to regulation for a single offering, the offering of well-being.[10] In this case, the worshiper receives the bulk of the meat from the sacrifice. The uneatable parts (the fat and the blood) are burned as an offering to Yahweh. The beast's breast meat belongs to the priests as a class, and the right thigh becomes compensation for the specific priest who performs the service. The economic benefits for the priests are clear; for this service they receive food as individuals and as a group. The Priestly tradition gives further rights to the priests.

> *The LORD spoke to Aaron: I have given you charge of the offerings made to me, all the holy gifts of the Israelites; I have given them to you and your sons as a priestly portion due you in perpetuity. This shall be yours from the most holy things, reserved from the fire: every offering of theirs that they render to me as a most holy thing, whether grain offering, sin offering, or guilt offering, shall belong to you and your sons. As a most holy thing you shall eat it; every male may eat it; it shall be holy to you. This also is yours: I have given to you, together with your sons and daughters, as a perpetual due, whatever is set aside from the gifts of all the elevation offerings of the Israelites; everyone who is clean in your house may eat them. All the best of the oil and all the best of the wine and of the grain, the choice produce that they give to the LORD, I have given to you. The first fruits of all that is in their land, which they bring to the LORD, shall be yours; everyone who is clean in your house may eat of it. (Numbers 18:8-13)*

The priests receive the right to eat the grain, sin, and guilt offerings, plus the first fruits donations, as well as a portion of the elevation offering. This provides the priests with a very sizable income for themselves and their families. Not only do the priests control the cultic practice, including the definition of who is clean and unclean, but they receive enough income to be considered among the wealthy. Although these regulations may have been in force earlier in Israel's history, they receive special attention in Persian-period Yehud because of the canonization of Pentateuchal law. However, there seems to be some indication that there were increasing financial rewards for the temple attendants in the early postexilic period. Consider the income of the Levites according to a Priestly passage:

> *To the Levites I have given every tithe in Israel for a possession in return for the service that they perform, the service in the tent of meeting. From now on the Israelites shall no longer approach the tent of meeting, or else they will incur guilt and die. But the Levites shall perform the service of the tent of meeting. (Numbers 18:21-23a)*

This provides a sizable income for this Levitical group in exchange for a service that had been handled by others previously. In comparison, the early Deuteronomistic regulation limited this income source sharply:

> *When you have finished paying all the tithe of your produce in the third year (which is the year of the tithe), giving it to the Levites, the aliens, the orphans, and the widows, so that they may eat their fill within your towns, then you shall say before Yahweh your God: "I have removed the sacred portion from the house, and I have given it to the Levites, the resident aliens, the orphans, and the widows, in accordance with your entire commandment that you commanded me." (Deuteronomy 26:12-13a)*

In this earlier version of the Levitical tithing law, the tithe seems to be an event applicable only one out of three years. In the P version of this legal discussion, found in Numbers, there is no indication that the tithe is not annual. Furthermore, P records that the Levites possess this tithe in its entirety; Deuteronomy commands that the tithe be shared by Levites and social programs for the poor within the cities. The later law of P shifts the benefits of this tax strictly to the Levites, disenfranchising the others who had received social welfare from this subsidy. Over time, priestly advantages increased.

Throughout all of these laws, the priests receive substantial power and privilege as well as direct economic benefit. The priesthood gathers its income from sources throughout the people; the authority of the priesthood to collect goods in exchange for religious services comes from none other than Yahweh. The God of Israel and Yehud requires popular financial support for the priests who run the temple and offer access to Yahweh. If the temple service mediates God's grace or embodies the worshiper with a vital sense of holiness essential to life, then grace and holiness require financial contributions to the priests. Not only do priests control the distribution of these religious goods but they receive financial compensation for their services, and thus the distribution of grace occurs in tandem with a centralization of wealth within the temple community of priests.

Priests and Politicians

The political power and the centralization of the priests brought them into close contact with the political leaders of Yehud. Their connections were diverse and often strong. Political leaders such as Nehemiah understood their own powers to include the ability to remove others from places of authority within the temple (Nehemiah 13:7-9). In that same case, the priest Eliashib had brought a neighboring colony's governor, Tobiah, into the temple courts and had allowed him to establish residence there. Priests considered themselves to have the power to house politicians, and politicians thought themselves capable of determining the actions of priests within the temple. This interchange marks the dimensions of both shared and contested power between the priests and the politicians throughout Yehud.

A second example occurs within Isaiah 56–66.[11] That document records conflict between priests and politicians among the immigrants, over against the native groups. The priests and the politicians hold distinct goals, although their intentions coalesce through the course of the text. They are separate groups who build a coalition to share their power in ways supportive of each other. Together, both of these groups who were descended from immigrants within the first reigns of Persian emperors combined their varying types of social influence and took control of the colony of Yehud, operating on behalf of the Persian Empire.

The agenda of the priests becomes visible in their sections of Isaiah 56–66. Their policy emphasizes the inclusion of foreigners into the cult (Isaiah 56:3, 6). Presumably these foreigners are chiefly the immigrants who had been born and raised in other parts of the Persian Empire, such as Babylonia. These priestly voices argue for the inclusion of eunuchs as well, breaking the boundaries established by prior law (Isaiah 56:4-5).[12] The priests also mention several specific worship practices: observing the Sabbath, joining in prayer, and offering sacrifices (Isaiah 56:4, 7). The priests also search after social justice, including attention to the hungry and homeless (Isaiah 58:6-8).

This agenda includes means of keeping the community together in physical and ideological terms. Through the maintenance of the homeless, these marginal persons remain within the community, attached to the other classes while not receiving sufficient social mobility to challenge their place. Through the practices of Sabbath and sacrifice, the priests demonstrate to the populace the proper means of relating to God, and they supervise such activity to ensure the propriety. The priests thus exercise control over the populace. The sacrificial system not only allows for similar control but also provides significant income for the priests.

Together, the priests and the political leaders assume top positions within the colony's hierarchies of power and influence. As such, their roles often overlap and coalesce. Zechariah's vision of cooperation between the high priest and the governor (Zechariah 3–4) provides one example of this overlapping of authority. When the two categories of social leaders cooperate in leading the people of Yehud, their abilities to guide the populace increase sharply.

Both priests and politicians base their authority in part upon a text and in part upon an unseen higher authority. An authority for priests resided within the Pentateuchal law's cultic regulations. Because the text gave to the priests certain rights, they could exercise corresponding functions within the temple system. The politicians, on the other hand, also had a textual basis for their action, but this came from places such as Zechariah's recorded vision as well as from governmental decrees and edicts from the Persian imperial court. In both cases, the texts' authority dwelt within those who generated the text, in whose name the priests and politicians claimed to act. The governor spoke with the authority of the emperor, asserting a right to speak in the emperor's name and to enforce imperial policy on the colonial level. The governor's authority was the authority of the emperor, but the populace had never (or only rarely) seen the emperor himself. Thus the people attributed to the governor the authority of the unseen emperor, whose authority came from the symbolic and ritual importance of the imperial office. Likewise, priests shared the authority of God and of Moses, both of whom were the putative originators of the priestly codes that they followed as authoritative. Again, God remained invisible to the people of Yehud, but the temple rituals made God known in symbolic and religious ways. God's presence with the priests empowered them to fulfill their tasks of ministry, and thus the priests' work was divinely ordained in the minds of the people. To question a priest would be to question God. God's authority manifested itself fully within the priests, who spoke for God and claimed God's authority to establish and regulate religion in Yehud.

There are indications that Yehud's high priesthood was hereditary from the start of the Persian period. As son succeeded father, the priesthood developed into a typically Yehudite institution. Thus the temple and the priesthood increasingly represented settled, stable leadership that worked within the middle of the community. The governorship appears to be quite a different matter altogether. Persia assigned a variety of governors to Yehud; there is no evidence at all of genetic relationships between any of them. Most of the governors had apparently served at least some time in foreign courts, especially the Persian imperial court; their assignment was to maintain order with the backing of the Persian Empire. The empire would send a loyal Jew with ethnic ties to Yehud but with no direct experience there. Thus each of the governors was, to one extent or another, an outsider. This prevented the establishment of a dynastic succession within the governmental community, but it made sure that the highest resident Persian authority was dependent upon the best kind of support from the emperor.

Over time, this produced a native, aristocratic leadership within the high priests and a foreign-imposed, erratic leadership in the political sphere. Conflicts would be inevitable with this separation of styles, but it allowed for Persian political control while at the same time Yehud developed a strong sense of self-identity, rooted in its own locally controlled institutions, the temple and its priesthood. The temple became the most markedly Yehudite institution through the postexilic period, and thus the priesthood became increasingly determinative of Yehudite culture, with a special freedom to influence religion and ideology within that culture.

The Priestly Capture of Religion

Throughout the period of Persian domination, the priests increasingly developed their own separate power base. Whereas the priesthood during the monarchy served at the pleasure of the kings and the political government, the Persian period allowed a sufficient separation of government and religion for the priesthood to establish itself much more completely as a distinct system of power and authority. The priesthood cooperated with the Persian-appointed governors, but they refused to allow the governors to coopt them into their own program. Certainly there would have been significant compromises on both sides, but the priesthood slowly gained in influence over the populace of Yehud, in large part because the politicians served shorter terms and were based upon an outside source of authority, whereas the priests could develop their strength through larger family systems of inherited power, enhanced by their perception as an internal authority.

With this kind of power at their disposal, the priests captured the religion of Yehud. Although the priesthood and the temple sacrificial system had been an enormously influential part of monarchic Israel's religion, the temple priests moved during the Persian period to dominate the religious expressions of the Yehudites. The pluralistic nature of the Persian Empire did not allow the capture to be complete, but the temple was able to accomplish significant gains in subsuming all religious expressions under its own program. Certainly the temple did become the chief expression of faith and operated with a potentiality for developing norms that no other religious group possessed.

One of the landmark achievements of these priests was a rewriting of Israel's historical traditions. The books of Chronicles retell and rewrite Israel's earlier history, from the Pentateuchal narratives through the history of the Israelite and Judean monarchies. Although Chronicles never succeeded in replacing the older historiographies, this new body of literature did achieve a canonization alongside them, despite its obvious nature as a reinterpretation of the same material.

Chronicles represents priestly historiography during the middle-to-late Persian period.[13] This literature emphasizes the temple as the central focus of Israelite and Judean life, displacing even the monarchy itself as a key social institution. In Chronicles, the temple becomes a massive operation and structure even from David's time, before the construction itself was done (1 Chronicles 23–26). The temple is central and employs thousands of persons with highly skilled jobs. The books of Samuel and Kings refrain from any mention of such things, at least in this exaggerated degree. Chronicles does not offer the reader the roguish David of the books of Samuel; instead, David's depiction emphasizes deep personal piety. David offers lengthy and theologically laden prayers, accompanied by sacrifices of immense proportions (1 Chronicles 29:10-22). This Persian-period priestly writing greatly expands the discussion of the First Temple's construction vis-à-vis the related texts from Kings (cf. 1 Kings 6–8 and 2 Chronicles 2–7).

The writing of the Chronicles offers one example of the priestly capture of religion in the Persian period. The priests rewrote history into a form that emphasized the temple and its sacrificial system of worship. By implication, the only acceptable expression of true religion in Yehud was therefore the temple. Other shrines and deities, frequently attacked during the monarchy and thus probably popular, cannot compete with this priestly organized vision of reality, in which the building of the First Temple climaxes God's involvement with the people of Israel and provides God with a permanent home. The leadership of ancient politicians, even the great David and Solomon, is reduced until all that is left is their contributions to the building of the temple. In a day when the priests and the politicians compete on somewhat equal footing for social influence, Chronicles argues radically for a shift toward priestly power. Within this text's ideology, the true goal of history is the temple, and politicians are relevant only when needed to support the temple and its worship. In the Persian period, the priests desired a greater standardization of religious practice and thus a greater control over the religion and the people than they had held in the monarchy. Chronicles uses ideology couched in historiography to work toward this shift. The priesthood had begun to capture the political ramifications of its religion.

The ability of priests to rewrite a political historical text represents one of the other shifts in the priestly social status. Priests increased their scribal activity. Although the monarchy may have experienced very little social distinction between the priests and the scribes, both of whom were in the employ of the government, the priests gained tighter control over scribal activity in the Persian Yehud. In the pluralistic society of the postexilic period, there must have been scribes in the employ of many groups, but the priests have control of writing for their own discrete purposes, perhaps for the first time in their history. This centralizes power, and they are able to propagate their own views in writing in ways impossible before.

Over time, Jerusalem and its temple religion developed the policy that God's speech came only through the earlier written words. Thus new revelation from God was impossible; only the priestly-scribal interpretation of past words could be normative for community life.[11] Although the fullness of this position lay centuries in Yehud's future, its roots begin at this time. As priests control writing, they endeavor to control the ideologies that achieve permanent, written status. Thus nascent Judaism begins its trek to becoming a people of a book, specially expressed in Torah. This shifts the locus of God's special presence from the present to the past; this move worked against the priestly impulse and was not begun for quite a while. The priestly agenda in Persian Yehud was to control the interpretation of the past through scribal activity and rewriting histories and to control the religious experiences of the present through temple worship according to the priestly regulations.

The priestly capture of religion becomes clearer through comparison of the other views of nascent Judaism in the Persian period. Other distinct positions vied for attention and popular acceptance throughout this time, but the priestly agenda grew in its own significance. Other forms of religion had been present in earlier Yahwism, such as that of the monarchy. There were wisdom and apocalyptic elements from much earlier times, for instance, but their presence was not felt as sharply in monarchic Judah as in postexilic Yehud.[15] In Judah, the monarchy exercised a political control over the temple that kept such divergent strands of religion together in the service of the state. In postexilic Yehud, the government no longer controlled the religion of the temple, and thus the priesthood took over control. However, Yehud's temple priests attempted this capture of religion in a pluralistic time, and their capture attained only a partial success. Although the priestly system of hierarchy and sacrificial worship succeeded in becoming the chief means for temple faith, other options flourished in increasing distance from the temple. The more control that the priests used to maintain their influence in the temple, the more that other religious options such as apocalyptic and wisdom sought other modes of expression. The priests captured the temple and ran it for their own benefit, but the other forms of religion became increasingly independent and allied themselves with different social sectors, not with the priests. The priestly capture of temple religion resulted in a fragmentation of the religion of nascent Judaism, and this fragmentation influenced the religion within a time of corresponding social and cultural pluralism.

This fragmentation served Judaism well in times to come, because it created a variety of different social bases for the divergent expressions of Yahwistic faith.[16] Some forms required priests and temples; others did not. As Judaism expanded into the Diaspora, the variety of expressions of the faith aided the process of transporting the religion and adapting the religion to new cultural settings. The Jerusalem temple priests controlled not only the Jerusalem temple but the sacrificial worship practices of a group of mercenary Jews on an island called Elephantine in the Nile; Persia employed these Jews as part of a garrison in Egypt. Since they wished to worship Yahweh in accordance with temple practices, the Jerusalem temple priests offered the proper instruction and permission to perform the rituals appropriately. This provided one basis for the expansion of the religion. Other forms of the religion did not require the temple and the sacrificial system, and this increased the variety with which Judaism expressed itself throughout a growing and pluralistic world.

The implications of this variety became even clearer four centuries after the end of Persian rule, when Roman forces attacked and destroyed the Second Temple. Had only priestly religion existed at that time, the religion would likely have ended, or at least undergone such a thoroughgoing transformation as to be unrecognizable to later retrospect. However, nascent Judaism had produced other forms of Yahwistic expression that did not depend upon the temple's presence and its sacrificial system. These other forms of religiosity produced the elements of Judaism (and Christianity) that flourished after the Second Temple's destruction. The diversity of religion in the midst of a pluralistic society, as begun in the Persian period, proved to be the saving factor to the religion and the impetus behind its continuing adaptive ability.

Although the priesthood would eventually end with the destruction of the Second Temple, those concerns were too far in the future for the consideration of Yehud in the Persian period. At this point in time, the priesthood had so consolidated its hold over the temple and over the religion of Yahweh in general that it was difficult even to consider other forms of the religion. Temple Yahwism was the form of the religion that produced the canonization of most of the extant texts and became the best understood and most representative form of the religion for centuries.

Conclusion

The cooperative separation of governmental and temple authority in the Persian administrative system allowed for the development of each in distinctive yet related patterns. The growth of priestly power in the Persian period intensified the priestly proprietorship of sacrificial worship. The priests then gained further control of scribes and offered the books of Chronicles, their own version of monarchic history, in which the temple was the apex of history and thus the recipient of huge amounts of labor and funding.

When the priests captured temple religion, other forms of religious expression separated themselves from the temple and thus from priestly control. These other forms never attained the thoroughgoing acceptance as did the temple worship, but in the long run they became essential to Yahwism's survival.

Notes

1. Nehemiah 13:4-9.

2. For a discussion of these models, see Philip J. Budd, "Holiness and Cult," in Clements, *The World of Ancient Israel*, 275–98.

3. Such was the tendency of the *Religionsgeschichtlicheschule*, among others.

4. The anti-Semitic assumptions of these evolutionistic models are obvious.

5. See especially Douglas, *Purity and Danger.*

6. Marvin Harris, *Cultural Materialism: The Struggle for a Science of Culture* (New York: Random House, 1979), assumes a similar distinction between "emics" and "etics."

7. The temple defines insiders and outsiders based on participation in the temple cult. Others throughout Yehud may have been very religious, participating in a variety of Yahwistic practices of piety or in other religions at local shrines, but the effect would be the same: the temple would define them as (at least partially) outsiders. Thus the temple defines on the basis of the externalities of religious expression within the temple, not upon the extent of religious devotion or other internal psychological factors. Such is not unique to the worship within the Second Temple, however; it is common for all religious services based in physical locations that provide ways to measure attendance or other forms of participation.

8. Whether this particular split continued into the postexilic period is debatable, although often supported. Certainly there was persistent conflict around the priesthood throughout the life of the Second Temple, as recorded in much later literature. For some prominent options within scholarship, see Aelred Cody, *A History of Old Testament Priesthood*, Analecta Biblica 35 (Rome: Pontifical Biblical Institute, 1969); and Hanson, *The People Called.*

9. For a particularly clear example, see Leviticus 14, containing legislation regarding certain

infectious diseases in persons and objects. The priest must examine the person or object to determine its cleanness and to recommend the length and type of remedy needed before the person could be restored to full participation in the community.

10. Similar regulations apply to other offerings.

11. See chapter 5, above.

12. In all probability, the original forms of the legislation against the inclusion of eunuchs date from the Judean monarchy (Leviticus 21:20; Deuteronomy 23:1), but these laws became part of the priestly canonization of Pentateuchal law. Isaiah 56–66 reflects the early years of Darius' reign, before the canonization. Emigration from Babylonia and Persia into Yehud would have peaked by 515 B.C.E.; after that, most Yehudites were born in Yehud and thus were not eunuchs. The discussion of including eunuchs would therefore have been a temporary emphasis, as the legislation indicates.

13. For current views on the books of the Chronicles, see Peter R. Ackroyd, *The Chronicler in His Age*, JSOTSup 101 (Sheffield: JSOT Press, 1991); Simon J. De Vries, *1 and 2 Chronicles*, FOTL 11 (Grand Rapids: Wm. B. Eerdmans Publishing Co., 1988); Jacob M. Myers, *I Chronicles: A New Translation with Introduction and Commentary*, AB 12 (Garden City, N.Y.: Doubleday & Co., 1965); idem, *II Chronicles: A New Translation with Introduction and Commentary*, AB 13 (Garden City, N.Y.: Doubleday & Co., 1965); and H. G. M. Williamson, *1 and 2 Chronicles*, NCBC (Grand Rapids: Wm. B. Eerdmans Publishing Co., 1982).

14. Greenspahn, "Why Prophecy Ceased," 37–49.

15. See chapters 11 and 12, below, for discussions of wisdom and apocalyptic, respectively.

16. Of course, there were also benefits to early Christianity in the last days of the Second Temple and the time following the Second Temple's destruction.

CHAPTER 11

SAGES AND WISDOM: INTELLECTUAL MAINTENANCE AND SOCIAL SYMBOLISM

IF YEHUD'S PRIESTHOOD SUCCEEDED in capturing and controlling the temple religion, it was not able to control all of the religious expressions of Yahwism throughout the colony. Other forms of religion developed out of Israel's religious and cultural heritage, flourishing in a pluralistic society where influences from many parts of the world were commonplace. Phenomena such as wisdom were not inventions of the Persian period; they had existed within Israel and Judah (as well as throughout the world) long before. Monarchic Judah, however, had maintained political control over the temple and its priesthood and also over the means of writing, in mostly successful attempts to dominate the monarchy's culture, including religion.[1] With both temple and scribes under the control of the state, they developed in tandem during the monarchy, but the period of Persian domination changed that balance. With foreign rule and less direct governmental interference in religion, the temple became autonomous and controlled the production of its own writings. The priesthood attempted the capture of Yehud's religion, and it succeeded in controlling the temple and in rewriting history to emphasize the centrality of the temple. At the same time, the other forces within Yehud's religion separated from temple control and developed in their own directions.

Thus in the postexilic period wisdom became its own phenomenon, inheriting the wisdom traditions of the preexilic temple and monarchy and expressing itself within the changing context of a pluralistic Yehud.[2] In religious terms, wisdom became an option for the experience and expression of faith, alongside other options such as the temple. Socially, wisdom's roots are in the intellectual circles of Jerusalem, especially those scribes whose livelihood might well have been in support of some other social group, such as the Persian government or the priestly temple bureaucracy. Wisdom grew among the learned, literate elite of Yehud's capital city, presenting a style of Yahwism increasingly distinct from that espoused by the temple priests.

Definitions of Wisdom

Scholars have experienced great difficulty in defining wisdom as literature, as theology, and as social group. Many commentators never offer a specific definition, but there is consensus around many of the important elements of wisdom. Thus R. N. Whybray describes wisdom as a discussion of the human world with a focus on the "potentiality and limitations of the individual."[3] Wisdom discerns what is best in life and decides how best to achieve these things. Wisdom's theological concerns deal with the ultimate questions of what is really best for humans, a concern that often turns to a consideration of creation. Morality is also a chief topic. Wisdom literature recognizes the limitations of human wisdom and assigns ultimate, complete wisdom only to God, thus building a possible bridge to the rest of Yehud's religious thought.

In a review of recent works on wisdom literature, James L. Crenshaw lists other descriptive elements of Israel's wisdom. Such elements include the concept that "wisdom is a primordial revelation which God implanted in the universe," which "announces the joyous news that God trusts men and women to steer their lives successfully."[4] Wisdom often deals with issues of order on the personal, social, and cosmic scales. At first, Israel's wisdom stressed the belief in order, but over time this wisdom moved to question and to critique that view, resulting in a crisis on the very form of faith that wisdom had propagated. The earlier wisdom saw less role for God, because of its strong self-confidence in the ability of humans to solve their own problems. Wisdom resulted from an intellectual tradition among the elites, not from a single school. At the same time, wisdom derived from the most literate segments of society, as proved by the elevated stylistic features of wisdom that argue persuasively for true artistry in its writing. Although some expressions of wisdom may have originated at the village level, all of the extant wisdom literature bears the marks of literate culture.

The social roots of wisdom writings have challenged scholars. Many have suggested an unbroken "wisdom school" running throughout the monarchy, surviving exile, and then flourishing again in the postexilic period under first Persian and then Greek rule. This class of sages transmitted ancient wisdom from one generation to the next, and the scribes among this group committed these traditions to writing. The group would have been open to receiving new wisdom traditions, from a variety of sources, during at least parts of its history, allowing new materials from other nations or other Israelite classes to add themselves to the growing corpus of canonical wisdom. Eventually this group's writings (or, more likely, a selected excerpting of them) became a part of the canon, accepted by official Judaism and then Christianity. Unfortunately there exists no direct evidence of a permanent wisdom school within ancient Israel and Yehud.[5]

However, the authorship of the Hebrew Bible's wisdom writings can be described at least in part. Scholars have long recognized foreign influences upon Israelite wisdom, especially from Egypt and Babylonia. The connections may well be strongest in the Book of Proverbs.[6] In these other nations, there exist sufficient records of the use of such literature to argue persuasively for their social function.[7] In Egypt and Babylonia, teachers used wisdom literature to educate ranking politicians, including the royal family and other governmental officials. Thus this suggests the ties of wisdom to education among the political groups in Yehud.

Gerhard von Rad had argued that Israel's wisdom literature dates from the time of the Solomonic enlightenment, when there was an intentional modeling of the Israelite monarchic state upon the example of Egypt.[8] Within that context of intentional cultural change and political transformation, Israel adopted large quantities of Egyptian wisdom literature as well as the attendant modes of instruction and used these with very few changes in Jerusalem. This led to a very quick development within Israelite culture, as it gained ancient insights from the established and advanced Egyptian society. However, very little of the Hebrew Bible's wisdom literature seems to derive from that monarchic period, especially from times as early as Solomon. Certainly Solomon's name becomes attached to several pieces of wisdom writing, but there is insufficient internal evidence from the texts themselves to argue that these assignations are accurate.[9]

In the Persian period, there must have been schools within Jerusalem to teach writing to the next generation of scribes, and it is reasonable to assume that the transmission of wisdom can be traced to these schools. However, these same scribes, products of scribal schools within the Persian colony of Yehud, would have been responsible for writing and/or copying all of the extant literature from the Hebrew Bible, including all of the non-wisdom literature. Writing was still a specialized skill within this period, and it was not taught as an ability appropriate to everyone. The few scribes were responsible for training the next generation of scribes as well as for doing their own work, for the temple, the government, the wealthy merchants, or others. On the other hand, it is dangerous to assume that scribalism was unified within Yehud. Perhaps not all scribes trained others, and not all scribes participated in the preservation of wisdom.

Even though it seems apparent that wisdom writing would belong within the educated classes of Yehud, and that it probably would be limited to Jerusalem, it remains difficult to construct a clear understanding of wisdom's social roots from simply the facts of its writing, its history, and its style. Other issues, such as content and social function, require attention before a fuller understanding of wisdom's social roots can be suggested.

The variety of wisdom literature also discourages easy definitions and descriptions of the material. Most lists of canonical wisdom literature include Proverbs, Job, and Qoheleth.[10] Some psalms are attributed wisdom functions, although this is much less clear. Later books that are clearly wisdom literature include the Wisdom of Solomon (often called Wisdom) and Ecclesiasticus, or the Wisdom of Jesus Ben-Sirach (often called Sirach or Ben-Sira).[11] These books derive from a later time but reflect many of the same concerns as the earlier wisdom literature.

Much wisdom literature represents a thought-centered mind-set. In other words, the good life and the proper relationship with created reality is possible for the person who thinks through the problems of life and acts on the basis of thought. Many scholars suggest that this reflects an absence of concepts of revealed religion. Whether or not this is true, clearly wisdom literature respects human thought as a significant means of knowing God and understanding life. Thus much wisdom literature lists the results of such sustained reflection upon life.

In many ways, the Book of Proverbs is the most classic of the extant wisdom literature and may exhibit the greatest age, at least in parts. It depicts definitions of basic Israelite religious terms at odds with the priestly establishment. For instance, there are only five references to "law" (Torah) within Proverbs.[12] In wisdom, those who keep the law have a better chance at living the good life, but the obedience to the law does not seem to be the same as living the good life. Other values represent themselves. One searches not after means to fulfill the law but instead after the sayings of the wise, in order to gain wisdom for oneself. Knowledge and understanding combine with wisdom as goals for human behavior, and the source of these goods is the speech of the wise rather than the legal codes of the Pentateuch.

This may represent a group within Yehud who were willing to reject the priestly temple hierarchy as a means toward God and toward attaining the good life on earth. On the other hand, it is also possible that this represents a group that follows in the temple cult but also searches for other truth. If so, then this group radically relativizes the temple as a source for divine truth, placing its own group's sayings as equal to the received traditions. In all likelihood, this group was also literate and educated and thus capable of producing this highly stylized literature. If so, then it is reasonable to suggest a locus for this wisdom group. In the Persian colony of Yehud, wisdom thought and literature flourished among the scribes and other literate members of Jerusalem society with strong Persian influence, who realized the constructed nature of the canonized Pentateuch and were unwilling to accept its authority as final. Instead, this group expressed its international exposure through a search for religious truths that transcend the particularities of the Jerusalem temple and the priestly-Mosaic legislation by which it operated its sacrifices. Those involved with the wisdom movement might well have been active within the temple, and might well have been faithful Yahwists by their own self-definition, but these scribes and others from the educated Jerusalem classes sought additional religious truth outside the temple system through the application of thought, non-temple tradition, and international resources.

This group also produced other literature during this time, in addition to Proverbs. Quite possibly, both Job and Qoheleth date from the later times of the Persian Empire, responding to the same pressures and religious situations as the Book of Proverbs. The Book of Job represents a very old story in its framework, with substantial theological and philosophical reflection contained in the speeches within. The book seems to negate the priestly assumptions of efficacious sacrifices and rewards for moral action and theological devotion to God. The experience of God, instead, becomes normative; the limited sacrifices stem properly from that. In other words, sacrifices never lead anyone to God, but they can properly come out of experience with God. Likewise, the Book of Job also critiques the wisdom movement out of which it derives. Wisdom attempts to discern the patterns within creation and to extol the virtues of knowing and understanding. Creating consternation among the wisdom group, Job argues persuasively that philosophical argumentation does not bring one closer to the good life or to God, as the dialogues with the friends indicate. Also, Job hears from God that there are strict limits to the abilities of human knowledge. The places where God acts most directly are outside the human realm of possible knowledge, and so thinking becomes an inadequate path toward God.[13]

The brief Book of Qoheleth presents other concerns still pertinent to the wisdom school. This orator's concerns with money are even greater than those of the other wisdom writers, once more betraying the high social class of wisdom. For Qoheleth, exploitation is an unchangeable status quo. The absurdity of life appears frequently throughout the book; it possessed a depressive nature not echoed by the more positive-toned wisdom literature such as Proverbs. Instead, Qoheleth examines the meaninglessness of a belabored life of toil and natural unpredictability, ending in pain and death. Because humans cannot control nature or even God through labor, toil, works, or faith, life progresses to death with no understanding of any sort of deeper pattern to existence. Qoheleth despairs of his ability to change the world, to make an impact upon his own surroundings, even upon himself. No matter what comes, the future remains unknowable; there is no security against the vagaries of the future, and the only certainty is life's cessation. Even what comes after death is unknowable, regardless of one's piety or faith. Again, Qoheleth questions the assumptions of the wisdom community: is it possible to know what one needs to know to live a better life?

The apocryphal or deuterocanonical wisdom books more clearly echo the philosophical tradition of Proverbs. Sirach reflects a Maccabean and later return to the praise of wisdom for its true abilities in teaching people to live better lives. The Wisdom of Solomon derives from slightly later, quite possibly in the last century B.C.E. Both books offer retellings of selected portions of prior Israelite history. That is, they consciously reflect on the religious traditions before their time and interpret those traditions in the light of their own contemporary philosophical stands. They are less concerned with developing religious ideology than with adapting religious traditions for use in their own time.

Of course, such can be said about all wisdom writings, at some level. Wisdom is a reflective process of systematic consideration of prior and current thought, looking for connections between them and explaining such connections with high literary style and sharp focuses on logic, coherence, and persuasion. It represents a social movement that seeks for coherence out of the combination of religious forces, adapting itself to a changing world by integrating new material while not completely abandoning the traditions of the past. This holds true even when the inherited traditions are themselves wisdom writings. In those cases, the wisdom tradition turns on itself in expressions of dissent.[14] First, however, it is necessary to examine further the social placement and function of the sages.

The Social Function of the Sage

Israelite and Yehudite sages operated at many locations within their society's structures.[15] Certainly there was some level of wisdom present in villages and among clans, tribes, and other family units. Likewise, the monarchy may have produced some sort of decentralized or at least extragovernmental educational system, which would have employed scribes throughout the kingdom and would have been likely places for wisdom traditions to develop over time. In Jerusalem, there would have been a school for the training of scribes, probably operating as an extended part of the royal court. The temple's scribes might also have produced wisdom literature, but the noncultic aspects of most wisdom literature tend to argue against such a location as affecting extant, canonical wisdom writings. With the growth of international trade during the more prosperous times of the monarchy and with the advent of colonialism with its incipient multiculturalism, society and government would have required multilingual scribes in increasing numbers as assistants to the merchants and the royal treasuries. Taxation and the monitoring of transported goods might well have been important responsibilities of scribes.

The international character of scribal education clearly impacted wisdom literature. Within the monarchic or colonial courts, employers would have required their trained scribes to know several languages and to be able to oversee the bureaucratic affairs with other nations and provinces. These scribes participated in an educational system that exposed them to many different languages and thus to the cultures and the official writings of other peoples. Most of the writing done by scribes would have been the production of lists and inventories, but there would also have been a need to read and write narrative texts, poetic pieces, and cultic legislation. In many ancient cultures, the teaching of such narrative writing involved religious texts as the reading material and the texts to be copied in scribal training.[16]

It seems reasonable, therefore, to suggest the following scenario. In Yehud, the Persian colonial government employed a number of scribes and thus also sponsored the school for the training of scribes. Because of the nature of provincial commerce throughout most of the Persian period, these Jerusalemite scribes would need to know not only Hebrew and Aramaic but possibly other local and regional languages, such as Egyptian, Babylonian, Persian, and Greek. There may well have been ample room for specialization; it seems unlikely that all scribes would have known all of these languages as well as the less frequently needed languages of smaller, less influential regions. Still, most scribes, if not all, were multilingual. Thus most scribes received a training that involved instruction in the religious texts of other peoples. These scribes then worked for the government as well as for the temple, local merchants, and other employers. They also formed strong class bonds through their academic training and through these common experiences within this rare and prestigious profession. Thus there were causes and opportunities for these scribes to integrate their experience of the world with their Yahwistic roots and the texts of other world religions. This task operated at the very heart of wisdom.

These scribes would therefore have been more aware than most Yehudites of the inherent subjectivity and the socially constructed nature of reality. All societies root themselves in basic assumptions about reality; these assumptions are not more "correct" than others, but they attain a certain agreement by diverse factions of the society, thus providing a grounding for social integration.[17] At times, societies legislate parts of their social assumptions, but usually there are other social constructions abounding even in the midst of such legislation. For example, ancient Israel legislated honor for one's father and mother (Deuteronomy 5:16). This asserted the appropriate action within common social relationships, the parent-child role set. Thus respect for one's parents became part of the socially constructed nature of reality; within such a culture, a variety of actions may have been judged as "honorable" in this regard, depending on the definitions agreed upon by the culture in question. But the constructed nature of reality shows itself at one other point in this example as well: the legislation assumed that father-child and mother-child relationships are both important, lifelong situations of social significance. Such was an assumption basic to that society.[18] Although other patterns of family relationships were possible, the biblical text (as well as ancient Israel) assumed that this pattern was significant, and thus the people constructed this reality through ways that were social, that is, through ways that involved common consensus and shared, communicated values.

Because the scribes of Yehud were more aware of other cultures through their multilingual scribal training, they may well have been more aware of the variations between them and the socially constructed nature of different systems of perceiving reality. However, their role was not as interpretive sociologists or ethnomethodological anthropologists who would analyze and describe their local communities. Instead, they were part of a specific social hierarchy in which they played a simple yet vital function, even if they did participate in such daily routines with the awareness that their life could be different from what it seemed to be within Yehudite culture.

Scribes existed only within an institutionalized, bureaucratic social organization. Unless there was sufficient differentiation of tasks to justify the concentration of time, skill, and training for the production of writing, there could not have been a group of scribes who specialized in literacy. Colonial Yehud was such a stratified society, and the scribes performed very specialized functions within this stratified world, operating within a complex system of roles and interrelationships. Much of their work, especially in prosaic and poetic writing, was to communicate the interrelationships of social interaction with those who had not yet learned it. Scribes, through their acceptance of the socially constructed world of Yehud and through their literate communicative abilities, constructed the appropriate symbols for the world and its role sets and shared these symbols with others. The net effect of such sharing was the maintenance of society. Scribes worked within a determined social system and worked to maintain that same system.

Much of the scribal contribution to social maintenance was in the support of institutions. Because the scribes contributed writing to a wide variety of social groups, they enabled these groups to keep better records and thus to enforce their will with written accounts. Temple priests pointed to the sacred law and legislation as recorded by scribes. Merchants examined the inventories and other scribal-produced records to make sure that all transactions were legal and fair. Governors kept records of prices and other local variables within their own province and wrote about those to other governors, searching either for standardization or for the advantages based in differences. In all these ways, these Yehudite scribes contributed to the maintenance of the society's power systems.

The scribes also participated in the ideological structure of the society. By functioning as record keepers and as the guardians of institutional memory, they embodied the power of the institutions to define reality. For example, because there were records to show that certain laws existed in the past, the populace experienced a reduced ability to question effectively the legal and cultic elites. It became increasingly difficult to argue with the written word, especially in the midst of a mostly nonliterate society. Scribes symbolized the power of the institution to define reality, and the scribes even reduced that reality into marks on tablets and papyri.

Nowhere was this clearer than in the case of religion. The temple scribes cooperated in the elites' definition of God through the production of texts. Literacy served as part of the social symbolic system of God's power and permanence. Writing produced a universe of discourse that is orderly and predictable.[19] Thus religion and scribes both produced senses of ordered universes for humans. Wisdom, as the written production of scribes, expressed the inherent stability of such universes, and it also manifested the upper-middle-class attitudes that the world must always stay as it is and that the hierarchies of privilege must remain stable to allow for individual progress.[20]

With such systems of privilege, scribes function as generalized experts within a society. Experts possess a certain knowledge that is not universal within a culture but that the society considers valuable. This knowledge is practical and necessary, but it is also rare and subject to control. Literacy within ancient Yehud forms a good example of a knowledge with practical usage that allows for the rise of experts, since more people would value the knowledge than would possess it. Experts function within hierarchies, since they are in the business of controlling knowledge in exchange for certain advantages. Thus they will accept payments or other social goods in transaction for their own ability and knowledge; the transactions occur when both parties understand the exchange as helping each party to rise up the social hierarchies.

The sociology of knowledge emphasizes that society influences what humans know. At one level, this occurs by society's definitions of categories and by the limits that society places upon experiences through behavioral norms and economic limitations. In more explicit cases, society influences human knowledge through authority. Through the regulation of speech, society controls what its populace hears and thus limits what the people know. In most cases, people only think the thoughts they have heard and, in cases of conflicts between ideas, people will identify as correct the thoughts heard from the highest authority within the person's social hierarchy. Scribes in an ancient society, who function as experts of knowledge, possess amazing abilities to shape popular thought through their pronouncements.

Experts of knowledge serve to objectify thought.[21] They present the opinions of the society's chief authorities as objective truth, somehow inherent in the nature of the universe and therefore immutable, immediately obvious to sense perception, even if the populace never receives the opportunity to verify such perception. The process and artifacts of writing symbolize well this objectification; the words once written become invariable and permanent, because they are "in black and white" or even "carved in stone."[22] Symbolically, writing makes thought objective and thus unquestionable as a base for authority.

Ancient scribes, such as those in Yehud, served as generalized experts. Because they knew how to write, the society assumed that they knew how to know. Their involvement in social hierarchies thus generalized into governmental, religious, and mercantile arenas. They also participated in the training of the next generation of scribes, and thus they worked to perpetuate their own ideology and their own source of authority.[23] Their elitist attitude was not surprising; they were highly valued colleagues of all the wealthiest and most powerful circles of Yehud, who needed the authority granted by writing and scribes.

This position among Yehud's elites also gave the scribes opportunity to develop, perpetuate, and record their own ideology. Because the scribes were generalized experts, people would assume that they had relevant, valuable knowledge about every topic of life, not just about the issues at hand. Their general advice about life and how to live it well would be considered important knowledge as well, and such were the roots of wisdom. Not only were these scribes persons who held the respect of the populace and who circulated among the elites, they were persons with the peculiar ability to propagate their worldview both because of the technology of communication at their disposal and also because of the popular perception that they knew how to know. The scribal worldview of order, harmony, and hierarchy permeated their writings and formed an important part of canonical wisdom literature.

Wisdom and the Editing of the Canon

Scribes produced wisdom literature as their own internal social understanding of the world, but they also produced all of the rest of the canonical religious literature of ancient Israel and Yehud. In other words, literate persons transmitted all of the texts of the canon, since they were the only ones who could read and write. Of course, there may have been different categories of scribes who were responsible for separate types of religious literature and religious thought, but the social indications would lead the interpreter to expect a relatively unified social class of scribes, especially when the number of literate persons within Yehud was so small. Canonization also occurred over so many centuries that it is difficult to evaluate the influence of scribal wisdom traditions upon each phase of canonical development. However, some factors in canonical editing become clear when seen in terms of scribal activity and the wisdom influences that would have affected it.

Wisdom was a worldview of a Yehudite literate and scribal elite. There was no direct indication of wisdom literature from the premonarchic, monarchic, or exilic periods. Although this negative evidence cannot positively rule out any presence of wisdom traditions during this earlier time, the strong lack of prior indications of wisdom argues for a wisdom "school" developing only in the Persian period and extending beyond. During the monarchy, there had been scribes, but they may well have existed under such tight control of the monarchy and in such small numbers that they never developed their own distinctive perspectives upon the world. If there was such a group, the temple's capture of religion may have erased all records of it. The only direct evidence of a community of sages appeared after the exile. Only in the Persian period and afterward did a class of scribes exist with joint and/or shared responsibilities for legal, governmental, and religious writing and also with the international experience that wisdom demonstrated. This argument about wisdom's social and historical roots both informs and receives support from an examination of canonization.

The Torah itself shows little sign of editing from a wisdom perspective.[24] Within these five books, no wisdom forms supplement the narrative themes and their development. International elements of scribal and wisdom worldview appear infrequently, if at all.[25] Above, the canonization of the Pentateuch was shown to be an act of Darius in the late sixth century (or early fifth century).[26] Either the wisdom emphasis of the scribal editors came much later or the canonization process under Darius' command was not amenable to a substantial reorientation of the literature. In either explanation, the effectiveness of a scribal community with wisdom interests would still be under development in 500 B.C.E. This correlates with the likely later dating for all extant canonical wisdom literature. After that time, Yehud's wisdom elements began to exert more influence.

Likewise, the major and minor prophets of the Hebrew canon show little evidence of wisdom editing in terms of content. Most of this part of the canon may well have been in place by the middle of the fifth century B.C.E.[27] However, the scribal wisdom school may well have been responsible for the organization of the material, especially the systematic ordering of the minor prophets by length, as well as a few ideological additions, such as Hosea 14:9. This shows the first strong evidence of wisdom's presence, hidden in the midst of prophetic texts that would have been assembled after the formation of the Pentateuch but within the middle of the Persian period.

With the growth of the wisdom school in Jerusalem, the next section of the canon, called the Writings, demonstrates very strong wisdom influences. The three wisdom books of the Hebrew and Protestant canon (Proverbs, Job, and Ecclesiastes) occur within the Writings. Furthermore, there is evidence of the intentional scribal editing of other texts within this part of the canon. For instance, the organization of the Psalter into five books, reminiscent of the Pentateuch's literary organization, may well betray the thinking of a textually-oriented mind. If the scribes assisted the temple in organizing the psalms into a Pentateuch-like form, then the scribal hand in Chronicles' rewriting of Samuel and Kings from the Prophets provides another instance of the same tendency. The scribes assisted the religious experts in redefining their topics and adding to the canonical literature further material consistent with their own concerns, but the scribes continued to exercise their own influence.[28] The international flavor of the short stories also represents the scribal tendencies. These stories' reflections on ways of living the good life come close to wisdom in theme, even though they are extremely dissimilar in form.[29] In the Writings, it is difficult to find literature that does not either represent a wisdom tradition or reflect some scribal involvement in ways much more obvious than in the Torah or the Prophets.

Outside the Hebrew canon, the wisdom tradition continued to shape a significant portion of the writings. The pluralistic, international mind-set at the root of wisdom, which had reached expression within the final stages of the canonical literature, continued in greater numbers in the remaining literature. Further wisdom books appeared, such as the Wisdom of Solomon and Sirach. The short stories also continued to gain popularity, expressing their internationalist views. The growth of apocalyptic appeared somewhat at odds with the wisdom tradition, but the scribes continued to give apocalyptic limited admission into the written traditions of the people.

The growth of scribalism as a distinct profession and social class within Yehud paralleled the development of the canon. Under Darius, the Pentateuch attained canonization with almost no scribal influences. The Prophets underwent minor scribal editing and wisdom additions in the middle of the Persian period. By the end of the Persian period, Yehud's scribes were producing major works of wisdom literature and were deeply involved in the editing of other texts; almost nothing gained inclusion in the canon's third section, Writings, without significant scribal and wisdom influence.[30]

The importance of wisdom, therefore, extended far beyond the literature that most clearly expressed its own ideology. Its influences outreached its own textual productivity and so appeared to have affected the bulk if not the whole of the canonical process. Wisdom's theology permeated much of the canon, and its assumptions about life became crucial to the understanding of one of the most prominent nonpriestly streams of thought in the Persian period.

Proverbs and the Theological Worldview of Wisdom

The theological worldview of wisdom proved to be of immense importance. Wisdom literature typically understood God to have implanted wisdom thought within the very structure of the universe, lying in wait for humans to discover the truths hidden just beneath the surface of observation. The Book of Proverbs provided the clearest examples of wisdom's assumptions about the order of life, but its own organization was far from obvious. It was not thematic or topical in any sense, but it did lend itself to a systematization of sorts when considered at the level of ideology.

The first chapters of the Book of Proverbs argued persuasively for the acceptance of wisdom's authority. The scribes' struggle became apparent from the beginning of their writings. Theirs was the power of the stylus, not the stronger, more obvious forms of coercion available to governors and priests. Instead, they needed to convince people of their authority, based upon their social location and the helpfulness of their discourse.

The Proverbs immediately started their appeals to authority. The superscription ascribed the book to Solomon, David's son, the king of Israel (Proverbs 1:1). Thus wisdom claimed to root its authority within that of the royalty. As a legitimating move of the postmonarchic period, the motivation was clear: the connection to an authority from the past that exceeded, at least in some ways, the moral and emotional authority of current governments. After an initial poem extolling wisdom and the wise, the book next enlisted the other native source of authority, the priests, through claiming that "the fear of Yahweh is the beginning of knowledge" (Proverbs 1:7). The literature called upon the hierarchies of the temple for support through relativizing them within wisdom; proper worship and correct attitudes toward God were part of wisdom. Wisdom denied the antithesis between wisdom and cult, even while subsuming cult within its own agenda;[31] proper religion, after all, was only the beginning of wisdom, which extended much farther than the temple could have suggested.

Most of the first nine chapters operate with a single metaphor governing the relationship of wisdom teacher and learner (and thus between narrator and reader). The father-son motif recurs to the point of dominance within these chapters.[32] This compares the authority of wisdom with the authority of the head of household within the Yehudite family. This inherent power relationship, combined with the emotional impact and the strong religious and cultural commands for respect and obedience, pushes forward the wisdom agenda within the context of a protective, hopeful relationship. Just as a father intends the best for his child, so the teacher wants the best for the learner, and the teacher knows best.[33] Since the topic is wisdom, the description of the best way to live life, the parental image would probably have seemed apt. It may also point to the use of Proverbs as an instructional book for the young, who were learning the skills of scribalism and also the rudiments of scribal social identity and wisdom thought.

The specific content of the proverbs beginning with chapter 10 focuses on everyday life. Many of the proverbs deal with the proper means of attaining riches. Wealth requires such virtues as diligence, prudence, integrity, wisdom, strength, truth, effective speech, and peacefulness. All of these characteristics qualify as self-descriptions of the wealthy and powerful; they understand themselves and their society in this way and they seek to preserve these values upon which they have based their own rise to power. There is a special focus on speech, especially upon the need for truth and for cautious speech. Good speech is equivalent to knowledge, thus representing the typical wisdom view connecting literacy, the social role of the expert, and wisdom ideology.

Beginning with chapter 25, the Book of Proverbs moves to more specific cases, especially with the role of the king and those in the king's presence. The king should have no evil advisers (Proverbs 25:5; 29:12, 16), and supplicants should approach the king's court with caution (Proverbs 25:6-7, 15; 29:26). Rulers should extract goods from their subjects but should not exploit them unduly (Proverbs 28:3, 15-16, 22; 30:11-14). This was an important lesson throughout the times of the Persian Empire's tendencies to exploit the colonies beyond their abilities to pay taxes. Above all, a ruler should maintain order (Proverbs 28:2; 29:2-4). The final poem (Proverbs 31:10-31), a skilled acrostic, portrays the ideal woman, whose performance as wife and mother has rendered her children happy and her husband wealthy. The elite men's values of peaceful life and the abundance of goods finds clear expression in this woman whose service to others (especially the men of her household) defines her own identity.

Throughout the book, Proverbs describes ways of safety in life. One should give proper respect to one's elders within the community. This reinforces the social hierarchies in place. One should practice the restraint of one's passions, because moderate, considered action is always best.[34] One must live effectively within the network of social relations, showing proper deference to one's betters and striving for respectability. The ideal social relations receive treatment at any cost; there should be reconciliation with estranged relatives and colleagues. The merchant implications are clear; everyone is a potential contact, and so all relationships must be conducted professionally. All of these ties to the social hierarchies represent wisdom's commitment to the maintenance of the status quo. This represents a type of propriety in life as well as in religion, in which one maintains the proper relationship of fear with respect to Yahweh.

At the same time that one conducts one's life in this manner of propriety, there are problems in the world that one must avoid. The Book of Proverbs often depicts the evils of the world as seductive woman, tempting persons to deviate from the proper path of action. The temptations of this other worldview are strong, but the book encourages these trainees to avoid such otherness. The fear of the unknown, of the nontraditional, is strong throughout Proverbs. Strictly speaking, there is little fear of the foreign; there are very few injunctions about other people groups. However, wisdom's desire to impress its own worldview upon its students is noted. Specifically, the proverbs fear laziness, deceit, and developing unorthodox views. These values were considered of such degrading potential that they were to be avoided at all costs. These negatively attributed values are precisely those that would be most effective in undermining the society. Proverbs attempts to maintain a hardworking, dedicated group with a closely defined orthodoxy and orthopraxy, and complete with a fixed hierarchy so that one knows to whom one answers in all tasks.

The Social Functions of Proverbs and Wisdom

At one level, the social function of the scribal sages and of their wisdom literature was the education of the young. Not only did they learn the appropriate skills of reading and writing but they also learned the values held by the elites of the Yehudite society. Education would have been an important goal. At the same time, scribal activity was its own reward, as the legal and religious usefulness of written texts proved themselves day after day in the service of the powers that be.

Proverbs and the similar forms of wisdom literature, however, had other more subtle purposes and effects. Proverbs presented a worldview of control, especially self-control. Yehud, as did all societies, required social control mechanisms of some sort. That is, in order for a society to remain stable, it must find ways to encourage its population to hold to the basic behavioral norms of that society. Force was too expensive as a long-term, widespread option, but the propagation of an ideology of control proved much more effective. Thus Proverbs supported obedience and restraint as proper goals for persons within Yehud. Such values made sense within a world of order, such as that social world with order enforced by the Persian Empire. Within that system, there were rewards for those who did right, as defined by the elites of the empire and its colonial administrative system. The strong sense of order within Proverbs thus maintained a hierarchy, communicating adherence to the rules of the powerful and respect for the hierarchy.

On still another level, this emphasis on order maintained the power of the scribes. Through the message that wisdom was the proper goal of life, they increased in value the one commodity that only they controlled: education. Wisdom itself became a social control mechanism by valuing education, which it then regulated and distributed at will to those who worked within the boundaries of the system as defined by the authors of wisdom literature. Thus the presence of wisdom literature worked to maintain the power of the educated classes, especially the scribes and those with a wisdom mind-set who knew the proverbs and could teach them, along with the skills to write, to the chosen few.

Job and Ecclesiastes proved that not all Hebrew Bible wisdom worked within these few assumptions, but Proverbs indicated the presence of a wisdom tradition based on the importance of world maintenance. The sages and scribes communicated the blessings of an orderly world in which the status quo never received a challenge. Within that world, the Persian Empire reigned supreme forever and the temple maintained its own ritual throughout eternity. Persons in families were happy and harmonious, and enough rich children went to school to keep the scribes well occupied. Values of obedience and self-control became highly praised, along with the rejection of new, challenging ideas that would lead people outside this world of diligence, prudence, and caution in seeking for advantage.

Notes

1. Consider David W. Jamieson-Drake, *Scribes and Schools in Monarchic Judah: A Socio-Archaeological Approach,* JSOTSup 109, SWBA 9 (Sheffield: Almond Press, 1991).

2. This is not to suggest that wisdom remained insulated from outside influences during the Persian period. Certainly the increased contact with Iranian forms of wisdom literature would have impacted the tradition. See James R. Russell, "The Sage in Ancient Iranian Literature," in *The Sage in Israel and the Ancient Near East,* ed. John G. Gammie and Leo G. Perdue (Winona Lake, Ind.: Eisenbrauns, 1990), 81–92; and idem, "Sages and Scribes at the Courts of Ancient Iran," in Gammie and Perdue, *The Sage in Israel,* 141–46. However, the influence does not seem to be direct, especially in the canonical wisdom books.

3. R. N. Whybray, "The Social World of the Wisdom Writers," in Clements, *The World of Ancient Israel,* 227.

4. James L. Crenshaw, "The Wisdom Literature," in *The Hebrew Bible and Its Modern Interpreters,* ed. Douglas A. Knight and Gene M. Tucker (Philadelphia: Fortress Press, 1985), 389.

5. Cf. James L. Crenshaw, "Education in Ancient Israel," *JBL* 104 (1989): 601–15.

6. Whybray, "Social World of the Wisdom Writers," in Clements, *The World of Ancient Israel*, 230–31.

7. The lack of such records from ancient Israel represents the priestly capture of religion. Once the priesthood became the group to define Yahwistic religion for the majority of Yehudites, they discouraged and repressed the presence of other religious expressions. Thus the extant records of the Hebrew Bible preserve little evidence for the use of wisdom during the monarchy; those records did not operate within the priestly agenda. Of course, the priestly capture of Yahwistic religion was only partially successful, and the pluralism of the Persian period allowed for the preservation of the canonical (and extracanonical) wisdom from that later time.

8. For a discussion of these views, see Whybray, "Social World of the Wisdom Writers," in Clements, *The World of Ancient Israel*, 229–35, esp. 231.

9. Still, scribalism and wisdom are always closely connected, and it is likely that Solomon's time saw the establishment of court schools for literacy training, in which some early forms of wisdom flourished. It is likely that these early wisdom pieces betrayed extensive Egyptian influences. However, it is exceedingly unclear whether any of this Solomonic wisdom literature is extant in the Hebrew Bible or whether the current texts' references to Israel's third king reflect only the habitual honoring of Solomon as Israel's first patron of writing and education.

10. Qoheleth is often known by the name "Ecclesiastes," especially in English texts.

11. Wisdom and Sirach are considered apocryphal books in Protestant tradition and deuterocanonical in Roman Catholic tradition.

12. Proverbs 6:23; 28:4, 7, 9; 29:9.

13. It is interesting that theological argumentation remains a path toward God, and in the Book of Job it is that path which succeeds when God visits Job with speech that leads, paradoxically, toward a restoration of blessedness and the good life.

14. See chapter 14, below, for a closer examination of Job and Ecclesiastes as examples of wisdom as dissent.

15. For an analysis of the variety of sages' roles, see Gammie and Perdue, *The Sage in Israel.*

16. For an important warning about the too-easy identification of wisdom with scribal productivity, see Hartmut Gese, "Wisdom Literature in the Persian Period," in *The Cambridge History of Judaism*, vol. 1, *Introduction, The Persian Period*, ed. W. D. Davies and Louis Finkelstein (Cambridge: Cambridge University Press, 1984), 190–99.

17. Berger and Luckmann, *Social Construction of Reality.*

18. Comparisons with other cultures point to the possibility of other constructed patterns. For instance, many non-Western people groups will not assume that the father-child relationship is one of importance but instead will assume that the mother's brother will take a major role in raising the child and relating to it through adulthood. This very different social system constructs its reality in a very different direction through a different set of assumptions about what relationships are "real" or automatically significant. Societies rarely make conscious choices about such matters, but there is strong ideological commitment to these types of patterns throughout cultures.

19. In earliest times, when literacy was extremely rare, it must have amazed the populace. A common citizen could approach a scribe and utter a sentence; the scribe would then make marks and send the tablet or scroll away, where others would know exactly what the commoner thought. This would have seemed magical or the result of technology and education far beyond the norm. It would have seemed magical for the second scribe to read the mind of the first simply on the basis of touching and examining the mysterious pattern of marks made by the first scribe. The populace would have held such abilities in the utmost awe.

20. To a large extent, wisdom relied upon the stability of the world at large as a backdrop for

individual accomplishment and acheivement. Only if the social rules remained stable and rewarded persons in established patterns could one rise through the ranks of society. Such was wisdom's goal, in many cases.

21. For a thorough discussion of objectification as a process within the sociology of knowledge, see Berger and Luckmann, *Social Construction of Reality.*

22. Note that the symbolism of writing's objectification of knowledge occurs within modern society as well as ancient; both societies use writing in the same way. The presence of modern proverbs such as "Don't believe everything you read" only confirms the power of writing; oral authorities need to attack written authority with such a proverbial saying, in order to emphasize the speaker's authority to define true knowledge.

23. Presumably, one of the functions of ancient scribal education would be to ensure that no one learned the skills of scribalism without also receiving an inculcation with the ideology and mind-set of the scribes, thus protecting the class of scribes from intrusion by divergent values. This is a prime function of much professional education, where the receipt of certain knowledge and abilities entitles one to join a class of practitioners.

24. Joseph Blenkinsopp, *Prophecy and Canon: A Contribution to the Study of Jewish Origins,* University of Notre Dame Center for the Study of Judaism and Christianity in Antiquity 3 (Notre Dame, Ind.: University of Notre Dame Press, 1977).

25. A possible exception is the Joseph cycle, in which the role of dreams becomes crucial in determining the right way to live. Even though it is important to know the right methods for interpreting dreams in order to reflect on the best ways of life within these stories, these are mantic means, not analytic wisdom/scribal attempts to comment on the values of life. This is shown clearly by the close parallel to the Daniel story, which is a short story and shares themes with other narratives, not with the wisdom literature of the postexilic period.

26. A postexilic date for the final edition of the Pentateuch is virtually required by the restoration themes in parts of the narratives as well as the Babylonian traces within the legal codes. See Spicer, "Postexilic Additions to Deuteronomy."

27. Later additions to the prophetic canon mention Greece and other elements that postdate 450 B.C.E. Similarly, the deuteroprophetic literature may well be significantly later, but these are perhaps better seen as late Persian or Hellenistic additions to a preexistent canon rather than the last stages of development of an open canon.

28. Note that scribes appear four times in Chronicles (1 Chronicles 2:55; 24:6; 27:32; 2 Chronicles 34:13), all at places where the older stories do not mention them. These are additions by the Chronicler to the original stories, representing a bias toward scribes and their role in society.

29. Suggestions about wisdom influences in such short stories are to be avoided. See James L. Crenshaw, "Method in Determining Wisdom Influence in 'Historical' Literature," *JBL* 88 (1969): 129–42. Even though any direct literary influences between wisdom literature and the short stories would be nearly impossible to prove and not helpful to suggest, it is possible to think of both wisdom and short stories as different types of responses to some of the same cultural and societal factors, and thus there may well have been underlying connections at the level of theme or assumptions. The fact remains that the short stories show evidence of intentional literary crafting, such as that done by scribes.

30. An interesting and related issue is that of translation. By the middle of the fifth century B.C.E., the Hebrew documents of the Torah and (presumably) the Prophets were becoming popular among the inhabitants of Yehud when read in Aramaic (see Nehemiah 8:1—9:3; consider also the presence of Aramaic texts within the canonical books of Ezra-Nehemiah and Daniel). This translation may well have been the duty of scribes, as the ones best trained in multiple languages and the practice of translation. Although there is no indication of the Persian-period production of

written translations into Aramaic or any other language, it appears likely that this would have served as the precursor for later, more formal translations under the direction of the scribal class and thus with the influence of wisdom and its pragmatism.

31. Leo G. Perdue, *Wisdom and Cult: A Critical Analysis of the Views of Cult in the Wisdom Literatures of Israel and the Ancient Near East*, SBLDS 30 (Missoula, Mont.: Scholars Press, 1977), esp. 347.

32. Carol A. Newsom, "Woman and the Discourse of Patriarchal Wisdom: A Study of Proverbs 1–9," in *Gender and Difference in Ancient Israel*, ed. Peggy L. Day (Minneapolis: Fortress Press, 1989), 142–60.

33. Of course, both of these metaphors depict dependent relationships of hierarchy.

34. The Greek notions of moderation echoed herein may indicate a date for the collection that is after 450 B.C.E., when Athens would have been able to have a significant influence upon Palestine as a whole.

CHAPTER 12

APOCALYPTIC VISIONS: RHETORIC OF VIOLENT OPPOSITION

THROUGHOUT ISRAEL'S MONARCHY, A number of individuals operated in a social role called prophecy.[1] In the Persian period, several more prophets spoke concerning the connection of politics, community life, and religion. These prophecies are extant in Isaiah 40–66, Haggai, Zechariah 1–8, and Malachi.[2] Prophets shared visions with people. Rarely were these visions actual visual portraits derived from some mystical experience by the prophet. More typically, the prophets expressed ideas about how society and human life could function. At times, the visions depicted life as affected by God's negative action that destroyed social institutions in attempts to build communities of justice and righteousness. Other visions emphasized the possibilities for faithful life that presented themselves to God's people as a result of God's salvific activity in the world. Throughout their works, the prophets offered a sense of alternative vision for their audiences. Prophecy produced an implicit critique of the status quo even at its mildest expressions because it offered another view of how life could be; at times prophecy directly condemned the status quo with great particularity.

To the range of Israelite and Yehudite social life, and especially in the midst of its social struggles during times of decision and action, prophecy claimed the voice of God and offered depictions of other ways of life that implied new options, favored by God, for the living of real life among the community.[3] Prophecy thus offered a critique of the ways of life that assumed a fixed number of options, thoroughly known by the members of the community. Prophecy pushed the borders of what the community considered to be possible.

Throughout Israel's and Yehud's history, prophecy functioned chiefly in relationship with governmental issues about the nature of the community. Although there are many examples of other prophetic functions throughout history, this seems to be the most common of the recorded forms from the postexilic period, at least. Third Isaiah offered the competing visions of the political organization of the Jerusalem community that three different political power groups were suggesting. Haggai and Proto-Zechariah both discussed the ramifications of the Persian-based political plan for building a temple in Jerusalem. Malachi debated the impact upon the temple life of certain changes in imperial policy toward the colonies and the funding of their temples. All of these Persian period prophets dealt significantly with political issues, although often in circumspect fashion. Certainly the prophets had interests other than politics, but their concern with the nature of community often expressed itself in issues close to politics.

In the Persian colony of Yehud, prophecy continued as a social institution that presented new options for the consideration of the community and claimed the divine prerogative for these options. Several prophets, as discussed above, operated within the first half of the colony's existence, but no prophecy from the second half of the Persian period survives to the modern day. It is unclear whether this indicates a decline or cessation in the occurrence of prophecy after the reign of Artaxerxes I or whether conditions for the recording of prophecy changed radically, perhaps correlating to the changing role of scribes within the society.[4] Regardless of the reasons for the canon's relative lack of prophets after the middle of the fifth century, there were other visions that gained currency within Yehud. These visions shared a character different from those offered by the prophets and participated in a notably different social reality. These apocalyptic visions gain in prominence through the Persian period and become substantial expressions of Yahwistic faith through the Hellenistic and Roman periods. Perhaps it is only the very beginnings of apocalyptic thought that appear in these Persian period texts, but the structure of apocalyptic takes hold in Persian Yehud, setting the standard forms for this type of expression in the following centuries.

The nature of apocalyptic vision demonstrates an inherent pessimism about human ability to choose new options for society. In this, it opposes both prophecy and wisdom, which are much more optimistic about human ability, although for different reasons and in distinct ways. Apocalyptic assumes God's approaching intervention in society to reverse its structures and to change radically the nature of human existence; thus apocalyptic emphasizes God's powerful role in shaping human events in the near future, in the midst of a despair about what God has done in the immediate past, if anything.

Reactions against Prophecy

Several texts within the Hebrew Bible offer very critical remarks about the prophets, accusing them of a variety of matters of infidelity and poor religion. Jeremiah 23:9-40 presents a text often dated to the postexilic period.[5] At first, this text limits its critique of the prophets to a comparison of the prophets of Samaria with those of Jerusalem, showing that neither did their jobs correctly. The text continues, however, to condemn the Jerusalemite prophets, using Yahweh's voice to command the people: "Do not listen to the words of the prophets who prophesy to you; they are deluding you. They speak visions of their own minds, not from the mouth of Yahweh" (Jeremiah 23:16). Repeatedly, the text proclaims that the prophets did not receive admission into Yahweh's councils and thus had no accurate information about Yahweh at all. Instead, the prophets made up sayings and prophecies on their own.

Zechariah 13:2-6 presented a different critique. Zechariah pictures a time when no prophets would willingly admit their vocation but instead would deny their work as prophets. None of the reasons for this shame were listed, but the extent of the animosity was clear. This writer in the Zechariah tradition understood prophets to be unrealistic, and his own views found expression in the themes and forms of the apocalyptic movement.

With these few indications, it is possible to assert that some elements of postexilic

Yehudite society were dissatisfied with prophecy and with its visions for action in community. This should not be surprising; prophecy had its detractors throughout its existence as an institution. Any presentation of alternate visions for community threatens those whose interest involves maintaining the society in its current form. In Yehud, the forces of social maintenance included governors, priests, and sages. These groups had often criticized the prophets for their variance from official policy. Throughout Israelite history, many prophets presented the views of the ruling class without question, legitimating the status quo through their prophetic voice.[6] This resulted in conflict between these "false" prophets and the "true" prophets who spoke the word of God, not the word of the people or the desires of the ruling classes; both "true" and "false" prophets became the target of the sort of accusations found in Jeremiah 23 and Zechariah 13. Perhaps the most that can be said about this postexilic disagreement with and devaluing of prophecy is that it may represent either the complaint of those with alternate vision that the prophets have allied themselves with the ruling class or the complaint of the ruling class that these prophets criticize them too much. Either of these opposite views seems possible, given the scarcity of evidence; perhaps all that can be known is that there were prophetic visions during the postexilic period and that these visions came under attack from part of the populace.

Despite the impossibility of determining the condition of prophecy in the last half of the Persian period, the rise of apocalyptic seems clear, if difficult to determine with precision. In the postexilic period, apocalyptic became another source for alternate visions of reality and community with God. Its own assumptions were quite different. Apocalyptic rarely presented the same concerns about politics that prophecy did; apocalyptic also tended to express its concerns in more cosmic terms. These probably represented a very different social location as well. Despite the many differences between prophecy and apocalyptic, both in social and literary terms, apocalyptic and prophecy both offered alternate visions of reality in community, and so the absence of recorded prophets in the second half of Yehud's Persian period coincided unsurprisingly with the growth of apocalyptic expression.

Definitions of Apocalyptic

The term "apocalyptic" has experienced many uses, and even within scholarship there has been a tendency to use the term in a variety of ways, often with limited precision. The variety of usages, however, expresses something important about the nature of apocalyptic. It is difficult to define this phenomenon of apocalyptic within only one set of parameters. That is, apocalyptic existed and functioned as a literary genre, as a religious worldview, and as a social expression within a community. All three of these operative categories are essential to the full understanding of the phenomenon; apocalyptic cannot be adequately defined and discussed within the confines of only one category. The confluence of these categories produces the only full description of apocalyptic. That having been said, the problem still remains. Constructing a definition that embraces genre, worldview, and social function proves difficult. The variety of apocalyptic literature makes that kind of definition a near impossibility, and such attempts run the risk of removing important pieces of apocalyptic from consideration because they do not fit into a given analytic schema. The problem requires a certain openness in the definitions until the patterns have demonstrated themselves more clearly from within.

Of the three definitional categories, genre, worldview, and social function, only one of them is currently accessible to the student of apocalyptic. A direct analysis of social function or of worldview is not possible; the evidence for those definitions exists within the people who wrote and read this literature, and they are no longer available for study. Genre is the only possible means for entry into the study at this point in time, because the literature is the only evidence in the investigator's possession. Thus it is necessary to begin with a literary definition. Philip R. Davies suggests the following definition of apocalyptic: "a literary communication of esoteric knowledge, purportedly mediated by a heavenly figure to (usually) a renowned figure of the past."[7] Although some examples of the apocalyptic literature may not meet all of the requirements of this definition, it still represents something essential about apocalyptic. Apocalyptic claims to possess some special heavenly knowledge about community, events, or God, and it attempts to share the secrets of this knowledge. Apocalyptic writers enter into the discussion of alternate visions of community by claiming that they have pertinent and vital information about such community. They also tend to claim that their information comes from God and that it is secret, special information not available to the masses. Whereas prophecy often assumes that the necessary evidence is in plain sight, only awaiting the proper insight and verbalization to express the direction of community life, apocalyptic assumes that the knowledge is *not* present within the world until God intervenes.

The definition of apocalyptic as a genre expressing esoteric knowledge necessitates a certain part of the apocalyptic worldview as well. Apocalyptic therefore assumes that there are heavenly secrets that are relevant to earthly phenomena and that heavenly beings wish at least certain humans to possess at least some of this information for their benefit.[8] This assumption about the accessibility of beneficial and secret heavenly information implies one of the important social dynamics of apocalyptic. An agent of heaven delivers secret information to the apocalyptic writer, and this secret information carries with it power. Apocalyptic produces a power differential of information, at least from the viewpoint of the apocalypticist. Thus apocalyptic flourishes among those who seek an advantage of secret information over others. It assumes that knowledge differentials produce power differentials, and that real social advantage, in addition to psychological advantages, accrues to those with the rare, special knowledge.

When assembled together, these pieces produce a significant understanding of apocalyptic. As a literary genre, it claims to receive and to communicate special esoteric knowledge received from heaven; this knowledge is meant for select individuals. As a worldview, it assumes the existence of heavenly beings who communicate knowledge to mortals in ways that are beneficial. Socially, apocalyptic functions to provide advantages for those who possess the special knowledge, over against those who are not initiated into the ways and information of the apocalyptic group.

Other attempts to define apocalyptic have, of course, produced alternate results. Davies has also noticed the connections of apocalyptic with mantic wisdom.[9] Manticism seeks to explain current events in esoteric ways. The dream interpretation of Joseph and Daniel provides biblical examples of this mode of envisioning reality. Rather than emphasizing a direct heavenly revelation, manticism focuses on technological interpretations of natural events. This technology can include divinations of many sorts. Davies argues that such mantic wisdom is more scribal than priestly; over time, it develops its own body of specialized knowledge about how to interpret various natural phenomena, from cloud formations to patterns in bird livers. With the proper techniques, interpretation becomes almost automatic. Of course, mantic interpretation of physical reality and thus its assertions about the nature of social community can be phrased within other forms. In the case of apocalyptic, the results of manticism may be couched as direct revelation from a heavenly being. In that case, the distinctions between other definitions of apocalyptic and a mantic emphasis become less clear, but this may only be a special case. If the connection with mantic wisdom is correct, then the parallels with apocalyptic should be found not within prophecy but within scribalism and divination, and the concerns will always be present rather than future.

The Rise of Apocalyptic

The imprecision in definitions virtually necessitates differences in explaining the development of apocalyptic. What factors within Israel's history and Yehud's experience contributed to the shape of apocalyptic? A frequent assertion has been the impact of Persian dualistic thought. As the exilic community came into contact first with Babylonian religions and patterns of thought and then with the Persian Empire's ideological features, the Yehudites began to borrow significant concepts from their imperial overlords. Persia thought in dualistic terms, many scholars assert. A "good" god opposed a "bad" god for control of the world, and there existed good and bad angels who fought for the ability to influence humans in forceful ways. Each good thought or deed possessed a parallel bad option, and humanity continually cycled between these. Apocalypticism's radicalization of options, often stressing dire ends to human existence, followed this dualistic pattern; if good was not happening in the present, then evil was in charge of human affairs, and this would only lead to increased evil until the world reached its destruction.

This opinion of Persian dualism's contribution to apocalypticism's development has been extremely influential, but it possesses several problems. First, there is little indication that Persian religion affected Yehud nearly as much as Babylonian religion and Canaanite religion did in ages past. Second, the characterization of Persian religion as dualistic proves problematic; most ancient and modern religions possessed at least some dualism, and Persian religion seems not to have been much different from other religions at this time. Third, dualism fails to explain the most characteristic features of apocalyptic thought or any of the specific views of the extant apocalyptic texts. The theory of Persian dualistic influence thus lacks historical basis and explanatory power.

Some others have argued that apocalyptic was simply a much later reapplication of prophecy, perhaps occurring as late as Maccabean times.[10] Over time, the inhabitants of Jerusalem increasingly understood prophecy as a set of predictions about the future. Some of these predictions, in the estimation of Hellenistic Jews, had come to pass, and others had not. Apocalyptic, in this view, restates and reinterprets the unfulfilled prophecies of ancient Israel and applies them to the Hellenistic Jewish community. Although this may well have affected some apocalyptic, it seems unlikely that this was a significant influence upon apocalyptic's shape and function. Apocalyptic lacks the flavor of documents constructed for specific statements about the immediate future. Instead, apocalyptic seems to be more general in its assertions and its alternate visions for life than one would expect for a direct application of unfulfilled prophecy.[11]

Other scholars have understood wisdom to be the source for apocalyptic. Whereas wisdom, as expressed in works such as Proverbs, demonstrated a fundamental belief in order on the social level, apocalyptic extended that same sense of order to the cosmos. God would move the very heavens to make them match God's own sense of values; creation would be forfeit in the path of God's renewed intentional activity.[12] In this sense, von Rad understood apocalyptic as a devolution of wisdom. Whereas wisdom proper gave concrete examples for how people should live in the real world, apocalyptic proved much less helpful in the search for real-life answers. Instead, apocalyptic wandered off into the cosmic realm, developing the same concerns on a scope far removed from daily issues.

Otto Plöger developed an explanation for apocalyptic's development that focused not on prior wisdom traditions but on the subsequent development of theocratic institutions.[13] Plöger saw the institutions deriving from the Maccabees as the best example of theocracy in Jerusalem, in which temple, cult, and law combine to form the political establishment. Against this theocracy, there formed small, nonpowerful groups of Hasidim, whose attitudes were pious, passive, and eschatological. These eschatologists developed apocalyptic stories such as Daniel, in which God is in control of the world and the full scope of human history, and humans wait with patience and pious activity to earn God's favor. Theocrats opted for human action in the present; eschatologists waited for God to act in the future. This essential difference produced a conflict between these two groups. The theocrats and the eschatologists developed into permanent antagonists; their conflict becomes the defining social event of the era as the entire society polarizes around these antithetic groups.

Plöger's explanation presents at least two major problems. First, Plöger studies the apocalyptic of the post-Maccabean period with much greater accuracy than he examines the earlier forms, such as those of the Persian and early Hellenistic periods. Second is the assumption of theocracy. Typically, theocracy combines political power and religious power into the same governing body, which thus controls all secular and religious influence over the community. However, a true theocracy could not develop within the Persian period because of the influence of Persian imperial control in Jerusalem. The Persian Empire exercised active political control over the colony of Yehud; the imperial structure severely limited the development of local political authorities. Thus no autonomous local political base could combine with a local religious power base to form a theocracy. Instead, the presence of Persian imperial control made it impossible for any local power group to assume complete authority; the resultant pluralism was the chief social characteristic of the Persian period.[14]

Despite the difficulties with Plöger's views, the high strong power of his theories has made them popular with many scholars. The theory seems promising with its combination of literature and society, working through many of the definitional problems experienced by many scholars of apocalyptic. Paul D. Hanson developed Plöger's theories and extended them into the Persian period.[15] Hanson asserted that the vision of the eschatologists was thoroughly separated from the pragmatic, reality-tested views of the hierocrats who controlled the temple in the early Persian period and beyond. Apocalyptic, on the other hand, reactualized ancient myths and presented no practical plans for organizing society. The social picture reflected this division; the hierocrats controlled the power centers of the society and the apocalypticists existed only along the social fringes.

Davies has disputed certain elements of Hanson's view.[16] The fringe-like nature of the apocalyptic literature did not require a fringe community for its production. Thus the connections between literature and society, long thought to be the most attractive feature of Hanson's and Plöger's theories, have proved to be elusive. Furthermore, the apocalyptic literature from ancient Jerusalem respected both the eschatological concerns and the values of the cult. There was no sharp divergence of these concerns, thus negating Hanson's hypotheses. In response, Davies presented a different suggestion: apocalyptic derives from disputes within the establishment.

Hanson identified apocalyptic's social location as the fringe, where apocalyptic communities lived at a distance from the rest of society. His analysis of these communities depended upon the sociological theories of revitalization movements. The theory of revitalization movements developed through studies of twentieth-century fringe communities in upheaval and transition through their interactions with newer technologies. Relative deprivation theory states that patterned change occurs in societies where one social group possesses a significantly lower standard of living than other groups.[17] In these cases, the disadvantaged group, once it realizes its own deprivation relative to the other groups, follows a leader in a revolt, with the goal being the overthrow of the government. Through this revitalization movement, a relatively unorganized group of lesser power and lower standard of living organizes itself in order to seek more goods and greater social advantage. This increases the target group's participation in the institutions of society, often through the creation of new institutions in which these fringe groups have a controlling interest. Social participation increases in the areas of politics, ideology, and economics. In all of these areas and more, the revitalization movement presses the poorer elements of the society into a higher state of involvement, through disruptive political maneuvers and economic and spiritual energizing.

Hanson understands the apocalyptic communities as revitalization movements. Forced onto the social fringe, they possess a much lower standard of living than that enjoyed by the ruling classes of Jerusalem. The rural parts of Yehud would have been rather unorganized politically, but leaders arose within these communities and began the process of revitalization. Through the introduction of apocalyptic ideas, these leaders encouraged political revolt against the Jerusalem hierocrats and thus brought about economic and spiritual renewal to the fringe communities.

Hanson's theories partake of the same problems that plague Plöger's work, in addition to some further difficulties. Apocalyptic expresses itself in sophisticated literary forms, arguing for roots within more educated and literary communities rather than uneducated and unorganized fringe communities. Thus Hanson's identification of the social location of apocalyptic must be questioned. Furthermore, relative deprivation theory and the descriptions of revitalization movements present their own problems. Sociologists have been extremely critical of these theories as explanations of social change. Certainly a wide variety of other communities experienced relative deprivation and yet did not undergo this pattern of revitalization. Hanson's theories about Yehud's development of apocalyptic, therefore, are based on inadequate sociological theories. The problems connecting the theory's predictions with Yehud's reality, such as the lack of sudden technological intrusion or the lack of any evidence of an attempted political overthrow, merely provide further questions about the helpfulness of this analysis.

The rise of apocalyptic, therefore, remains unexplained by the dominant theories available in recent scholarship. Persian dualism and prophetic reapplication have been widely recognized as inadequate as explanatory theories. Plöger and Hanson have presented views dividing theocracy and eschatology as competing forces within the society that produced apocalyptic, and Hanson has refined those theories using relative deprivation theory and descriptions of revitalization movements. Despite the popular currency of these theories, the sociological foundations are questionable and the correspondence between the theories and the actual realities of ancient Yehud are insufficient to serve as effective explanatory tools.

Apocalyptic and Social Class

Many of the theories of apocalyptic's development assume that apocalyptic derives from fringe communities in Yehud. Certainly Yehud's centralization and the Persian Empire's development of Jerusalem as an urban center of political and religious control over the colony of Yehud established the possibilities for fringe groups, kept out of the power circles in Jerusalem. However, the existence of such fringe elements does not prove that such were the roots for apocalyptic's development. The social class of apocalyptic's origin may well have left its mark upon the texts. Thus the social origin is relevant but perhaps cannot be so easily defined, as many other theories have suggested.

Although relative deprivation theory has lost its recognition as a reliable, useful theory within sociology, there is some support for a variant: the concept of perceived relative deprivation.[18] Persons who feel themselves to have significantly less than others within their sphere of acquaintance can experience a sense of lack that can lead to dissatisfaction, possibly resulting in a motivation for social change. This can occur whether such persons actually own fewer possessions or not. That is, persons with relatively high standards of living, but who are poorer than their colleagues, often feel a sense of inadequacy and dissatisfaction, whereas people living in poverty who have little contact with wealth may not feel the same sense of mobilizing dissatisfaction with their personal economic condition. The key factor is comparison with others in personal experience, not with far-reaching economic realities.

If perceived relative deprivation is a relevant causation in the development of the dissatisfaction endemic to apocalyptic, then the search for the genre's social roots shifts. Yehud's rural areas may well have been relatively undifferentiated in economic measures, but Jerusalem itself contained a wide variety of economic strata. The ruling classes controlled the resources of the Persian colonial government and the temple as they passed through the city; the benefits and profits from the distribution of these resources were sizable. However, not everyone in Jerusalem was wealthy. The uppermost classes employed a variety of laborers and others to serve their needs. This created an immense gulf of wealth, power, advantage, and privilege within the city of Jerusalem. Furthermore, there were many persons in the middle of Jerusalem's economic spectrum. These would have included minor functionaries within the priestly apparatus, scribes in government employ, merchants, and a variety of others. These persons would have had intimate contact with the wealthiest segments of Yehudite society, and yet they themselves experienced a much lower standard of living. Theirs is the greatest perceived relative deprivation.

Apocalyptic expresses itself with sophisticated literary forms. As a genre, apocalyptic could have flourished only within circles of sufficient education and erudition to produce this kind of literature. Again, this evidence indicates Jerusalem as the source of apocalyptic and points toward the scribes and others who occupied the middle sectors of Jerusalemite society. They experienced a lesser lifestyle than that of their employers, and they expressed their dissatisfaction with the uneven economic distribution with apocalyptic literature. This perceived relative deprivation was an important conditioning factor for the rise of Yehud's scribal apocalyptic.

Apocalyptic literature, through all its periods, demonstrates a knowledge of the international scene. Daniel's visions, for instance, betray a sophisticated knowledge of international imperial history (Daniel 7). Deutero-Zechariah discusses the fate of many neighboring regions (Zechariah 9:1-8). This internationalism points toward the scribes and governmental officials of Jerusalem, since they would have had the greatest exposure to international events, history, and thought.

From these indications, the most reasonable social location for apocalyptic's origins is a Jerusalemite group of middle-class scribes and governmental officials.[19] They experience their own lifestyles, as wealthy and powerful as they may be in comparison with the entire population of Yehud, as significantly and disturbingly less than those of their superiors. These middle-class, middle-management discontents argued for the destruction of their own society and for the radical restructuring of values and social structures as a response to their own frustrations with a status quo in which they participated and from which they benefited but which they felt they could not control and use to their own advantage and for the right purposes within society. They were not fringe elements within the society; rather, they were integral to the power structures of Yehudite society. Their dissatisfaction with the uses of power by the even more privileged and with their own opportunities for advancement within the system brought about extreme frustration at the system itself, expressing itself in a rhetoric of apocalyptic violence. Because they lost hope at rising through the ranks, they abandoned the mind-sets typical of wisdom and participated in apocalyptic's vision of wholesale destruction that equalizes the whole society by leveling it.

Social Control and the Rhetoric of Violence

The apocalyptic groups from Jerusalem experienced the wealth and power of Yehudite society but felt themselves alienated within the system.[20] These bureaucrats and other officials would have participated in the system but would have felt very little control over that system. They did not have enough power to influence the system to their own ends. Even though they benefited from the structures in which they operated, they could not shift the emphases of those same bureaucratic systems. They lost a sense of self-determination and of self-control.[21] Thus they participate in a radical condemnation of the leaders of the society and they wish a destruction of the system in order to establish a better order on earth and in the cosmos.

Apocalyptic experiences and expresses the irrationality of human organizational systems. Thus they understand power in its positive and negative applications. Systems adhere not for rational reasons but because of the power of the institutions.[22] Apocalyptic derives from those who must work within that system and whose livelihood depends upon it but who cannot control the system. They experience directly the irrationality of the system. Bureaucracies define themselves and identify their goals in terms of efficiency and, in most cases, of service to the interest of at least one constituency.[23] However, the institution often rewards internal loyalty more than the effective delivery of services, creating an inherent contradiction between the internal organizational priorities and the externally expressed goals of the institution. Those caught in the midst of these inconsistencies experience the irrationality of the institution. Such would have been the case for many of the scribes and governmental officials within Yehud.

Desperation results from the perceived absence of a means of social control within these systems. Without any means of shaping the direct power bases of decision making within bureaucratic institutions, individuals vie for control of rhetoric. These middle-management knowledge experts shape the discourse of their social institutions through their control of rhetoric. Apocalyptic, therefore, represents such a rhetoric of desperation, in which the knowledge experts despair of changing their institutions from within but attempt to control those very institutions through such use of rhetoric. It is not surprising, therefore, that the rhetoric includes sharp condemnations of the leaders and the institutions of the status quo. The harshness of these denunciations moves the discourse into a rhetoric of violence. A rhetoric of power attempts to wrest control of the institution and put it in the hands of the knowledge experts so they can reorganize the system's priorities and advantage structures to benefit them, since they have despaired of working for effective change within the system. Such rhetoric of power argues strenuously for the reconceptualization of the society and the institution, through advancing new concepts and categories in which the leaders can understand and interpret their reality.

This rhetorical reconstruction of reality operates within the terms familiar to the knowledge experts and provides a transition from wisdom literature to apocalyptic per se. Within apocalyptic itself, the rhetoric of power and of rethinking reality becomes a rhetoric of violence. The potential power of new social organization moves into threats and condemnations. Apocalyptic claims God's own intervention in order to reorganize society. No longer is there a hope that humans will rethink their own systems and change from within; instead, the only hope is that God will intervene and change the systems directly. The literature that presents the threat of this sudden, forced change commits a rhetorical violence upon the leaders, cutting off the possibilities of considering them as partners from within the rhetorical world constructed by the apocalypticists.

Thus the literature of apocalyptic is a literature not only of dissent but of social separation; it restructures reality by defining separate groups and claiming for them, in God's name, radically divergent futures.[24] The apocalypticists will survive (in some of the texts, at least), while the leaders fall into destruction. The literature produces the social split that legitimates the attempted takeover of the social structures by the middle-management knowledge experts. Their attempts, however, possess no power base outside their rhetoric; the leaders still firmly control the social means of production. The rhetoric of the knowledge experts, however, can significantly shake the society and its assumptions about itself; it legitimates a resistance and a restructuring at lower levels, thus shifting the results of the bureaucracy as a whole.

Apocalyptic, therefore, is a dangerous genre. It exists within a rhetorical discourse of violence that legitimates the internal destruction of social systems by those within the social institutions themselves. It legitimates the abuse of a system in order to manifest the inherent contradictions, and it pushes for continuation of division between the elite leaders and the knowledge experts. Apocalyptic reacts to the irrationalities of a bureaucratic system by appealing to power beyond reason. No longer do the apocalypticists attempt to persuade their colleagues; instead, they await God's intervention to destroy their employing enemies.

Wisdom and Apocalyptic

This analysis of apocalyptic allows for a clear understanding of the relationship between wisdom and apocalyptic. Both derive from the same social location: the knowledge experts of Jerusalem, who operate within the middle management of the imperial-colonial bureaucracies. Unable to change the systems in which they work and yet benefiting from the same systems, they undertake a variety of responses. The sages produce wisdom literature in their attempts to perpetuate their society and their institutions. They sense the benefits that they receive from being among the wealthier elements of Yehud. Wisdom literature presents advice to persons about how to succeed within this structured, hierarchical society. The directions and the means of benefit are clearly presented and discussed. Sages possess a shared hope of advancing through this system to reach even greater levels of influence within a system that they perceive as relatively benign. The apocalypticists perceive the benefits of the system but sense the inconsistencies even more strongly, and they feel themselves victimized by the irrationalities of the system, even though they depend upon the system for their own survival. They sense no hopes for advancement; they feel that their superiors will never move aside to allow a redress to the perceived relative deprivation but will continue to apply power against these experts in continuing repression. Thus the system provides no hope for the apocalypticists, and they react with despair. They construct apocalyptic thought and literature as an attempt to create a rhetorical power that legitimates their own dissatisfaction by claiming God's displeasure at the system led by their superiors. Destruction of the system seems inevitable because of the system's irrational inconsistencies and its misapplication of power.

Both wisdom and apocalyptic seek hidden knowledge. For sages, this knowledge hides within the structure of reality and presents itself eagerly to the observant sage. Knowledge provides solutions to the problems of life. Such knowledge makes itself available to everyone, although only some find it, and it will benefit all. Any person can succeed in the sages' society, if the person seeks and finds the required knowledge. Apocalypticists, on the other hand, find a hidden knowledge that limits itself to those who are righteous. Apocalyptic knowledge does not belong to the masses or to their superiors. The knowledge is not universally helpful; it tells of the destruction of some and thus comforts only the apocalypticists. The sages' knowledge can provide equality by raising the standard of living for all, whereas the apocalypticists seek a knowledge that differentiates and creates a power basis for their subversive action. But apocalyptic action can never progress far; apocalypticists themselves are too dependent upon the system to desire an overthrow.[25] Instead, they languish in the middle, awaiting the day when God will act and taking comfort in their knowledge of when and how that day will arrive.

Wisdom thus demonstrates a worldview of social order. According to the sages, humans can solve their own problems with the knowledge awaiting them within the world, available to all. If people work together in the appropriate structures, accepting the status quo and working within its strictures, benefits will accrue to all through this embrace of each person's place within society. Apocalypticists reject their place within society and thus possess a worldview of social chaos. The institutions themselves are evil, and the secret knowledge is that God will destroy the institutions and the power structures, along with all of the social roles that cohere with them. Humans cannot solve their own problems, because of the corruption of the systems; only God can solve the problems through destructive intervention. God gives the secret knowledge of that destruction.

Apocalyptic results in a stringent attempt at social control and a set of radical moves toward that control, at least at the rhetorical level. Apocalypticists resign themselves to life in the midst of chaos while they wait for God's intervention. The chaos of their fear springs into existence when they experience relative perceived deprivation, the very embodiment of their sense that the world does not reward the righteous and the skilled. They sponsor a hatred of those who produce such chaos by controlling them and assuming privilege into themselves, while asserting that God will use chaos to act in the world and to reorganize it into a new cosmic order. The powers that be are so corrupt and so powerfully entrenched that only God can shake them loose, and only through the most drastic means.

The Worldview of Apocalyptic

God desires the destruction of Jerusalem in order to destroy the leaders who rule corruptly. Zechariah 14 describes Jerusalem's destruction in physical terms. Nations surround Jerusalem, looting the houses, raping the women, and taking the inhabitants into exile. But only half of the people leave; the other half remain. God divides the society in half, sentencing the rulers to complete destruction and removing them from the city (Zechariah 14:1-4, 12-15). After that, the remaining half shall live forever in security, participating in the proper worship of Yahweh (Zechariah 14:10-11, 16). In this revised Jerusalem, rain will fall only on the just and those who worship properly (Zechariah 14:17-18). In typical apocalyptic fashion, God will restructure the very cosmos so that human values and the work of nature are in perfect harmony. This marks the apocalyptic dissatisfaction with life in a world in which nature favors all alike, without making those distinctions, and in which social institutions give advantage to those less deserving.

Isaiah 24–27 presents images of utter destruction. God will send destruction upon all creation, including nature and human productions, and even upon the hosts of heaven (Isaiah 24:1-23). The aliens living in the city palace will be destroyed (Isaiah 25:2-5), which perhaps refers to the Persian-connected leadership strata within colonial Yehud's capital, Jerusalem. After the destruction, God prepares a momentous feast upon the very mountain of Zion, where once the evil city stood (Isaiah 25:6-9). The apocalypticists will be saved by God because they have rejected human leaders in favor of God (Isaiah 26:13); apocalyptic usually condemns the leaders and expresses an opposition between human leaders and the divine will and activity.

The Book of Daniel tells a short story about a mantic wisdom hero who divines the future through the interpretation of dreams. The short story itself depicts the leaders of Babylonia and Persia as foolish and evil. The full weight of apocalyptic thought does not appear within the short story but within the attendant visions. In those visions (Daniel 7–8; 10–12), the apocalypticist wishes for the destruction of empires and their systems of control. Daniel recognizes that evil will increase throughout the world (Daniel 12:4, 10), but in the end Yahweh will triumph over all of the forces of evil, embodied within the imperial bureaucracies, and will bring reward for those who have remained faithful in their positions of service (Daniel 12:12). Daniel himself functions as a representative of the apocalypticists' self-understanding. Daniel is a bureaucrat trapped within the system of an evil empire. He remains pious and oriented toward God, although he himself is able to bring about only the most minor alterations within the system itself. Apocalyptic awaits the intervention of God to change the systems of the world in wholesale fashion through destruction.

These various examples of canonical apocalyptic show the dissatisfaction with life expanded to a cosmic scale. These apocalypticists operate within structures but desire a divine destruction of those structures so that the proper life can take place, by God's direction. The rhetoric creates division, showing the difference between those within God's will and those outside it. Apocalyptic resorts to images of violence in order to accomplish this social division, and thus it legitimates violence at the social level within the apocalyptic communities themselves. Their rejection of their leaders is clear and complete, and God shares the rejection of the evil superiors. Apocalyptic is extremely aware of the internationally enmeshed system of government within colonial administration, and they desire the removal of foreign rule and the imposition of God's own desire in an idyllic world to come. Apocalyptic lives within a pluralistic and bureaucratic world. Finding both distasteful and evil, apocalyptic argues for a world affected by neither pluralism nor bureaucracy. In response, apocalyptic wishes the destruction of the whole social order to remove this evil, and yet apocalyptic realizes its own context within the present day, including its own position of advantage within the world system.

Notes

1. Many scholars have focused on the social description of ancient Israelite prophecy. For examples, see Robert R. Wilson, *Prophecy and Society in Ancient Israel* (Philadelphia: Fortress, 1980); David L. Petersen, *The Roles of Israel's Prophets*, JSOTSup 17 (Sheffield: JSOT Press, 1981); Thomas W. Overholt, *Channels of Prophecy: Social Dynamics of Prophetic Activity* (Minneapolis:

Fortress Press, 1989); and Don C. Benjamin, "An Anthropology of Prophecy," *BTB* 21 (1991): 135–44. Frank Moore Cross, *Canaanite Myth and Hebrew Epic* (Cambridge: Harvard University Press, 1973); Hanson, *Dawn of Apocalyptic,* and idem, *The People Called,* assume that prophecy and monarchy are coextensive, but that assertion overstates the evidence. Saul and others participated in prophet-like behavior before the establishment of the monarchy; this early form of prophecy is still poorly understood. Similarly, several prophets operated over the next century after the downfall of the monarchy, including Jeremiah, Ezekiel, Deutero-Isaiah, Trito-Isaiah, Haggai, Proto-Zechariah, and Malachi. With this large number of postmonarchic prophets, prophecy must be able to operate outside the monarchic context that provided so many foci for their speech. Still, the growth of other forms of visionary expression in postexilic times must be noticed.

2. See chapters 3 and 5, above.

3. For a description of prophecy as a social institution tied to social debate, see Jon L. Berquist, "The Social Setting of Early Postexilic Prophecy" (Ph.D. diss., Vanderbilt University, 1989), 260–98.

4. In the second case, scribes gained autonomy and produced texts that legitimated the status quo, such as Proverbs; they did not record the prophetic critiques of the society, but did perform their own critical rethinkings of social assumptions, as present in scribal wisdom texts such as Job and Ecclesiastes. See chapter 15 below.

5. Robert P. Carroll, *Jeremiah, A Commentary,* OTL (Philadelphia: Westminster Press, 1985), 450, discusses the connection to Zechariah 13:2-6. William L. Holladay, *Jeremiah 1 (1–25),* Hermeneia (Philadelphia: Fortress Press, 1986), 625, disagrees with a postexilic dating in favor of about 600 B.C.E. See also Petersen, *Late Israelite Prophecy,* 27–33.

6. For examples, see 1 Kings 22 and Jeremiah 28. See James L. Crenshaw, *Prophetic Conflict: Its Effect upon Israelite Religion,* BZAW 124 (Berlin: Walter de Gruyter, 1971).

7. Philip R. Davies, "The Social World of Apocalyptic Writings," in Clements, *The World of Ancient Israel,* 254.

8. Ibid. Cf. Wilson, *Prophecy and Society,* 14–31, who argues that prophecy as well assumes the existence of heavenly knowledge that is beneficial for humans to possess.

9. Davies, "Social World of Apocalyptic Writings," Clements, *The World of Ancient Israel,* 260.

10. Ibid., 255–60.

11. As a comparison, consider documents from Qumran, such as the Habakkuk pesher, which reinterpret prophecy and apply it to the realities of one sect within Hellenistic-period Judaism. This pesher's clarity about specific applications stands in stark contrast to the canonical apocalyptic writings.

12. Two assumptions seem to be at work here. First, God's work at creation stopped, but now restarts; God had left the world on its own, resulting in chaos, but God will intervene. Second, all the universe should be ordered around human existence; the stars should have a pattern that expresses human organization and God's own valuation of various human existence. These assumptions seem to reflect accurately much of the ethos of apocalyptic.

13. Plöger, *Theocracy and Eschatology.*

14. Pluralism, not theocracy, seems more descriptive of most of the Hellenistic period as well.

15. Hanson, *Dawn of Apocalyptic.*

16. Davies, "Social World of Apocalyptic Writings," in Clements, *The World of Ancient Israel,* 256–60.

17. David F. Aberle, "A Note on Relative Deprivation Theory as Applied to Millenarian and Other Cult Movements," in *Millennial Dreams in Action: Essays in Comparative Study,* ed. Sylvia L. Thrupp, Comparative Studies in Society and History Supplements 2 (The Hague: Mouton, 1962), 209–10.

18. For the distinction between relative deprivation and the more recent emphasis on *perceived* relative deprivation, see Graham Allan, "A Theory of Millennialism: The Irvingite Movement as

an Illustration," *British Journal of Sociology* 25 (1974): 297. See also Charles Y. Glock, "On the Origin and Evolution of Religious Groups," in *Religion in Sociological Perspective: Essays in the Empirical Study of Religion*, ed. Charles Y. Glock (Belmont, Calif.: Wadsworth, 1973), 210–20; Bernard Barber, "Acculturation and Messianic Movements," *American Sociological Review* 6 (1941): 667; Leslie Spier, Wayne Suttles, and Melville J. Herskovits, "Comments on Aberle's Thesis of Deprivation," *Southwestern Journal of Anthropology* 15 (1959): 84–88; Yonina Talmon, "Millenarian Movements," *European Journal of Sociology* 7 (1966): 166; Norman Cohn, *The Pursuit of the Millennium: Revolutionary Millenarians and Mystical Anarchists of the Middle Ages*, rev. ed. (New York: Oxford University Press, 1970), 282; Takie Sugiyama Lebra, "Millenarian Movements and Resocialization," *American Behavioral Scientist* 16 (1972): 212–15; and Michael Barkun, "Movements of Total Transformation: An Introduction," *American Behavioral Scientist* 16 (1972): 146. See also Anthony F. C. Wallace, "Revitalization Movements," *American Anthropologist* 58 (1956): 265–75.

19. This interpretation is not far from Davies' suggestion that apocalyptic sprang from inner-establishment disputes.

20. This alienation itself may have roots within the education of this group. As scribes and other experts, they would have learned a wide variety of options, thus relativizing their own assumptions about reality. If they did not accept the societal presumptions, then they might well have experienced a sense of anomie or of alienation, perceiving themselves fundamentally separate from the values of the society itself. This would have enhanced their dissatisfaction with the very status quo that benefited them in so many measures of economics and prestige.

21. For studies on the effects of bureaucratization, see C. Wright Mills, *The Sociological Imagination* (Oxford: Oxford University Press, 1959); Vilfredo Pareto, *The Rise and Fall of the Elites: An Application of Theoretical Sociology* (Totowa, N.J.: Bedminster Press, 1968); and Eva Etzioni-Halevy, *The Knowledge Elite and the Failure of Prophecy*, Controversies in Sociology 18 (London: George Allen & Unwin, 1985).

22. For these reasons, functionalism becomes an unsatisfactory explanation of institutional life. In its place have arisen some interesting alternatives within neofunctionalism, for which see Jeffrey C. Alexander, ed., *Neofunctionalism*, Key Issues in Sociological Theory 1 (Beverly Hills, Calif.: SAGE Publications, 1985); and S. N. Eisenstadt and M. Curelaru, *The Form of Sociology—Paradigms and Crises* (New York: John Wiley & Sons, 1976). See also S. N. Eisenstadt, "Macro-Societal Analysis—Background, Development and Indications," in *Macro-Sociological Theory: Perspectives on Sociology Theory, Volume 1*, ed. S. N. Eisenstadt and H. J. Helle, SAGE Studies in International Sociology 33 (London: SAGE Publications, 1985), 13; and Edward Shils, "The Integration of Society," in *The Constitution of Society*, ed. Edward Shils (Chicago: University of Chicago Press, 1972), 41–45.

23. For example, modern governmental bureaucracies in the United States identify themselves as in the service of the people, with an emphasis on efficient delivery of such services. However, the bureaucracies tend to place much of their energy into the organization of the bureaucracy and the maintenance of the structures, as well as endemic infighting as individuals position themselves for enhanced power within the system. Correspondingly, resources expended in institutional power conflicts are not expended on delivery of services; the weight of the bureaucracy can take more of the institutional resources than the delivery of the services themselves. The amount of energy and resources spent on institutional concerns can increase when the institution attempts to serve several potentially oppositional constituencies, such as in the case of academic institutions that serve interests of faculty, students, trustees, and donors. If the constituencies conflict, then the energy expended on internal organizational matters and redistributions of power can overwhelm the delivery of services.

24. For this reason, apocalyptic literature and speech can be extremely effective in forming group solidarity, since it requires the construction of firm social boundaries. Apocalyptic divides

communities into insiders and outsiders—those who survive (by God's grace or by other fortuitous occurrence) and those who face certain destruction—and thus strengthens ties among its audience, which consists entirely of insiders who survive the terrors of the destruction depicted in the apocalyptic rhetoric. The sense of survival exhilarates; when shared, this sense of survival bonds the community together.

25. In comparison, social movements such as the Maccabees or the Zealots of later times derive from social classes with much less dependence upon the social structures, and thus they can reject the societies in a much broader way. These movements can work for revolution, whereas apocalypticists do not disturb the structural and infrastructural levels of society while, at the same time, conducting rhetorical violence at the superstructural or ideological level.

CHAPTER 13

SONGS OF JOY AND PAIN: POPULAR IMAGES OF A DIFFERENT WORLD

PSALMS AND SONGS OF the Hebrew canon provide another entry into the social matrix of colonial Yehud.[1] In the early decades of the Second Temple, the priests and their scribes developed the Book of Psalms as a collection of many of the songs used within the temple worship services. These songs expressed a wide variety of experiences and emotions, usually connecting them implicitly to Yahweh's presence and activity in the world through the temple. These extant songs provide a glimpse into the popular religion as provided by the priesthood for the masses.

As such, the songs connect the aspirations and the fears of the populace with the desires of the temple for social control. The priesthood exercised its control through a variety of means, including the ideology of Yahwism, the economic transfers of the sacrificial system, the symbols and rituals of the temple service, and the legal structures expressed within the law. The songs presented the ideology in distilled form. It should not be thought, however, that these songs are doctrinal in character. Instead, some of the songs contribute little in explicit theology. They speak of Yahweh and of the temple's concerns by connecting them to the people's lived reality.

Yehud's priestly songs would thus have immense applicability to real-life situations among the colonial populace. Within the songs are traces of the Persian Empire's domination of individual lives. When the people felt loss, there were lament psalms with which to bemoan their lack and to find words of encouragement that would bring them back to Yahweh. In times of joy and thanksgiving, the people could find psalms that would allow them to bring that thanksgiving into the temple worship, extolling the worthiness of Yahweh for blessing them. A wide range of emotions thus became permissible within temple worship, and the priesthood gained access to these important times of joy and crisis within individuals' lives. For many of the inhabitants of Yehud, the psalms may have been the most important and vital place where life and religion came together.[2]

Functions of Praise Psalms

Many of Yehud's psalms proclaim praise and thanksgiving for Yahweh's acts of blessing. These psalms ascribe glory to Yahweh and mention the specific beneficial acts that Yahweh has done for the individual or group reciting the psalm. These acts range from the cosmic praise of God's creation (Psalm 8) to God's involvement in producing another year's crop (Psalm 67).

These psalms of praise and thanksgiving express a strong degree of social solidarity.[3] The shared singing of songs produces a degree of solidarity; the language of many of these songs enhances the effect.

Let the nations be glad and sing for joy,
for you judge the peoples with equity
and guide the nations upon earth. . . .
Let the peoples praise you, O God;
let all the peoples praise you.
The earth has yielded its increase;
God, our God, has blessed us.
May God continue to bless us;
let all the ends of the earth revere him.
(Psalm 67:4-7)

This psalm of thanksgiving depicts God as the ruler of the whole world, thus placing all humans together within the same category as the recipients of God's graciousness. The repetitions of "the peoples," intensified by the repeated use of "all," further the idea that the speakers are united into a solidified society that even reaches beyond national boundaries.[4] The text connects God's continued blessings to the common reverence of God, probably referring to the activity of the whole people in the temple ritual.

The creation language of many of the psalms conducts the same bridging of national boundaries to form a community of discourse and thus intensifies the connectedness of those participating within the ritual. The radical inclusion perhaps has no direct social referent, but the rhetoric allows for feelings of connectedness and solidarity. Talk of unity throughout the world heightens feelings of oneness with neighbors and like-minded folk. Such feelings of unity appear within the mention of creation.

O Yahweh, our Lord,
how majestic is your name in all the earth!
You have set your glory above the heavens.
Out of the mouths of babes and infants
you have founded a bulwark because of your foes,
to silence the enemy and the avenger.
When I look at your heavens, the work of your fingers,
the moon and the stars that you have established;
what are human beings that you are mindful of them,
mortals that you care for them?
Yet you have made them a little lower than God,
and crowned them with glory and honor.
You have given them dominion over the works of your hands;
you have put all things under their feet,

all sheep and oxen,
and also the beasts of the field,
the birds of the air, and the fish of the sea,
whatever passes along the paths of the seas.
O Yahweh, our Lord,
how majestic is your name in all the earth!
(Psalm 8)

Texts such as these represent humans in radical dependence upon God who creates them but also extol humans as God's favored creations. Because of Yahweh's high valuation of humans, there is reason to feel good about the role of humans in the world and the societies they create. The support for God's creation supports humanity's social institutions as well.[5] These psalms inculcate a harmonious worldview that contradicts any need for reform or critique of the society. Social maintenance takes place through the use of these psalms.

Many of the psalms retell the story of Israel's origins or detail parts of the subsequent history. These recitations of shared history also work toward social solidarity. Although they contain a great deal of information about the history of Israel, these psalms appear to function in a nondidactic manner. They may teach about the history, but their primary function is to create a shared identity through the shared performance of the song and through the recognition of common origins. There are many examples of such historical psalms. For instance, a psalm devoted to the recitation of the exodus from Egypt begins and ends with emphases on the relevance for Yehud:

O give thanks to Yahweh, call on his name,
make known his deeds among the peoples.
Sing to him, sing praises to him;
tell of all his wonderful works.
Glory in his holy name;
let the hearts of those who seek Yahweh rejoice.
Seek Yahweh and his strength;
seek his presence continually.
Remember the wonderful works he has done,
his miracles, and the judgments he uttered,
O offspring of his servant Abraham,
children of Jacob, his chosen ones.
He is Yahweh our God;
his judgments are in all the earth.
He is mindful of his covenant forever,
of the word that he commanded, for a thousand generations.
. . . .

So he brought his people out with joy,
his chosen ones with singing.
He gave them the lands of the nations,
and they took possession of the wealth of the peoples,

that they might keep his statutes and observe his laws.
Praise Yahweh!
(Psalm 105:1-8, 43-45)

The introduction to this psalm emphasizes the community that gathers together to worship. Together they will proclaim the proper praise that is due Yahweh; together they will perform the psalm. The psalm concludes with an implicit application to the worshiping community. Those who share the history are those to whom God has given the land; these people should obey God's law, as taught by the priests. History and law become inextricably tied together in such a psalm. Thus the community shares not only the unifying worship of the psalm's recitation and the shared history within the psalm's content but also the legal codes administered by the priests. The multiple supports for communal solidarity reinforce each other to create a sense of a shared society that is inherently good and right, beyond questioning because it is rooted in God's own activity.

In a postexilic time, when the ethnic ties between the various inhabitants of Yehud are even weaker than at earlier times within the history, these psalms of historical reminiscence become a vital way of building community. They create a sense of shared history, a sense that may be fictional but is nonetheless effective in establishing a reality of community.

These psalms of praise also serve to legitimate violence. The images of violence and retribution in the psalms are strong; they picture a disturbed world in which God acts to restore social order and right relationship through violence.

"Often have they attacked me from my youth"
—let Israel now say—
"often have they attacked me from my youth,
yet they have not prevailed against me.
The plowers plowed on my back;
they made their furrows long."
Yahweh is righteous;
he has cut the cords of the wicked.
May all who hate Zion
be put to shame and turned backward.
Let them be like the grass on the housetops
that withers before it grows up,
with which reapers do not fill their hands
or binders of sheaves their arms,
while those who pass by do not say,
"The blessing of Yahweh be upon you!
We bless you in the name of Yahweh!"
(Psalm 129)

The worshiping assembly has experienced attacks from others. The nature of the attacks is obscure; it may be military, socioeconomic, or otherwise. Probably the ambiguity is part of the nature of this psalm, allowing its use in multiple settings. Yahweh has intervened and has solved the problem, whatever it may be. Now the worshipers ask God for vengeance, calling forth curses upon the agricultural fertility of their attackers. Those who hate Jerusalem become destined for shame, for exclusion from social participation. Yahweh's blessings do not come to those who attack God's people in Zion.

This text radically excludes others from the community in life-threatening ways. Nowhere does the text suggest that violence and deprivation are wrong actions; instead, the psalm insists that answering violence with forcible deprivation of the means of life is an appropriate social and religious goal. In such ways, psalms legitimate violence, especially the violence committed by the community to its enemies, as defined by the worship service itself. Once the priests have identified the enemy, the rhetoric of worship orients the people toward accepting acts against these enemies.

In particular, the psalms legitimate violence committed in the service of social order. The psalms, as with other aspects of priestly religion, argue strenuously for a harmonious society in which every inhabitant of Yehud knows her or his place. The psalms identify this desire for harmony with the will of God. The praise of God is therefore a praise of social order. Yahweh keeps society stable, and thus should Yahweh be praised.

We give thanks to you, O God;
we give thanks; your name is near.
People tell of your wondrous deeds.
At the set time that I appoint
I will judge with equity.
When the earth totters, with all its inhabitants,
it is I who keep its pillars steady. Selah.
I say to the boastful, "Do not boast,"
and to the wicked, "Do not lift up your horn;
do not lift up your horn on high,
or speak with insolent neck."
For not from the east or from the west
and not from the wilderness comes lifting up;
but it is God who executes judgment,
putting down one and lifting up another.
For in the hand of Yahweh there is a cup
with foaming wine, well mixed;
he will pour a draught from it,
and all the wicked of the earth
shall drain it down to the dregs.
But I will rejoice forever;
I will sing praises to the God of Jacob.
All the horns of the wicked I will cut off,
but the horns of the righteous shall be exalted.
(Psalm 75)

Anyone who would challenge the status quo receives condemnation through this psalm of praise to the social order. The text depicts God as the enforcer of the social order, seeking out those who violate it with lethal punishment in hand. The psalmist singles out for special attention those who boast. Such braggarts violate the social order by thinking of themselves in ways other than those by which society defines them. They desire changes in relative social standing, perhaps thinking themselves more deserving or more meritorious than others who are better recognized. Braggarts question the social standards by which such rankings are made and assert that the society's systems are wrong, at least in their own case. In this psalm, God destroys persons who critique the social order in this fashion.

The psalm also establishes an equivalency between righteousness and exaltation; those who are religiously correct will receive earthly favor in terms of recognition and presumably power and economic advantages as well, but those whom the priestly system defines as evil lose everything. This radical collapse of religious and secular categories asserts that the community is right to act against the evil ones in its midst. Even God rejects the unrighteous, and so human prejudice against them cannot be wrong.

Throughout the psalm, the audience hears a legitimation of violence against those who disrupt the social order. Violence against the outsiders, as defined by the temple, is good and righteous. The community can rightly ignore those who should live in shame; the typical commands to the community to care for its own may be violated for these unworthy ones. This mobilizes a high level of sanctions against those who argue against the society's structures. In general, psalms of praise legitimate the social order and at times will allow a rhetoric of violence against those who oppose the society's status quo.

Functions of Laments

In occasions of praise and thanksgiving, the support of the social order seems unsurprising. Good times provide ample opportunity to avoid critique of society's organization, since things seem to be working as is. In times of prosperity, many persons support the ruling classes because of the benefits they receive from the structures. However, the lament psalms represent a different set of life experiences. In the laments, the pain of individuals and of the community going through times of loss becomes connected to the religious values of the temple in powerful ways. Laments channel the energy present in life's crises and focus it through the temple. Given the legitimizing role of the praise and thanksgiving psalms, what, then, is the social function of these lament psalms?

Laments reflect life crises, and thus they reflect times of instability and uncertainty, when the social rules seem to break down, at least for a while. In the minds of its members, society exists as a construct, a set of rules, perspectives, and assumptions upon which the members have agreed at least in sufficient substance that social cooperation becomes possible. Crises threaten the social presumptions and thus the social construction of reality, because they place individuals and communities in disconfirming situations. The praise psalms, for instance, insist that God cares for the righteous. If so, then why is there tragedy in the lives of pious Yahwists, and why does Jerusalem itself suffer from time to time? In these times of threatened social or social-psychological breakdown, the temple used psalms to acknowledge people's anomie and to encourage them to embrace the social order once more.

In theological perspective, the lament psalms respond to personal and communal crises with theodicy, the defense of God for the presence of pain and suffering in the world.[6]

Theodicy encourages people to strengthen their faith in God in the face of evidence that argues against God's power or beneficence. Thus the lament psalms equate God and the social order, arguing for belief in and support of both, even when life presents disconfirming experiences. Through these times of doubt and questioning, the psalms work toward social reintegration. Negative experiences are inconsistent with the highly integrated society that the praise psalms portray, in which the righteous receive God's blessings always. When bad things happen, they threaten the entire system of belief in God, worship in the temple, and obedience to the social order. Lament psalms offer a picture of a reintegrating society, in which social order and God's concern will manifest themselves even if they seem absent.

Fools say in their hearts, "There is no God."
They are corrupt, they commit abominable acts;
there is no one who does good.
God looks down from heaven on humankind
to see if there are any who are wise,
who seek after God.
They have all fallen away, they are all alike perverse;
there is no one who does good,
no, not one.
Have they no knowledge, those evildoers,
who eat up my people as they eat bread,
and do not call upon God?
There they shall be in great terror,
in terror such as has not been.
For God will scatter the bones of the ungodly;
they will be put to shame, for God has rejected them.
O that deliverance for Israel would come from Zion!
When God restores the fortunes of his people,
Jacob will rejoice; Israel will be glad.
(Psalm 53)

Psalm 53 condemns people who violate the social order and the precepts of the religion of Yahweh. God has rejected these people and they will be put to shame, removed from the social order and the social protection. Yet this psalm portrays a time when salvation has not yet come to God's people and the social order has not been restored. Instead, the psalm promises that such a time will come in the near future. God will act, despite all of the evidence to the contrary, and then there will be the kind of restoration that brings joy to the inhabitants of Jerusalem. The psalm uses a future promise to relativize and thus to deny the present experience of the audience.

Psalm 74 deals with disconfirming events on a national scale. The psalm begins with the plea, "O God, why do you cast us off forever? Why does your anger smoke against the sheep of your pasture?" (Psalm 74:1). The psalmist asks God to remember the congregation and then describes the destruction done to the sanctuary of the temple in great detail (Psalm 74:3-9). Then the psalm moves into royal language and creation terminology to extol the praises of God, ending in another plea for God to remember (Psalm 74:12-18). The psalm concludes with a direct request for God to act:

Do not deliver the soul of your dove to the wild animals;
do not forget the life of your poor forever.
Have regard for your covenant,
for the dark places of the land are full of the haunts of violence.
Do not let the downtrodden be put to shame;
let the poor and needy praise your name.
Rise up, O God, plead your cause;
remember how the impious scoff at you all day long.
Do not forget the clamor of your foes,
the uproar of your adversaries that goes up continually.
(Psalm 74:19-23)

The people beg God for effective intervention to restore the social order. God has granted the people a covenant, representing the fullness of the social order, but some of the people violate that covenant in violent, destructive ways. The dark places of the land have become full of violence; the social order is breaking down in the fringes of Yehud. This indicates that Jerusalem's ability to enforce order throughout the reaches of its colonial responsibility is ineffective, and there is chaos that Jerusalem's government cannot control.[7] The victims of such uncontrolled violence are downtrodden and deserve God's help because they praise God, thus trusting in God's ability to restore society. The psalm concludes with an appeal to God's honor; the presence of the unrighteous in the world not only disrupts the social order but sullies God's own reputation.

Many other lament psalms follow a pattern of a plea to God for help in time of need, ending either with an energetic assignation of disaster to the enemies or with an assertion of God's goodness and willingness to provide social order. The disaster awaiting the enemies ranges from shame (Psalms 6:10; 35:26; 40:14-15; 83:16-17), the removal of privilege (Psalms 57:4; 62:9-10; 140:8), death by sword or arrow (Psalms 7:12-13; 17:13; 63:10; 64:7), or injury (Psalms 3:7; 10:15; 36:12). A variety of praises to God and the social order also appear, such as rejoicing in Yahweh (Psalms 10:18; 13:6; 64:10), praising the king (Psalms 61:6; 63:11), and paying vows (Psalms 54:6; 56:12; 61:8). Through all of these images, the psalm argues that God will restore the social order and thus be worthy of the praises now offered. The social chaos of the present is only temporary. This institutionalizes the pain and suffering while denying it an independent existence in the present.

The legitimation of God's rule and the social order can even proceed through the direct condemnation of God's lack of activity in the world.[8] This communicates the assumption that God can and will act for social order in the future. Such approaches typically emphasize the innocence of the suffering, thus stressing that God is morally required to take action.

If we had forgotten the name of our God,
or spread out our hands to a strange god,

would not God discover this?
For he knows the secrets of the heart.
Because of you we are being killed all day long,
and accounted as sheep for the slaughter.
Rouse yourself! Why do you sleep, O Lord?
Awake, do not cast us off forever!
Why do you hide your face?
Why do you forget our affliction and oppression?
For we sink down to the dust;
our bodies cling to the ground.
Rise up, come to our help.
Redeem us for the sake of your steadfast love.
(Psalm 44:20-26)

Because God has not acted in the past, calamity has come upon the people, but the religion of Yahweh calls the people to believe that God will intervene soon, now that the people have issued the proper call. God will set everything right in the future. These strong psalms admit Yahweh's culpability for the current calamities but do not deal seriously with this critique of God's own character. Instead, the immediate future once more functions as the substitute for the present pains. Because God will soon act, there is little need to dwell on the people's negative experiences of the moment. Such pain is only transitory; God's action is the only relevant permanence.

Challenges to Authority

Within the worldview of these songs of joy and pain, it is exceedingly difficult to critique the status quo or even to question the beneficence of God in the midst of conflicting human experience. Both praise and lament psalms legitimate the social order. The psalms do function as a reorientation of human experience and possible attributions of causation. Praise psalms derive from experiences of joy and abundance; they point toward Yahweh's blessing for those who obey as the cause for all human joy. Thus people do not cause their own happiness. Joy is a gift from God, contingent upon obedience to the priestly regulations and to the other rules of social life. Likewise, lament psalms also reorient the people from their experiences of present pain to faith in the future activity of God. Laments encourage people to deny their pain and to focus on God's ultimate goodness, not even upon the theological problems of theodicy. Because God will soon correct human pain and suffering, humans should not act themselves to change their society. Instead, waiting for God is the only appropriate solution.

Still, some of these psalms function toward dissent, in at least very mild forms. The lament psalms clearly portray the pains that humans cause other humans. At one level, these texts invalidate any denial of suffering, but the texts at the same time force that denial by emphasizing God's goodness. Psalms can focus anger, as Psalm 137 unleashes anger on the Babylonians who stole and killed children during the exiling. Rarely do the psalms focus any of that anger, whether a destructive psychological force or a positive sociological motivation for change, anywhere within the system, but the potential exists. The psalms sacralize suffering as a preparation for God's activity, but there is still the proclamation of pain as real and present that echoes through these psalms.

The lament psalms at first seem to allow strong critiques of the social status quo and of God's role in the world. However, these psalms actually govern the expression of negative emotions, channeling them in "safe" directions that end with devotion to God and a belief in Yahweh's (eventual) beneficence. These psalms allow for the expression of a wide range of emotion, but they do not allow for the existence of long-lasting moods of dissension. They move into the status quo quickly. The psalms disallow the space needed for separation from the social institutions of power that would allow the growth of a truly different view of reality. Instead, the psalms—even the psalms that express the deepest discontent with the realities of life—bring everything in life within the systems of power within Yehudite society.

The laments rhetorically attempt to disallow dissension and to create a harmonious world in which even the sharpest pains of life and the greatest questions of theodicy receive their final answer in God's beneficial activity. Even if it seems that God has left behind the people, this seeming distance is only temporary, for God will always act to support the social order and to eliminate the seeming inconsistencies brought about by human power and its abuse. Laments, just as do the praise psalms, bind the community together by ignoring the truly lasting sources of pain and oppression as well as the locations of abuse and the incoherencies of power-based society. Instead, the psalms present a God who solves all inconsistencies within a sphere of love and concern, providing short-term psychological benefit in the place of long-term social change.

Notes

1. See Gunther Wanke, "Prophecy and Psalms in the Persian Period," in Davies and Finkelstein, *The Cambridge History of Judaism,* 1:184–86.

2. See Walter Brueggemann, "Psalms and the Life of Faith: A Suggested Typology of Function," *JSOT* 17 (1980): 3–32, who argues for psalms of orientation, disorientation, and reorientation.

3. When one considers the ritual context of temple worship in which these psalms were probably performed, one realizes the ability of the psalms to induce social solidarity. See Kertzer, *Ritual, Politics, and Power.*

4. This allows for the inclusion of the Persian Empire's core as well as a variety of the colonies beyond Yehud, thus binding the empire together as well as unifying the colony of Yehud as a separate group.

5. Cf. Coote and Ord, *In the Beginning.*

6. For a sociological description of theodicy, see Berger, *Sacred Canopy,* 53–59. A biblical and theological discussion of this issue can be found in James L. Crenshaw, ed., *Theodicy in the Old Testament,* Issues in Religion and Theology 4 (Philadelphia: Fortress Press, 1983).

7. The government's inability to enforce stability must be questioned. This text, prepared by the temple, argues that forces of darkness have challenged the governmental authority within the fringes and that Jerusalem cannot restore order, thus the people must wait for God's action. The social situation itself may be different. Jerusalem seems to have been capable of enforcing its will throughout Yehud when it so desired, but the colonial administration may have allowed some chaotic elements to exist at its borders, just as modern governments allow certain amounts of crime to

exist in certain areas. The government then claims that the crime is inevitable, when in reality governmental decisions allow the crime to continue to exist as long as it threatens only those whom the government thinks appropriate. In other words, Psalm 74:20 may be an attempt to appease persons in outlying areas who experience social chaos by persuading them that the chaos is God's fault but will soon be corrected.

8. For a parallel in prophets' rhetorical support of their own legitimacy to function as prophets, see Jon L. Berquist, "Prophetic Legitimation in Jeremiah," *VT* 39 (1989): 129–39.

CHAPTER 14

WISDOM AS DISSENT: UNDERMINING SOCIETY'S ASSUMPTIONS

YEHUD'S DEVELOPING WISDOM TRADITION grew as a result of a new scribal class within Jerusalem who functioned as generalized knowledge experts.[1] Over time, they produced their own body of wisdom literature, informed by the scribes' involvement with religious, governmental, and legal institutions within Yehud as well as the scribes' international connections. Wisdom developed as a set of things to be known in order to figure out the best way to live. Through mastery of the proper body of knowledge, one reaches one's own conclusions about the nature of the good life and the means of reaching it. Thus these thinkers of the wisdom tradition produced documents such as Proverbs, providing practical guides about how to live well and how to succeed in the world of ancient Yehud. These proverbs dealt mostly with realia of daily life, rarely going beyond everyday activities to discuss greater principles.[2]

Other wisdom literature, however, considered a wider range of issues, from God's involvement in creation to the ultimate questions of aging and death. These broader discussions carried with them a different social basis. The wisdom of daily social order, such as the Book of Proverbs, emphasized the importance of maintaining a status quo in which the ruling class continued its dominance in issues of power and theology alike. Some wisdom literature, such as Job and Ecclesiastes, operated as dissent literature within ancient Yehud. Such literature disagreed with important social and religious doctrines, debating the value of widely accepted institutions and presumptions. Although wisdom of order and wisdom of dissent alike would have stemmed from the same social strata of professional scribes, the social orientation of these texts differed greatly. Dissent wisdom argued against the status quo in ways impossible for wisdom of social order. The dissent wisdom produced one of Yehud's clearest voices outside the mainstream of canonical religious thought, and as such it reflected the thoughts of a much more dissatisfied group than that responsible for Proverbs.

Books such as Job and Ecclesiastes prove difficult to date with precision. For Job, the literary conflicts between the core and the frame only serve to complicate the matter. The connections between the narrative frame and the canon's short stories are obvious, as they share similar form.[3] Since these other short stories derive from Yehud's colonial period, it seems reasonable to suggest that Job's frame also represents this period. The connections between Job's core of discourse and the typical forms of speech favored by the Yehudite wisdom tradition also appear to date this material to colonial Yehud. If these indications are right, then the assemblage of the entire Book of Job probably occurred within the time of Persia's domination, quite possibly late within that period, partly in response to the development of the classical wisdom tradition as a somewhat official position among the elites of Jerusalem.[4]

The Book of Ecclesiastes presents problems for dating as well. It seems to possess some Greek influences, and many scholars have thus dated it post–330 B.C.E. However, Greek influences would have been rampant in Yehud long before Alexander's conquest of the Persian imperial core. During the middle of the fifth century B.C.E., the growth of trade between Jerusalem and Athens (as well as other Greek city-states) would have allowed a significant interchange of ideas, and these ideas would have been most clearly felt within the wisdom traditions of scribes who needed to learn about other languages and cultures. Ecclesiastes, then, seems to reflect a late Persian setting, once more as a response to the official scribal positions developing in Jerusalem.[5]

Literature as Dissent

Literature, as a product of a society's elite scribes, often expresses the views of the status quo, but literature can also dissent against the views of the majority. The ideology of such literature can present a distinctly different worldview and set of social assumptions, thus challenging the majority social construction of reality. Through such functions, it is possible for literature to operate as dissent. The contradictions of specific social perspectives are clear within certain canonical texts.

> *The words of Agur son of Jakeh. An oracle.*
> *Thus says the man: I am weary, O God,*
> *I am weary, O God. How can I prevail?*
> *Surely I am too stupid to be human;*
> *I do not have human understanding.*
> *I have not learned wisdom,*
> *nor have I knowledge of the holy ones.*
> *Who has ascended to heaven and come down?*
> *Who has gathered the wind in the hollow of the hand?*
> *Who has wrapped up the waters in a garment?*
> *Who has established all the ends of the earth?*
> *What is the person's name?*
> *And what is the name of the person's child?*
> *Surely you know!*
>
> *(Proverbs 30:1-4)*

These sayings of Agur operate as dissent within the wisdom tradition.[6] Wisdom emphasizes that relevant knowledge for human existence is attainable and that the parts of God's reality that humans need to know for daily life are discernible from the observation of the world. These sayings appear near the end of the Book of Proverbs, which expresses the standard views of wisdom, but these sayings do not reflect the typical wisdom expressions. Instead, Agur's sayings dissent strongly from that wisdom tradition by denying the knowability of the depths of faith. Agur asserts that he himself has not attained sufficient wisdom. He clearly writes in the style of wisdom; his questions reflect the same type of argumentation found in other wisdom writings. Despite the typicality of his form, his content argues against the knowability of necessary facts for human existence: "I am too stupid to be human" (Proverbs 30:2).

Agur continues to question further the basis for wisdom. There are facets to the world that no human has experienced; the reaches of nature remain unknowable to humans, who cannot hold the wind and contain the waters. The text ends with a twist that brings the argument to the reader. Who can know such things? Is there anyone who can? If so, can you, the reader, even know the name of such a one? This attacks the sensibilities of the wisdom reader, whose training produced the assumptions that all things needful are knowable. The reader must join Agur in admitting ignorance, the very lack of wisdom with which Agur begins his sayings.

Through such means, this text attacks the presuppositions of wisdom. It subverts the structures of wisdom's social construction of reality. Agur's sayings stop short of suggesting alternate ways of being; they merely present challenges that break down the system constructed by wisdom. This dissent literature operates by pointing toward the intrinsic contradictions with the system of wisdom literature and thought. After deconstructing certain elements of wisdom's underlying assumptions, the text ends with a question that echoes a challenge to the reader to find some other way of being. In this way, the dissent literature moves beyond the page, where it functions as literature, to address and alter the social realities of the readers' communities.

Such is the work of dissent literature. It first attacks the sensibilities of a standard literature's readers, and then the dissent begun at the literary level moves into the social dimension, questioning the assumptions by which a society organizes itself. The case of Agur's sayings begins to demonstrate the challenge against scribalism. The literature asserts the unknowability of certain elements of the natural world and then forces the reader to admit ignorance. This reader thus asserts the antithesis of the wisdom worldview that emphasizes knowability. Such a reader, presumably part of a wisdom community who would be reading such texts, then realizes, first, that not everything relevant is knowable and, second, that not everything can be taught and learned within the environment of the scribal school. Thus the literature moves to undermine the institution. Dissent literature not only works at an intellectual, ideological level but it disrupts the social connections based on ideological commitments.

Problems with Job

The Book of Job offers perhaps the best example of wisdom dissent literature, and yet the problems in the interpretation of Job are immense; they complicate greatly any attempts to understand the functions of dissent wisdom. Job proves to be a difficult book for exegesis on many counts. The language differs in many ways from the prose and poetry of the rest of the canon. Many words present lexical ambiguities. The form of extended philosophical argumentation offers few comparative opportunities within canonical literature.[7] Dating the Book of Job is extraordinarily troublesome. The relationship of the book's frame and core plagues scholarship to this day. The theological issues surrounding the text as a whole have received far too little attention within the secondary literature, given the complexity of the task of describing the text's theological presuppositions. With these problems combined, Job presents a formidable object for detailed exegesis.

Perhaps the most seriously exegetical problem is the relationship of the core and the frame. Job 1–2 and 42 present a narrative about Job; Job 3–41 contains poetic and philosophical arguments between Job, three friends, a man named Elihu, and Yahweh. The formal differences between the core and the frame are clear. The narrative reads rather well as its own separate story. The philosophical arguments reach their own resolution with God's final speech; many scholars consider the closing narrative to be anticlimactic with regard to the intervening poetic discourse. The frame begins with a description of Satan's and God's discussion concerning Job, but Satan does not appear as an issue for debate within the poetic sections. In the poetic arguments, Job asserts that God does not keep a perfect quid pro quo justice within the world, but the narrative closes with a restoration to Job of all that he had lost. Thus the core and the frame offer divergent theologies, ideologies, and interpretations of the character Job.

The poetic argumentation in the core of the Book of Job offers the more classical wisdom formulations. Speech is the key category of action throughout this core; there is no action of significance whatsoever. Instead, the book progresses through the debate between Job and his friends, followed by speeches by Elihu and Yahweh. Job's friends offer rather standard developments of typical Israelite wisdom ideologies. To these proffered orthodoxies, Job responds with sharp denunciations of the underlying assumptions of wisdom theology.

The wisdom and priestly traditions of colonial Yehud shared several elements of their worldviews. Both social groups assumed that there was and should be an underlying cosmic order, undergirded by the nature of God. Although wisdom typically grounded this order in God's functions at creation and priestly theology referred instead to God's establishment of the law, both emphasized the importance of this essential order. Both wisdom and priestly theology concluded that God worked for justice in the world. Thus those who obeyed God and lived within the strictures of the natural order would receive the benefits of the good life, whether as a natural result or as a consequence of divine blessing. Both ideologies assumed a perfect correlation between correct action and positive results in personal (and corporate) life. Job denied this common position, while his partners in debate encouraged him to accept it.

Then Bildad the Shuhite answered:
"How long will you say these things,
and the words of your mouth be a great wind?
Does God pervert justice?
Or does the Almighty pervert the right?
If your children sinned against him,
he delivered them into the power of their transgression.
If you will seek God
and make supplication to the Almighty,

if you are pure and upright,
surely then he will rouse himself for you
and restore to you your rightful place.
Though your beginning was small,
your latter days will be very great.
For inquire now of bygone generations,
and consider what their ancestors have found;
for we are but of yesterday, and we know nothing,
for our days on earth are but a shadow.
Will they not teach you and tell you
and utter words out of their understanding?

. . . .

See, God will not reject a blameless person,
nor take the hand of evildoers.
He will yet fill your mouth with laughter,
and your lips with shouts of joy.
Those who hate you will be clothed with shame,
and the tent of the wicked will be no more."
(Job 8:1-10, 20-22)

Job's friend Bildad offers this discourse reflecting the standards of typical wisdom thought. It was unthinkable that God could pervert justice (Job 8:3). Wisdom theology equated God with the dispensing of justice; Bildad rightly recognizes the absurdity of any other position within the context of wisdom thought. Thus his conclusions are certain within that context. The suffering of Job's children must have been punishment from God who maintains the order of justice in the world, and thus the children must have sinned in order to deserve the punishment that God gave them. Sin, punishment, suffering, and the will of God thus become intertwined in the wisdom and priestly ideology. On the basis of this powerful ideology, Bildad can offer a prediction: if Job repents from the sin that is obvious on the basis of his current suffering, then God will bless Job's future.

Bildad also supports the framework within which wisdom operates. Because all necessary things are knowable, there exists a body of knowledge developed through the generations and passed down to contemporaries. Within the social order of wisdom, this body of knowledge provided the content for the service of education and ideation that the scribes performed. The function of scribes was the transmission of this accumulated knowledge. Job, however, not only denies the ideology of the wisdom tradition but strikes at the heart of the social system. He has refused the wisdom of the ancestors. If everyone followed Job's example, then the social system of scribes as educators would break down and fall apart. The ideology and the social structure both insist that the teachers and scribes have vital knowledge that is right by definition. It is taught because it is right and it is right because it is taught. Job's focus on experience denies tradition and thus dissents from the social structure of scribal wisdom.

Bildad's assertion of social order grounded in God's action and his defense of the social institution of scribal wisdom set the stage for Job's response. Job questions the very social order that Bildad supports, insisting instead on power as the source for God's ability and on randomness as the only relevant moral standard for Yahweh's actions.

> *"God will not turn back his anger;*
> *the helpers of Rahab bowed beneath him.*
> *How then can I answer him,*
> *choosing my words with him?*
> *Though I am innocent, I cannot answer him;*
> *I must appeal for mercy to my accuser.*
> *If I summoned him and he answered me,*
> *I do not believe that he would listen to my voice.*
> *For he crushes me with a tempest,*
> *and multiplies my wounds without cause;*
> *he will not let me get my breath,*
> *but fills me with bitterness.*
> *If it is a contest of strength, he is the strong one!*
> *If it is a matter of justice, who can summon him?*
> *Though I am innocent, my own mouth would condemn me;*
> *though I am blameless, he would prove me perverse.*
> *I am blameless; I do not know myself;*
> *I loathe my life.*
> *It is all one; therefore I say,*
> *he destroys both the blameless and the wicked.*
> *When disaster brings sudden death,*
> *he mocks at the calamity of the innocent.*
> *The earth is given into the hand of the wicked;*
> *he covers the eyes of its judges—*
> *if it is not he, who then is it?"*
> *(Job 9:13-24)*

The chief characteristic of God, according to Job, is not justice but anger. This violates the assumptions of typical wisdom literature. Not only does emotion dominate God's responses but the poet compares God's activity to that of the helpers of Rahab, the chaos leviathan.[8] Answering God, therefore, is absurd; there is no basis for reason with such a one (Job 9:14-16). God's speech is not a discourse of rationality but instead a rhetoric of violent power (Job 9:17-20). Any attempt on Job's part would lead inevitably to God's discrediting; the Deity does not play fair but uses rhetorical strength to strong-arm the truth. Job then denies completely God's justice, a foundational precept of wisdom and priestly theologies. God destroys both the innocent and the evil (Job 9:22). The distinctions and the categories on which the sages and the priests base their ideologies are meaningless; they collapse into one blur. Furthermore, God actively disturbs the order presumed by the forces of Yehud's social stability. God mocks the pain of the innocent (Job 9:23) and obscures the sight of the judges (Job 9:24), making right deliberation impossible. God's action in the world destroys the possibilities for justice.

Through this speech, Job succeeds in denying one of the fundamental assumptions of wisdom and priestly theology. Job argues against justice as an operative concept within the world or as an apt description of God's intentions and activity. Without this ideological basis, the sages and the priests have no warrant for establishing their own social structures that divide and organize society on the basis of God's natural and legal desire for justice. In fact, God actively opposes any human perceptions that might lead to justice, and thus the social systems based upon such presuppositions must necessarily fail. This ideological shift negates the institutions at the social level.

Furthermore, Job shifts the image of God as presented by the sages and the priests. The priestly image of God as lawgiver, who delivered legal codes with instructions for life to Moses upon the mountain, coalesces with the wisdom portrayal of God as creator, who imbued all nature (including human existence) with inherent rules about how to live the good life. Both of these images, although differing in the details, depict God as hierarchical and prior, both above and before the current situations in Yehud. Also, both portrayals show God's desire for order and justice. Job's view of God is much more present and active; God works in the present to obscure justice. God is neither logical nor orderly; there is no internal divine commitment to the law or to the order of nature. Instead, God is emotional and randomly destructive. Such a God provides no basis for the promulgation of law or wisdom; neither make any sense if this is the nature of God. Instead, the only sensible option is Job's stubborn arguing, a perpetual struggling with God over the very definitions of right and wrong that seem to be the issue between Job and his friends. The theological debate over the nature of God seems to parallel a disagreement about the proper role of social institutions, especially those rooted in hierarchies of access to God or of knowledge about reality.

The defense of this hierarchy is of supreme importance to Job's friends. Eliphaz heatedly argues in favor of the established patterns.

> *Then Eliphaz the Temanite answered:*
> *"Should the wise answer with windy knowledge,*
> *and fill themselves with the east wind?*
> *Should they argue in unprofitable talk,*
> *or in words with which they can do no good?*
> *But you are doing away with the fear of God,*
> *and hindering meditation before God.*
> *For your iniquity teaches your mouth,*
> *and you choose the tongue of the crafty.*
> *Your own mouth condemns you, and not I;*
> *your own lips testify against you.*
> *Are you the firstborn of the human race?*
> *Were you brought forth before the hills?*
> *Have you listened in the council of God?*
> *And do you limit wisdom to yourself?*
> *What do you know that we do not know?*
> *What do you understand that is not clear to us?*
> *The gray-haired and the aged are on our side,*
> *those older than your father.*

Are the consolations of God too small for you,
or the word that deals gently with you?
Why does your heart carry you away,
and why do your eyes flash,
so that you turn your spirit against God,
and let such words go out of your mouth?
What are mortals, that they can be clean?
Or those born of woman, that they can be righteous?
God puts no trust even in his holy ones,
and the heavens are not clean in his sight;
how much less one who is abominable and corrupt,
one who drinks iniquity like water!
I will show you; listen to me;
what I have seen I will declare—
what sages have told,
and their ancestors have not hidden,
to whom alone the land was given,
and no stranger passed among them.
The wicked writhe in pain all their days,
through all the years that are laid up for the ruthless.
Terrifying sounds are in their ears;
in prosperity the destroyer will come upon them.
They despair of returning from darkness,
and they are destined for the sword.
They wander abroad for bread, saying, 'Where is it?'
They know that a day of darkness is ready at hand;
distress and anguish terrify them;
they prevail against them, like a king prepared for battle.
Because they stretched out their hands against God,
and bid defiance to the Almighty,
running stubbornly against him
with a thick-bossed shield;
because they have covered their faces with their fat,
and gathered fat upon their loins,
they will live in desolate cities,
in houses that no one should inhabit,
houses destined to become heaps of ruins;
they will not be rich, and their wealth will not endure,
nor will they strike root in the earth;
they will not escape from darkness;
the flame will dry up their shoots,
and their blossom will be swept away by the wind.
Let them not trust in emptiness, deceiving themselves;
for emptiness will be their recompense.
It will be paid in full before their time,
and their branch will not be green.

They will shake off their unripe grape, like the vine,
and cast off their blossoms, like the olive tree.
For the company of the godless is barren,
and fire consumes the tents of bribery.
They conceive mischief and bring forth evil
and their heart prepares deceit."
(Job 15)

The opening move of Eliphaz within this declaration argues the worthlessness of Job's approach (Job 15:2-6). Eliphaz charges that Job, through unprofitable talk, undermines the religion of Yahweh. This position clearly identifies the support of God's justice with the worship of God; other views are sin. From this perspective, the very voicing of Job's position proves its own worthlessness, because it questions what must be unquestionable within the social construction of reality favored by the priests and the sages. These social systems devalue Job's speculation as emptiness. Of course, the presence of Job's discourse within the canon creates a space for this kind of speculation; the juxtaposition of Job's questioning with Eliphaz's defense of the status quo merely strengthens the sense that the society here stretches itself to include Job as dissent literature within the wisdom tradition.

Eliphaz then moves to a more personal attack against Job (Job 15:7-16). His first argument is that Job is not one of the elders, and thus his attempts at knowledge are bound to fail in the face of the sages' accumulated wisdom. Job cannot know anything that the wise do not already know; therefore his discourse is faulty wherever it disagrees with established wisdom. Age, wisdom, and the word of God are equivalent expressions of authority and correctness within Eliphaz's understanding. Contradicting any of these authorities undermines the others, and so the attack on God's justice not only rejects the official religion but also sets oneself against the powerful elements of the society, such as the priests and the sages.

Eliphaz's defense of established religion's social ideology next attempts to demonstrate the social realities that the position adduces as its best evidence (Job 15:17-30). From within this perspective, the examination of society creates an obvious and consistent defense. In other words, wisdom considers itself and its categories self-evident, as do most ideologies. The elements of power used to enforce this ideology are clear only from outside the ideology itself. Pain, destruction, and poverty are symptoms of God's displeasure, the sure result of wickedness. However, the powerful members of society are in a position to ensure these very results, since they control the powers that can punish and impoverish those with whom they disagree. Wisdom creates its own plausibility structure, since the elites can diminish the standard of living for those who do not follow its precepts.[9] Thus power becomes the ultimate criterion of correctness in theological disputes. Because the powerful can control wealth, they can control the definitions of the behavior that attains wealth and then can reward such behavior in the appropriate fashion. In the same fashion, the powerful, such as Eliphaz in Job 15, can control such factors as the availability of bread (Job 15:23) and the desolation of cities (Job 15:28).

Eliphaz, however, considers these issues to be self-evident. Because the impious are impoverished, God must hate what the community defines as impiety. There is no cognizance that the community controls both the definition of piety and the definition of poverty. The sages never realize that the society does not demand the ideology; in a sense, the ideology shapes the society in ways that make the ideology more plausible and thus more effective in shaping society. Job, on the other hand, argues that the unknowability of God's intentions, resulting in human perceptions of randomness, denies the possibility of objectivity in human institutions, especially those hierarchies based in sure knowledge of God, whether through revealed law or discovered wisdom.

The Challenge of God

After many chapters, God interrupts the dialogue between Job and his friends with a lengthy statement (Job 38–41). Yahweh details some of what God knows that Job, and by extension other humans, does not know. The list contains items such as the size of the cosmos, the cause for the movement of the sun, the location of weather before it precipitates, the reason for the stability of constellations, the reproductive cycles of various wild animals, means of taming other wild animals, methods for flight, and the mysteries of Behemoth and Leviathan. Job responds in humility to this theophanic disclosure of might; he repents (Job 42:1-6).

Yahweh's point in the argument is that God's knowledge is far beyond humans. There may well be justice within God, but the specific details are unknowable to humans because of the great difference of perspective. God knows so much more than humans that human knowledge is radically limited. Ironically, God's pronouncement is in fundamental agreement with Job, but it partakes of the forms against which Job had argued for the bulk of the text. Job argued against the authority structures of the priests and the sages, but Yahweh provides the same content in direct revelation, according to the priests' authority structure, and in riddle language concerning creation, such as the speech forms of the sages. Thus Yahweh's speech tends to be more convincing in its sheer rhetorical power than Job's discourse, even though Job more directly addresses the issues of Yahweh's justice and the knowability of human institutions. The text as a whole, then, attempts to convince the sages and the priests of the extent of Yahweh's knowledge and the radically relativized ability to know that humans possess. God appears at the end of the book and challenges the sages and the priests to accept these new theological presuppositions, as Job had set forth throughout the book's core.

The Warp of the Frame

After the core, one further chapter redirects many of the issues presented in the dialogues (Job 42). Job expresses his humility and his willingness to repent. Immediately, Yahweh gives Job a chance to sacrifice in order to assuage the divine wrath against his friends. Job then receives blessings again in greater amounts than his previous wealth. This ending has troubled many interpreters. Whereas the beginning of the book asks whether Job will serve God without reward, the conclusion gives him the rewards anyway, negating the original problem. Just as God and Job agree within the speeches, God clearly shows favor for Job's thought, admitting that Job had spoken correctly about God.

If God and Job agree on the content issues within the text, why is there tension between them at the end of Yahweh's speech? Of what does Job repent at the start of the frame (Job 42:6)? Perhaps the subtle difference is that Job knows that God is random, whereas God argues that humans cannot know whether God is consistent or not. Job suggests that humans should know that God has limits; even God does not know everything. Yahweh's speech implies that God is omniscient, but that humans' knowing is radically limited. Thus Yahweh's speech is slightly more orthodox than Job's, but Yahweh's is in some senses more radical in its social ramifications. God argues that people cannot know such a wide variety of things that one must question human ability to create social institutions. Of course, this itself argues in favor of the priestly dimensions of Yehudite faith; their dependence upon revelation instead of reason provides a way around the impasse.

Thus the ending frame moves in the direction of a priestly solution to the book as a whole. Job sacrifices for his friends, bringing them a removal of God's anger. Through repentance and sacrifice, Job receives God's favor, and God's favor brings Job great bounty in earthly goods. Herein exists the greatest tension between the core and the frame. The book's core argues against the sages and the priests, combining these two systems of hierarchical privilege based upon special knowledge about God and reality. The frame, however, warps the intent of the core, shifting back into a sacerdotal mindset and reinforcing the status quo. With the frame in place, it becomes possible to read the Book of Job as a morality tale of faith. If one sticks with God even in the midst of loss and then one repents, one receives blessing. This warps the antiestablishmentarian feeling of the core discourses, which argue against systems of hierarchy and in favor of God's randomness and unknowability. The frame returns to the reader a method for controlling God: if one sacrifices, then God will bless. Thus Job forms an incoherent book, and perhaps intentionally so.[10] At core, however, the condemnation of the hierarchies is clear. Job denies God's justice and predictability and thus threatens the social structures in which the sages and the priests construct advantages for themselves. The frame shifts the book into something more palatable for the masses, who may have accepted the core as a popular tale. The frame warps the meaning and shifts the emphasis toward obedience toward God and the hierarchies of sacrifice. Perhaps the frame was the price for canonical inclusion, or a nervous attempt toward moralizing this shocking text that persuades the reader of God's complicity in the injustices of the world.

Ecclesiastes

The Book of Ecclesiastes also proves troublesome, but it provides a clear voice of dissent within the wisdom tradition. Although it claims authorship by Solomon, the third and final king of the united monarchy of Israel and Judah, it reflects the same concerns as does the Book of Job and seems to derive from colonial Yehud.[11] In many ways, Ecclesiastes directly rejects wisdom, or at least wisdom as defined by the tradition of Proverbs. In this, Ecclesiastes is similar to Job; neither book recognizes the ultimate value of knowledge but searches for other values that can be known.

I, the Teacher, when king over Israel in Jerusalem, applied my mind to seek and to search out by wisdom all that is done under heaven; it is an unhappy business that God has given to human beings to be busy with. I saw all the deeds that are done under the sun; and see, all is vanity and a chasing after wind.

What is crooked cannot be made straight,
and what is lacking cannot be counted.

I said to myself, "I have acquired great wisdom, surpassing all who were over Jerusalem before me; and my mind has had great experience of wisdom and knowledge." And I applied my mind to know wisdom and to know madness and folly. I perceived that this also is but a chasing after wind.

For in much wisdom is much vexation,
and those who increase knowledge increase sorrow.
(Ecclesiastes 1:12-18)

The author of Ecclesiastes rejects wisdom as an ultimate value and clearly asserts the negative effects of knowledge. Yet even this forms a type of knowledge; the author knows that knowledge causes sorrow. Wisdom itself is an unhappy business; it is not a panacea through which one easily finds the way to the good life. Ecclesiastes may even argue that wisdom leads one away from the good life by leading one into intellectual machinations that deceive and frustrate rather than allowing one to live life. Such would be a radical denunciation of the wisdom tradition and the scribes who fostered it and benefited from the widespread acceptance of wisdom doctrines. The worthlessness of intellectual activity seems to be one of Ecclesiastes' main points.

Like Job, Ecclesiastes points out the severe limits of knowability. One can only know what is present; absence cannot be known. This limit proves increasingly problematic over time, as one tries to grow in knowledge. The entirety of any system proves impossible to know without understanding the limits of the system and the types of absence that surround it. Thus the inability to know what is not means that one cannot fully know what is, because one can never determine the extent of presence without knowing the neighboring absence. Even when one endeavors to know not only wisdom but also folly, so that the limits of each are fully known through the experience of the other, this too is pointless.

The Book of Ecclesiastes contains other relativizations of wisdom and knowledge, based in the same frustrations with the wisdom tradition.

Dead flies make the perfumer's ointment give off a foul odor;
so a little folly outweighs wisdom and honor.
(Ecclesiastes 10:1)

Even if one attains a great deal of wisdom, the limits are still unavoidable. Because one's wisdom cannot be infinite or pure, there will always be room for other thought, and these other thoughts can spoil the value of the correct thoughts that one can attain. A small degree of folly ruins a huge amount of wisdom. Small amounts of the unknowable relativize the worth of what is known. Thus the greatest amount of wisdom, short of the infinite, voids itself upon contact with the minor follies unavoidable in human life.

Wisdom, for all its benefits, cannot protect itself against its own self-cancellation when confronted with the realities of human existence. In this sense, Ecclesiastes knows the problems connected with wisdom's agenda, which includes the discernment of ways to live the good life through the study of texts and thoughts. Real life, however, often proves disagreeable to analysis and to reduction to textual formulae, no matter their complexity. This reflects a basic philosophical problem. Texts of wisdom or other knowledge tend to be word games, resolvable within their own contexts and full of the sorts of intriguingly complex self-referential statements in which scholars can spend their lives. However, the correlation of these word games to real life is tenuous at best, and in most cases the connections are absent altogether. Ecclesiastes recognizes this philosophical limitation to the wisdom project through two repeated features of the text: the theme of absurdity and the treatment of aging.

Ecclesiastes contains a refrain, repeated thirty-one times within the book, including an inclusio in Ecclesiastes 1:2 and 12:8. This refrain announces that all is vanity or absolute vanity. Other translations of the Hebrew word *hebel* include "absurdity" or "emptiness."[12] The book emphasizes that various types of effort in life, whether through labor, through intellectual mastery of wisdom, or through the proper worship of God, result in the same unsatisfying end. In the long run, all effort is worthless; nothing escapes the sentence of absurdity. Wisdom especially falls victim to this critique. Attempts to know better ways to live life inevitably fail; instead, Ecclesiastes' only advice is that "there is nothing better for mortals than to eat and drink, and find enjoyment in their toil."[13] This hedonistic moral replaces wisdom's standard attempts to define the correct life, usually with moderation and integrity as well as hard work. Ecclesiastes' view is that such things are meaningless; only pleasure endures.

Aging and death receive special attention in Ecclesiastes. Death has an equalizing power in Ecclesiastes. Just as all are born, so all die (Ecclesiastes 3:2). Death captures the wise and the foolish alike; death's unwillingness to show preference removes all privileged positions within society (Ecclesiastes 2:16); this frustrates the powerful, because they find it impossible to gain any ultimate advantage. Death leaves everyone powerless; even those who on earth had power to oppress and to hurt (Ecclesiastes 8:8). Thus the aging process and the resultant death remove the distinctions between people and thus rule out the opportunities for advantage and privilege. Nothing that gives benefit is meaningful in the face of death; everything is absurd and valueless. Thus death relativizes the gains and the struggles of human existence.

Since death is so destructive of human organization of reality, it should be avoided. It would be stupid to live life in such a way as to make death come more quickly, and thus moderation is to be recommended (Ecclesiastes 7:16-18). However, there are things in life that are worse than death. The day of death is better than the day of birth, since it is better to reach an end and to cease the possibilities for doing wrong (Ecclesiastes 7:1). An evil woman who entraps a man is worse than death as well (Ecclesiastes 7:26). Dying is not the ultimate tragedy; there are things that can be lost more precious even than life.

Likewise, the length of one's years is not of absolute value. The quality of life is more important than its quantity. Without enjoyment, longevity is meaningless (Ecclesiastes

6:3, 6). Ecclesiastes realizes that the end of life contains pain and darkness (Ecclesiastes 11:9; 12:1). Life is not without pain; thus pain is a necessary prerequisite to the continuation of life that allows the existence of more pleasure and enjoyment as well. Although this may be absurd, the author recognizes that it is inevitably true. Thus it is best to endure some pain while still enjoying life as much as one can, but sheer length of life without enjoyment is absurd as well. A lengthy poem details the decreasing abilities brought on by age (Ecclesiastes 11:7—12:8).

After death, nothing is known. One's spirit may become eternal or may not; such cannot be known (Ecclesiastes 3:21). No earthly achievements or abilities follow one into death (Ecclesiastes 9:10). Death removes privileges; it is a place and time of hopelessness (Ecclesiastes 9:4-5). Nothing remains.

Through all of these issues, Ecclesiastes dissents from the majority opinions expressed in the wisdom literature. Whereas most wisdom thought points toward concrete suggestions for living life well, Ecclesiastes denies the possibility of good living beyond eating and drinking. Wisdom typically supports life within the social order, suggesting practices for daily life that allow one to work effectively in the context of the wider social institutions. Wisdom also assumes a wide variety of social privileges within a structure of social class; Ecclesiastes denies these variations in the face of meaninglessness for all and death at the end that equalizes differences.

Ecclesiastes dissents from the wisdom consensus, but the dissent never reaches its strength. Ecclesiastes maintains an ability to undermine the systems of privilege but never suggests any replacement or any other form of social organization. This author argues strenuously against the social institutions. The ideology of enjoyment would have serious consequences for society if it was followed, certainly resulting in the downfall of all institutions. But Ecclesiastes does not provide an alternative structure. Enjoyment, by itself, would not produce a new social structure; instead, it makes all social structures untenable. It can function as a significant value system only in cases when others in the society do not hold it. That is, the ability of one group to follow an ethic of enjoyment and form a leisure class depends upon the presence of others dedicated to an ethic of work and personal responsibility. Enjoyment without labor is meaningful only for the elite.

This points toward the social location of Ecclesiastes. One of the elites, unwilling to accept the contradictions of life, retreats into a solipsistic ethic of enjoyment, expecting others to continue providing for the needs of life. From such a context, everything is meaningless, and death equalizes everyone—an issue of concern for those who have maintained their privilege throughout life. It may be possible that the Book of Ecclesiastes even functioned as a legitimation of the power of the elites; it could not be immoral for them to hold onto their wealth since everything on earth is only transitory anyway.[14] In this sense, Ecclesiastes is hardly dissent literature; it argues for society's wealthiest to stay at home, mourn their own future passing in the years before it actually arrives, and to realize that at death they will lose their privileges. Yet the radically different view of God and society—a view bordering at times on an anarchy of the elites—was well outside the mainstream of wisdom thought. It supported the social order through assuming the division between elites and workers, but it broke down the theological framework by which many of the inhabitants of Yehud managed to maintain their inequalities of power.

Dissent Literature

The dissent literature of the Hebrew Bible includes two examples with connections to the wisdom schools of colonial Yehud: Job and Ecclesiastes. The Book of Job offers discourses dissenting about the knowability of God, framed within a narrative with traditional sacrificial values. Ecclesiastes dissents about the value of human effort, arguing that all is meaningless and that death removes all distinctions anyway. Both books argue against hierarchies and systems of privilege, especially those grounded in revelation and wisdom.

Often dissent literature provides alternatives for life. Throughout the history of Israel and Yehud, visionaries such as prophets and apocalypticists offered alternative visions of the way that society and personal life could be. Some of these eschatological visions operate as dissent literature, because of the strong critique of the status quo combined with a clear sense of another way of constructing society. Job and Ecclesiastes, however, do not offer such alternatives. As dissent literature, these texts do not offer a reorientation of society, because they do not possess alternatives for action.

Instead, these two examples of wisdom dissent literature perform their dissent through undermining the ideological structures of their contemporary status quo. Job argues for the unknowability of God. This breaks the assumption of wisdom, that observation of the world can lead to an appropriate knowledge of God, and also violates the assumption of priestly and cultic law, that revelation provides a path to knowing God. If God is unknowable, then there is no basis for social hierarchies based upon those sorts of knowledge. Thus Job works against such hierarchies as those engineered by the sages and the priests. Ecclesiastes asserts the meaninglessness of life and the equalization of all persons in death, thus relativizing the worth of any efforts, including the effort to know God. If all human effort is equivalently meaningless, then there seems to be little basis for constructing social hierarchies and social systems. Both Job and Ecclesiastes remove or at least undermine the ideological foundations for many of the sages' sources of institutional power.

In this way, this wisdom literature could operate as a continuing source of critique and dissent with regard both to the literature and to the society. If this literature presented a highly concretized plan for an alternative community, its life as literature would be limited to specific historical contexts. Instead, Job and Ecclesiastes question the underlying assumptions of the knowability of God and the relevance of human activity. This radical questioning of basic assumptions allows for few responses from any society; they thus insinuate themselves into the value systems of many social institutions and undermine the self-evidency of their plausibility structures.

Job and Ecclesiastes disagree with other wisdom literature that humans can construct a good society through hierarchies of privilege and knowledge. Yet both of these texts operate clearly within the confines of wisdom literature, placing great value upon the effort to understand the world and organize one's participation in it according to the best possible thought about it and about God's intention. At that level, this dissent literature functions within the status quo, supporting the sages' continuing quest for truth even when that truth leads in directions away from the standard forms.

Notes

1. Cf. the views expressed in Gammie and Perdue, *The Sage in Israel.*

2. The canonical Book of Proverbs, of course, began with an extended treatise about the nature of wisdom and its opponent, folly. This strand of wisdom thought was obviously capable of more theoretical and theological discussions such as these, but overall Proverbs focuses on specific, concrete ethical issues.

3. See chapter 16, below.

4. On Job, see Marvin H. Pope, *Job,* AB 15 (Garden City, N.Y.: Doubleday & Co., 1965); Roland E. Murphy, *Wisdom Literature: Job, Proverbs, Ruth, Canticles, Ecclesiastes, and Esther,* FOTL 13 (Grand Rapids: Wm. B. Eerdmans Publishing Co., 1981); Norman C. Habel, *The Book of Job, A Commentary,* OTL (Philadelphia: Westminster Press, 1985); J. Gerald Janzen, *Job,* Interpretation (Atlanta: John Knox Press, 1988); D. J. A. Clines, *Job 1–20,* WBC 17 (Dallas, Tex.: Word Books, 1989); David Penchansky, *The Betrayal of God: Ideological Conflict in Job,* Literary Currents in Biblical Interpretation (Louisville, Ky.: Westminster/John Knox Press, 1990); Leo G. Perdue and W. Clark Gilpin, eds., *Voices from the Whirlwind: Interpreting the Book of Job* (Nashville, Tenn.: Abingdon Press, 1991); and Leo G. Perdue, *Wisdom in Revolt: Metaphorical Theology in the Book of Job,* JSOTSup 112 (Sheffield: JSOT Press, 1991).

5. See R. B. Y. Scott, *Proverbs and Ecclesiastes,* AB 18 (Garden City, N.Y.: Doubleday & Co., 1965); John J. Collins, *Proverbs and Ecclesiastes,* Knox Preaching Guides (Atlanta: John Knox Press, 1980); Murphy, *Wisdom Literature;* James L. Crenshaw, *Ecclesiastes, A Commentary,* OTL (Philadelphia: Westminster Press, 1987); R. N. Whybray, *Ecclesiastes,* OTG (Sheffield: JSOT Press, 1989); and Michael V. Fox, *Qohelet and His Contradictions,* JSOTSup 71 (Sheffield: Almond Press, 1989).

6. See James L. Crenshaw, "Clanging Symbols," in *Justice and the Holy: Essays in Honor of Walter Harrelson,* ed. Douglas A. Knight and Peter J. Paris (Atlanta: Scholars Press, 1989), 51–64.

7. The argumentation forms a shifting pattern of metaphors with the effect of destabilizing and disassembling the wisdom tradition from within that tradition. See Perdue, *Wisdom in Revolt.*

8. Job 9:13; 26:12; Psalms 87:4; 89:10; Isaiah 30:7; 51:9.

9. For the concept of a plausibility structure, see Berger, *Sacred Canopy.* For comments on the abilities of elites to control the results that they "predict," see Etzioni-Halevy, *Knowledge Elite.*

10. Cf. Penchansky, *The Betrayal of God.*

11. Another possible connection is in Ecclesiastes 7:10 ("Do not say, 'Why were the former days better than these?'") which is similar to Haggai 2:3, 9; Zechariah 8:11; and Malachi 3:4.

12. The expression *hᵃbel hᵃbalim* is often mistranslated as "vanity of vanities" or "absurdity of absurdities." The form is the Hebrew superlative and would be better rendered as "ultimate vanity," "absolute absurdity," or the like.

13. Similar admonitions are found in Ecclesiastes 3:13; 5:18; 8:15; and 9:7.

14. Note that Ecclesiastes is a wisdom response almost identical to apocalyptic. In apocalyptic, middle management wishes the destruction of the whole world in an attempt to reequalize society and start over. For Ecclesiastes, the elites realize that their destruction in death equalizes them, but they do not long for the day when they lose their privilege.

CHAPTER 15

STORIES OF THE LARGER WORLD: IMAGINING OTHER LIVES

DURING THE TIME OF colonial Yehud, the new genre of the short story became popular, and that popularity continued through at least the Hellenistic period. These brief narratives provide glimpses into alternative social realities and suggest other ways of living life, often with values markedly different from those asserted by the priests, the sages, and the governors of the colony. The short stories seek a different way of life. They search for expressions of correct living, in which people receive their deepest needs. In religious terms, this need could be termed redemption, salvation, or blessing; the short stories themselves rarely operate in such explicitly religious terms. Instead, the narratives examine basic issues of daily life and offer an implicit commentary about the way life could—and quite possibly should—be.

After a fashion, these short stories share many of the characteristics of wisdom literature. The social impetus behind both short stories and wisdom seems to be the consideration of how to live the good life. The form of expression differs sharply. Whereas wisdom contains brief aphorisms or lofty philosophical discourse, the short stories develop characters and plots to show the interactions of different social worlds. Furthermore, the short stories develop notions that are contrary to the mainstream of thought, whereas the wisdom of the Book of Proverbs represents part of that mainstream. Job and Ecclesiastes depict a kind of wisdom in which the text dissents from the dominant worldview without suggesting alternatives. Herein lies the chief topical difference between dissent wisdom and the short stories. Dissent wisdom avoids examining alternatives; instead, it undermines the assumptions of society in general. Short stories, on the other hand, describe alternative communities, allowing the readers to draw connections between this other world and the different real world in which they live.

These stories operate as fiction, and perhaps they should be categorized as historical fiction. Usually there is a rich framework of dates and historical contexts, although the details at times seem vague or obscured.[1] The functionality of these short stories depends on personal connections with the characters and on generalizability. If the text is to suggest an alternative social world that seems relevant and attractive to the reader, at least in part, then there must be some positive connection with one or more of the story's characters. The reader must be able to identify self with a character and begin to transfer the values of the story into the values of the real world. On the other hand, the identification must be sufficiently ambiguous to allow some generalizability. The story must present situations that are almost stereotypical, so that they can be prototypical of the readers' actions in the world. The ambiguities of the text allow for variation in application and thus provide the grounds for subversion of the existing social order. The vague historical contextings of these stories meet the twin goals of identification and generalizability.

The short stories from the period of Yehud probably include Ruth, Esther, Jonah, and Daniel. Each of these stories presents a different set of life problems and solutions. Although there are significant differences in each story's portrayal of God, the social-ideological structure of each story falls into a recognizable pattern. The story presents a problem within the social world and, through the course of the plot, develops a solution to that problem. The point of the story lies within the strategies for solving the problem. As religious literature, defined as such by placement in the canon, the stories present a range of different ways in which one can act socially to solve problems with theological correctness. In other words, these stories depict different ways in which God can work through the normal processes of human life to solve their social problems. Taken as a whole, the short stories depict the variety of God's involvements in human life, whether recognized by the characters or not. With God's involvement in bringing people into better life so varied, the social implication is clear: there is no such thing as a privileged social strategy for solving problems, since God operates within and responds to so many different strategies. Thus the short stories offer a range of alternative communities, depicted in fiction as different options throughout Israel's history. These alternative communities begin to infringe upon the reality of Yehud, offering values for contemporary life that differed from the mainstream of the sages, priests, and governors.

Pluralism and the Short Stories

Colonial Yehud institutionalized pluralism. The intrusion of the Persian Empire into the political arena of Palestine permanently displaced the native monarchy of Jerusalem and began the development of Yehud as a secondary state, a colony run for the benefit of the empire. The Persian Empire allowed no independent political operations that would interfere with its long-range exploitation of Yehudite economy. This meant that no local politicians could gain enough power to mandate opinions on local matters. The political apparatus needed to enforce religious or social opinion throughout the colonial populace. Thus independent social groups, such as priests and sages, attempted to persuade the populace of the correct social attitudes and behaviors. Although they were mostly successful, they did not have the support of the political establishment behind them in the same way that such collusion would have been possible during the monarchy.

The entry of the Persian Empire as a displacing force within Yehudite politics meant that no social group had the ability to enforce its own social position. This resulted inevitably in a plurality of opinions and options. No position, not even that of the priests, could exterminate the others and operate as an exclusive option. This pluralism within local society paralleled the pluralism growing within the international community. The very existence of internationalistic influences within Jerusalem was part of this societal shift. Jerusalem's commerce with the wider world increased throughout the Persian period, especially through contact with Greece throughout the late fifth and the fourth centuries. This brought a wide variety of new ideas into Yehud and decentered the older notions from the Yahwistic temple and the Davidic monarchy. These other ideas gained currency throughout the populace, affecting the ways in which the people perceived their religion.

In this context, it is not surprising that the short stories take place in a wide variety of narrative settings. The Book of Ruth contains scenes in Israel and in Moab, a neighboring enemy state. Jonah, Daniel, and Esther take place in the Assyrian, Babylonian, and Persian imperial courts, respectively. Not all of the significant characters in these stories are from Israel or Yehud; some of the protagonists are even foreigners. The scope of the narrative range is much greater than ever before in Israelite literature. These short stories depict a much larger world with much greater variation, and the stories in many ways operate on the basis of that diversity and difference. Questions of ethnicity and religious variation come to the fore in several of the stories. These stories deal directly with the changes in faith as a result of an international, pluralistic world.

The short stories reflect the multiform adaptations of faith to such a pluralistic world. Together, the canonical stories offer a range of reflections on pluralism, responding to the question of how to live a life of faith in the midst of a pluralistic world. The answers are extremely diverse, and perhaps even mutually contradictory, but they fit well the realities of pluralism. If people must choose how to live out their own faith because there is no central, dominant social institution that can define a unified exclusive faith, then there will be a variety of answers. These short stories all show successful faith options, implying that God sees and honors these different expressions of faith. In this sense, the results of these life choices in the short stories can be called salvation; they are the result of the combination of human choice in life plus God's activity in response, leading into better life circumstances as a result of the human activity. Such is the nature of God's presence with the people in a pluralistic world, and such is the character of salvation.

Ruth

The Book of Ruth sets itself within the times of Israel's judges, before the monarchy. A Bethlehemite family leaves Israel during a time of drought and immigrates to Moab, where the men of the family die. The family's mother, Naomi, returns to Bethlehem, accompanied by one of her daughters-in-law, the Moabitess Ruth. Once back in Israel, Naomi and Ruth need to find ways to survive. Ruth chooses a short-term solution, involving the backbreaking labor of gleaning. She also pursues a long-term solution, the seduction and marriage of a man of means. For this purpose, she singles out Boaz, a distant relative of Naomi. Throughout harvest season, as long as gleaning remains a viable option, Ruth waits, but at the end of the harvest she approaches a drunken Boaz on the threshing floor at night with sexual suggestions. In the morning, Boaz offers marriage and through complex legal proceedings establishes his legal right to obtain the family property. This solves the problem of survival. Boaz and Ruth have a son, whom Naomi nurses and whom the women of the community name Obed. Thus Naomi's lack, which she had defined as the lack of a man because she was dried up, is solved as well.[2]

The story deals with issues of gender roles and family structure. Initially, the family includes father, mother, and two sons; the family soon adds two daughters-in-law. Then, death transforms the family, so that there are only mother and two daughters-in-law, one of whom leaves. This pair of mother-in-law and daughter-in-law operates as the relationship of highest significance for most of the story. This was a relationship relatively undefined within the culture and would not have been considered to be a family relationship that implied protection. By the end of the story, the family includes Boaz and Ruth, an absent father and a foreign mother, whose child nursed at his grandmother's breast and received a name from the women of the community. The story, in the process of solving the problems and the lacks described at the beginning, transforms the normal Israelite family at the start to something almost thoroughly unrecognizable as a family at the end. Yet the transformation is salvific; it solves the problems of lack of food and lack of the stability created by family connections.

Throughout the story, the characters add roles that transcend the boundaries of gender distinctions.[3] Ruth, the Moabitess daughter-in-law, becomes the provider of food for her small family of two. She takes on a male role of field labor so that she can eat; the role leads toward the solution. Ruth also takes the role of sexual aggressor in her pursuit of Boaz. Naomi functions later as the matchmaker, a typically male role. The women of the community name the child, taking over the male role of naming. In this way, the story argues against standard definitions of gender and the limitations that the society places upon roles as part of its social construction of gender. When the women take on male roles, then they bring themselves into self-sufficiency and they solve their own problems, without even mentioning the name of God.

The Book of Ruth also focuses on ethnicity issues. The family at the beginning experiences hardship within Israel, but the experiences of the family become fatal, at least for the men, in the foreign land of Moab. When Naomi returns from her time there, she has lost all of her men and she brings back with her only a daughter-in-law. To this point, the foreign land operates within the traditions of Israelite literature; it is an evil place from which no good comes. Interactions with the foreign lead to ruin. Such was the case, at least, within this story's beginning. But Ruth becomes the story's salvation. She solves the problems, both in the short and in the long term. She bears the child that solves Naomi's last problem. The Moabitess Ruth even becomes an ancestress of David, the messiah who would be king of Israel. Israel's laws forbade the inclusion of Moabites in the assembly of worship. King David, who danced before the ark, was one-eighth Moabite. King Solomon, who built the temple himself and dedicated it under command from Yahweh, was one-sixteenth Moabite. Thus the story legitimates the inclusion of foreigners, arguing even that they are the only way to solve life's problems.

The story defines the initial problem as the lack of food and the lack of proper relationships within the community, through men. The story solves those problems through food and through a son, as mediated by Boaz. Boaz's role as mediator rather than as solution becomes clear as he disappears from the story before the end. The practical strategies for solving the problems are twofold. First, there is a sense of inclusion. Where the tradition demands that the community reject foreigners, the Book of Ruth insists on their inclusion. The ethnic inclusion becomes an essential part of the story's drive toward a conclusion. The characters who accept Ruth more fully are those who work toward solving the problems. Second, the characters practice the addition of social roles in patterns that deviate from the social norm and form a new family structure. The story deconstructs the old style of family and builds a new one that looks quite different from anything known before. The social roles of breadwinner, nurse, husband, and namer have all shifted into directions that are not recognizable within typical Yehudite society.

The Book of Ruth senses God's activity within the world as people go beyond the limits placed upon them by society. The social definitions of ethnicity and gender are not only unhelpful but they block the successful solution of life's problems. Inclusion and the violation of role limits become the proper ways of living out one's faith in the midst of a pluralistic world.

Jonah

The Book of Jonah, although part of the Prophets within the Hebrew canon, represents a short story or a historical fiction in its genre, and its themes tie it to the Persian period. According to the story, God calls a prophet, Jonah, to travel east and to preach repentance to Nineveh, the Assyrian capital. In response, Jonah quickly travels west, away from Nineveh and from the prophetic assignment. While in the midst of Jonah's traveling, God causes a storm to engulf Jonah's boat.[4] Jonah sleeps through the storm, but the sailors recognize that some god is angry with them. They try everything else they can think of, but soon they have no recourse but to believe that Jonah is the culprit. After orthodox prayer to Yahweh, these heathen sailors toss Jonah overboard; they then worship God again and offered sacrifices.

Jonah, in the meantime, finds himself inside a large fish that Yahweh appoints for the purpose of transit. The second chapter of the book recounts Jonah's prayer of thanksgiving, but this may well be a later addition to the story. Jonah eventually reaches Nineveh, where he preaches a short sermon: "Forty days more, and Nineveh's changed" (Jonah 3:4).[5] After a single occurrence of this meager sermon, Jonah leaves the city and takes a place on a hillside overlooking it, waiting for the destruction to come. But the people of Nineveh repent, from the king to the lowest person on the social ladder, and even the cattle. God then changes the mind and repents of the disaster that God would have done. This angers Jonah, who wished that the destruction would have come upon his enemies. God causes a bush to grow for Jonah's shade and then causes an insect to eat it. God uses this as a lesson to teach Jonah about care for creation; how much more should God care for Nineveh?

This story represents a dissenting voice within several traditions. First, it portrays a reluctant, argumentative prophet, spoofing the earlier stories of prophets who forcefully speak the appointed words of God in highly ineffective attempts to change their societies. Jonah's hesitant speech changes the wicked city of Nineveh despite the prophet's wishes. But the deviation from the mainstream does not stop there. Jonah disagrees with God about who should be saved from the destruction that God threatens.

The strategy of salvation in this story is the recognition and embrace of universalism. Once the Ninevites admit that they must worship Yahweh, they are saved. Jonah, paradoxically, does not repent and does not attain salvation, as measured by any improvement in his life. This failure to attain salvation is connected to his failure to accept Yahweh's universalism. This disgruntled prophet wishes a nationalistic deity who plays favorites and who works for Jerusalem's salvation instead of for the benefit of the whole world. God's own activities frustrate such wishes. The theological message of the book is clear: God wishes to save the world, and those who would work with God must be willing to work on behalf of the entire world.

The narrative underscores this theological point through its use of humor. Jonah's sermon is more a caricature of a sermon than an actual attempt to convert the Ninevites. The story shows the inhabitants of this great city as a comic bunch, who do not know how to pray and who misunderstand even the most basic of theological points, such as the unchangeability of Yahweh's decision. Ironically, they turn out to be right about this; they may know more about correct theology than Israel itself did. They clothe even their cattle in sackcloth and ashes in their attempt to assuage God's anger, violating the Israelite understanding of God as one concerned with humans in ways not true about animals. The Ninevites are described as stupid, foolish persons, who do not know their right hand from their left. God chooses to save such foolish persons with outrageously bad theology.

The salvation of the story comes without a temple, without a sermon, without even hearing the name of Yahweh. The Ninevites do not worship properly, do not pray to Yahweh, and do strange things with their animals. The strategy for salvation as presented in this story is so radically universalistic that the only operative factor is God's choice to save. Jonah, then, faces another choice: whether to participate in this universalism or not. His choice to resist God results in his own misery on the fringes of human society.

The message for the story's hearers in colonial Yehud seems clear. God works throughout the world, not just in Jerusalem. Those who desire God to work for Jerusalem but not for the rest of world are wrong. God will resist them. The proper relationship with God requires participation in an international web of order; those who desire Jerusalem's ascendancy violate God's desire. The social implications for life in a pluralistic world are clear. Temples, sages, priests, and geography—even the name of Yahweh and the proper theology—are irrelevant in the faith. To live faith in this pluralistic world, one must accept the pluralism and embrace it in radical, outrageous ways that would seem stupid and foolish to most Jerusalemites. This radical acceptance of pluralism dissents from much of the religious traditions of Jerusalem and of the Hebrew canon, which emphasize that there is some core of faith to which persons must adhere in order to be part of the Yahwistic community.

Daniel

The Book of Daniel contains extended apocalyptic visions, but it also contains a short story very much of the same character as these others. This short story in Daniel 1–6 tells of a beautiful and bright Israelite boy taken from the Jerusalemite royalty upon Babylonia's capture of Judah in the early sixth century B.C.E. The Babylonian Empire captured Daniel and three of his friends for three years of court education to be followed by a lifetime of service in the imperial bureaucracy. Daniel continually displays resistance to many cultural nuances of Babylonian life, although he shows loyal acceptance of the general goals of the imperial training and service. He first rejects the non-kosher food, refuses to worship a statue, and later insists on keeping his regular prayer time. Daniel survives the punishments meted out to him for his resistance on these items, and he also survives death repeatedly. Throughout all of this time, he becomes a skilled interpreter of dreams, and his service to the imperial Babylonian court is immense, even if it does go mostly unrecognized because he predicts the downfall of that empire.

The story depicts ways to live in a pluralistic world such as the Babylonian imperial court. For the audience, the concern shifts to the Persian imperial court, but many of the issues are precisely the same. How does one maintain religious identity? How does one survive the persecutions directed toward religious minority? How does one climb the social hierarchies in ways effective for one's career? Daniel provides answers to such questions. He participates fully in imperial administration. This example is clear: there is no inconsistency between faithful Yahwism and the service of a foreign empire. What matters in life is not one's political orientation or whether one serves the oppressor of Israel, but simply one's personal piety.

Daniel maintains his integrity within the religion by focusing on regular and private acts of piety toward Yahweh. He keeps a kosher diet, despite the temptations of foreign food. This distinguishes him from others and marks him as different, but such is part of being a faithful worshiper of Yahweh in a foreign land. He gains in his career despite such differences, because Yahweh helped him do his work well as a reward for his piety. Not only does Daniel keep kosher, but he also refuses to worship idols and he prays regularly toward Jerusalem. Supposedly, this reinforces his "real" allegiance, but the facts of his service to the Babylonian Empire remain unchallenged. These acts of piety mark Daniel as one who worships God correctly and who thus receives God's favor. The Persian period date of Daniel may be reflected in the fact that scripture reading is not one of the acts of piety that Daniel performs, even though he is a scribe who knows how to read. Later Jews in foreign areas, perhaps as early as the Hellenistic period and certainly by the Roman, frequently carried with them small scrolls with scriptural texts for their meditation and reflection in prayer.

Thus the strategy for salvation in the narrative of Daniel is piety. Through observance of food laws and through regular, visible prayer, Daniel receives God's favor. This piety becomes the necessary mark of a faithful Jew when away from Jerusalem. Politics and temple worship are not requisite; only piety demonstrates the proper internal characteristics to maintain the proper relationship with God. Piety proves to be a popular solution to the problem of living faith in pluralistic Persia and the later empires, because it is portable and accessible. Even in Jerusalem, piety becomes an increasingly important part of the religion through the next centuries.

Esther

The Book of Esther relates a narrative from the Persian imperial court. The Persian emperor Ahasuerus (probably Xerxes) deposes his queen and searches throughout the empire for another one. His aides select suitable virgins from each of the provinces. Out of these, the emperor selects Esther, a Jew, as the next queen. Esther conspires with her cousin, Mordecai. The bulk of the story revolves around Mordecai's battle with his enemy, Haman, for the favor of the emperor. Haman seems to win the emperor's ear and orders the extermination of all the Jews throughout the Persian Empire on a future date. Mordecai appeals to Esther for help, and Esther takes matters into her own hands. She sets a banquet for the emperor and Haman, during which she accuses Haman of trying to murder her. Ahasuerus orders the execution of Haman and then crafts a law to save the Jews: on the date scheduled for the Jews' extermination, the Jews would be allowed and encouraged to defend themselves and to kill their enemies. Later, Esther convinces Ahasuerus to extend that decree for a second day. Throughout the empire, the Jews kill seventy-five thousand of their enemies. This provides the basis for the Feast of Purim, to be celebrated annually.

This story tells plainly of the salvation of the Jews from certain destruction by the Persian Empire as a result of the political activity of one Jewish woman, Esther. This one woman persuaded the emperor to change a decree and thus to permit the continuation of all Jews. Such a political triumph would have been beyond the abilities of any other politician, even a high-ranking official such as Mordecai, who was not able to approach the emperor concerning the matter.[6] Esther's ability derived from her position as queen. Her access to the emperor was more influential than that of any of the politicians. Thus her political effectiveness stemmed from her sexual relationship with the emperor. Because they were sexually involved and because he felt protective of her, he was willing to kill her enemy, Haman, and to reverse the imperial decree of death issued under Haman's counsel. Thus Esther's sexuality became an important ingredient in the salvation of the Jews.

Esther's ethnic loyalties also proved critical. After the announcement of the decree calling for the extermination of the Jews, Mordecai approached Esther with a challenge. His message to her was as follows:

> *Do not think that in the king's palace you will escape any more than all the other Jews. For if you keep silence at such a time as this, relief and deliverance will rise for the Jews from another quarter, but you and your father's family will perish. Who knows? Perhaps you have come to royal dignity for just such a time as this. (Esther 4:13-14)*

Esther faced a choice. Since her ethnicity was not widely known, she could have escaped the destruction planned for her ethnic group. To reveal her opposition to this plan could reveal her Jewishness, thus placing her at risk of her life as well. Mordecai encouraged her to prioritize her ethnic loyalties higher than her own personal safety. This forms an integral part of the salvation for the entirety of the Jews. The story depicts ethnic loyalty as an essential virtue, overarching other values. Loyalty saves lives and produced a saved community that continues throughout history; if even one fewer person had been loyal in the past, the ethnic group might not have survived.

Ethnic loyalty becomes so highly important in the light of the planned extermination that there are no limits to loyalty's means. In the story of Esther, her ethnic loyalty persuades the emperor to forbid the extermination of the Jews but also to legalize the murder of seventy-five thousand imperial citizens. These seventy-five thousand deaths are the price for ethnic loyalty. Although the survival of the Jews is certainly important, the text never dwells on the murders of others. Ethnic loyalty limits the perception of death's evil to only those with a certain ethnicity. In many ways, this short story represents the opposite of Jonah's universalism, in which the evil Assyrians receive God's mercy and life instead of destruction when they repent. In Esther, thousands of Persians die, never receiving God's mercy or salvation, for those are limited to the Jews alone. Ethnic loyalty encourages the reader to see the proper moral actions, those that lead to salvation, within the consideration of the survival of only one's own group rather than the world as a whole.

Salvation becomes an odd term within the context of Esther. God never appears in the book. God is not a character and God does not act, nor do any of the story's characters pray to God or mention God's name. No characters of the narrative pray, worship, or participate in theological discourse. God's absence resounds through the text. Yet salvation seems an apt description of the sudden, fortuitous avoidance of certain genocide. The Jews receive salvation instead of destruction. This provides for the survival of the group and the continuation of their faith, even though their faith does not appear within the text. Certainly the text's use as a justification for and explanation of the contemporary Festival of Purim grounds the text within the cultic functioning of later Judaism, but there is no internal indication that this is a religious text. The subsequent communities' recognition of the book allows the observation that this secularism is also an acceptable response to pluralism, as long as such secularism takes place within the context of ethnic loyalty.

Thus the Book of Esther presents a strategy for salvation as clear as those of the other short stories. Through the appropriate application of sexuality and through the high prioritization of ethnic loyalty, Esther cooperates with Mordecai and works through Ahasuerus to save the Jews as an ethnic group. There are no limits to the exploitation of ethnic loyalty. The deaths of seventy-five thousand individuals is not only an acceptable price to pay; the ideology of ethnic loyalty is so great that the text never considers that the deaths of others would be at all negative.

Similarly, the use of sexuality to gain one's goals is subsumed under ethnic loyalty. Because there might be advantage for one's ethnic group through attaining high position within the imperial court, one should attain such position, even if that means the use of one's sexuality to achieve such goals. The text contains no censure, nor even any embarrassment, that Esther gains the rank of queen because she expended her virginity in a night that the emperor considered memorable, not that she set up a seduction of the emperor and then framed her enemy Haman on a charge of sexual impropriety concerning her. These sexual exploits and exploitations are part of the natural occurrences of life within this text, just as much as the power politics between Haman and Mordecai. Politics, sex, and even genocide become convenient tools for salvation, in the interest of ethnic loyalty.

The Effects of Pluralism on the Popular Imagination

These four stories represent a new tradition within the variety of genres used within the Hebrew Bible. The short stories are distinctive formulations of the postexilic period. The first appearances of these stories was in the Persian period, but more were written in subsequent years. The Hellenistic period saw the publication of stories such as Susanna and Judith, both of which share many thematic elements with these stories from the Persian colony of Yehud.

Taken together, these four Persian-period stories communicate a range of responses to the growth of pluralism. Ruth argues for the violation of social customs in transcending limitations of gender and ethnicity. Jonah presents the importance of embracing pluralism to the point of salvation for the foreign enemies, in a system where none of the patterns of privilege function. For Daniel, salvation results from piety, including adherence to food and prayer laws. Esther recounts the salvific virtues of sexuality and of genocide in the service of ethnic loyalty. All of these reflect acceptable responses to the challenges of faith within a pluralistic world, even though these stories do express mutually contradictory options for action within that world.

Many themes resonate throughout these stories. All of them deal with the larger world of imperial-colonial relationships. Of these four, only the Book of Ruth is set within Israel, and it concerns the interrelationships of Israel with its neighbor, Moab. The other three stories take place within imperial settings, and two of them transpire directly within imperial courts. These stories are thoroughly at home in an enlarged world with complicated international relationships that affect individual lives, even on the private level.

Ethnicity figures within many of these stories. For Ruth, the story concerns Ruth's ethnicity and contradicts the legalistic, priestly condemnation of Moabites. The story argues that Ruth's ethnic identification should not be an issue in her inclusion within Israel. The Book of Jonah takes things one step farther, describing the salvation of Israel's worst enemies, the Assyrians. These foreigners deserve salvation through personal attention from God. Esther, however, addresses ethnic issues in a very different vein. For the Book of Esther, ethnic loyalty is paramount, and that means the rejection of other ethnic groups and the exploitation of religious means (such as fasting) as well as political imperial means in order to attack the enemies of the Jews.

At the same time, there are also gender issues in many of these texts.[7] Ruth transcends the limits of society's assigned gender roles in order to bring salvation. Esther functions specifically as a woman to gain her ends. Both Ruth and Esther use their sexuality in order to achieve their ends, their shared goal of the survival of their people, even though these two women define that in different ways. These stories reflect a time of pluralism in which the society questioned the proper role for women and presented an increasingly wide range of options about the definition of women's roles. Esther then argues for the valuation of women in high roles, whether inside or outside the traditional power hierarchies, and Ruth argues for the valuation of poorer women who take a variety of roles, both male and female, in order to survive.

The short stories contain another shared dimension. None of them focus on the temple or on wisdom. They portray alternative senses of community and social organization in which the standard religious authority structures of colonial Yehud seem oddly absent. In Jonah's case, the salvation of a foreign people does not require much of anything in theological terms, except the willingness and decisive action of God. The short stories represent a time when the society's self-understanding depended less upon the priests and the sages. Pluralism broke down the monopoly of the older authority structures and resulted in a wider variety of religious expression.

In keeping with the realities of pluralism, various responses embody this shared core in different ways. Even though the authors of these diverse short stories hold a partially common worldview, there are significant differences. In a sense, the different views represent different perceived worlds and different universes of discourse, but there is still a shared core. These differing partial universes shape the interpretation of the core.[8] All of these stories represent ways of dealing with the realities of a pluralistic world. Jonah wishes to convert the world, whereas Esther recognizes genocide as an acceptable solution. Ruth sees the dissolution of social norms and gender roles to be effective in bringing about personal salvation from problems; Daniel views only piety as sufficient for success in life. Pluralism brought about the range of responses to pluralism.

The short stories point toward a society that shared a common core of faith in Yahweh and a common desire to live successfully as Jews in a pluralistic world. Each group expressed that in different ways. Each of the stories represents a form of dissent against the forces of social maintenance. Ruth attacks priestly legislation about ethnic limitations. Jonah violates the centrality of the temple and of proper theology. Daniel operates willingly as a functionary for the very government that brought about the exile, and he resists the government on religious grounds. Esther favors government-sponsored genocide but never mentions God. Furthermore, none of the stories places any emphasis on the local governors, the priests, and the sages—the very forces of social maintenance. These stories operate as critique of the status quo and oppose the easy solutions proffered by the temple priests and the scribal schools. The pluralism so thoroughly affected Yehud that there was no single voice of dissent to oppose the patterns of social stratification. Instead, there were many attempts to critique it from a variety of different social positions. In this sense, the short stories represent the fragmentation of the social world built by the priests and the sages with the support of the governors.

The short stories would have proved popular with the inhabitants of Yehud and with Jews throughout the Diaspora. They present alternative portraits of community, in which people live out their faith in opposition to temple, to governor, and to sage. As these stories circulated within the communities of Jews throughout the world, the ability of the temple to maintain social control diminished. The canonization of these divergent views represents the failure of the temple to maintain social order in the long run. Instead, the forces of social order increasingly became separate worlds with less connection to the life of the whole people.

Paradoxically, religion became increasingly private and public at the same time. The ethnic concern of Esther at a public level is recognizable in the political forces of Jerusalem throughout the Hellenistic and Roman periods. Likewise, the privatization of religion means that the piety of Daniel became more common as an expression of individual faith throughout the passing centuries. The group of persons gathered at the temple to worship as a community became less important as religion became both more public and more private. As these short stories attest, the religion of Yehud moved toward several extremes at once, gaining in breadth but losing its monolithic voice of the temple priesthood.

Notes

1. For example, the Persian emperors in the Book of Daniel and similar political details in Judith seem intentionally misconstrued. See André LaCocque, *The Feminine Unconventional:*

Four Subversive Figures in Israel's Tradition, Overtures to Biblical Theology 26 (Minneapolis: Fortress Press, 1990), 31–32.

2. A genealogical note explains that Ruth is David's great-grandmother.

3. For a fuller discussion of role changes in the Book of Ruth, see Jon L. Berquist, "Role Dedifferentiation in the Book of Ruth," *JSOT* 57 (1993): 23–37.

4. The boat and the sailors mark this story as later than the Assyrian period. Jewish navigation of the seas became a possibility only through Greek trade in the second half of the Persian period.

5. Most translations render *hpk* as "overthrown," but this is an overinterpretation of this frequent word that means to change in nature or in appearance, or to turn. See Berquist, "Social Setting of Early Postexilic Prophecy," 182–84.

6. At least, the narrative presents Mordecai's claim to be unable to act effectively in the political arena.

7. The Greek version of Daniel includes the story of Susanna, whom Daniel rescues. That short story elevates the value of woman's purity in the face of inappropriate male sexual attention. If this story is included with the Persian period short stories, then a very different view of a female sexuality joins Ruth and Esther. Similarly, the story of Judith portrays a very strong, courageous, and manipulative woman. For discussions of these women, see Toni Craven, *Artistry and Faith in the Book of Judith* (Atlanta: Scholars Press, 1983); idem, "Women Who Lied for the Faith," in *Justice and the Holy: Essays in Honor of Walter Harrelson*, ed. Douglas A. Knight and Peter J. Paris (Atlanta: Scholars Press, 1989), 35–49; Carey A. Moore, *Judith*, AB 40 (Garden City, N.Y.: Doubleday & Co., 1985); LaCocque, *The Feminine Unconventional;* James C. VanderKam, ed., *"No One Spoke Ill of Her": Essays on Judith* (Atlanta: Scholars Press, 1992); Jon L. Berquist, *Reclaiming Her Story: The Witness of Women in the Old Testament* (St. Louis: Chalice Press, 1992); and Martha J. Steussy, *Gardens in Babylon: Narrative and Faith in the Greek Legends of Daniel*, SBLDS 141 (Atlanta: Scholars Press, 1993).

8. Berger and Luckmann, *Social Construction of Reality*, 125.

CHAPTER 16

THE EFFECTS OF THE PERSIAN PERIOD

THROUGHOUT THE PERSIAN PERIOD, the small western colony of Yehud maintained its identity, even though that identity fluctuated and changed with the varying influences of the imperial core and the internal dynamics of society. During this time of slightly more than two centuries, the Persian Empire grew from a petty kingdom to the largest empire that the world had known to that point and then fell to its long-standing enemy, Greece. Persia's speedy trek from a dream to an empire to a memory found itself preserved in the tales of Greek historians as well as in the numerous documents and monuments left by these rulers and by their subjects throughout the empire.

Persia's legacy extends beyond the artifacts and stories of the imperial core, however. The imperial domination of Persia's many colonies left its mark on the development of those smaller-scale societies.[1] When Alexander conquered the Persian Empire and brought a new Hellenistic organization and mind-set to much of the known western and eastern worlds, the new Greek rulers inherited a functioning administrative system and ruled over peoples whose social character had been shaped by Persian control. Much of Greece's influence in the centuries after Persia's defeat expanded upon the Persian influences already in place and assumed the Persian styles of imperial presence.[2]

The Persian Empire created controlled environments in which independent yet related cultures could grow. This benign support depended on two factors: the colonial society must maintain its political and economic allegiance to the Persian Empire, and it must provide sufficient political stability and internal social control that it does not represent a threat to the empire itself. Within these restrictions, most colonial societies found opportunities to flourish. Thus colonial Yehud took advantage of the Persian system of administration to create its own distinctive temple system as a dominant social institution, to establish the training of sages with distinctive traditions as a significant social influence, and to canonize large portions of still-extant scripture. During the years of the Pax Persica, Yehud developed into a society with a religion very strongly connected to subsequent and even modern forms of religion. The roots of formative Judaism and early Christianity are clearly evident in the religious changes and innovations of the Persian period.[3]

Colonialism

The political influences of the Persian Empire upon Yehud fall under the rubric of imperial-colonial relations. Persia developed Yehud as a secondary state. As such a secondary state, Persia allowed Yehud to function on its own as long as it provided extensive support for the empire's core in taxation and labor. For Persia, Yehud's existence depended upon its benefit to the empire as a whole, or at least to the imperial core and its attendant bureaucracy. At times, the taxation was sufficiently limited to allow for Yehud to develop economically; at other times, the exploitation was severe enough to bankrupt significant portions of Yehud's populace. Local autonomy was only partial but was still significant, allowing the formation of a local elite who could control the burden of the imperial intrusion so that it fell less heavily on themselves. This added internal variety in the application of external imperial forces. The exact balance of these forces shifted over time.

The reign of Cyrus as the first Persian emperor (539–530 B.C.E.) saw relatively few changes from the less centralized administrative policies of the Babylonian Empire. Cyrus' modes of dealing with the outer reaches of the empire included military means and propaganda extolling his own goodness and right to rule. Cyrus directed his military efforts eastward, and so Yehud did not experience any military campaigns during his reign. The propaganda did influence Yehud's religious thought through the writings of Deutero-Isaiah; this added a significant expectation of return to Yehud's theology and interpreted the advent of the Persian Empire as a blessing from God for the purpose of restoring Yehud. This shifted power toward the political and priestly elements of Yehud's society. Under Cyrus, emigration from Babylonia to Yehud began, but sporadically. Over time, this movement of population would create a new upper class in Jerusalem, but that did not happen to a significant degree until near the end of the sixth century B.C.E. Still, the beginnings of immigration created a social division into the immigrants and the natives, and these two groups continued an antagonism for generations. The ideological difference between these groups included the assertion that the Persian imperial bureaucracy function in the Yehudites' best interests and according to the will of God.

Cambyses became the next emperor of Persia (530–522 B.C.E.). His chief influence upon Yehud was a military campaign against Egypt, even though this had little direct impact upon the Jerusalem area because the army avoided Palestine. Presumably, immigration continued, but this was a time of slow development in a stable imperial context. The immigrant and native populations may have assimilated to some degree, but tensions were far from over. Within a context of little imperial intervention, Yehud chose not to build a temple in Jerusalem. Cyrus had permitted such an action in 538 B.C.E., yet the local authorities in Yehud did not act upon that possibility. In fact, there developed a substantial resistance to a temple that expressed itself later.

The reign of Darius (522–486 B.C.E.) brought about the farthest-reaching changes for Yehud and for the Persian Empire. Borders expanded and the empire conquered Egypt, passing through Yehud on its way. By the end of Darius' reign, Persia defined itself as over against Greece as its chief military opponent; this antagonism lasted throughout the rest of the Persian Empire and became its undoing. Internally, Darius reorganized the empire, increasing the efficiency of colonial administration and working toward greater ideological control of the provinces. Haggai, Zechariah, and Third Isaiah wrote during the period to encourage the construction of the temple and to calm local Yehudite fears about the passage of the army and the intrusion of the empire into local affairs. Third Isaiah represented the conflict between the natives and the immigrants about the construction of the temple, siding with the immigrants, including the politicians and the priests who supported Persia in the construction project. The temple became a symbol for the local worship of Yahweh but also for Persia's economic, political, and ideological domination of Yehud. Under Darius, Yehud constructed the physical and social apparatus by which Yahwism would be the official religion of the colony, with powers to enforce its positions, even if those powers were not absolute. The governorship and the priesthood became tightly linked partners in the administration of the society. As the society developed, however, the governorship became a lesser partner in the control of society. The priesthood continued as a local form of authority, and thus it grew more connections and more local persuasiveness than the governorship, which depended upon immigrants from Persia in each generation. This set the stage for the priestly capture of official religion throughout the reigns of Darius and Xerxes.

In part, Darius' creation of a law code aided the priesthood's rise to power. Darius ordered and supported the assemblage of legal materials from many cultures throughout the empire in order to create official bodies of law. Quite possibly, this administrative endeavor was responsible for the canonization of the Pentateuch. This began the transition to a religion of texts and of interpretation of those texts, although this process continued for centuries.

Darius also ordered and funded the construction of a Jerusalem temple, which provided a power basis for the priesthood as well as an opportunity for enhanced administrative attention from the Persian Empire, who used the temple as a base for its local bureaucracy. Although there was substantial local opposition to this construction because it gave Persia more local control, the power of the Persian Empire combined with the influences of local persons and institutions among Yehud who would benefit from the increased presence of the empire and its enhanced support of certain activities. The collusion between the local immigrants and the Persian imperial bureaucracy in the construction of the temple created a base of permanent power within Yehud.

Persia's next emperor, Xerxes (486–465 B.C.E.), reversed several of Darius' policies. Xerxes ended funding for colonial temples and thus forced Yehud to take control of its own religious system and priesthood. This separated the close connection between the priesthood and the governors; the sundering of this coalition left the priesthood with the greater internal authority, in no small part because the people themselves chose to fund and support it, and thus responded more easily to its use of authority. Internally, the prophet Malachi represented a voice for an increased acceptance of pluralism within the community, even though Malachi still urged the unity of the society in support of the temple and its practice of worship. This furthered the strength of the temple as the chief institution within Yehud.

Artaxerxes I (465–423 B.C.E.) sent two memorable governors to Yehud: Ezra and Nehemiah. Xerxes and Artaxerxes both operated under a policy of depletion of colonial resources. They shifted much higher imperial priorities to the Persian core and increased the taxation of the provinces. Ezra and Nehemiah therefore protected Yehud's resources, carefully shepherding them to preserve the means of production. At the same time, both of them dealt with a powerful elite class who hoarded an increasing portion of the society's resources.

The later emperors of the Persian Empire (from 423 B.C.E. to 330 B.C.E.) spent less of its resources governing Yehud and more of its time struggling against Greece. Correspondingly, there were times when Egypt may have been a greater influence upon Yehud than Persia was, and throughout the period Greek commerce grew in importance. Economically, the empire was in a slow decline, and taxation was increased in the colonies to compensate. At the same time, the imperial core lost much of its ability to project military force to collect these increased taxes. This combination probably made the collection of taxes sporadic. Throughout the second half of the Persian Empire's existence, its domination of life in Yehud would have decreased. Persia was still the major political influence, but the rise of internal diversification and internal disputes would have proved of increasing importance throughout the period.

Pluralism

The Persian Empire displaced local political authority, making it dependent upon the will of the foreign empire. The local political apparatus in Yehud lost the ability to act autocratically; Yehud's governmental policies were relativized by the desire of the Persian Empire to show a profit from its inclusion of the colony of Yehud. The removal of absolute local control, combined with Persia's lack of desire to manipulate all facets of colonial social life, caused the growth of pluralism. With the breakdown of the strong connection of priestly and political authority, the temple became the dominant social and religious institution but without means of absolute enforcement of its will. Thus the temple was a persuasive institution that could not block other social groups. The increase of Yehud's international contacts and influences throughout the Persian period spurred the pluralism further, allowing the growth of a wide variety of visions and interpretations within the growing body of Yehudite religious expression.

In the early Persian period, Darius' promulgation of law codes allowed the publication of the Pentateuch as the Law of the King as well as the Torah of God. This canonization of scripture made a stable foundation for Israelite religion.[4] However, the rapidly changing social conditions resulted in a religion in constant transition. Other materials quickly came to the forefront. Canonization could not stop pluralism. In fact, the growth of literature that became canonical occurred at a phenomenal pace throughout this period. Once the priesthood could no longer control the religion absolutely, other religious expressions developed their own texts. Sages and scribes recorded wisdom literature, both as support for social order and as dissent literature. Apocalyptic visions were published as well as a number of short stories depicting variations upon possible communities. The priests continued their publishing, including the development of psalms as hymns for the populace.

Through the various texts from this period that the canon preserved, it is possible to reconstruct much more of the popular religion than for most periods in Israel's history.

The psalms represent songs that the people in general sang during their temple worship; the short stories are tales told by the people who dreamed of other ways to organize their lives. Still, the extant literature is biased against popular religion. Those movements within Yehud that opposed the status quo too strongly probably had their records destroyed. Religious thoughts in Yehud that took hold only through the lower classes may never have received access to writing in the first place, and so they were never recorded. Inscriptionary evidence from the Yehud area indicates the worship of Yahweh and Asherah as co-deities, but the textual evidence from the Hebrew Bible as well as all the evidence from Persian sources does not indicate this religious belief. The popular religion remains mysterious. All of the evidence points only toward official religion, even if that was more open to pluralism, variety, and dissent than ever before.

Persian domination of Yehud created the conditions of colonialism, with all of its negative ramifications for the independence of the people. It also created a pluralistic environment in which the priests and the temple captured the religion but could not enforce their capture. Other views of Yahwism flourished. Some of them reinforced the religious and social establishment, at least in part, while others very strongly opposed the standard Yahwism of the temple. Yahwism developed into a nonmonarchic religion and centered around the temple, but only loosely, as many other forms of faith became prominent as well. The growth of canon established the bounds of official religion and created a constant force to expand those boundaries to include newer material. Throughout all of these developments, Yahwism in Yehud increased its range of expressions and created the setting for the transition into even later forms of religion.

The Foundations for Judaism

The Persian period witnessed the transition of Yahwism into new forms. Some of these forms became even more prominent in later years as the religion shifted into formative Judaism. During the Persian domination, Yehud constructed a temple and developed the canon of Torah as well as several other canonical scriptures. Both of these developments set the stage for formative Judaism.

The inhabitants of Yehud opposed the construction of a temple in Jerusalem. There is no indication that the Babylonian Empire forbade the building of a temple, yet during the half century of Babylonian domination the inhabitants of Jerusalem chose not to build a temple. Cyrus clearly allowed the temple construction in 539 B.C.E., but there was no effort to build a temple then or for the next seventeen years. Construction began only after Darius issued a decree, commanded the construction project, funded it from the imperial treasury, and sent an army to check on progress as part of the military campaign against Egypt. The Persian Empire wanted a temple in Jerusalem; the local populace did not. There were residents of Jerusalem who supported the temple, in large part because of their loyalty to Persia and their identification of Persian imperial decisions and the will of God. These persons also stood to benefit from the temple construction through the increased presence of the imperial bureaucracy as well as through the enhanced worship practice.

The temple functioned not only as a site of religious worship but also as a center for Persian administration. Taxation was ordered by the empire and collected within the temple. This coordination of governmental and priestly functions replicated the pattern of many other communities throughout the Persian Empire and the ancient Near East, including monarchic Israel and Judah. The change during the Persian period occurred when the governorship and the priesthood developed in separate directions, neither having absolute power. This freed the priesthood and the temple personnel, and they developed independently of the political forces. This pattern of a politically allied but independently powerful temple lasted throughout the history of the Second Temple.[5]

There were governors of immense importance as well. Ezra and Nehemiah recognized the influence of the elite and formed an assembly of powerful residents who governed much of the local matters. Such a group or Great Assembly became influential throughout formative Judaism. Even though the political apparatus did not allow the coalescence of state and religious authority, there were councils of elders and other such groups who controlled much regional and community life, in part based in religious authority.

The development of canon throughout the Persian period established formative Judaism as a people of a book. The priestly influence within Yahwism emphasized that the past times of God's direct interaction with the people were times in the past. God no longer dealt directly with human individuals. Instead, God spoke to subsequent generations through the scriptures and through those qualified to interpret the scriptures.[6] This shifted the attention of the religion from new expressions to the restatement and reapplication of the old. From this innovative understanding of the nature of faith came writings such as Mishnah and Talmud.

The canon continued to develop variety. Wisdom, apocalyptic, and short stories were genres that did not exist in written form before the Persian period but that continued production of new literature throughout the Hellenistic period. This enhanced variety sensitized the religion to pluralism and internationalism. Although the temple and priestly form of religion remained centered in Jerusalem, Judaism became a religion that could exist away from the temple as a result of the canon, and perhaps especially as a result of the canon's increasing inclusion of these internationalistic and pluralistic strands.[7] Judaism became a Diaspora religion during the Persian period, in no small part because of the separation of the religion from the local Jerusalem government, the pluralism of the religion that kept it temple-centered but participating in other partial universes of discourse, and the development of a canon that encouraged variety in religious expression.

The Foundations for Early Christianity

Just as the roots of formative Judaism trace themselves to the seeds of the Persian period, the ramifications of colonial Yehud's religious development for early Christianity should not be underestimated. Christianity, of course, developed as a particular strand of formative Judaism. Thus Christianity experienced many of the same influences as Judaism.

Christianity also flourished as a nongovernmental religion, at least until Constantine. Christianity's concept of canon extended into the development of the New Testament as an extension of the older Jewish canon, which Christianity did not abandon. The effects of canonization upon the religion are clear within Christianity. Despite its divergence from Judaism, it did not replace the prior canon but extended it. After the first century of Christianity, however, its canon closed as well. More literature appeared, but it was excluded, as part of an ideology that the formative acts of the religion were over and that God did not speak directly to humans. The interpretation and application of the canonical materials, expanded to include the New Testament, were sufficient guides for faith. Christianity grew, as did Judaism, as a religion of the Diaspora, flourishing in many different geographical locations without strong attachment to any single one of them. The Persian period's acceptance of pluralism continued into early Christianity, which accepted several different narratives about its founder, Jesus, and placed four contradictory stories into its canon of the New Testament. Only well after the completion of the canon were there strong moves to limit the interpretation to single perspectives. Instead, the very early church respected the pluralism of its own experience and rejected creedal statements.[8]

Early Christianity told its stories about its founder in the narrative form of the Gospels, but some of the earliest collections of Jesus sayings may well have been within a wisdom tradition. A sayings source such as Q would have included short aphorisms from Jesus, functioning somewhat like dissent wisdom. Jesus undermined the assumptions by which the status quo operated. The innovations of Jesus and the early church often expressed themselves in these abbreviated critiques of reality as typically perceived. The ethical admonitions certainly fit into this category. At the same time, this tradition of dissent wisdom was not the only form in which earliest Christianity functioned. The parables portrayed literature not unlike the short stories, offering reorientations of reality through depicting alternative formations of community.[9] Apocalyptic strands also appeared within the early church and the New Testament (Mark 13). Throughout time, the church developed more explicit theological statements about Jesus, but these were relatively slow in forming.

Part of the success of the Jesus movement was a focus upon popular religion.[10] The tradition denounces the religion of the Pharisees and the scribes, those who were the most representative voices of the official religion. Instead, the followers of Jesus argued for a religion that was much more accessible to the people, embodying images of God that were much closer to lived experience of the masses. The gulf between official and popular religion left a large opportunity for a new movement within Judaism to emerge, and Christianity took advantage of this opportunity to stress the kind of religion that could be appropriated by average people. The inability of the Jewish religious core to censure popular religion sped the growth of nascent Christianity, which spread quickly among the popular religion of the Jews. This accounts for the amalgamated genres of the New Testament, in which wisdom, short stories, theological discourse, and apocalyptic mingle together. Although these had been separate movements during the Persian period and remained distinct through much of official formative Judaism, the popular religion blurred many of these more technical differentiations into a generalized religion. Christianity flourished first among these social groups of lower classes and adherents of popular religion, and so many of the genres blur even in the Gospels' retellings of the stories.

Conclusion

Both formative Judaism and nascent Christianity developed within the context of a society and a religion that had been shaped by the Persian Empire's domination of Jerusalem and the surrounding colony of Yehud. The intervening centuries changed many of the details, but the influence remained. The Hellenistic kingdoms and, to a lesser extent, the Roman Empire carried over many of the governmental patterns of the Persians, and so the continued emphases on commerce, social pluralism, and religious tolerance created a long-standing stability within Jerusalem's political and social organization. The social atmosphere that gave rise to Persian-period Yahwism was mostly the same sort of social atmosphere that contexted formative Judaism and nascent Christianity. Thus both of these religions began as nongovernmental religions, existing in a context of radical pluralism that gave rise to a multiplicity of faith expressions, and their roots trace back to the domination of colonial Yehud by the Persian Empire.

Notes

1. See Dandamaev and Lukonin, *Culture and Social Institutions.*

2. By contrast, Assyria and Babylonia governed with a much higher reliance upon military force, genocide, and forced emigration. Persia and Greece tended toward more subtle forms of control with higher levels of local autonomy and a concentration on trade and other economic forms of imperial management, though not to the exclusion of force.

3. See Grabbe, *Judaism from Cyrus to Hadrian,* 1:100–112.

4. The growth of Samaritan religion in a slightly later period reflects this common acceptance of the Pentateuch that did not necessitate the acceptance of other literature considered canonical by the Jerusalem establishment. Samaria's social evolution must have differed in certain significant ways after the establishment of the official Pentateuchal canon by Darius.

5. The history of Judaism as a religion separate from the state political apparatus continued through the present.

6. Greenspahn, "Why Prophecy Ceased," 37–49.

7. This may explain Samaritanism's lack of growth. Because it accepted only the Pentateuch and rejected the internationalistic and pluralistic documents, it never developed beyond a regional religion.

8. Perhaps even the early creeds represent an embrace of a narrowed range of pluralistic options within the one faith. See David W. Odell-Scott, *A Post-Patriarchal Christology* (Atlanta: Scholars Press, 1991).

9. Bernard Brandon Scott, *Hear Then the Parable: A Commentary on the Parables of Jesus* (Minneapolis: Fortress Press, 1989).

10. For analysis of the range of popular movements within Jesus' time, see Richard A. Horsley, with John S. Hanson, *Bandits, Prophets, and Messiahs: Popular Movements at the Time of Jesus* (San Francisco: Harper & Row, 1985).

APPENDIX
METHODS FOR STUDYING POSTEXILIC SOCIETY

THE COLONY OF YEHUD and the Persian Empire existed as an intricately connected social system. Sociological analysis of Yehud and Jerusalem without its larger context would therefore be misleading at best. The sociological investigation of Persian-period Yehud must therefore take into account Persian imperial history and society as influential factors in the colony's internal development.[1]

Once the identification of Yehud as colony and Persia as empire has been made, the investigation of their interrelationship can explore a wealth of studies, theories, and models from sociology, anthropology, economics, and political science. These social-scientific methods have long examined the nature and development of similar empire-colony systems throughout world history, providing both parallels for comparison and theories for application. To provide a setting for the study of these parallels and theories, this appendix will first focus on the nature of sociological investigation itself, especially the discipline of historical sociology. It will then examine the prominent theories for imperial-colonial relations and will conclude with some comments about the purpose and limits of historical sociological investigation of Yehud.

The Object of Sociological Investigation

Sociology is the systematic investigation of human societies. As such, its findings can be generalized throughout human history, since humans have always organized themselves into social groupings of various types. However, the task is much more difficult than it may seem at first, since those groupings are amazingly diverse. Nevertheless sociology has developed a large number of analytic tools and methods that allow some commonality of approach to societies of widely varying organization.

Chief among these analytic tools is a division of the elements of human social life into three broad categories: infrastructure, structure, and superstructure.[2] Infrastructure refers to the material and economic factors of a society, such as geography, climate, food supply, technology, and population. Structure includes political organization, family and kinship patterns, power relationships, modes of production, behavioral patterns, and available roles. A society's superstructure contains its mental and symbolic aspects, including art, music, beliefs, values, philosophy, religion, ideology, and its assumptions about the nature of reality. All of these factors are extremely important in the constitution of any society, and the interrelationships between these sectors of social phenomena should be obvious. The distinction between them is an analytic device, valuable for its helpfulness in describing and investigating social relations.

Sociological investigation of a society necessarily involves all three of these sectors as well as the relationships between them. Although various sociological studies and methods may lean toward a closer examination of one of them, the combination of all three produces a full human society. In the study of Yehud or any other society, the interconnection of the analytic sectors is an essential part of the task of sociological description and explanation.

Historical Sociology

The analysis of a society's infrastructure, structure, and superstructure often proves to be a daunting task. Certainly modern societies provide a complexity of situation that can seem to overwhelm the available evidence, even though the tools for the study of a modern society are immense. The sociological investigation of a modern society can rely upon a wealth of evidence. Infrastructure can be studied through extensive climatological and agricultural investigation as well as close attention to the effects of technology's use upon the environment and thus upon the conditions for human existence. On the structural level, modern sociologists can study organizational flow charts and other such evidence based upon close examination of the ways humans interact with each other on a daily basis. These types of study approach most closely to what many people perceive as modern sociology, such as studies of patterns of television viewership distributed by age and gender or connections between ethnicity and social class. Surveys of popular opinion provide description of superstructural realities in a society, as also do anecdotal evidence of persons' perceptions of their lives. Through all of these means and many more, modern sociologists access a plethora of evidence as they research society to arrive at descriptions and explanations of social phenomena.

Sociologists who study ancient societies face a different set of problems.[3] The available evidence is much less because of the distance of the society. Surveys of popular opinion and participant observation of social practices can no longer be accomplished. The nature of the available evidence forces historical sociologists to rely on other types of evidence and other methods to accomplish their goals of description and explanation. Despite the methodological difficulties inherent in the study of ancient societies, the discipline of historical sociology has experienced a dramatic rise throughout recent decades.[4] Both historians and sociologists have furthered the rise of historical sociology as both groups admit the relevance and necessity of each other. Scholars of modern social situations increasingly realize that historical grounding of modern society, necessitating the move to the study of historical sociological roots. At the same time, historians who have been increasingly disenchanted with more traditional forms of historiography have moved toward social history and the examination of forms of daily life, complete with the influences of institutions and customs upon human society.

Historical sociology studies ancient human societies through a reliance upon the texts, records, remains, and artifacts that the society produced. Since it is impossible to study the society itself, sociologists examine the *effects* of the society in question. This is just as true for the sociologist as for the historian; neither has direct access to ancient history but only to the remains and effects of ancient civilization. Historical sociology depends on the same evidence as ancient history but combines this evidence with an understanding of the typical patterns of human societies.[5] In the case of colonial Yehud and imperial Persia, the historical evidence allows for sociological analysis that reflects the nature of other empires and colonies in other locations and periods. By an examination of the patterns of imperial-colonial relationships, the specific structures of Yehud in the Persian Empire become more clear.[6]

Empire and Colony

Eisenstadt and the Growth of Empires

The works of Shmuel Noah Eisenstadt have contributed greatly to the understanding of complex ancient and modern societies. Eisenstadt offered an extensive and generalized perspective on the historical processes of institution building. Humans tend to construct boundaries to social systems, using ideology, power, and material resources. Since such systems and boundaries are always fragile, their construction requires regulative mechanisms, such as bureaucracy, rituals, and law. Boundary mechanisms, in other words, can derive from any of the three sectors of social phenomena (infrastructure, structure, and superstructure). In more complex societies, these mechanisms can become autonomous.[7] In such cases, institutions form in order to continue the implementation of social boundaries. A boundary mechanism, such as religious ritual, may begin as an impromptu attempt to legitimate a specific social action, but as societal complexity grows and such boundary mechanisms become increasingly autonomous, the religious ritual may well develop into an organized priesthood that discerns and enforces official distinctions between the holy and the profane.

Eisenstadt's special emphasis on historical empires bears special relevance to the situation of the Persian colony of Yehud. The building of institutions, such as those developing from boundary mechanisms, depends upon the level and distribution of resources. The society's elites struggle for control of such resources, using visions and rhetoric. In such ways, the elites exercise control of the society through organizations as well as through coercion. The differential control of resources results in heterogeneity and conflict, requiring further attempts by the elites to maintain control and to enforce boundaries.[8] According to Eisenstadt, the social complexity of empires requires high societal differentiation, resulting in a political elite.[9] Imperial political elites possess new, broader goals, capable of harnessing the enhanced resources available to them as societal differentiation increases. This growth of the elite class also results in a more clearly delineated center and periphery, along with the growth of multiple autonomous centers. The growing split between the center and the periphery creates the central contradiction of any empire.[10]

Empires can come into existence only when social differentiation has produced such resources as material goods, technology, social control, or ideology that have not yet been monopolized or appropriated by any group. These free-floating resources create a reservoir of generalized power, embodying possibilities for social organization that have not yet been institutionalized. Elites with broader goals move to take control of these free-floating resources and thus use the nonappropriated power of these resources to consolidate control over the society at large. Typically, the empire's more traditional power bases attempt to limit access to these resources, while the more entrepreneurial elites diffuse their new culture throughout the empire's geographic area. In other words, imperial elites are likely to have a broad power base, rooted in specific innovations that create advantage over a large area, whereas the traditional, "old-fashioned," aristocratic groups continue to wield power based in the previous sources of power. Usually the empire's cities form the area for the congregation of the elites with their newer power bases, whereas traditional authority resides in more rural areas, often tied to agriculture.

Religion often flourishes within empires, for connected reasons. Religion forms a boundary mechanism within the superstructural sector that develops into an autonomous institution through the development of an empire, as certain elites use the religion for their own legitimation. New priesthoods allow the imposition of religious ideologies throughout a large geographic area, and thus the religion and its concepts form a strong group of free-floating resources. Those elites who gain the approval of the religion find themselves in situations of increasing power; in this sense, imperial religion tends to be highly politicized.[11] Imperial religion thus tends to widen its referents, finding new social settings as the elites push the growth of legitimating religion to the borders of the empire. This removes the religion from its original settings, and the disembedment of religion from its former social setting can cause an increased formalization, leading to codified sacred books and schools for interpreting texts. The texts themselves function as free-floating religious resources.[12]

Thus, in Eisenstadt's theoretical framework, both material causes and ideological factors have their place as possible loci of free-floating resources. These resources create the potential, and the power of the elites shape that potential into imperial institutions.[13] This system envisions an equilibrating function for society; the move to empire can be swift, but the path is predictable.[14]

Colonies within Empires

Within Eisenstadt's view of imperial development, the key factor is the elites' appropriation of free-floating resources. This leads to a centralization of far-reaching bases for power and to an institutionalization of the use of these resources. Since the institutionalization involves a centralization as part of a more general differentiation of control of resources, the empire will develop a core and a periphery. Of course, the core may encompass much more than just a capital city or province, and the periphery will be quite heterogeneous in its nature. Still, such a view of empires emphasizes the collection of resources within the center, placing relatively little emphasis on the periphery as part of the empire.

Donald V. Kurtz and Margaret Showman have argued that the periphery often consists of inchoate states.[15] These colonial states lack sufficient authority or ability to govern themselves and their populations; the functions of truly autonomous government reside within the imperial center. Such peripheries still maintain some local control, however. Often, colonial power relies on the less material of the free-floating resources. For example, imperial control may depend upon food production or military might, whereas the selection of local leaders may be more sensitive to principles of religion. Such local leaders, lacking the basis for true government, turn to more symbolic forms of legitimation in order to support their own functions within the governmental apparatus. Thus colonies and colonial administration do not necessarily derive all of their power from the empire; instead, the periphery possesses different kinds of authority, often involving fewer material resources.

Secondary State Development

Whereas Eisenstadt and other related theorists focus on empires with only little attention to their subsequent effects on colonies, other sociologists and anthropologists have emphasized the development of states within conditions of imperial domination. This shift of emphasis creates a different image of the process of state formation through their realization that not all states develop as pristine states, that is, as states with no significant external influences.[16] Colonies provide one example of state development under intrusive circumstances, and such secondary states develop in patterns of their own.[17]

Barbara J. Price has explained secondary state development in terms of economic intrusion and exploitation. According to her, secondary states occur when other states expand by "the capture by a foreign elite of the capital and labor—the surplus energy of an impacted population."[18] The resultant centralization follows the application of military force necessary to mobilize the society into a nonbeneficial project. In other words, an empire conquers an area and organizes it in order to maximize the empire's extraction of resources. In the ancient world, the resources in question are usually agricultural but can include a wide range of other resources and skills.[19] The intrusive empire would desire the maintenance of order; thus the empire would allow the growth of limited power bases in the colony for the purpose of increased control. The imperial state encourages economic intensification if it is practical to increase the flow of resources from the secondary state. In general, the empire will take all cost-effective steps to exploit the colony to the fullest degree made possible by the presence of resources.[20] Romila Thapar offers a divergent view, noticing that many imperial states do not maximize exploitation. Instead, the intrusion and the subsequent restructure occur only to the degree necessary to establish hegemony over the resources in question. Although the imperial center dominates this newly annexed colony, a complete redistribution of resources is not likely.[21] In Thapar's view, the impoverishment of a colony is not as likely as the limited domination.

Together, Price and Thapar offer an important analysis of the development of a secondary state.[22] Both agree that the flow of wealth will be from the colony to the empire and that the imperial state will organize the colony politically and economically for imperial rather than local benefit. A key variable will be the extent of the economic exploitation as well as the political reorganization and military enforcement required to attain the empire's goals. Certainly the presence of an imperial state causes patterned changes in the development of the secondary region, creating the conditions in which its evolution will continue.[23]

Core and Periphery

Empires, then, exist as a mixed entity. Whereas simpler forms of state organization make possible a homogeneity, empires assume difference between areas, classes, and other sorts of groupings. This differentiation between elements of society thus necessitates the comparison of imperial core and periphery.[24] The core identifies the locations of greatest power and privilege, whether measured in terms of politics, economy, military, or ideology. Usually these various spheres of power coalesce into a clearly defined core. As an example, consider Jerusalem during the pan-Israelite monarchies of David and Solomon. Although there were other important sites throughout the region, Jerusalem was the political capital and the site of the monarchy's palace and throne, but it was also the chief location for tax collection, an important trading center, and the site of the region's most important temple, along with its associated priesthood. In each way, the core exercised influence and control over its peripheral areas within the rest of the monarchy. In the periphery, trade was scarce, taxation meant the *removal* of local resources rather than the accumulation of them, there was no control over military might, and the temple's demands often required movement from the periphery to the core.[25]

In ancient empires, a common distinction between the core and the periphery is the flow of food. Typically, the periphery contains peasants who produce food and send their surplus to the governing core, in which the inhabitants live as merchants or other types of elites but not as peasants. Even though the peasants produce enough foodstuffs for their own existence, they do not form a complete society; they exist within relationships with the core, which offers military protection, trade, and ideology.[26] The core and the periphery involve different ways of life as well as different roles within the society as a whole.[27]

World-systems theorists offer a more comprehensive view of core-periphery relations.[28] This theory, operative mostly within political anthropology and macroeconomics, emphasizes the interconnectedness of separate states and social structures, examining their modes of interaction through trade, military conquest, and other means.[29] The large scale of history moves not in terms of subsequent political states and empires but in terms of the cumulative effects of civilization as it waxes and wanes throughout systematic change.

World-systems theory introduces the concept of the semiperiphery. Christopher Chase-Dunn and Thomas D. Hall define four possible elements of the semiperiphery: (1) it may mix organizational forms of the core and periphery; (2) it may be geographically located between the core and the periphery; (3) it may mediate between the core and the periphery; and (4) it may exhibit institutional forms that are intermediate between the core and the periphery.[30] This provides a most helpful way to understand Jerusalem's role as a center of colonial administration within the Persian Empire. Although Jerusalem was far from the imperial core and exhibited markedly different organizational forms in comparison to the Persian capital cities, it was distinct from the rural areas of the periphery itself. Also, core-periphery mediation quite aptly describes the functions of the Jerusalem elite as they administered imperial policy. Chase-Dunn and Hall note that semiperipheral regions are often "unusually fertile zones for social innovation" because of their in-between status.[31]

David Wilkinson expands on the notion of semiperiphery. The semiperiphery, an area recently engulfed by the core, is "a zone characterized by military subjection, powerlessness, relative poverty, technological backwardness, and low cultural prestige."[32] Wilkinson notes a tendency for cores to incorporate their peripheries over time, transforming them into semiperipheries or into completely depleted areas, at the same time as the cores themselves decline and power shifts to a new core.

The work of these various social scientists clarifies the interplay of life between core and periphery (as well as semiperiphery). The dynamic flow of power, resources, and ideology between imperial cores and colonial semiperipheries and peripheries requires a rethinking of the role of Jerusalem and Yehud within the Persian Empire. No longer can they be considered by themselves; the interrelationship of the whole world is a prerequisite for understanding the more local affairs of postexilic Yehud.[33]

The Construction and Maintenance of Society

Tendencies such as those inherent in core-periphery relations combine to produce societies. The dynamics of power, resources, and ideology interact to create and construct societies in specific ways.[34] But how do societies establish themselves in enduring ways? Certainly institutionalization produces a powerful force for continuation, but there are other factors. The maintenance of society requires that individuals continue to live mostly within the confines of that social structure. No society is completely integrated, with no questioning and challenge of the status quo. However, some integration is necessary or else the society will immediately dissipate. Thus the maintenance of society requires that individuals invest themselves in the society, at least to the degree that most persons limit their lived critiques of the social structure.

Clifford Geertz, one of the chief phenomenological anthropologists, understands culture as the "web of significance" that humans spin.[35] Within this signifying culture, persons construct symbol systems that help them to understand and to fit into their social systems. The symbol systems are coherent, both in the sense that they establish relatively consistent means of perceiving reality and in the sense that they work to keep society together. A large element of such a web of significance is religion. Geertz defines religion as "(1) a system of symbols which acts to (2) establish powerful, pervasive, and long-lasting moods and motivations in men by (3) formulating conceptions of a general order of existence and (4) clothing these conceptions with such an aura of factuality that (5) the moods and motivations seem uniquely realistic."[36] These religious concepts are then used to understand all perceived reality.[37] Through this religious perception of reality, the social structure receives affirmation, and individuals are less likely to question the societal systems so affirmed.[38]

Similarly, the individualist focus of symbolic interactionism emphasizes humans' construction of their own ways of experiencing reality.[39] Symbolic interactionism is similar to phenomenology in its emphasis on the symbols by and through which humans construct perceptions of their world. This symbolic orientation to the world and the social system is an important base for understanding the mechanisms of acceptance and enforcement of social order and thus for comprehending society itself.[40] Religion functions as a symbol system that embodies an individual's worldview.[41] Along with other ideological resources, religion serves to legitimate the world as commonly perceived, producing integrated symbolic universes.[42] Symbolic universes also require plausibility structures, which are the specific social bases and processes required to maintain the symbolic universe.[13] Thus the structural and infrastructural components support and are supported by the superstructural level of ideological world construction.[14]

Ritual reminds people of the legitimations for reality and its institutions. When myths are rooted in ritual, there is a strong combination of ideology and action. Such legitimation is powerful and can justify otherwise intolerable situations "by legitimating marginal situations in terms of an all-encompassing sacred reality."[15] Symbolic interactionism and the social construction of reality thus provide a nuanced framework for understanding symbols and ideology and for interpreting their influence on social systems.[16]

The Persian Empire constructed Yehudite society as an imperial colony, in ways consistent with standard theories of colonial development. As a semiperiphery, Yehud retained the ability to control its own internal life to some extent, especially in religious matters; the result was a maintenance of Yehudite society through a variety of imperial and colonial/local means, including religion. A full study of the construction and maintenance of Yehudite society must include not only the political machinations that constructed the society but also the superstructural and ideological elements that maintained the society in cooperation with structural and infrastructural plausibility structures.[17]

Of course, not all social elements work together for social maintenance. In other words, all societies are imperfectly integrated, and conflict is inherent. The unavoidability of conflict means that societies will contain elements working in opposite directions of legitimation and plausibility. The ideological struggles, as well as the political battles and the economic exploitation, mediate the conflict present within all societies. The maintenance of Yehudite society, therefore, involves not only the factors that support the status quo but also those forces that oppose it, attempting to assert an alternative social reality.[18]

The Benefits and Problems of Comparison

The theories discussed above and offered for use in the study of the Persian Empire's colony of Yehud will be helpful only on one contingency: the applicability of examples and models from other societies for the study of this particular ancient society. Anthropological theories proceed from the assumption that social systems throughout the history of the world are roughly comparable and thus that categorizations of a wide range of cultures can be beneficial for understanding any other culture.[49] In what ways and under what conditions are such comparisons beneficial?

Robert Wilson's primer on sociological methodology focuses on comparative anthropological approaches as the source of "useful analogies from studies of modern societies" at the level of philology, genre, or social structures.[50] He offers six useful guides for the application of anthropological methods to biblical studies:

1. Know the limits of the method.
2. Use only work of competent social scientists, relying on peer evaluation to determine this.

3. Understand the theoretical background of the theories used.
4. Use a wide range of societies for anthropological comparison.
5. Beware of interpretive schemata in the data used.
6. Use the biblical text as the controlling factor.[51]

These strictures are helpful, but they still open the interpreter to such a wide range of anthropological data that misinterpretation of the data seems likely. The first three guidelines are more difficult than most biblical sociologists have recognized. Furthermore, they seem to assume that anthropology and sociology are consistent fields, whereas in actuality they exist as deeply fractured disciplines without unanimous consensus about methods and goals.

Shemaryahu Talmon points out the dangers implicit in any comparative approach. By attending to the similarities under the assumption of basic similarities between human societies, the particular nature of individual societies is lost.[52] It is thus necessary to begin with establishing the basic similarity of the two situations to be compared. Comparisons should only be attempted between comparable societies, particularly those sharing temporal proximity. This moves in a direction opposite from Wilson's fourth guideline, which searches for safety in numbers of comparisons rather than in a selectivity of comparative data. Talmon emphasizes the need to examine total societal phenomena as objects for comparison, not only isolated aspects of the culture.[53] Gottwald later echoes these cautions that holistic, contextual comparison, rather than "superficial juxtaposition," be attempted.[54]

Anthropology's strong point is its reliance on actual cultures, but its weakness is its dependence upon comparison of separate situations for generalizability.[55] Comparative material is valuable in its indications of cultural tendencies, and thus its role in reconstructions and interpretations of ancient societies can be highly suggestive and yet potentially misleading.[56] Thus the dangers of anthropological and sociological approaches must be remembered throughout such study of an ancient culture.

Although there are dangers inherent in these methods, there are also great rewards in results. Perhaps the greatest benefit of these approaches is their emphasis on people as producers of the biblical texts as well as the societies and their artifacts. In this way, the interpreter gains analytical frameworks in which to examine the relationships between biblical texts, the archaeological examination of the remains of the societies, and the historical relationships of various peoples. Rightly used, sociological methods can ground the interpretation of texts within the fuller range of human motivations, allowing an understanding of human belief and the action of writing religious texts that reflect lived reality and integrate religion with the rest of life.

Areas for Investigation

Much sociological investigation proceeds with the help of models. The analysis of multiple social situations allows the construction of models, which are analytical devices that attempt to predict and explain human social behavior. Gary Herion rightly asserts that these models are hypothetical; thus they cannot be used as substitutes for data. At best, models provide new directions of questioning, which may or may not be substantiated by the data itself.[57] For the study of Persian Yehud, the models include the various sociological theories discussed above, and the data that these models must explain include biblical texts, historical writings of other ancient peoples, and archaeological findings. If the models provide new questions and suggestions about how to explain the evidence, and if the evidence truly finds better explanations through the use of these models, then sociological interpretation has performed successfully.

A Strategy for Sociological Investigation

This discussion of method, then, provides us with a strategy for examining the data about Yehud during the time of the Persian Empire. First, we notice an analytical distinction between the construction of the society (including the political, economic, and ideological factors that shaped the social reality as it existed) and the maintenance of that same society (including the forces that moved toward the replication of the status quo and those that worked against it). Thus this book divides itself into separate sections on social construction (a mostly diachronic study of the factors of change) and social maintenance (a mostly synchronic study of the institutions of importance throughout Yehud's existence as a society).

Within both sections, this analysis derives its questions from a model of an imperial core in relationship with a colonial periphery (or semiperiphery). The various forces of this relationship are examined to see how much of the biblical, historical, and archaeological evidence can find explanation in the context of these social models. The sociological and anthropological theories of secondary state development and international imperial underdevelopment of peripheral resources receive special attention as possible explanations for the construction of Yehudite society into its unique organizational pattern. Then, the ideological basis for the conceptualization of that society and its alternatives, as well as the structural and infrastructural bases for that conceptualization, are the focus of specific examination as this study shifts toward the maintenance of Yehudite society. The combination of construction and maintenance forms the specific situation of Yehud during the era of Persian domination, 539–333 B.C.E.

Notes

1. Also, one cannot adequately analyze religion apart from an investigation of the culture and society in which that religion exists. See Richard A. Horsley, "Empire, Temple and Community—but No Bourgeoisie! A Response to Blenkinsopp and Petersen," in Davies, *Second Temple Studies*, 1:163–64.

2. Harris, *Cultural Materialism*, provides a detailed analysis of the interaction of these categories in many societies. Harris, however, takes the analytic distinction a step farther and argues that the infrastructure causes the other categories of social life in at least enough cases that the only effective sociological research strategy is the assumption of infrastructural causation. Such preconceptions of causation, however, are limiting.

3. For other positive assessments of the possibility of historical sociology, see Charles Tilly, *As Sociology Meets History* (New York: Academic Press, 1981).

4. For an overview and analysis of recent scholarship in historical sociology, see Dennis Smith, *The Rise of Historical Sociology* (Philadelphia: Temple University Press, 1991).

5. Arguments in favor of historical sociology can be found in Philip Abrams, *Historical Sociology* (Ithaca, N.Y.: Cornell University Press, 1982); Anthony Giddens, *New Rules of Sociological Method: A Positive Critique of Interpretative Sociologies* (New York: Basic Books, 1976); Larry J. Griffin, "Temporality, Events, and Explanation in Historical Sociology: An Introduction," *Sociological Methods and Research* 20 (1992): 403–27; and Jill Quadaguo and Stan J. Knapp, "Have Historical Sociologists Forsaken Theory? Thoughts on the History/Theory Relationship," *Sociological Methods and Research* 20 (1992): 481–507. For arguments against historical sociology and its current practice, see John H. Goldthorpe, "The Uses of History in Sociology: Reflections on Some Recent Tendencies," *British Journal of Sociology* 42 (1991): 211–30.

6. For a review of explicitly Marxist theories, see Anthony Brewer, *Marxist Theories of Imperialism: A Critical Survey* (London: Routledge & Kegan Paul, 1980).

7. S. N. Eisenstadt, *Revolution and the Transformation of Societies: A Comparative Study of Civilizations* (New York: Free Press, 1978); and idem, "Macro-Societal Analysis," 16–19. See also Eisenstadt and Curelaru, *Form of Sociology;* and Bertrand Badie and Pierre Birnbaum, *The Sociology of the State,* trans. Arthur Goldhammer (Chicago: University of Chicago Press, 1983), 30.

8. Eisenstadt, "Macro-Societal Analysis," 19–23. Eisenstadt analyzed revolutions as a special case of social transformation due to conflict and heterogeneity. See Eisenstadt, *Revolution,* 2–3, 19. For a middle-range theoretical portrayal of other types of radical social change, see Juan J. Linz, "Crisis, Breakdown, and Reequilibration," in *The Breakdown of Democratic Regimes,* ed. Juan J. Linz and Alfred Stepan (Baltimore: Johns Hopkins University Press, 1978), 3–124.

9. Peter Skalník, "Some Additional Thoughts on the Concept of the Early State," in *The Study of the State,* ed. Henri J. M. Claessen and Peter Skalník, New Babylon Studies in the Social Sciences 35 (The Hague: Mouton, 1981), 340, argues that studies of the state overemphasize the elites of the society, reflecting a "tendency towards seeing the state as a more self-generating phenomenon than it really is." Although the present work focuses much attention on the imperial elites, it also strives to show the local elites (who are part of the imperial "middle class") and the work by others against the formation of the state. These drives toward dissolution and the focus on colonial life attempt to correct a bias toward examining the highest levels of imperial life. The core-periphery distinction places both in context, paralleling the emphasis in *class formation* in Skalník's work (p. 344).

10. Eisenstadt, *Political Systems of Empires,* ix–xv. It should be noted that Eisenstadt mostly deals with empires in the medieval period, but he does state that his discussion is valid "to a lesser extent" in Achaemenid Persia (p. 11). More recently, Eisenstadt has discussed the flaws inherent in his dependence on functionalism, although he still recognizes his categorization as a neofunctionalist. See S. N. Eisenstadt, "Systemic Qualities and Boundaries of Societies: Some Theoretical Considerations," in Alexander, *Neofunctionalism,* 99–112.

11. Eisenstadt, *Political Systems of Empires,* 96–121, 141–42, 185, 308.

12. Ibid., 14–47, 61–67, 87–91.

13. See Bruce G. Trigger, "Generalized Coercion and Inequality: The Basis of State Power in the Early Civilizations," in *Development and Decline: The Evolution of Sociopolitical Organization,* ed. Henri J. M. Claessen, Pieter van de Velde, and M. Estellie Smith (South Hadley, Mass.: Bergin & Garvey, 1985), 46–61.

14. A summary of anthropological and sociological work on historical empires can also be found in Michael W. Doyle, *Empires* (Ithaca, N.Y.: Cornell University Press, 1986). For a consideration

of literary images of the Roman Empire, see Loveday Alexander, ed., *Images of Empire,* JSOTSup 122 (Sheffield: JSOT Press, 1991).

15. Donald V. Kurtz and Margaret Showman, "The Legitimation of Early Inchoate States," in Claessen and Skalník, *The Study of the State,* 179–91.

16. For general works on state evolution, see Claessen, van de Velde, and M. Estellie Smith, *Development and Decline;* Ted C. Lewellen, *Political Anthropology: An Introduction* (South Hadley, Mass.: Bergin & Garvey, 1983); Cohen and Service, *Origins of the State;* and Morton H. Fried, *The Evolution of Political Society: An Essay in Political Anthropology,* Studies in Anthropology (New York: Random House, 1967).

17. For some of these patterns, see the following chapters in *Political Development and Social Change,* ed. Jason L. Finkle and Richard W. Gable (New York: John Wiley & Sons, 1966): David E. Apter, "System, Process, and the Politics of Economic Development," 441–57; S. C. Dube, "Bureaucracy and Nation Building in Transitional Societies," 403–8; Fred W. Riggs, "Bureaucrats and Political Development: A Paradoxical View," 409–29; Lester G. Seligman, "Elite Recruitment and Political Development," 329–38; Edward Shils, "Alternative Courses of Political Development," 458–78; Edward Shils, "The Intellectuals in the Political Development of the New States," 338–65; and Neil J. Smelser, "Mechanisms of Change and Adjustments to Change," 28–43. See also Christine Ward Gailey and Thomas C. Patterson, "State Formation and Uneven Development," in *State and Society: The Emergence and Development of Social Hierarchy and Political Centralization,* ed. John Gledhill, Barbara Bender, and Mogens Trolle Larsen, One World Archaeology 4 (London: Unwin Hyman, 1988), 77–90.

18. Price, "Secondary State Formation," 171.

19. Agricultural intensification almost always produces a hierarchicalization that provides the class formation necessary for early state development, according to R. A. L. H. Gunawardana, "Social Function and Political Power: A Case Study of State Formation in Irrigation Society," in Claessen and Skalník, *The Study of the State,* 133–54.

20. Price, "Secondary State Formation," 171–81.

21. Romila Thapar, "The State as Empire," in Claessen and Skalník, *The Study of the State,* 411–12, 425. See also Sudharshan Seneviratne, "Kalinga and Andhra: The Process of Secondary State Formation," in Claessen and Skalník, *The Study of the State,* 334; Abraham I. Pershits, "Tribute Relations," in *Political Anthropology: The State of the Art,* ed. S. Lee Seaton and Henri J. M. Claessen, World Anthropology (The Hague: Mouton, 1979), 149–56; K. Ekholm and J. Friedman, "'Capital' Imperialism and Exploitation in Ancient World Systems," in *Power and Propaganda: A Symposium on Ancient Empires,* ed. Mogens Trolle Larsen, Mesopotamia 7 (Copenhagen: Akademisk Forlag, 1979), 41–58; and Carneiro, "Political Expansion as an Expression of the Principle of Competitive Exclusion," 205–23.

22. A different yet related balance is found by Ronald E. Cohen, "Evolution, Fission, and the Early State," in Claessen and Skalník, *The Study of the State,* 87–115.

23. For an overview of state evolution theory, see Haas, *Evolution of the Prehistoric State.*

24. For Eisenstadt's views on cores and peripheries, see S. N. Eisenstadt, "Observations and Queries about Sociological Aspects of Imperialism in the Ancient World," in *Power and Propaganda: A Symposium on Ancient Empires,* ed. Mogens Trolle Larsen, Mesopotamia 7 (Copenhagen: Akademisk Forlag, 1979), 21–34; and S. N. Eisenstadt and Luis Roniger, "The Study of Patron-Client Relations and Recent Developments in Sociological Theory," in *Political Clientelism, Patronage and Development,* ed. S. N. Eisenstadt and René Lemarchand, Contemporary Political Sociology 3 (Beverly Hills, Calif.: SAGE Publications, 1981), 271–95. Other views receive helpful summaries in Anton L. Allahar, *Sociology and the Periphery: Theories and Issues* (Toronto: Garamond Press, 1989).

25. Evidence for the peripheries of the Persian Empire can be found in Sancisi-Weerdenburg and Kuhrt, *Achaemenid History IV: Centre and Periphery.*

26. Wolf, *Peasants,* 3–4; and Robert Redfield, *Peasant Society and Culture: An Anthropological Approach to Civilization* (Chicago: University of Chicago Press, 1956), 29, 60–69.

27. Clifford Geertz argues that peripheral figures also depend on the symbolics of the core; it would be impossible for anyone to understand a figure who did not partake of core symbols, since that is the only common ground for cultural communication. Although Geertz assumes homogeneous culture, his argument rightly emphasizes the importance of the cultural core in setting the language and the agenda for social debate throughout the society. See especially his "Centers, Kings, and Charisma: Reflections on the Symbolics of Power," in *Local Knowledge: Further Essays in Interpretive Anthropology,* ed. Clifford Geertz (New York: Basic Books, 1983), 121–46.

28. World-systems theorists often point to the works of Immanuel Wallerstein as seminal, especially his *The Modern World-System,* 3 vols. (New York: Academic Press, 1974–88).

29. Also instructive is the assertion that the trade of luxury goods indicates relations between elites (including their constructions of social hierarchies), whereas the exchange of basic goods indicates more general relationships between states. See Barry K. Gills and Andre Gunder Frank, "5000 Years of World System History: The Cumulation of Accumulation," in *Core/Periphery Relations in Precapitalist Worlds,* ed. Christopher Chase-Dunn and Thomas D. Hall (Boulder, Colo.: Westview Press, 1991), 67–112.

30. Christopher Chase-Dunn and Thomas D. Hall, "Conceptualizing Core/Periphery Hierarchies for Comparative Study," in *Core/Periphery Relations in Precapitalist Worlds,* ed. Christopher Chase-Dunn and Thomas D. Hall (Boulder, Colo.: Westview Press, 1991), 21.

31. Ibid., 30. They also notice the distinction between "spread effects" (in which peripheral areas become more like the core) and "backwash effects" (which intensify the underdevelopment of the semiperiphery) (31, 37 n. 17).

32. David Wilkinson, "Cores, Peripheries, and Civilizations," in Chase-Dunn and Hall, *Core/ Periphery Relations in Precapitalist Worlds,* 122.

33. For another study of the peripheral relationships in the Achaemenid Empire, see Torben Holm-Rasmussen, "Collaboration in Early Achaemenid Egypt: A New Approach," in *Studies in Ancient History and Numismatics presented to Rudi Thomsen* (Copenhagen: Aarhus University Press, 1988), 29–38.

34. For an introduction to the specific analysis of ideological construction of colonies within empires, see the following chapters in *State Formation and Political Legitimacy,* ed. Ronald Cohen and Judith D. Toland, Political Anthropology 6 (New Brunswick, N.J.: Transaction Books, 1988): Henri J. M. Claessen, "Changing Legitimacy," 23–44; Ronald Cohen, "Legitimacy, Illegitimacy, and State Formation," 69–84; Joan Vincent, "Sovereignty, Legitimacy, and Power: Prolegomena to the Study of the Colonial State," 137–54; and Roy Willis, "Public and Personal Ideology in an Early State," 85–94. An interesting parallel can be found in Michael Kearney, "Borders and Boundaries of State and Self at the End of Empire," *Journal of Historical Sociology* 4 (1991): 52–74.

35. Clifford Geertz, "Thick Description: Toward an Interpretive Theory of Culture," in *The Interpretation of Cultures: Selected Essays,* ed. Clifford Geertz (New York: Basic Books, 1973), 5.

36. Clifford Geertz, "Religion as a Cultural System," in *The Interpretation of Cultures: Selected Essays,* ed. Clifford Geertz (New York: Basic Books, 1973), 90.

37. Ibid., 123; and idem, "Ethos, World View, and the Analysis of Sacred Symbols," in *The Interpretation of Cultures: Selected Essays,* ed. Clifford Geertz (New York: Basic Books, 1973), 129–31.

38. Geertz' important contributions to the anthropological and ethnographic study of religion

have gone almost without critique by scholars of religion. From an anthropological view, there have been few responses to Geertz, but see the invaluable postmodern comments of Aletta Biersack, "Local Knowledge, Local History: Geertz and Beyond," in *The New Cultural History*, ed. Lynn Hunt, Studies on the History of Society and Culture (Berkeley and Los Angeles, Calif.: University of California Press, 1989), 72–96. Much more work of this type is necessary to place Geertz' anthropological notions of religion in the proper methodological context.

39. It should be noted that this is a reversal of an earlier view common in sociological theory, that human behavior was not rational. This view of human irrationality was often tied to the idea, also a part of symbolic interactionism, that people do not respond to actual events but to perceived events. Human irrational reaction to perceived nonactual events was maintained by Vilfredo Pareto in the first two decades of this century. See Charles H. Powers, *Vilfredo Pareto*, Masters of Social Theory 5 (Newbury Park, Calif.: SAGE Publications, 1987), 43–45. For one of the first clear statements of methodological individualism, see George Caspar Homans, "The Present State of Sociological Theory," in *Certainties and Doubts: Collected Papers, 1962–1985*, ed. George Caspar Homans (New Brunswick, N.J.: Transaction Books, 1987), 237–54; and idem, "Bringing Men Back In," 15. See the impact of Homans' thoughts in Eisenstadt and Curelaru, *Form of Sociology*, 198; and Christopher Lloyd, *Explanation in Social History* (Oxford: Basil Blackwell, 1986), 18.

40. Eisenstadt and Curelaru, *Form of Sociology*, 200–201, 268; Karl Mannheim, *Essays on the Sociology of Knowledge*, ed. Paul Kecskemeti (New York: Oxford University Press, 1952), 180; Berger and Kellner, *Sociology Reinterpreted*, 38, 45; Berger and Luckmann, *Social Construction of Reality;* and Berger, *Sacred Canopy*. Also relevant here is Burkart Holzner, *Reality Construction in Society* (Cambridge, Mass.: Schenkman Publishing, 1968). For a critique of Berger's theories of social construction, see Ivan H. Light, "The Social Construction of Uncertainty," *Berkeley Journal of Sociology* 14 (1969): 189–99.

41. J. Christopher Crocker, "The Social Functions of Rhetorical Forms," in *The Social Use of Metaphor: Essays on the Anthropology of Rhetoric*, ed. J. David Sapir and J. Christopher Crocker (Philadelphia: University of Pennsylvania Press, 1977), 64; and James W. Fernandez, "The Performance of Ritual Metaphors," in *The Social Use of Metaphor: Essays on the Anthropology of Rhetoric*, ed. J. David Sapir and J. Christopher Crocker (Philadelphia: University of Pennsylvania Press, 1977), 126. Berger, *Sacred Canopy*, 8–18; and Berger and Luckmann, *Social Construction of Reality*, 34, 129–30.

42. Berger and Luckmann, *Social Construction of Reality*, 90–120; and Berger, *Sacred Canopy*, 29, 44. Religious legitimations of anomic situations are called theodicy, a social phenomenon treated at length in Berger, *Sacred Canopy*, 53–79. The same relationship can be seen in nonreligious myth, ritual, symbol, and ideology. See Myron J. Aronoff, "Ideology and Interest: The Dialectics of Politics," in *Ideology and Interest: The Dialectics of Politics*, ed. Myron J. Aronoff, Political Anthropology Yearbook 1 (New Brunswick, N.J.: Transaction Books, 1980), 7–24; David E. Apter, "Ideology and Discontent," in *Ideology and Discontent*, ed. David E. Apter (New York: Free Press, 1964), 15–18; Kertzer, *Ritual, Politics, and Power;* and W. Lance Bennett, "Myth, Ritual, and Political Control," *Journal of Communication* 30/4 (1980): 168.

43. Berger and Luckmann, *Social Construction of Reality*, 154; and Holzner, *Reality Construction in Society*, 13. For religion, this often includes ecclesial structures (Berger, *Sacred Canopy*, 46–48).

44. Within the structural components of society are ritualized actions, which serve to support the superstructural worldviews.

45. Berger, *Sacred Canopy*, 44.

46. Symbolic interactionism has recently developed in numerous distinct directions. One interesting work combines symbolic interactionist and Marxist approaches with existentialist philoso-

phy and theology, and thus opens many new channels for understanding how one's symbols, especially one's religious symbols, work to create one's world and worldview (Richard Quinney, *Social Existence: Metaphysics, Marxism, and the Social Sciences,* Sage Library of Social Research 141 [Beverly Hills, Calif.: SAGE Publications, 1982]).

47. For a discussion of the mechanics of legitimation and its connection to state development in a variety of situations, see Cohen and Toland, *State Formation and Political Legitimacy.* Writing serves as a particularly strong force for the legitimation of the status quo. See the following chapters in *State and Society: The Emergence and Development of Social Hierarchy and Political Centralization,* ed. John Gledhill, Barbara Bender, and Mogens Trolle Larsen, One World Archaeology 4 (London: Unwin Hyman, 1988): John Gledhill, "Introduction: The Comparative Analysis of Social and Political Transitions," 1–29; Michael Harbsmeier, "Inventions of Writing," 253–76; and Mogens Trolle Larsen, "Introduction: Literacy and Social Complexity," 173–91.

48. This proposal for a research strategy attempts a synthesis of integration and conflict approaches. For a related but different synthesis, see Haas, *Evolution of the Prehistoric State,* 86–129.

49. The work of Mary Douglas on the Leviticus purity laws has often been regarded as a seminal work in the application of anthropological approaches to biblical problems. However, she has applied to the texts the same categories of "clean" and "unclean" that are derived from the Hebrew Bible; thus, her anthropology does not enlighten the text (Richard Elliott Friedman, "The Prophet and the Historian: The Acquisition of Historical Information from Literary Sources," in *The Poet and the Historian: Essays in Literary and Historical Criticism,* ed. Richard Elliott Friedman, HSM 26 [Chico, Calif., Scholars Press, 1983], 4).

50. Robert R. Wilson, *Sociological Approaches to the Old Testament,* Guides to Biblical Scholarship, Old Testament Series (Philadelphia: Fortress Press, 1984), 6.

51. Ibid., 28–29.

52. Shemaryahu Talmon, "The 'Comparative Method' in Biblical Interpretation—Principles and Problems," VTSup 29 (1978): 322-23.

53. Ibid., 324–29.

54. Norman K. Gottwald, "Sociological Method in the Study of Ancient Israel," in *Encounter with the Text: Form and History in the Hebrew Bible,* ed. Martin J. Buss, Semeia, Supplement 8 (Philadelphia: Fortress Press, 1979), 71.

55. For a discussion of the necessity of the comparative method, see Frank S. Frick, *The Formation of the State in Ancient Israel,* SWBA 4 (Sheffield: Almond Press, 1985), 15–17; Joseph R. Rosenbloom, "Social Science Concepts of Modernization and Biblical History: The Development of the Israelite Monarchy," *JAAR* 40 (1972): 444; Frank S. Frick, "Social Science Methods and Theories of Significance for the Study of the Israelite Monarchy: A Critical Review Essay," *Semeia* 37 (1986): 10–11; and Gillian Feeley-Harnik, "Is Historical Anthropology Possible?: The Case of the Runaway Slave," in *Humanizing America's Iconic Book: The SBL Centennial Addresses, 1980,* ed. Gene M. Tucker and Douglas A. Knight (Chico, Calif.: Scholars Press, 1982), 98–99, 126.

56. James W. Flanagan, "History as Hologram: Integrating Literary, Archaeological and Comparative Sociological Evidence," *SBL Seminar Papers* 24 (1985): 298–304; and Shemaryahu Talmon, "The 'Comparative Method' in Biblical Interpretation," 320–56.

57. Gary A. Herion, "The Impact of Modern and Social Science Assumptions on the Reconstruction of Israelite History," *JSOT* 34 (1986): 7–8. Herion continues to point out several specific theories about influences upon ancient religion that develop from these modernist assumptions: urbanization, politicization, and economic determinism.

BIBLIOGRAPHY

Texts from the Postexilic Period

Achtemeier, Elizabeth. *Nahum-Malachi.* Interpretation. Atlanta: John Knox Press, 1986.

Ackroyd, Peter R. *The Chronicler in His Age.* JSOTSup 101. Sheffield: JSOT Press, 1990.

———. "Chronicles-Ezra-Nehemiah: The Concept of Unity." *ZAW* 100 Supplement (1988): 189–202.

———. *Exile and Restoration: A Study of Hebrew Thought of the Sixth Century B.C.* OTL. Philadelphia: Westminster Press, 1968.

———. "Haggai." In *Harper's Bible Commentary,* edited by James L. Mays, 745–46. San Francisco: Harper & Row, 1988.

———. "Studies in the Book of Haggai." *Journal of Jewish Studies* 2 (1951): 163–76; 3 (1952): 1–13.

Amsler, Samuel. *Aggée, Zacharie 1–8.* CAT 11c. Neuchâtel: Delachaux et Niestlé, 1981.

Anderson, Gary A. *Sacrifices and Offerings in Ancient Israel: Studies in Their Social and Political Importance.* HSM 41. Atlanta: Scholars Press, 1987.

Aytoun, W. R. "The Rise and Fall of the 'Messianic' Hope in the Sixth Century." *JBL* 39 (1920): 24–43.

Baldwin, Joyce G. *Haggai, Zechariah, Malachi: An Introduction and Commentary.* Tyndale Old Testament Commentaries. Downers Grove, Ill.: Inter-Varsity Press, 1972.

Barnes, W. Emery. *Haggai, Zechariah and Malachi.* Cambridge Bible. Cambridge: Cambridge University Press, 1934.

Berquist, Jon L. "Haggai." In *Mercer Commentary on the Bible,* edited by Watson E. Mills et al., 789–92. Macon: Mercer University Press, 1995.

———. "Malachi." In *Mercer Commentary on the Bible,* edited by Watson E. Mills et al., 799–802. Macon, Ga.: Mercer University Press, 1995.

———. "Prophetic Legitimation in Jeremiah." *VT* 39 (1989): 129–39.

———. "Reading Difference in Isaiah 56–66: The Interplay of Literary and Sociological Strategies." *Method and Theory in the Study of Religion* 7/1 (January 1995): 19–38.

———. *Reclaiming Her Story: The Witness of Women in the Old Testament.* St. Louis: Chalice Press, 1992.

———. "Role Dedifferentiation in the Book of Ruth." *JSOT* 57 (1993): 23–37.

———. "The Social Setting of Early Postexilic Prophecy." Ph.D. diss., Vanderbilt University, 1989.

———. "The Social Setting of Malachi." *BTB* 19 (1989): 121–26.

———. "Zechariah." In *Mercer Commentary on the Bible,* edited by Watson E. Mills et al., 793–98. Macon: Mercer University Press, 1995.

Beuken, W. A. M. *Haggai-Sacharja 1–8: Studien zur Überlieferungsgeschichte der frühnachexilischen Prophetie.* Studia semitica neerlandica 10. Assen: Van Gorcum, 1967.

Beyse, Karl-Martin. *Serubbabel und die Königserwartungen der Propheten Haggai und Sacharja: Eine historische und traditionsgeschichtliche Untersuchung.* Stuttgart: Calwer Verlag, 1972.

Bič, Miloš. *Die Nachtgesichte des Sacharja: Eine Auslegung von Sacharja 1–6.* Biblische Studien 42. Neukirchen-Vluyn: Neukirchener Verlag, 1964.

Blenkinsopp, Joseph. *Ezra-Nehemiah, A Commentary.* OTL. Philadelphia: Westminster Press, 1988.

———. *A History of Prophecy in Israel from the Settlement in the Land to the Hellenistic Period.* Philadelphia: Westminster Press, 1983.

———. "Interpretation and the Tendency to Sectarianism: An Aspect of Second Temple History." In *Jewish and Christian Self-Definition,* edited by E. P. Sanders, 1–26. Philadelphia: Fortress Press, 1981.

———. "A Jewish Sect of the Persian Period." *CBQ* 52 (1990): 5–20.

———. "The Mission of Udjahorresnet and Those of Ezra and Nehemiah." *JBL* 106 (1987): 409–21.

———. *Prophecy and Canon: A Contribution to the Study of Jewish Origins.* University of Notre Dame Center for the Study of Judaism and Christianity in Antiquity 3. Notre Dame, Ind.: University of Notre Dame Press, 1977.

———. "Second Isaiah—Prophet of Universalism." *JSOT* 41 (1988): 83–103.

———. "The 'Servants of the Lord' in Third Isaiah: Profile of a Pietistic Group in the Persian Epoch." *Proceedings of the Irish Biblical Association* 7 (1983): 1–23.

Brueggemann, Walter. "Psalms and the Life of Faith: A Suggested Typology of Function." *JSOT* 17 (1980): 3–32.

Bulmerincq, Alexander von. *Der Prophet Maleachi.* 2 vols. Vol. 1, *Einleitung in das Buch des Propheten Maleachi.* Dorpat, 1926. Vol. 2, *Kommentar zum Buche des Propheten Maleachi.* Tartu: J. G. Krüger, 1932.

Carroll, Robert P. "Coopting the Prophets: Nehemiah and Noadiah." In *Priests, Prophets and Scribes: Essays on the Formation and Heritage of Second Temple Judaism in Honour of Joseph Blenkinsopp,* JSOTSup 149, edited by Eugene Ulrich, John W. Wright, Robert P. Carroll, and Philip R. Davies, 87–99. Sheffield: JSOT Press, 1992.

———. *Jeremiah, A Commentary.* OTL. Philadelphia: Westminster Press, 1985.

Chary, Théophane. *Aggée—Zacharie—Malachie.* Sources Bibliques. Paris: J. Gabalda, 1969.

Clements, R. E., ed. *The World of Ancient Israel: Sociological, Anthropological and Political Perspectives.* Cambridge: Cambridge University Press, 1989.

Clines, D. J. A. *Ezra, Nehemiah, Esther.* NCBC. Grand Rapids: Wm. B. Eerdmans Publishing Co., 1984.

———. *Job 1–20.* WBC 17. Dallas, Tex.: Word Books, 1989.

Cody, Aelred. *A History of Old Testament Priesthood.* Analecta Biblica 35. Rome: Pontifical Biblical Institute, 1969.

Coggins, R. J. *Haggai, Zechariah, Malachi.* OTG. Sheffield: JSOT Press, 1987.

Collins, John J. *Proverbs and Ecclesiastes.* Knox Preaching Guides. Atlanta: John Knox Press, 1980.

Coote, Robert B., and David Robert Ord. *In the Beginning: Creation and the Priestly History.* Minneapolis: Fortress Press, 1991.

Craven, Toni. *Artistry and Faith in the Book of Judith.* Atlanta: Scholars Press, 1983.

———. "Women Who Lied for the Faith." In *Justice and the Holy: Essays in Honor of Walter Harrelson,* edited by Douglas A. Knight and Peter J. Paris, 35–49. Atlanta: Scholars Press, 1989.

Crenshaw, James L. "Clanging Symbols." In *Justice and the Holy: Essays in Honor of Walter Harrelson,* edited by Douglas A. Knight and Peter J. Paris, 51–64. Atlanta: Scholars Press, 1989.

———. *Ecclesiastes, A Commentary.* OTL. Philadelphia: Westminster Press, 1987.

———. "Education in Ancient Israel." *JBL* 104 (1989): 601–15.

———. "Method in Determining Wisdom Influence in 'Historical' Literature." *JBL* 88 (1969): 129–42.

———. *Old Testament Wisdom: An Introduction.* Atlanta: John Knox Press, 1981.

———. "Prohibitions in Proverbs and Qoheleth." In *Priests, Prophets and Scribes: Essays on the*

Formation and Heritage of Second Temple Judaism in Honour of Joseph Blenkinsopp, JSOTSup 149, edited by Eugene Ulrich, John W. Wright, Robert P. Carroll, and Philip R. Davies, 115–24. Sheffield: JSOT Press, 1992.

———. *Prophetic Conflict: Its Effect upon Israelite Religion.* BZAW 124. Berlin: Walter de Gruyter, 1971.

———, ed. *Theodicy in the Old Testament.* Issues in Religion and Theology 4. Philadelphia: Fortress Press, 1983.

Cross, Frank Moore. *Canaanite Myth and Hebrew Epic.* Cambridge: Harvard University Press, 1973.

Dahood, Mitchell. *Psalms II: 51–100.* AB 17. Garden City, N.Y.: Doubleday & Co., 1968.

Davies, Philip R. "Defending the Boundaries of Israel in the Second Temple Period: 2 Chronicles 20 and the 'Salvation Army.'" In *Priests, Prophets and Scribes: Essays on the Formation and Heritage of Second Temple Judaism in Honour of Joseph Blenkinsopp*, JSOTSup 149, edited by Eugene Ulrich, John W. Wright, Robert P. Carroll, and Philip R. Davies, 43–54. Sheffield: JSOT Press, 1992.

———, ed. *Second Temple Studies: 1. Persian Period.* JSOTSup 117. Sheffield: JSOT Press, 1991.

Dentan, Robert C. "Malachi." In *The Interpreter's Bible*, 12 vols., edited by G. A. Buttrick et al., 6: 1117–44. New York: Abingdon Press, 1956.

De Vries, Simon J. *1 and 2 Chronicles.* FOTL 11. Grand Rapids: Wm. B. Eerdmans Publishing Co., 1989.

Dods, Marcus. *The Post-Exilian Prophets: Haggai, Zechariah, Malachi.* Edinburgh: T. & T. Clark, 1881.

Duhm, B. "Anmerkungen zu den Zwölf Propheten. IX. Buch Maleachi." *ZAW* 31 (1911): 178–84.

Elliger, Karl. *Das Buch der zwölf kleinen Propheten.* Vol. 2, *Die Propheten Nahum, Habakuk, Zephania, Haggai, Sacharja, Maleachi.* 5th ed. ATD 25. Göttingen: Vandenhoeck & Ruprecht, 1964.

Eskenazi, Tamara Cohn. *In an Age of Prose: A Literary Approach to Ezra-Nehemiah.* SBLMS 36. Atlanta: Scholars Press, 1989.

Eskenazi, Tamara Cohn, and Kent H. Richards, eds. *Second Temple Studies: 2. Temple Community in the Persian Period.* JSOTSup 175. Sheffield: Sheffield Academic Press, 1994.

Eybers, I. H. "The Rebuilding of the Temple according to Haggai and Zechariah." In *Studies in Old Testament Prophecy*, edited by W. C. van Wyk, 15–26. Potchefstroom: Pro Rege Press, 1975.

Fischer, James A. "Notes on the Literary Form and Message of Malachi." *CBQ* 34 (1972): 315–20.

Fishbane, Michael. "Form and Reformulation of the Biblical Priestly Blessing." *Journal of the American Oriental Society* 103 (1983): 115–21.

Fox, Michael V. *Qohelet and His Contradictions.* JSOTSup 71. Sheffield: Almond Press, 1989.

Galling, Kurt. "Die Exilswende in der Sicht des Propheten Sacharja." *VT* 2 (1952): 18–36.

———. "The 'Gōlā-List' according to Ezra 2 || Nehemiah 7." *JBL* 70 (1951): 149–58.

———. *Studien zur Geschichte Israels im persischen Zeitalter.* Tübingen: J. C. B. Mohr (Paul Siebeck), 1964.

Gammie, John G. *Holiness in Israel.* Overtures to Biblical Theology. Philadelphia: Fortress Press, 1989.

Gammie, John G., and Leo G. Perdue, eds. *The Sage in Israel and the Ancient Near East.* Winona Lake, Ind.: Eisenbrauns, 1990.

Glazier-McDonald, Beth. *Malachi: The Divine Messenger.* SBLDS 98. Atlanta: Scholars Press, 1987.

———. "Malachi 2:12: *'ēr wĕ 'ōneh*—Another Look." *JBL* 105 (1986): 295–98.

Gottwald, Norman K. *The Hebrew Bible: A Socio-Literary Introduction.* Philadelphia: Fortress Press, 1985.

Grabbe, Lester L. "The Jewish Theocracy from Cyrus to Titus: A Programmatic Essay." *JSOT* 37 (1987): 117–24.

Greenspahn, Frederick E. "Why Prophecy Ceased." *JBL* 108 (1989): 37–49.

Habel, Norman C. *The Book of Job, A Commentary.* OTL. Philadelphia: Westminster Press, 1985.

Halpern, Baruch. *The Constitution of the Monarchy in Israel.* HSM 25. Chico, Calif.: Scholars Press, 1981.

———. "The Ritual Background of Zechariah's Temple Song." *CBQ* 40 (1978): 167–90.

Hanson, Paul D. "Compositional Techniques in the Book of Haggai." Paper presented as part of the Israelite Prophetic Literature Section at the Annual Meeting of SBL, Chicago, 20 November 1988.

———. *The Dawn of Apocalyptic: The Historical and Sociological Roots of Jewish Apocalyptic Eschatology.* Rev. ed. Philadelphia: Fortress Press, 1979.

———. "In Defiance of Death: Zechariah's Symbolic Universe." In *Love and Death in the Ancient Near East: Essays in Honor of Marvin H. Pope,* edited by John H. Marks and Robert M. Good, 173–79. New Haven, Conn.: Four Quarters Publishing Co., 1987.

———. "From Prophecy to Apocalyptic: Unresolved Issues." *JSOT* 15 (1980): 3–6.

———. "Israelite Religion in the Early Postexilic Period." In *Ancient Israelite Religion: Essays in Honor of Frank Moore Cross,* edited by Patrick D. Miller, Jr., Paul D. Hanson, and S. Dean McBride, 485–508. Philadelphia: Fortress Press, 1987.

———. "Malachi." In *Harper's Bible Commentary,* edited by James L. Mays, 753–56. San Francisco: Harper & Row, 1988.

———. *The People Called: The Growth of Community in the Bible.* San Francisco: Harper & Row, 1986.

———. "Zechariah." In *Interpreter's Dictionary of the Bible Supplementary Volume,* edited by Keith Crim, 982–83. Nashville: Abingdon Press, 1968.

Harrelson, Walter. "The Trial of the High Priest Joshua: Zechariah 3." *Eretz-Israel* 16 (1982): 116*–24*.

Hayes, John H. "Wellhausen as a Historian of Israel." *Semeia* 25 (1982): 37–60.

Hildebrand, David R. "Temple Ritual: A Paradigm for Moral Holiness in Haggai 2:10-19." *VT* 39 (1989): 154–68.

Hill, Andrew E. "Dating the Book of Malachi: A Linguistic Reexamination." In *The Word of the Lord Shall Go Forth: Essays in Honor of David Noel Freedman in Celebration of His Sixtieth Birthday,* edited by Carol L. Meyers and M. O'Connor, 77–89. Winona Lake, Ind.: Eisenbrauns, 1983.

Hillers, Delbert R. *Treaty-Curses and the Old Testament Prophets.* Biblica Orientalia 16. Rome: Pontifical Biblical Institute, 1964.

Holladay, William L. *Jeremiah 1 (1–25).* Hermeneia. Philadelphia: Fortress Press, 1986.

Horsley, Richard A., with John S. Hanson. *Bandits, Prophets, and Messiahs: Popular Movements at the Time of Jesus.* San Francisco: Harper & Row, 1985.

Horst, Friedrich. *Die zwölf kleinen Propheten Nahum bis Maleachi.* Handbuch zum Alten Testament 14. Tübingen: J. C. B. Mohr (Paul Siebeck), 1938.

Janzen, J. Gerald. *Job.* Interpretation. Atlanta: John Knox Press, 1988.

Jemielity, Thomas. *Satire and the Hebrew Prophets.* Literary Currents in Biblical Interpretation. Louisville, Ky.: Westminster/John Knox Press, 1992.

Jones, Douglas Rawlinson. *Haggai, Zechariah and Malachi.* Torch Bible Commentary. London: SCM Press, 1962.

Kessler, Werner. "Studie zur religiösen Situation im ersten nachexilischen Jahrhundert und zur Auslegung von Jesaja 56–66." *Wissenschaftliche Zeitschrift der Martin-Luther-Universität* 6 (1956): 41–74.

Knight, Douglas A., ed. *Julius Wellhausen and His "Prolegomena to the History of Israel." Semeia* 25. Chico, Calif.: Scholars Press, 1982.

———. "Wellhausen and the Interpretation of Israel's Literature." *Semeia* 25 (1982): 21–36.

Knight, Douglas A., and Gene M. Tucker, eds. *The Hebrew Bible and Its Modern Interpreters.* Philadelphia: Fortress Press, 1985.

Koch, Klaus. "Haggais unreines Volk." *ZAW* 79 (1967): 52–66.

———. *The Prophets.* Vol. 2, *The Babylonian and Persian Periods.* Translated by Margaret Kohl. Philadelphia: Fortress Press, 1982.

Kodell, Jerome. *Lamentations, Haggai, Zechariah, Malachi, Obadiah, Joel, Second Zechariah, Baruch.* Old Testament Message 14. Wilmington, Del.: Michael Glazier, 1982.

Kuenen, Abraham. *The Prophets and Prophecy in Israel.* Translated by Adam Milroy. Amsterdam: Philo Press, 1969.

LaCocque, André. *The Feminine Unconventional: Four Subversive Figures in Israel's Tradition.* Overtures to Biblical Theology 26. Minneapolis: Fortress Press, 1990.

Marti, Karl. *Dodekapropheton.* Kleiner Handkommentar zum Alten Testament 13. Tübingen: J. C. B. Mohr, 1904.

Mason, Rex. *The Books of Haggai, Zechariah, and Malachi.* Cambridge Bible Commentary. Cambridge: Cambridge University Press, 1977.

———. "The Prophets of the Restoration." In *Israel's Prophetic Tradition: Essays in Honour of Peter R. Ackroyd,* edited by Richard Coggins, Anthony Phillips, and Michael Knibb, 137–54. Cambridge: Cambridge University Press, 1982.

———. "The Purpose of the 'Editorial Framework' of the Book of Haggai." *VT* 27 (1977): 413–21.

Matthews, J. G. "Tammuz Worship in the Book of Malachi." *Journal of the Palestine Oriental Society* 11 (1931): 42–50.

May, Herbert Gordon. "A Key to the Interpretation of Zechariah's Visions." *JBL* 57 (1938): 173–84.

———. "'This People' and 'This Nation' in Haggai." *VT* 18 (1968): 190–97.

McEvenue, Sean E. "The Political Structure in Judah from Cyrus to Nehemiah." *CBQ* 43 (1981): 353–64.

McKenzie, John L. *Second Isaiah.* AB 20. Garden City, N.Y.: Doubleday & Co., 1968.

McKenzie, Steven L., and Howard N. Wallace. "Covenant Themes in Malachi." *CBQ* 45 (1983): 549–63.

Meyers, Carol L., and Eric M. Meyers. *Haggai, Zechariah 1–8.* AB 25B. Garden City, N.Y.: Doubleday & Co., 1987.

———, and Eric M. Meyers. *Zechariah 9–14.* AB 25C. New York: Doubleday & Co., 1993.

Meyers, Eric M. "The Persian Period and the Judean Restoration: From Zerubbabel to Nehemiah." In *Ancient Israelite Religion: Essays in Honor of Frank Moore Cross,* edited by Patrick D. Miller, Jr., Paul D. Hanson, and S. Dean McBride, 509–21. Philadelphia: Fortress Press, 1987.

———. "Priestly Language in the Book of Malachi." *Hebrew Annual Review* 10 (1986): 225–37.

———. "The Use of Tôrâ in Haggai 2:11 and the Role of the Prophet in the Restoration Community." In *The Word of the Lord Shall Go Forth: Essays in Honor of David Noel Freedman in Celebration of His Sixtieth Birthday,* edited by Carol L. Meyers and M. O'Connor, 69–76. Winona Lake, Ind.: Eisenbrauns, 1983.

Moore, Carey A. *Judith.* AB 40. Garden City, N.Y.: Doubleday & Co., 1985.

Morgenstern, Julian. "A Chapter in the History of the High Priesthood." *American Journal of Semitic Languages and Literature* 55 (1938): 1–24, 183–97, 360–77.

———. "Jerusalem—485 B.C." *HUCA* 27 (1956): 101–79, 28 (1957): 15–47, 31 (1960): 1–29.

Murphy, Frederick J. *The Religious World of Jesus: An Introduction to Second Temple Palestinian Judaism.* Nashville: Abingdon Press, 1991.

Murphy, Roland E. *Wisdom Literature: Job, Proverbs, Ruth, Canticles, Ecclesiastes, and Esther.* FOTL 13. Grand Rapids: Wm. B. Eerdmans Publishing Co., 1981.

Murray, D. F. "The Rhetoric of Disputation: Re-examination of a Prophetic Genre." *JSOT* 38 (1987): 95–121.

Myers, Jacob M. *I Chronicles: A New Translation with Introduction and Commentary.* AB 12. Garden City, N.Y.: Doubleday & Co., 1965.

———. *II Chronicles: A New Translation with Introduction and Commentary.* AB 13. Garden City, N.Y.: Doubleday & Co., 1965.

———. *The World of the Restoration.* Englewood Cliffs, N.J.: Prentice-Hall, 1968.

Neufeld, E. "The Rate of Interest and the Text of Nehemiah 5:11." *JQR* 44 (1953–54): 194–204.

Newsom, Carol A. "Woman and the Discourse of Patriarchal Wisdom: A Study of Proverbs 1–9." In *Gender and Difference in Ancient Israel,* edited by Peggy L. Day, 142–60. Minneapolis: Fortress Press, 1989.

Nickelsburg, George W. E., and Michael E. Stone. *Faith and Piety in Early Judaism: Texts and Documents.* Philadelphia: Fortress Press, 1983.

Nowack, W. *Die kleinen Propheten.* 3d ed. Göttinger Handkommentar zum Alten Testament 3/4. Göttingen, 1922.

O'Brien, Julia M. *Priest and Levite in Malachi.* SBLDS 121. Atlanta: Scholars Press, 1990.

Odell-Scott, David W. *A Post-Patriarchal Christology.* Atlanta: Scholars Press, 1991.

Orelli, Conrad von. *The Twelve Minor Prophets.* Translated by J. S. Banks. Edinburgh: T. & T. Clark, 1893.

Overholt, Thomas W. *Channels of Prophecy: Social Dynamics of Prophetic Activity.* Minneapolis: Fortress Press, 1989.

Penchansky, David. *The Betrayal of God: Ideological Conflict in Job.* Literary Currents in Biblical Interpretation. Louisville, Ky: Westminster/John Knox Press, 1990.

Perdue, Leo G. *Wisdom and Cult: A Critical Analysis of the Views of Cult in the Wisdom Literatures of Israel and the Ancient Near East.* SBLDS 30. Missoula, Mont.: Scholars Press, 1977.

———. *Wisdom in Revolt: Metaphorical Theology in the Book of Job.* JSOTSup 112. Sheffield: JSOT Press, 1991.

Perdue, Leo G., and W. Clark Gilpin, eds. *Voices from the Whirlwind: Interpreting the Book of Job.* Nashville: Abingdon Press, 1991.

Perowne, T. T. *Malachi.* Cambridge Bible. 2d ed. Cambridge: Cambridge University Press, 1901.

Petersen, David L. *Haggai and Zechariah 1–8, A Commentary.* OTL. Philadelphia: Westminster Press, 1984.

———. "Introduction: Ways of Thinking about Israel's Prophets." In *Prophecy in Israel: Search for an Identity,* edited by David L. Petersen, Issues in Religion and Theology 10, 1–21. Philadelphia: Fortress Press, 1987.

———. *Late Israelite Prophecy: Studies in Deutero-Prophetic Literature and in Chronicles.* SBLMS 23. Missoula, Mont.: Scholars Press, 1977.

———. "Malachi and the Language of Divorce, Malachi 2:10-16." Paper presented as part of the Israelite Prophetic Literature Section at the Annual Meeting of SBL, Boston, Mass., 6 December 1987.

———. "Max Weber and the Sociological Study of Ancient Israel." *Sociological Inquiry* 49 (1979): 117–49.

———. *The Roles of Israel's Prophets.* JSOTSup 17. Sheffield: JSOT Press, 1981.

———. "Zechariah's Visions: A Theological Perspective." *VT* 34 (1984): 195–206.

———. "Zerubbabel and Jerusalem Temple Reconstruction." *CBQ* 36 (1974): 366–72.

Petitjean, A. "La Mission de Zorobabel et la Reconstruction du Temple." *Ephemerides Theologicae Lovanienses* 42 (1966): 40–71.

Pfeiffer, Egon. "Die Disputationsworte im Buche Maleachi (Ein Beitrag zur formgeschichtlichen Struktur)." *Evangelische Theologie* 19 (1959): 546–68.

Plöger, Otto. *Theocracy and Eschatology.* Translated by S. Rudman. Richmond, Va.: John Knox Press, 1968.

Pope, Marvin H. *Job.* AB 15. Garden City, N.Y.: Doubleday & Co., 1965.

Procksch, Otto. *Die kleinen prophetischen Schriften nach dem Exil.* Stuttgart: Vereinsbuchhandlung, 1916.

von Rad, Gerhard. *Old Testament Theology.* Translated by D. M. G. Stalker. 2 vols. New York: Harper & Row, 1962–65.

Radday, Yehuda T., and Moshe A. Pollatschek. "Vocabulary Richness in Post-Exilic Prophetic Books." *ZAW* 92 (1980): 333–46.

Redditt, Paul L. "Once Again, The City in Isaiah 24–27." *Hebrew Annual Review* 10 (1986): 317–35.

Rudolph, Wilhelm. *Haggai—Sacharja 1–8—Sacharja 9–14—Maleachi.* Kommentar zum Alten Testament 13/4. Gütersloh: Gütersloher Verlagshaus Gerd Mohn, 1976.

Sauer, Georg. "Serubbabel in der Sicht Haggais und Sacharjas." In *Das ferne und nahe Wort. Festschrift Leonhard Rost,* edited by F. Maass, BZAW 105, 199–207. Berlin: Alfred Töpelmann, 1967.

Schiffman, Lawrence H. *From Text to Tradition: A History of Second Temple and Rabbinic Judaism.* New York: KTAV, 1991.

Schottroff, Willy. "Zur Sozialgeschichte Israels in der Perserzeit." *Verkündigung und Forschung* 27/1 (1982): 46–68.

Schultz, Carl. "The Political Tensions Reflected in Ezra-Nehemiah." In *Scripture in Context: Essays on the Comparative Method,* Pittsburgh Theological Monograph Series 34, edited by Carl D. Evans, William W. Hallo, and John B. White, 221–44. Pittsburgh: Pickwick Press, 1980.

Scott, Bernard Brandon. *Hear Then the Parable: A Commentary on the Parables of Jesus.* Minneapolis: Fortress Press, 1989.

Scott, R. B. Y. *Proverbs and Ecclesiastes.* AB 18. Garden City, N.Y.: Doubleday & Co., 1965.

Sellin, Ernst. *Das Zwölfprophetenbuch übersetzt und erklärt.* Kommentar zum Alten Testament 12/2. Leipzig: Deichert, 1930.

Silberman, Lou H. "Wellhausen and Judaism." *Semeia* 25 (1982): 75–82.

Smith, Daniel L. *The Religion of the Landless: The Social Context of the Babylonian Exile.* Bloomington, Ind.: Meyer-Stone Books, 1989.

Smith, John Merlin Powers. *Malachi.* International Critical Commentary. New York: Charles Scribner's Sons, 1912.

Smith, Morton. *Palestinian Parties and Politics That Shaped the Old Testament.* New York: Columbia University Press, 1971.

Smith, Ralph L. *Micah-Malachi.* WBC 32. Waco, Tex.: Word Books, 1984.

Sperling, S. David. "Rethinking Covenant in Late Biblical Books." *Biblica* 70 (1989): 50–73.

Spicer, Laura Rey. "Postexilic Additions to Deuteronomy." Paper presented as part of the SBL Southwest Regional Meeting, Dallas, 14 March 1993.

Spoer, Hans H. "Some New Considerations towards the Dating of the Book of Malachi." *JQR* 20 (1908): 167–86.

Stendebach, Franz Josef. *Prophetie und Tempel: Die Bücher Haggai—Sacharja—Maleachi—Joel.* Stuttgarter Kleiner Kommentar, Altes Testament 16. Stuttgart: Verlag Katholisches Bibelwerk, 1977.

Steussy, Martha J. *Gardens in Babylon: Narrative and Faith in the Greek Legends of Daniel.* SBLDS 141. Atlanta: Scholars Press, 1993.

Talmon, Shemaryahu. "The 'Comparative Method' in Biblical Interpretation—Principles and Problems." *VT Supplements* 29 (1978): 320–56.

———. "The Emergence of Jewish Sectarianism in the Early Second Temple Period." In *Ancient Israelite Religion: Essays in Honor of Frank Moore Cross*, edited by Patrick D. Miller, Jr., Paul D. Hanson, and S. Dean McBride, 587–616. Philadelphia: Fortress Press, 1987.

Torrey, C. C. "The Prophecy of Malachi." *JBL* 17 (1898): 1–15.

Ulrich, Eugene. "Ezra and Qoheleth Manuscripts from Qumran (4QEzra and 4QQoh^{a,b}). In *Priests, Prophets and Scribes: Essays on the Formation and Heritage of Second Temple Judaism in Honour of Joseph Blenkinsopp*, JSOTSup 149, edited by Eugene Ulrich, John W. Wright, Robert P. Carroll, and Philip R. Davies, 139–57. Sheffield: JSOT Press, 1992.

VanderKam, James C. "Ezra-Nehemiah or Ezra and Nehemiah?" In *Priests, Prophets and Scribes: Essays on the Formation and Heritage of Second Temple Judaism in Honour of Joseph Blenkinsopp*, JSOTSup 149, edited by Eugene Ulrich, John W. Wright, Robert P. Carroll, and Philip R. Davies, 55–75. Sheffield: JSOT Press, 1992.

———, ed. *"No One Spoke Ill of Her": Essays on Judith*. Atlanta: Scholars Press, 1992.

Verhoef, Pieter A. *The Books of Haggai and Malachi*. New International Commentary on the Old Testament. Grand Rapids: Wm. B. Eerdmans Publishing Co., 1987.

Vriezen, Th. C. "How to Understand Malachi 1:11." In *Grace upon Grace: Essays in Honor of Lester J. Kuyper*, edited by James I. Cook, 128–36. Grand Rapids: Wm. B. Eerdmans Publishing Co., 1975.

Vuilleumier, René. *Malachie*. CAT 11c. Neuchâtel: Delachaux et Niestlé, 1981.

Wallis, G. "Die Nachtgesichte des Propheten Sacharja. Zur Idee einer Form." *VT Supplements* 29 (1978): 377–91.

Wanke, Gunther. "Prophecy and Psalms in the Persian Period." In *The Cambridge History of Judaism*. Vol. 1, *Introduction, The Persian Period*, edited by W. D. Davies and Louis Finkelstein, 162–88. Cambridge: Cambridge University Press, 1984.

Waterman, Leroy. "The Camouflaged Purge of Three Messianic Conspirators." *JNES* 13 (1954): 73–78.

Welch, Adam C. *Post-Exilic Judaism*. Baird Lecture, 1934. Edinburgh: William Blackwood & Sons, 1935.

———. "The Share of N. Israel in the Restoration of the Temple Worship." *ZAW* 48 (1930): 175–87.

Wellhausen, Julius. *Prolegomena to the History of Ancient Israel*. New York: Meridian Books, 1957.

Westermann, Claus. *Isaiah 40–66, A Commentary*. OTL. Philadelphia: Westminster Press, 1965.

Whybray, R. N. *Ecclesiastes*. OTG. Sheffield: JSOT Press, 1989.

———. *Isaiah 40–66*. NCBC. Grand Rapids: Wm. B. Eerdmans Publishing Co., 1975.

———. "Thoughts on the Composition of Proverbs 10–29." In *Priests, Prophets and Scribes: Essays on the Formation and Heritage of Second Temple Judaism in Honour of Joseph Blenkinsopp*, JSOTSup 149, edited by Eugene Ulrich, John W. Wright, Robert P. Carroll, and Philip R. Davies, 102–14. Sheffield: JSOT Press, 1992.

Williamson, H. G. M. *Ezra and Nehemiah*. OTG. Sheffield: JSOT Press, 1987.

———. *1 and 2 Chronicles*. NCBC. Grand Rapids: Wm. B. Eerdmans Publishing Co., 1982.

Wilson, Robert R. *Genealogy and History in the Biblical World*. New Haven, Conn.: Yale University Press, 1977.

———. *Prophecy and Society in Ancient Israel*. Philadelphia: Fortress Press, 1980.

———. *Sociological Approaches to the Old Testament*. Guides to Biblical Scholarship, Old Testament Series. Philadelphia: Fortress Press, 1984.

Wolff, Hans Walter. *Haggai: A Commentary*. Translated by Margaret Kohl. Minneapolis: Augsburg Press, 1988.

Wright, John W. "From Center to Periphery: 1 Chronicles 23–27 and the Interpretation of Chronicles in the Nineteenth Century." In *Priests, Prophets and Scribes: Essays on the Formation and Heritage of Second Temple Judaism in Honour of Joseph Blenkinsopp,* JSOTSup 149, edited by Eugene Ulrich, John W. Wright, Robert P. Carroll, and Philip R. Davies, 20–42. Sheffield: JSOT Press, 1992.

The History of the Persian Empire During the Achaemenid Period

Ackroyd, Peter R. "The History of Israel in the Exilic and Post-Exilic Periods." In *Tradition and Interpretation,* edited by G. W. Anderson, 320–50. Oxford: Clarendon Press, 1979.

———. *Israel under Babylon and Persia.* New Clarendon Bible, Old Testament 4. Oxford: Oxford University Press, 1970.

———. "The Jewish Community in Palestine in the Persian Period." In *The Cambridge History of Judaism.* Vol. 1, *Introduction, The Persian Period,* edited by W. D. Davies and Louis Finkelstein, 130–61. Cambridge: Cambridge University Press, 1984.

———. "Two Old Testament Historical Problems of the Early Persian Period." *JNES* 17 (1958): 13–27.

Ahlström, Gösta W. *The History of Ancient Palestine from the Paleolithic Period to Alexander's Conquest,* edited by Diana Edelman. JSOTSup 146. Sheffield: JSOT Press, 1993.

Alexander, Loveday, ed. *Images of Empire.* JSOTSup 122. Sheffield: JSOT Press, 1991.

Avigad, N. *Bullae and Seals from a Post-Exilic Judaean Archive.* Monographs of the Institute of Archaeology at the Hebrew University of Jerusalem 4. Jerusalem: Hebrew University Press, 1976.

Balcer, Jack M. "Ionia and Sparda under the Achaemenid Empire; The Sixth and Fifth Century B.C.: Tribute, Taxation and Assessment." In *Le tribut dans l'empire perse,* Travaux de l'Institut d'Etudes Iraniennes de l'Université de la Sorbonne Nouvelle 13, edited by Pierre Briant and Cl. Herrenschmidt, 2–24. Paris: Université de la Sorbonne, 1988.

———. *Sparda by the Bitter Sea: Imperial Interaction in Western Anatolia.* Brown Judaic Studies 52. Chico, Calif.: Scholars Press, 1984.

Bengtson, Herrmann. "The Persian Empire and the Greeks ca. 520 B.C." In *The Greeks and the Persians from the Sixth to the Fourth Centuries,* edited by Herrmann Bengtson, translated by John Conway, 1–25. New York: Delacorte Press, 1968.

———, ed. *The Greeks and the Persians from the Sixth to the Fourth Centuries.* Translated by John Conway. New York: Delacorte Press, 1968.

Bentzen, Aage. "Quelques remarques sur la mouvement messianique parmi les Juifs aux environs l'an 520 avant Jésus-Christ." *Revue d'histoire et de philosophie religieuse* 10 (1930): 493–503.

Bickerman, E. J. "The Edict of Cyrus in Ezra I." In *Studies in Jewish and Christian History, Volume I,* edited by E. J. Bickerman, 72–108. Leiden: E. J. Brill, 1976.

———. "The Historical Foundations of Postbiblical Judaism." Reprinted in *Emerging Judaism: Studies on the Fourth and Third Centuries B.C.E.,* edited by Michael E. Stone and David Satran, 9–45. Philadelphia: Fortress Press, 1989.

———. "La seconde année de Darius." *Revue Biblique* 88 (1981): 23–28.

Boardman, John; N. G. L. Hammond; D. M. Lewis; and M. Ostwald, eds. *The Cambridge Ancient History.* Vol. 4, *Persia, Greece and the Western Mediterranean, c. 525 to 479 B.C.* 2d ed. Cambridge: Cambridge University Press, 1988.

Bresciani, Edda. "Egypt and the Persian Empire." In *The Greeks and the Persians from the Sixth to the Fourth Centuries,* edited by Herrmann Bengtson, translated by Phyllis Johnson, 333–53. New York: Delacorte Press, 1968.

Bright, John. *A History of Israel.* 3d ed. Philadelphia: Westminster Press, 1981.

———. *The Kingdom of God: The Biblical Concept and Its Meaning for the Church.* Nashville: Abingdon Press, 1953.

Broshi, Magen. "Estimating the Population of Ancient Jerusalem." *Biblical Archaeology Review* 4 (1978): 10–15.

Burn, A. R. *Persia and the Greeks: The Defence of the West, 546–478 B.C.* 2d ed. Edited by D. M. Lewis. Stanford: Stanford University Press, 1984.

Cameron, George G. "Darius, Egypt, and the 'Lands Beyond the Sea.'" *JNES* 2 (1943): 307–13.

———. "Persepolis Treasury Tablets Old and New." *JNES* 17 (1958): 161–76.

———. "A Photograph of Darius' Sculptures at Behistan." *JNES* 2 (1943): 115–16.

Cook, John Manuel. *The Persian Empire.* London: J. M. Dent & Sons, 1983.

———. "The Rise of the Achaemenids and Establishment of Their Empire." In *The Cambridge History of Iran.* Vol. 2, *The Median and Achaemenian Periods,* edited by Ilya Gershevitch, 200–91. Cambridge: Cambridge University Press, 1985.

Crown, Alan D. "Toward a Reconstruction of the Climate of Palestine 8000 B.C.–0 B.C." *JNES* 31 (1972): 312–30.

Culican, William. *The Medes and the Persians.* London: Thames & Hudson, 1965.

Dandamaev, M[uhammad] A. *A Political History of the Achaemenid Empire.* Leiden: E. J. Brill, 1989.

———. "Social Stratification in Babylonia (7th–4th Centuries B.C.)." In *Wirtschaft und Gesellschaft im Alten Vorderasien,* edited by J. Harmatta and G. Komoróczy, 433–44. Budapest: Akadémiai Kiadó, 1976.

———. "State and Temple in Babylonia in the First Millennium B.C." In *State and Temple Economy in the Ancient Near East,* 2 vols., Orientalia Lovaniensia Analecta 5–6, edited by Edward Lipiński, 2:589–96. Louvain: Departement Oriëntalistiek, 1979.

———. "Der Tempelzehnte in Babylonien während des 6. bis 4. Jh. v. u. Z." In *Beiträge zur Alten Geschichte und deren Nachleben: Festschrift für Franz Altheim,* edited by Ruth Stiehl and Hans Erich Stier, 1:82–90. Berlin: Walter de Gruyter, 1969.

Dandamaev, M[uhammad] A., and Vladimir G. Lukonin. *The Culture and Social Institutions of Ancient Iran.* Cambridge: Cambridge University Press, 1989.

Davies, W. D., and Louis Finkelstein, eds. *The Cambridge History of Judaism.* Vol. 1, *Introduction, The Persian Period.* Cambridge: Cambridge University Press, 1984.

Farkas, Ann. "The Behistun Relief." In *The Cambridge History of Iran.* Vol. 2, *The Median and Achaemenian Periods,* edited by Ilya Gershevitch, 828–31. Cambridge: Cambridge University Press, 1985.

Frye, Richard N. *The Heritage of Persia.* Cleveland: World Books, 1962.

———. *The History of Ancient Iran.* Handbuch der Altertumswissenschaft III/7. Munich: C. H. Beck, 1984.

Gershevitch, Ilya, ed. *The Cambridge History of Iran.* Vol. 2, *The Median and Achaemenian Periods.* Cambridge: Cambridge University Press, 1985.

Grabbe, Lester L. *Judaism from Cyrus to Hadrian.* Vol. 1, *The Persian and Greek Periods.* Minneapolis: Fortress Press, 1992.

Hallock, Richard T. "The Evidence of the Persepolis Tablets." In *The Cambridge History of Iran.* Vol. 2, *The Median and Achaemenian Periods,* edited by Ilya Gershevitch, 588–609. Cambridge: Cambridge University Press, 1985.

———. "The 'One Year' of Darius I." *JNES* 19 (1960): 36–39.

Heichelheim, Fritz M. "Ezra's Palestine and Periclean Athens." *Zeitschrift für Religions- und Geistesgeschichte* 3 (1951): 251–53.

Hayes, John H., and Paul K. Hooker. *A New Chronology for the Kings of Israel and Judah and Its Implications for Biblical History and Literature.* Atlanta: John Knox Press, 1988.

Hoglund, Kenneth G. *Achaemenid Imperial Administration in Syria-Palestine and the Missions of Ezra and Nehemiah.* SBLDS 125. Atlanta: Scholars Press, 1992.

Holm-Rasmussen, Torben. "Collaboration in Early Achaemenid Egypt: A New Approach." In *Studies in Ancient History and Numismatics presented to Rudi Thomsen*, 29–38. Copenhagen: Aarhus University Press, 1988.

Jamieson-Drake, David W. *Scribes and Schools in Monarchic Judah: A Socio-Archaeological Approach.* JSOTSup 109; SWBA 9. Sheffield: Almond Press, 1991.

Kaufmann, Yehezkel. *History of the Religion of Israel.* Vol. 4, *From the Babylonian Captivity to the End of Prophecy.* Translated by C. W. Efroymson. New York: Ktav, 1977.

Kent, Roland G. "Old Persian Texts. I. The Darius Suez c Inscription." *JNES* 1 (1942): 415–21.

———. "Old Persian Texts. III. Darius' Behistan Inscription, Column V." *JNES* 2 (1943):105–14.

———. "Old Persian Texts. IV. The Lists of Provinces." *JNES* 2 (1943): 302–6.

———. "Old Persian Texts. V. Darius' Behistan Inscription, Column V: A Correction." *JNES* 3 (1944): 232–33.

———. "Old Persian Texts. VI. Darius' Naqš-i-Rustam B Inscription." *JNES* 4 (1945): 39–52.

Kippenberg, Hans G. *Religion und Klassenbildung im antiken Judäa: Eine religionssoziologische Studie zum Verhältnis von Tradition und gesellschaftlicher Entwicklung.* Studien zur Umwelt des Neuen Testaments 14. Göttingen: Vandenhoeck & Ruprecht, 1982.

Kreissig, Heinz. *Die sozialökonomische Situation in Juda zur Achämenidenzeit.* Schriften zur Geschichte und Kultur des Alten Orients 7. Berlin: Akademie, 1973.

Kuhrt, Amélie. "The Cyrus Cylinder and Achaemenid Imperial Policy." *JSOT* 25 (1983): 83–97.

Kuhrt, Amélie, and Heleen Sancisi-Weerdenburg, eds. *Achaemenid History III: Method and Theory. Proceedings of the London 1985 Achaemenid History Workshop.* Leiden: Nederlands Instituut voor het Nabije Oosten, 1988.

Lemche, Niels Peter. *Ancient Israel: A New History of Israelite Society.* Biblical Seminar 5. Sheffield: JSOT Press, 1988.

Lewis, D. M., et al., eds. *The Cambridge Ancient History.* Vol. 5, *The Fifth Century B.C.* 2d ed. Cambridge: Cambridge University Press, 1986.

Lipiński, E. "Les temples néo-assyriens et les origines du monnayage." In *State and Temple Economy in the Ancient Near East*, edited by Edward Lipiński, Orientalia Lovaniensia Analecta 5–6, 2:565–88. Louvain: Departement Oriëntalistiek, 1979.

Margalith, Othniel. "The Political Role of Ezra as Persian Governor." *ZAW* 98 (1986): 110–12.

Meuleau, Maurice. "Mesopotamia under Persian Rule." In *The Greeks and the Persians from the Sixth to the Fourth Centuries*, edited by Herrmann Bengtson, translated by Robert F. Tannenbaum, 354–85. New York: Delacorte Press, 1968.

Miller, J. Maxwell, and John H. Hayes. *A History of Ancient Israel and Judah.* Philadelphia: Westminster Press, 1986.

Noth, Martin. *The History of Israel.* 2d ed. Translated by P. R. Ackroyd. New York: Harper & Row, 1960.

Olmstead, A. T. *History of the Persian Empire.* Chicago: University of Chicago Press, 1948.

Petit, Thierry. "L'évolution sémantique des termes hébreux et araméens *pḥh* et *sgn* et accadiens *pāḫatu* et *šaknu.*" *JBL* 107 (1988): 53–67.

Pirradaziš: Bulletin of Archaemenid Studies. 1990.

Porten, Bezalel. *Archives from Elephantine: The Life of an Ancient Jewish Military Colony.* Berkeley and Los Angeles: University of California Press, 1968.

Reich, Nathaniel Julius. "The Codification of the Egyptian Laws by Darius and the Origin of the 'Demotic Chronicle.'" *Mizraim* 1 (1933): 178–85.

Sancisi-Weerdenburg, Heleen, ed. *Achaemenid History I: Sources, Structures and Synthesis.* Leiden: Nederlands Instituut voor het Nabije Oosten, 1987.

Sancisi-Weerdenburg, Heleen, and J. W. Drijvers, eds. *Achaemenid History V: The Roots of the European Tradition.* Leiden: Nederlands Instituut voor het Nabije Oosten, 1990.

Sancisi-Weerdenburg, Heleen, and Amélie Kuhrt, eds. *Achaemenid History II: The Greek Sources. Proceedings of the Groningen 1984 Achaemenid History Workshop.* Leiden: Nederlands Instituut voor het Nabije Oosten, 1987.

———, and Amélie Kuhrt, eds. *Achaemenid History IV: Centre and Periphery. Proceedings of the Groningen 1986 Achaemenid History Workshop.* Leiden: Nederlands Instituut voor het Nabije Oosten, 1990.

——— and Amélie Kuhrt, eds. *Achaemenid History VI: Asia Minor and Egypt: Old Cultures in a New Empire. Proceedings of the Groningen 1988 Achaemenid History Workshop.* Leiden: Nederlands Instituut voor het Nabije Oosten, 1991.

Stager, Lawrence E. "Climatic Conditions and Grain Storage in the Persian Period." *Harvard Theological Review* 64 (1971): 448–50.

Stern, Ephraim. "The Persian Empire and the Political and Social History of Palestine in the Persian Period." In *The Cambridge History of Judaism.* Vol. 1, *Introduction, The Persian Period,* edited by W. D. Davies and Louis Finkelstein, 70–87. Cambridge: Cambridge University Press, 1984.

———. "The Province of Yehud: The Vision and the Reality." *The Jerusalem Cathedra* 1 (1981): 9–21.

Stolper, Matthew W. "The Governor of Babylon and Across-the-River in 486 B.C." *JNES* 48 (1989): 283–305.

———. "A Note on the Yahwistic Personal Names in the Murašû Texts." *Bulletin of the American Schools of Oriental Research* 222 (1976): 25–28.

Tod, Marcus N. "The Economic Background of the Fifth Century." In *The Cambridge Ancient History.* Vol. 5, *Athens: 478–401 B.C.*, edited by J. Bury, S. A. Cook, and F. E. Adcock, 1–32. Cambridge: Cambridge University Press, 1927.

de Vaux, Roland. *Ancient Israel.* 2 vols. New York: McGraw-Hill Book Co., 1965.

Weinberg, J. P. "Die Agrarverhältnisse in der Bürger-Tempel-Gemeinde der Achämenidenzeit." In *Wirtschaft und Gesellschaft im alten Vorderasien,* edited by J. Harmatta and G. Komoróczy, 473–86. Budapest: Akadémiai Kiadó, 1976.

———. "Demographische Notizen zur Geschichte der nachexilischen Gemeinde in Juda." *KLIO: Beiträge zur Alten Geschichte* 54 (1972): 45–59.

Weinberg, Saul S. "Post-Exilic Palestine: An Archaeological Report." *Proceedings of the Israel Academy of Sciences and Humanities* 4 (1971): 78–97.

Weisberg, David B. *Guild Structure and Political Allegiance in Early Achaemenid Mesopotamia.* New Haven, Conn.: Yale University Press, 1967.

Widengren, Geo. "The Persian Period." In *Israelite and Judean History,* edited by John H. Hayes and J. Maxwell Miller, 489–538. Philadelphia: Westminster Press, 1977.

———. "The Persians." In *Peoples of Old Testament Times,* edited by D. J. Wiseman, 312–57. Oxford: Clarendon Press, 1973.

Sociological Methodology

Aberle, David F. "A Note on Relative Deprivation Theory as Applied to Millenarian and Other Cult Movements." In *Millennial Dreams in Action: Essays in Comparative Study,* edited by Sylvia L. Thrupp, Comparative Studies in History and Society Supplements 2, 209–14. The Hague: Mouton, 1962.

Abrams, Philip. *Historical Sociology.* Ithaca, N.Y.: Cornell University Press, 1982.

Alexander, Jeffrey C., ed. *Neofunctionalism.* Key Issues in Sociological Theory 1. Beverly Hills, Calif.: SAGE Publications, 1985.

Allahar, Anton L. *Sociology and the Periphery: Theories and Issues.* Toronto: Garamond Press, 1989.

Allan, Graham. "A Theory of Millennialism: The Irvingite Movement as an Illustration." *British Journal of Sociology* 25 (1974): 296–311.

Apter, David E. "Ideology and Discontent." In *Ideology and Discontent,* edited by David E. Apter, 15–46. New York: Free Press, 1964.

Aronoff, Myron J. "Ideology and Interest: The Dialectics of Politics." In *Ideology and Interest. The Dialectics of Politics,* edited by Myron J. Aronoff, Political Anthropology Yearbook 1, 1–29. New Brunswick, N.J.: Transaction Books, 1980.

Badie, Bertrand, and Pierre Birnbaum. *The Sociology of the State.* Translated by Arthur Goldhammer. Chicago: University of Chicago Press, 1983.

Barber, Bernard. "Acculturation and Messianic Movements." *American Sociological Review* 6 (1941): 663–69.

Barkun, Michael. "Movements of Total Transformation: An Introduction." *American Behavioral Scientist* 16 (1972): 145–52.

Benjamin, Don C. "An Anthropology of Prophecy." *BTB* 21 (1991): 135–44.

Bennett, W. Lance. "Myth, Ritual, and Political Control." *Journal of Communication* 30/4 (1980): 166–79.

Berger, Peter L. *The Sacred Canopy: Elements of a Sociological Theory of Religion.* New York: Doubleday & Co., 1967.

Berger, Peter L., and Hansfried Kellner. *Sociology Reinterpreted: An Essay on Method and Vocation.* Garden City, N.Y.: Doubleday & Co., 1981.

Berger, Peter L., and Thomas Luckmann. *The Social Construction of Reality: A Treatise in the Sociology of Knowledge.* New York: Doubleday & Co., 1966.

Berquist, Jon L. "Social Change: Functionalism versus Historical Materialism." In *Survey of Social Science: Sociology,* edited by Frank N. Magill, 1779–85. Pasadena: Salem Press, 1994.

Biersack, Aletta. "Local Knowledge, Local History: Geertz and Beyond." In *The New Cultural History,* Studies on the History of Society and Culture, edited by Lynn Hunt, 72–96. Berkeley and Los Angeles: University of California Press, 1989.

Bilde, Per, et al., eds. *Centre and Periphery in the Hellenistic World.* Studies in Hellenistic Civilization 4. Aarhus: Aarhus University Press, 1993.

Brewer, Anthony. *Marxist Theories of Imperialism: A Critical Survey.* London: Routledge & Kegan Paul, 1980.

Burke, Peter. *Sociology and History.* Controversies in Sociology 10. London: George Allen & Unwin, 1980.

Carneiro, Robert L. "Political Expansion as an Expression of the Principle of Competitive Exclusion." In *Origins of the State: The Anthropology of Political Evolution,* edited by Ronald E. Cohen and Elman R. Service, 205–23. Philadelphia: Institute for the Study of Human Issues, 1978.

Chase-Dunn, Christopher, and Thomas D. Hall, eds. *Core/Periphery Relations in Precapitalist Worlds.* Boulder, Colo.: Westview Press, 1991.

Claessen, Henri J. M., and Peter Skalník, eds. *The Study of the State.* New Babylon Studies in the Social Sciences 35. The Hague: Mouton, 1981.

Claessen, Henri J. M.; Pieter van de Velde; and M. Estellie Smith, eds. *Development and Decline: The Evolution of Sociopolitical Organization.* South Hadley, Mass.: Bergin & Garvey, 1985.

Cohen, Ronald E. "Evolution, Fission, and the Early State." In Claessen and Skalník, *The Study of the State*, 87–115.

Cohen, Ronald E., and Elman R. Service, eds. *Origins of the State: The Anthropology of Political Evolution.* Philadelphia: Institute for the Study of Human Issues, 1978.

Cohen, Ronald E., and Judith D. Toland, eds. *State Formation and Political Legitimacy.* Political Anthropology 6. New Brunswick, N.J.: Transaction Books, 1988.

Cohn, Norman. *The Pursuit of the Millennium: Revolutionary Millenarians and Mystical Anarchists of the Middle Ages.* Rev. ed. New York: Oxford University Press, 1970.

Crocker, J. Christopher. "The Social Functions of Rhetorical Forms." In *The Social Use of Metaphor: Essays on the Anthropology of Rhetoric,* edited by J. David Sapir and J. Christopher Crocker, 33–66. Philadelphia: University of Pennsylvania Press, 1977.

Douglas, Mary. *Purity and Danger: An Analysis of the Concepts of Pollution and Taboo.* New York: Praeger Publishers, 1966.

Doyle, Michael W. *Empires.* Ithaca, N.Y.: Cornell University Press, 1986.

Eisenstadt, S. N. "Macro-Societal Analysis—Background, Development and Indications." In *Macro-Sociological Theory: Perspectives on Sociological Theory, Volume 1,* SAGE Studies in International Sociology 33, edited by S. N. Eisenstadt and H. J. Helle, 7–24. London: SAGE Publications, 1985.

———. "Observations and Queries about Sociological Aspects of Imperialism in the Ancient World." In *Power and Propaganda: A Symposium on Ancient Empires,* Mesopotamia 7, edited by Mogens Trolle Larsen, 21–34. Copenhagen: Akademisk Forlag, 1979.

———. *The Political Systems of Empires: The Rise and Fall of the Historical Bureaucratic Societies.* Rev. ed. New York: Free Press, 1969.

———. *Revolution and the Transformation of Societies: A Comparative Study of Civilizations.* New York: Free Press, 1978.

———. "Systemic Qualities and Boundaries of Societies: Some Theoretical Considerations." In *Neofunctionalism,* Key Issues in Sociological Theory 1, edited by Jeffrey C. Alexander, 99–112. Beverly Hills, Calif.: SAGE Publications, 1985.

Eisenstadt, S. N., and M. Curelaru. *The Form of Sociology—Paradigms and Crises.* New York: John Wiley & Sons, 1976.

Eisenstadt, S. N., and Luis Roniger. "The Study of Patron-Client Relations and Recent Developments in Sociological Theory." In *Political Clientelism, Patronage and Development,* Contemporary Political Sociology 3, edited by S. N. Eisenstadt and René Lemarchand, 271–95. Beverly Hills, Calif.: SAGE Publications, 1981.

Ekholm, K., and J. Friedman. "'Capital' Imperialism and Exploitation in Ancient World Systems." In *Power and Propaganda: A Symposium on Ancient Empires,* Mesopotamia 7, edited by Mogens Trolle Larsen, 41–58. Copenhagen: Akademisk Forlag, 1979.

Etzioni, Amitai. *A Comparative Analysis of Complex Organizations: On Power, Involvement, and Their Correlates.* Glencoe, Ill.: Free Press, 1961.

Etzioni-Halevy, Eva. *The Knowledge Elite and the Failure of Prophecy.* Controversies in Sociology 18. London: George Allen & Unwin, 1985.

Feeley-Harnik, Gillian. "Is Historical Anthropology Possible? The Case of the Runaway Slave." In *Humanizing America's Iconic Book: The SBL Centennial Addresses, 1980,* edited by Gene M. Tucker and Douglas A. Knight, 95–126. Chico, Calif.: Scholars Press, 1982.

Fernandez, James W. "The Performance of Ritual Metaphors." In *The Social Use of Metaphor: Essays on the Anthropology of Rhetoric,* edited by J. David Sapir and J. Christopher Crocker, 100–131. Philadelphia: University of Pennsylvania Press, 1977.

Finkle, Jason L., and Richard W. Gable, eds. *Political Development and Social Change.* New York: John Wiley & Sons, 1966.

Flanagan, James W. *David's Social Drama: A Hologram of Israel's Early Iron Age.* SWBA 7. JSOTSup 73. Sheffield: Almond Press, 1988.

———. "History as Hologram: Integrating Literary, Archaeological and Comparative Sociological Evidence." *SBL Seminar Papers* 24 (1985): 291–314.

Frick, Frank S. *The Formation of the State in Ancient Israel.* SWBA 4. Sheffield: Almond Press, 1985.

———. "Social Science Methods and Theories of Significance for the Study of the Israelite Monarchy: A Critical Review Essay." *Semeia* 37 (1986): 9–52.

Fried, Morton H. *The Evolution of Political Society: An Essay in Political Anthropology.* Studies in Anthropology. New York: Random House, 1967.

Friedman, Richard Elliott. "The Prophet and the Historian: The Acquisition of Historical Information from Literary Sources." In *The Poet and the Historian: Essays in Literary and Historical Biblical Criticism,* HSM 26, edited by Richard Elliott Friedman, 1–12. Chico, Calif.: Scholars Press, 1983.

Gailey, Christine Ward, and Thomas C. Patterson. "State Formation and Uneven Development." In *State and Society: The Emergence and Development of Social Hierarchy and Political Centralization,* One World Archaeology 4, edited by John Gledhill, Barbara Bender, and Mogens Trolle Larsen, 77–90. London: Unwin Hyman, 1988.

Geertz, Clifford. "Centers, Kings, and Charisma: Reflections on the Symbolics of Power." *Culture and Its Creators: Essays in Honor of Edward Shils,* edited by Joseph Ben-David and Terry Nichols Clark, 150–71. Chicago: University of Chicago Press, 1977.

———. "Ethos, World View, and the Analysis of Sacred Symbols." In *The Interpretation of Cultures: Selected Essays,* edited by Clifford Geertz, 126–41. New York: Basic Books, 1973

———. "Religion as a Cultural System." In *The Interpretation of Cultures: Selected Essays,* edited by Clifford Geertz, 87–125. New York: Basic Books, 1973.

———. "Thick Description: Toward an Interpretive Theory of Culture." In *The Interpretation of Cultures: Selected Essays,* edited by Clifford Geertz, 3–30. New York: Basic Books, 1973.

Giddens, Anthony. *New Rules of Sociological Method: A Positive Critique of Interpretative Sociologies.* New York: Basic Books, 1976.

Gills, Barry K., and Andre Gunder Frank. "5000 Years of World System History: The Cumulation of Accumulation." In *Core/Periphery Relations in Precapitalist Worlds,* edited by Christopher Chase-Dunn and Thomas D. Hall, 67–112. Boulder, Colo.: Westview Press, 1991.

Gledhill, John; Barbara Bender; and Mogens Trolle Larsen, eds. *State and Society: The Emergence and Development of Social Hierarchy and Political Centralization.* One World Archaeology 4. London: Unwin Hyman, 1988.

Glock, Charles Y. "On the Origin and Evolution of Religious Groups." In *Religion in Sociological Perspective: Essays in the Empirical Study of Religion,* edited by Charles Y. Glock, 207–20. Belmont, Calif.: Wadsworth Publishing Co., 1973.

Goldthorpe, John H. "The Relevance of History to Sociology." In *Sociological Research Methods,* 2d ed., edited by Martin Bulmer, 162–74. New Brunswick, N.J.: Transaction Books, 1984.

———. "The Uses of History in Sociology: Reflections on Some Recent Tendencies." *British Journal of Sociology* 42 (1991): 211–230.

Gottwald, Norman K. "Sociological Method in the Study of Ancient Israel." In *Encounter with the Text: Form and History in the Hebrew Bible,* Semeia Supplement 8. Edited by Martin J. Buss, 69–81. Philadelphia: Fortress Press, 1979.

Griffin, Larry J. "Temporality, Events, and Explanation in Historical Sociology: An Introduction." *Sociological Methods and Research* 20 (1992): 403–27.

Gunawardana, R. A. L. H. "Social Function and Political Power: A Case Study of State Formation in Irrigation Society." In Claessen and Skalník, *The Study of the State,* 133–54.

Haas, Jonathan. *The Evolution of the Prehistoric State.* New York: Columbia University Press, 1982.

Hall, Thomas D., and Christopher Chase-Dunn. "Forward into the Past: World-Systems Before 1500." *Sociological Forum 9/2* (1994): 295–306.

Harris, Marvin. *Cultural Materialism: The Struggle for a Science of Culture.* New York: Random House, 1979.

Herion, Gary A. "The Impact of Modern and Social Science Assumptions on the Reconstruction of Israelite History." *JSOT* 34 (1986): 3–33.

Hochstadt, Steve. "Social History and Politics: A Materialist View." *Social History* 7 (1982): 75–83.

Holzner, Burkart. *Reality Construction in Society.* Cambridge, Mass.: Schenkman Publishing, 1968.

Homans, George Caspar. "Bringing Men Back In." In *Certainties and Doubts: Collected Papers, 1962–1985,* edited by George Caspar Homans, 1–16. New Brunswick, N.J.: Transaction Books, 1987.

———. *Certainties and Doubts: Collected Papers, 1962–1985.* Chicago: University of Chicago Press, 1987.

———. *The Human Group.* New York: Harcourt, Brace & Co., 1950.

———. "The Present State of Sociological Theory." In Homans, *Certainties and Doubts,* 237–54.

Jones, Gareth Stedman. "From Historical Sociology to Theoretical History." *British Journal of Sociology* 27 (1976): 295–305.

Kearney, Michael. "Borders and Boundaries of State and Self at the End of Empire." *Journal of Historical Sociology* 4 (1991): 52–74.

Kertzer, David I. *Ritual, Politics, and Power.* New Haven, Conn.: Yale University Press, 1988.

Kurtz, Donald V., and Margaret Showman. "The Legitimation of Early Inchoate States." In *The Study of the State,* edited by Henry J. Claessen and Peter Skalník, 177–200. Paris: Mouton Press, 1981.

Larsen, Mogens Trolle, ed. *Power and Propaganda: A Symposium on Ancient Empires.* Mesopotamia 7. Copenhagen: Akademisk Forlag, 1979.

Laslett, Peter. "The Wrong Way through the Telescope: A Note on Literary Evidence in Sociology and in Historical Sociology." *British Journal of Sociology* 27 (1976): 319–42.

Lebra, Takie Sugiyama. "Millenarian Movements and Resocialization." *American Behavioral Scientist* 16 (1972): 195–217.

Lewellen, Ted C. *Political Anthropology: An Introduction.* South Hadley, Mass.: Bergin & Garvey, 1983.

Light, Ivan H. "The Social Construction of Uncertainty." *Berkeley Journal of Sociology* 14 (1969): 189–99.

Linz, Juan J. "Crisis, Breakdown, and Reequilibration." In *The Breakdown of Democratic Regimes,* edited by Juan J. Linz and Alfred Stepan, 3–124. Baltimore, Md.: Johns Hopkins University Press, 1978.

Lloyd, Christopher. *Explanation in Social History.* Oxford: Basil Blackwell, 1986.

Mannheim, Karl. *Essays on the Sociology of Knowledge.* Edited by Paul Kecskemeti. New York: Oxford University Press, 1952.

Mills, C. Wright. *The Sociological Imagination.* London: Oxford University Press, 1959.

Pareto, Vilfredo. *The Rise and Fall of the Elites: An Application of Theoretical Sociology.* Totowa, N.J.: Bedminster Press, 1968.

Pershits, Abraham I. "Tribute Relations." In *Political Anthropology: The State of the Art,* edited by S. Lee Seaton and Henri J. M. Claessen, World Anthropology, 149–56. The Hague: Mouton, 1979.

Powers, Charles H. *Vilfredo Pareto.* Masters of Social Theory 5. Newbury Park, Calif.: SAGE Publications, 1987.

Price, Barbara J. "Secondary State Formation: An Explanatory Model." In *Origins of the State: The Anthropology of Political Evolution,* edited by Ronald E. Cohen and Elman R. Service, 161–86. Philadelphia: Institute for the Study of Human Values, 1978.

Quadaguo, Jill, and Stan J. Knapp. "Have Historical Sociologists Forsaken Theory? Thoughts on the History/Theory Relationship." *Sociological Methods and Research* 20 (1992): 481–507.

Quinney, Richard. *Social Existence: Metaphysics, Marxism, and the Social Sciences.* Sage Library of Social Research 141. Beverly Hills, Calif.: SAGE Publications, 1982.

Redfield, Robert. *Peasant Society and Culture: An Anthropological Approach to Civilization.* Chicago: University of Chicago Press, 1956.

Rosenbloom, Joseph R. "Social Science Concepts of Modernization and Biblical History: The Development of the Israelite Monarchy." *JAAR* 40 (1972): 437–44.

Seneviratne, Sudharshan. "Kalinga and Andhra: The Process of Secondary State Formation." In Claessen and Skalník, *The Study of the State,* 317–38.

Shils, Edward. "Center and Periphery." In *The Constitution of Society,* edited by Edward Shils, 93–109. Chicago: University of Chicago Press, 1972.

———. "The Integration of Society." In *The Constitution of Society,* edited by Edward Shils, 3–52. Chicago: University of Chicago Press, 1972.

———. "Society and Societies: The Macrosociological View." In *The Constitution of Society,* edited by Edward Shils, 53–68. Chicago: University of Chicago Press, 1972.

Smith, Dennis. *The Rise of Historical Sociology.* Philadelphia: Temple University Press, 1991.

Spier, Leslie; Wayne Suttles; and Melville J. Herskovits. "Comments on Aberle's Thesis of Deprivation." *Southwestern Journal of Anthropology* 15 (1959): 84–88.

Talmon, Shemaryahu. "The 'Comparative Method' in Biblical Interpretation—Principles and Problems." *VT Supplements* 29 (1978): 320–56.

Talmon, Yonina. "Millenarian Movements." *European Journal of Sociology* 7 (1966): 159–200.

Thapar, Romila. "The State as Empire." In Claessen and Skalník, *The Study of the State,* 409–26.

Tilly, Charles. *As Sociology Meets History.* New York: Academic Press, 1981.

Trigger, Bruce G. "Generalized Coercion and Inequality: The Basis of State Power in the Early Civilizations." In *Development and Decline: The Evolution of Sociopolitical Organization,* edited by Henri J. M. Claessen, Pieter van de Velde, and M. Estellie Smith, 46–61. South Hadley, Mass.: Bergin & Garvey, 1985.

Wallace, Anthony F. C. "Revitalization Movements." *American Anthropologist* 58 (1956): 265–75.

Wallerstein, Immanuel. *The Modern World-System.* 3 vols. New York: Academic Press, 1974–88.

Wardell, Mark L., and Stephen P. Turner, eds. *Sociological Theory in Transition.* Boston: Allen & Unwin, 1986.

Weber, Max. *Ancient Judaism.* Glencoe, Ill.: Free Press, 1952.

Wilson, Bryan R. "An Analysis of Sect Development." In *Patterns of Sectarianism: Organisation and Ideology in Social and Religious Movements,* edited by Bryan R. Wilson, 22–45. London: Heinemann, 1967.

———. *Magic and the Millennium: A Sociological Study of Religious Movements of Protest among Tribal and Third-World Peoples.* New York: Harper & Row, 1973.

———. *Religion in Sociological Perspective.* Oxford: Oxford University Press, 1982.

Wilson, Robert R. *Sociological Approaches to the Old Testament.* Guides to Biblical Scholarship, Old Testament Series. Philadelphia: Fortress Press, 1984.

Wolf, Eric R. *Peasants.* Foundations of Modern Anthropology. Englewood Cliffs, N.J.: Prentice-Hall, 1966.

SUBJECT AND NAME INDEX

SCRIPTURE INDEX

HEBREW BIBLE

APOCRYPHA

NEW TESTAMENT